D0914999

226
C

Ð 125-17

The Salvation Army
School For Officers' Training
Library
Chicago, Illinois

B 125-17

THE EXPOSITOR'S BIBLE. Edited by Rev.
W. R. NICOLL, D.D., Editor of *London Expositor*.

1ST SERIES IN 6 VOLS.
MACLAREN, Rev. Alex.—COLOSSIANS—PHILEMON.
DODS, Rev. Marcus.—GENESIS.
CHADWICK, Rev. Dean.—ST. MARK.
BLAIKIE, Rev. W. G.—SAMUEL, 2 VOLS.
EDWARDS, Rev. T. C.—HEBREWS.

2D SERIES IN 6 VOLS.
SMITH, Rev. G. A.—ISAIAH, VOL. I.
ALEXANDER, Bishop.—EPISTLES OF ST. JOHN.
PLUMMER, Rev. A.—PASTORAL EPISTLES.
FINDLAY, Rev. G. G.—GALATIANS.
MILLIGAN, Rev. W.—REVELATION.
DODS, Rev. Marcus.—1ST CORINTHIANS.

3D SERIES IN 6 VOLS.
SMITH, Rev. G. A.—ISAIAH, VOL. II.
GIBSON, Rev. J. M.—ST. MATTHEW.
WATSON, Rev. R. A.—JUDGES—RUTH.
BALL, Rev. C. J.—JEREMIAH. CHAP. I-XX.
CHADWICK, Rev. Dean.—EXODUS.
BURTON, Rev. H.—ST. LUKE.

4TH SERIES IN 6 VOLS.
KELLOGG, Rev. S. H.—LEVITICUS.
STOKES, Rev. G. T.—ACTS, VOL. I.
HORTON, Rev. R. F.—PROVERBS.
DODS, Rev. Marcus.—GOSPEL ST. JOHN, VOL. I.
PLUMMER, Rev. A.—JAMES—JUDE.
COX, Rev. S.—ECCLESIASTES.

5TH SERIES IN 6 VOLS.
DENNEY, Rev. J.—THESSALONIANS.
WATSON, Rev. R. A.—JOB.
MACLAREN, Rev. A.—PSALMS, VOL. I.
STOKES, Rev. G. T.—ACTS, VOL. II.
DODS, Rev. Marcus.—GOSPEL ST. JOHN, VOL. II.
FINDLAY, Rev. C. G.—EPHESIANS.

6TH SERIES IN 6 VOLS.
RAINY, Rev. R.—PHILIPPIANS.
FARRAR, Archdeacon F. W.—1ST KINGS.
BLAIKIE, Rev. W. G.—JOSHUA.
MACLAREN, Rev. A.—PSALMS, VOL. II.
LUMBY, Rev. J. R.—EPISTLES OF ST. PETER.
ADENEY, Rev. W. F.—EZRA—NEHEMIAH-ESTHER.

7TH SERIES IN 6 VOLS.
MOULE, Rev. H. C. G.—ROMANS.
FARRAR, Archdeacon F. W.—2D KINGS.
BENNETT, Rev. W. H.—1ST AND 2D CHRONICLES.
MACLAREN, Rev. A.—PSALMS, VOL. III.
DENNEY, Rev. James.—2D CORINTHIANS.
WATSON, Rev. R. A.—NUMBERS.

8TH AND FINAL SERIES IN 7 VOLS.
FARRAR, Archdeacon F. W.—DANIEL.
SKINNER, Rev. John.—EZEKIEL.
BENNETT, Rev. W. H.—JEREMIAH.
HARPER, Rev. Prof.—DEUTERONOMY.
ADENEY, Rev. W. F.—SOLOMON AND LAMENTATIONS.
SMITH, Rev. G. A.—THE MINOR PROPHETS, 2 VOLS.

☞—About 400 pages in each Volume. Price for either series, six volumes, $6.00. (Orders for 2 or more series at same rate will be sent by Express, prepaid. Separate vols. $1.50, postpaid.) Descriptive circular sent on application.

THE GOSPEL

ACCORDING TO

ST. MARK.

BY THE VERY REV.

G. A. CHADWICK, D.D.,

Dean of Armagh,

AUTHOR OF "CHRIST BEARING WITNESS TO HIMSELF," "AS HE THAT SEWETH," ETC.

NEW YORK:

A. C. ARMSTRONG AND SON.

CONTENTS.

1207

CHAPTER I.

THE BEGINNING OF THE GOSPEL.

"The beginning of the gospel of Jesus Christ, the Son of God. Even as it is written in Isaiah the prophet, Behold, I send My messenger before Thy face, who shall prepare Thy way; The voice of one crying in the wilderness, Make ye ready the way of the Lord, Make His paths straight; John came, who baptized in the wilderness and preached the baptism of repentance unto remission of sins. And there went out unto him all the country of Judæa, and all they of Jerusalem; and they were baptized of him in the river Jordan, confessing their sins. And John was clothed with camel's hair, and had a leathern girdle about his loins, and did eat locusts and wild honey."—MARK i. 1–6 (R.V.).

THE opening of St. Mark's Gospel is energetic and full of character. St. Matthew traces for Jews the pedigree of their Messiah; St. Luke's worldwide sympathies linger with the maiden who bore Jesus, and the village of His boyhood; and St. John's theology proclaims the Divine origin of the Eternal Lord. But St. Mark trusts the public acts of the Mighty Worker to do for the reader what they did for those who first "beheld His glory." How He came to earth can safely be left untold: what He was will appear by what He wrought. It is enough to record, with matchless vividness, the toils, the energy, the love and wrath, the defeat and triumph of the brief career which changed the world. It will prove itself to be the career of "the Son of God."

In so deciding, he followed the example of the Apostolic teaching. The first vacant place among the

I

Twelve was filled by an eye-witness, competent to tell what Jesus did "from the baptism of John to the day when He was received up," the very space covered by this Gospel.   That " Gospel of peace," which Cornelius heard from St. Peter (and hearing, received the Holy Ghost) was the same story of Jesus " after the baptism which John preached."   And this is throughout the substance of the primitive teaching.   The Apostles act as men who believe that everything necessary to salvation is (implicit or explicit) in the history of those few crowded years.   Therefore this is "the gospel."

Men there are who judge otherwise, and whose gospel is not the story of salvation wrought, but the plan of salvation applied, how the Atonement avails for us, how men are converted, and what privileges they then receive.   But in truth men are not converted by preaching conversion, any more than citizens are made loyal by demanding loyalty.   Show men their prince, and convince them that he is gracious and truly royal, and they will die for him.   Show them the Prince of Life, and He, being lifted up, will draw all men unto Him; and thus the truest gospel is that which declares Christ and Him crucified.   As all science springs from the phenomena of the external world, so do theology and religion spring from the life of Him who was too adorable to be mortal, and too loving to be disobeyed.

Therefore St. Paul declares that the gospel which he preached to the Corinthians and by which they were saved, was, that Christ died for our sins and was buried and rose again, and was seen of sufficient witnesses (I Cor. xv. I-8).

And therefore St. Mark is contented with a very brief record of those wondrous years ; a few facts, chosen with a keen sense of the intense energy and burning force which they reveal, are what he is inspired to call the gospel.

He presently uses the word in a somewhat larger sense, telling how Jesus Himself, before the story of His life could possibly be unfolded, preached as " the gospel of God" that "the time is fulfilled, and the kingdom of God is at hand," and added (what St. Mark only has preserved for us), " Repent, and believe in the gospel" (i. 14-15). So too it is part of St. Paul's "gospel" that God shall judge the secrets of men by Jesus Christ" (Rom. ii. 16). For this also is good news of God, " the gospel of the kingdom." And like "the gospel of Jesus Christ," it treats of His attitude toward us, more than ours toward Him, which latter is the result rather than the substance of it. That He rules, and not the devil ; that we shall answer at last to Him and to none lower; that Satan lied when he claimed to possess all the kingdoms of the earth, and to dispose of them ; that Christ has now received from far different hands " all power on earth"; this is a gospel which the world has not yet learned to welcome, nor the Church fully to proclaim.

Now the scriptural use of this term is quite as important to religious emotion as to accuracy of thought. All true emotions hide their fountain too deep for self-consciousness to find. We feel best when our feeling is forgotten. Not while we think about finding peace, but while we approach God as a Father, and are anxious for nothing, but in everything by prayer and supplication with thanksgiving make known our requests, is it promised that the peace of God which passeth all understanding shall guard our hearts and our thoughts (Phil. iv. 7). And many a soul of the righteous, whom

faith in the true gospel fills with trembling adoration, is
made sad by the inflexible demand for certain realised
personal experiences as the title to recognition as a
Christian.   That great title belonged at the first to all
who would learn of Jesus : the disciples were called
Christians.   To acquaint ourselves with Him, that is
to be at peace.

Meantime, we observe that the new movement which
now begins is not, like Judaism, a law which brings
death ; nor like Buddhism, a path in which one must
walk as best he may : it differs from all other systems
in being essentially the announcement of good tidings
from above.

Yet " the beginning of the gospel of Jesus Christ "
is a profound agitation and widespread alarm.   Lest the
soothing words of Jesus should blend like music with
the slumber of sinners at ease in Zion, John came
preaching repentance, and what is more, a baptism of
repentance ; not such a lustration as was most familiar
to the Mosaic law, administered by the worshipper to
himself, but an ablution at other hands, a confession
that one is not only soiled, but soiled beyond all
cleansing of his own.   Formal Judaism was one long
struggle for self-purification.   The dawn of a new
system is visible in the movement of all Judæa towards
one who bids them throw every such hope away, and
come to him for the baptism of repentance, and expect
a Greater One, who shall baptize them with the Holy
Ghost and with fire.   And the true function of the
predicted herald, the best levelling of the rugged ways
of humanity for the Promised One to traverse, was in
this universal diffusion of the sense of sin.   For Christ
was not come to call the righteous, but sinners to
repentance.

In truth, the movement of the Baptist, with its double aspect, gathers up all the teaching of the past. He produced conviction, and he promised help. One lesson of all sacred history is universal failure. The innocence of Eden cannot last. The law with its promise of life to the man who doeth these things, issued practically in the knowledge of sin; it entered that sin might abound; it made a formal confession of universal sin, year by year, continually. And therefore its fitting close was a baptism of repentance universally accepted. Alas, not universally. For while we read of all the nation swayed by one impulse, and rushing to the stern teacher who had no share in its pleasures or its luxuries, whose life was separated from its concerns, and whose food was the simplest that could sustain existence, yet we know that when they heard how deep his censures pierced, and how unsparingly he scourged their best loved sins, the loudest professors of religion rejected the counsel of God against themselves, being not baptized of Him. Nevertheless, by coming to Him, they also had pleaded guilty. Something they needed; they were sore at heart, and would have welcomed any soothing balm, although they refused the surgeon's knife.

The law did more than convict men; it inspired hope. The promise of a Redeemer shone like a rainbow across the dark story of the past. He was the end of all the types, at once the Victim and the Priest. To Him gave all the prophets witness, and the Baptist brought all past attainment to its full height, and was " more than a prophet " when he announced the actual presence of the Christ, when he pointed out to the first two Apostles, the Lamb of God.

AT THE JORDAN.

"And he preached, saying, There cometh after me He that is mightier than I, the latchet of whose shoes I am not worthy to stoop down and unloose. I baptized you with water ; but He shall baptize you with the Holy Ghost. And it came to pass in those days, that Jesus came from Nazareth of Galilee, and was baptized of John in the Jordan. And straightway coming up out of the water, He saw the heavens rent asunder, and the Spirit as a dove descending upon Him : and a voice came out of the heavens, Thou art My Beloved Son, in Thee I am well pleased."—MARK i. 7–11 (R.V.).

IT was when all men mused in their hearts whether John was the Christ or no, that he announced the coming of a Stronger One. By thus promptly silencing a whisper, so honourable to himself, he showed how strong he really was, and how unselfish "a friend of the Bridegroom." Nor was this the vague humility of phrase which is content to be lowly in general, so long as no specified individual stands higher. His word is definite, and accepts much for himself. " The Stronger One than I cometh," and it is in presence of the might of Jesus (whom yet this fiery reformer called a Lamb), that he feels himself unworthy to bend to the dust and unbind the latchets or laces of his shoe.

So then, though asceticism be sometimes good, it is consciously not the highest nor the most effective goodness. Perhaps it is the most impressive. Without a miracle, the preaching of John shook the nation as widely as that of Jesus melted it, and prepared men's hearts for His. A king consulted and feared him. And when the Pharisees were at open feud with Jesus, they feared to be stoned if they should pronounce John's baptism to be of men.

Yet is there weakness lurking even in the very

quality which gives asceticism its power. That stern seclusion from an evil world, that peremptory denial of its charms, why are they so impressive? Because they set an example to those who are hard beset, of the one way of escape, the cutting off of the hand and foot, the plucking out of the eye. And our Lord enjoins such mutilation of the life upon those whom its gifts betray. Yet is it as the halt and maimed that such men enter into life. The ascetic is a man who needs to sternly repress and deny his impulses, who is conscious of traitors within his breast that may revolt if the enemy be suffered to approach too near.

It is harder to be a holy friend of publicans and sinners, a witness for God while eating and drinking with these, than to remain in the desert undefiled. It is greater to convert a sinful woman in familiar converse by the well, than to shake trembling multitudes by threats of the fire for the chaff and the axe for the barren tree. And John confessed this. In the supreme moment of his life, he added his own confession to that of all his nation. This rugged ascetic had need to be baptized of Him who came eating and drinking.

Nay, he taught that all his work was but superficial, a baptism with water to reach the surface of men's life, to check, at the most, exaction and violence and neglect of the wants of others, while the Greater One should baptize with the Holy Ghost, should pierce the depths of human nature, and throughly purge His floor.

Nothing could refute more clearly than our three simple narratives, the sceptical notion that Jesus yielded for awhile to the dominating influence of the Baptist. Only from the Gospels can we at all connect the two. And what we read here is, that before Jesus came, John expected his Superior; that when they met, John declared his own need to be baptized of Him, that he, nevertheless, submitted to the will of Jesus, and thereupon heard a voice from the heavens which must for ever have destroyed all notion of equality; that afterwards he only saw Jesus at a distance, and made a confession which transferred two of his disciples to our Lord.

The criticism which transforms our Lord's part in these events to that of a pupil is far more wilful than would be tolerated in dealing with any other record. And it too palpably springs from the need to find some human inspiration for the Word of God, some candle from which the Sun of Righteousness took fire, if one would escape the confession that He **is** not of this world.

But here we meet a deeper question: Not why Jesus accepted baptism from an inferior, but why, being sinless, He sought for a baptism of repentance. How is this act consistent with absolute and stainless purity?

Now it sometimes lightens a difficulty to find that it is not occasional nor accidental, but wrought deep into the plan of a consistent work. And the Gospels are consistent in representing the innocence of Jesus as refusing immunity from the consequences of guilt. He was circumcised, and His mother then paid the offering commanded by the law, although both these actions spoke of defilement. In submitting to the likeness of sinful flesh He submitted to its conditions. He was present at feasts in which national confessions led up to sacrifice, and the sacrificial blood was sprinkled to make atonement for the children of Israel, because of all their sins. When He tasted death itself, which passed upon all men, for that all have sinned, He

carried out to the utmost the same stern rule to which
at His baptism He consciously submitted. Nor will
any theory of His atonement suffice, which is content
with believing that His humiliations and sufferings,
though inevitable, were only collateral results of contact with our fallen race. Baptism was avoidable, and
that without any compromise of His influence, since the
Pharisees refused it with impunity, and John would
fain have exempted Him. Here at least He was not
"entangled in the machinery," but deliberately turned
the wheels upon Himself. And this is the more impressive because, in another aspect of affairs, He
claimed to be out of the reach of ceremonial defilement, and touched without reluctance disease, leprosy
and the dead.

Humiliating and penal consequences of sin, to these
He bowed His head. Yet to a confession of personal
taint, never. And all the accounts agree that He never
was less conscience-stricken than when He shared the
baptism of repentance. St. Matthew implies, what St.
Luke plainly declares, that He did not come to baptism
along with the crowds of penitents, but separately.
And at the point where all others made confession, in
the hour when even the Baptist, although filled with
the Holy Ghost from his mother's womb, had need to
be baptized, He only felt the propriety, the fitness of
fulfilling all righteousness. That mighty task was not
even a yoke to Him, it was an instinct like that of
beauty to an artist, it was what became Him.

St. Mark omits even this evidence of sinlessness.
His energetic method is like that of a great commander,
who seizes at all costs the vital point upon the battle
field. He constantly omits what is subordinate
(although very conscious of the power of graphic

details), when by so doing he can force the central thought upon the mind. Here he concentrates our attention upon the witness from above, upon the rending asunder of the heavens which unfold all their heights over a bended head, upon the visible descent of the Holy Spirit in His fulness, upon the voice from the heavens which pealed through the souls of these two peerless worshippers, and proclaimed that He who had gone down to the baptismal flood was no sinner to be forgiven, but the beloved Son of God, in whom He is well pleased.

That is our Evangelist's answer to all misunderstanding of the rite, and it is enough.

How do men think of heaven ? Perhaps only as a remote point in space, where flames a material and solid structure into which it is the highest bliss to enter. A place there must be to which the Body of our Lord ascended and whither He shall yet lead home His followers in spiritual bodies to be with Him where He is. If, however, only this be heaven, we should hold that in the revolutions of the solar system it hung just then vertically above the Jordan, a few fathoms or miles aloft. But we also believe in a spiritual city, in which the pillars are living saints, an all-embracing blessedness and rapture and depth of revelation, whereinto holy mortals in their highest moments have been "caught up," a heaven whose angels ascend and descend upon the Son of man. In this hour of highest consecration, these heavens were thrown open—rent asunder—for the gaze of our Lord and of the Baptist. They were opened again when the first martyr died. And we read that what eye hath not seen nor ear heard nor heart conceived of the preparation of God for them that love Him, He hath already revealed to them by His Spirit. To others there is only cloud or "the infinite azure," as to the the crowd by the Jordan and the murderers of Stephen.

Now it is to be observed that we never read of Jesus being caught up into heaven for a space, like St. Paul or St. John. What we read is, that while on earth the Son of man is in Heaven (John iii. 13),* for heaven is the manifestation of God, whose truest glory was revealed in the grace and truth of Jesus.

Along with this revelation, the Holy Spirit was manifested wondrously. His appearance, indeed, is quite unlike what it was to others. At Pentecost He became visible, but since each disciple received only a portion, "according to his several ability," his fitting symbol was "tongues parting asunder like as of fire." He came as an element powerful and pervasive, not as a Personality bestowed in all His vital force on any one.

So, too, the phrase which John used, when predicting that Jesus should baptize with the Holy Ghost, slightly though it differs from what is here, implies † that only a portion is to be given, not the fulness. And the angel who foretold to Zacharias that John himself should be filled with the Holy Ghost, conveyed the same limitation in his words. John received all that he was able to receive : he was filled. But how should mortal capacity exhaust the fulness of Deity ? And Who is this, upon Whom, while John is but an awe-stricken beholder, the Spirit of God descends in all completeness, a living organic unity, like a dove? Only the Infinite is capable of receiving such a gift, and this

---

* Cf. the admirable note in Archdeacon Watkins' "Commentary on John."

† By the absence of the article in the Greek.

is He in Whom dwelleth all the fulness of the Godhead bodily. No wonder then that "in bodily form"
as a dove, the Spirit of God descended upon Him
alone. Henceforward He became the great Dispenser,
and "the Spirit emanated from Him as perfume from
the rose when it has opened."

At the same time was heard a Voice from heaven.
And the bearing of this passage upon the Trinity
becomes clear, when we combine the manifestation of
the Spirit in living Personality, and the Divine Voice,
not from the Dove but from the heavens, with the
announcement that Jesus is not merely beloved and
well-pleasing, but a Son, and in this high sense the
only Son, since the words are literally "Thou art the
Son of Me, the beloved." And yet He is to bring many
sons unto glory.

Is it consistent with due reverence to believe that
this voice conveyed a message to our Lord Himself?
Even so liberal a critic as Neander has denied this.
But if we grasp the meaning of what we believe, that
He upon taking flesh "emptied Himself," that He increased in wisdom during His youth, and that there
was a day and hour which to the end of life He knew
not, we need not suppose that His infancy was so
unchildlike as the realisation of His mysterious and
awful Personality would make it. There must then
have been a period when His perfect human development rose up into what Renan calls (more accurately
than he knows) identification of Himself with the object
of His devotion, carried to the utmost limit. Nor is
this period quite undiscoverable, for when it arrived it
would seem highly unnatural to postpone His public
ministry further. Now this reasonable inference is
entirely supported by the narrative. St. Matthew

indeed regards the event from the Baptist's point of vision. But St. Mark and St. Luke are agreed that to Jesus Himself it was also said, " *Thou* art My beloved Son." Now this is not the way to teach us that the testimony came only to John. And how solemn a thought is this, that the full certitude of His destiny expanded before the eyes of Jesus, just when He lifted them from those baptismal waters in which He stooped so low.

THE TEMPTATION.

" **And** straightway the Spirit driveth Him forth into the wilderness. And He was in the wilderness forty days tempted of Satan ; and He was with the wild beasts ; and the angels ministered unto Him."— MARK i. 12, 13 (R.V.).

ST. MARK has not recorded the details of our Lord's temptations, and lays more stress upon the duration of the struggle, than the nature of the last and crowning assaults. But he is careful, like the others, to connect it closely with the baptism of Jesus, and the miraculous testimony then borne to Him.

It is indeed instructive that He should have suffered this affront, immediately upon being recognised as the Messiah. But the explanation will not be found in the notion, which Milton has popularised, that only now Satan was assured of the urgent necessity for attacking Him :

"That heard the adversary . . . and with the voice **Divine**
Nigh thunderstruck, the exalted Man, to whom
Such high attest was given, awhile surveyed
With wonder."

As if Satan forgot the marvels of the sacred **infancy.** As if the spirits who attack all could have failed to identify, after thirty years of defeat, the Greater One whom the Baptist had everywhere proclaimed. No. But Satan admirably chose the time for a supreme effort. High places are dizzy, and especially when one has just attained them; and therefore it was when the voice of the herald and the Voice from the heavens were blended in acclaim, that the Evil One tried all his arts. He had formerly plunged Elijah into despair and a desire to die, immediately after fire from heaven responded to the prophet's prayer. Soon after this, he would degrade Peter to be his mouth-piece, just when his noblest testimony was borne, and the highest approval of his Lord was won. In the flush of their triumphs he found his best opportunity; but Jesus remained unflushed, and met the first recorded temptation, in the full consciousness of Messiahship, by quoting the words which spoke to every man alike, and as man.

It is a lesson which the weakest needs to learn, for little victories can intoxicate little men.

It is easy then to see why the recorded temptations insist upon the exceptional dignity of Christ, and urge Him to seize its advantages, while He insists on bearing the common burden, and proves Himself greatest by becoming least of all. The sharp contrast between His circumstances and His rank drove the temptations deep into His consciousness, and wounded His sensibilities, though they failed to shake His will.

How unnatural that the Son of God should lack and suffer hunger, how right that He should challenge recognition, how needful (though now His sacred Personality is cunningly allowed to fall somewhat into the background) that He should obtain armies and splendour.

This explains the possibility of temptation in a sinless nature, which indeed can only be denied by assuming that sin is part of the original creation. Not because we are sinful, but because we are flesh and blood (of which He became partaker), when we feel the pains of hunger we are attracted by food, at whatever price it is offered. In truth, no man is allured by sin, but only by the bait and bribe of sin, except perhaps in the last stages of spiritual decomposition.

Now, just as the bait allures, and not the jaws of the trap, so the power of a temptation is not its wickedness, not the guilty service, but the proffered recompense; and this appeals to the most upright man, equally with the most corrupt. Thus the stress of a temptation is to be measured by our gravitation, not towards the sin, but towards the pleasure or advantage which is entangled with that. And this may be realised even more powerfully by a man of keen feeling and vivid imagination who does not falter, than by a grosser nature which succumbs.

Now Jesus was a perfect man. To His exquisite sensibilities, which had neither inherited nor contracted any blemish, the pain of hunger at the opening of His ministry, and the horror of the cross at its close, were not less intense, but sharper than to ours. And this pain and horror measured the temptation to evade them. The issue never hung in the scales; even to hesitate would have been to forfeit the delicate bloom of absolute sinlessness ; but, none the less, the decision was costly, the temptation poignant.

St. Mark has given us no details ; but there is immense and compressed power in the assertion, only his, that the temptation lasted all through the forty days. We know the power of an unremitting pressure, an incessant importunity, a haunting thought. A very trifling annoyance, long protracted, drives men to strange remedies. And the remorseless urgency of Satan may be measured by what St. Matthew tells us, that only after the forty days Jesus became aware of the pains of hunger. Perhaps the assertion that He was with the wild beasts may throw some ray of light upon the nature of the temptation. There is no intimation of bodily peril. On the other hand it seems incredible that what is hinted is His own consciousness of the supernatural dignity from which

> " The fiery serpent fled, and noxious worm ;
> The lion and fierce tiger glared aloof."

Such a consciousness would have relieved the strain of which their presence is evidently a part. Nay, but the oppressive solitude, the waste region so unlike His blooming Nazareth, and the ferocity of the brute creation, all would conspire to suggest those dread misgivings and questionings which are provoked by " the something that infects the world."

Surely we may believe that He Who was tempted at all points like as we are, felt now the deadly chill which falls upon the soul from the shadow of our ruined earth. In our nature He bore the assault and overcame. And then His human nature condescended to accept help, such as ours receives, from the ministering spirits which are sent forth to minister to them that shall be heirs of salvation. So perfectly was He made like unto His brethren.

THE EARLY PREACHING AND THE FIRST DISCIPLES.

"Now after that John was delivered up, Jesus came into Galilee preaching the gospel of God, and saying, The time is fulfilled, and the kingdom of God is at hand : repent ye, and believe in the gospel. And passing along by the sea of Galilee, He saw Simon and Andrew the brother of Simon casting a net in the sea ; for they were fishers. And Jesus said unto them, Come ye after Me, and I will make you to become fishers of men. And straightway they left the nets, and followed Him. And going on a little further, He saw James the son of Zebedee, and John his brother, who also were in the boat mending the nets. And straightway He called them : and they left their father Zebedee in the boat with the hired servants, and went after Him."—MARK i. 14-20 (R.V.).

ST. MARK has shown us the Baptist proclaiming Christ. He now tells us that when John was imprisoned, Jesus, turning from that Judean ministry which stirred the jealousy of John's disciples (John iii. 26), " came into Galilee, preaching." And one looks twice before observing that His teaching is a distinct advance upon the herald's. Men are still to repent ; for however slightly modern preachers may heal the hurt of souls, real contrition is here taken over into the gospel scheme. But the time which was hitherto said to be at hand is now fulfilled. And they are not only to believe the gospel, but to " believe in it." Reliance, the effort of the soul by which it ceases equally to be self-confident and to despair, confiding itself to some word which is a gospel, or some being who has salvation to bestow, that is belief in its object. And it is highly important to observe that faith is thus made prominent so early in our Lord's teaching. The vitalizing power of faith was no discovery of St. Paul ; it was not evolved by devout meditation after Jesus had passed from view, nor introduced into His system when opposition forced Him to bind men to Him in a

2

stronger allegiance.   The power of faith is implied in
His earliest preaching, and it is connected with His
earliest miracles.   But no such phrase as the power of
faith is ever used.   Faith is precious only as it leans
on what is trustworthy.   And it is produced, not by
thinking of faith itself, but of its proper object.   Therefore Christ did not come preaching faith, but preaching
the gospel of God, and bidding men believe in that.

Shall we not follow His example ?   It is morally
certain that Abraham never heard of salvation by faith,
yet he was justified by faith when he believed in Him
Who justifieth the ungodly.   To preach Him, and His
gospel, is the way to lead men to be saved by faith.

Few things are more instructive to consider than
the slow, deliberate, yet firm steps by which Christ
advanced to the revelation of God in flesh.   Thirty
years of silence, forty days of seclusion after heaven
had proclaimed Him, leisurely intercourse with Andrew
and John, Peter and Nathanael, and then a brief
ministry in a subject nation, and chiefly in a despised
province.   It is not the action of a fanatic.   It exactly
fulfils His own description of the kingdom which He
proclaimed, which was to exhibit first the blade, then
the ear, then the full corn in the ear.   And it is a
lesson to all time, that the boldest expectations possible
to faith do not justify feverish haste and excited longings for immediate prominence or immediate success.
The husbandman who has long patience with the seed
is not therefore hopeless of the harvest.

Passing by the sea of Galilee, Jesus finds two fishermen at their toil, and bids them follow Him.   Both are
men of decided and earnest character; one is to become
the spokesman and leader of the Apostolic band, and
the little which is recorded of the other indicates the

same temperament, somewhat less developed.   Our Lord now calls upon them to take a decided step.   But here again we find traces of the same deliberate progression, the same absence of haste, as in His early preaching.   He does not, as unthinking readers fancy, come upon two utter strangers, fascinate and arrest them in a moment, and sweep their lives into the vortex of His own.   Andrew had already heard the Baptist proclaim the Lamb of God, had followed Jesus home, and had introduced his brother, to whom Jesus then gave the new name Cephas.   Their faith had since been confirmed by miracles.   The demands of our Lord may be trying, but they are never unreasonable, and the faith He claims is not a blind credulity.

Nor does He, even now, finally and entirely call them away from their occupation.   Some time is still to elapse, and a sign, especially impressive to fishermen, the miraculous draught of fishes, is to burn into their minds a profound sense of their unworthiness, before the vocation now promised shall arrive.   Then He will say, From henceforth ye shall catch men : now He says, I will prepare you for that future, I will make you to become fishers of men.   So ungrounded is the suspicion of any confusion between the stories of the three steps by which they rose to their Apostleship.

A little further on, He finds the two sons of Zebedee, and calls them also.   John had almost certainly been the companion of Andrew when he followed Jesus home, and his brother had become the sharer of his hopes.   And if there were any hesitation, the example of their comrades helped them to decide—so soon, so inevitably does each disciple begin to be a fisher of other men—and leaving their father, as we are gracefully told, not desolate, but with servants, they also follow Jesus.

Thus He asks, from each group, the sacrifice involved in following Him at an inconvenient time. The first are casting their nets and eager in their quest. The others are mending their nets, perhaps after some large draught had broken them. So Levi was sitting at the receipt of toll. Not one of the Twelve was chosen to that high rank when idle.

Very charming, very powerful still is the spell by which Christ drew His first apostles to His side. Not yet are they told anything of thrones on which they are to sit and judge the tribes of Israel, or that their names shall be engraven on the foundations of the heavenly city besides being great on earth while the world stands. For them, the capture of men was less lucrative than that of fish, and less honourable, for they suffered the loss of all things and were made as the filth of the earth. To learn Christ's art, to be made helpful in drawing souls to Him, following Jesus and catching men, this was enough to attract His first ministers ; God grant that a time may never come when ministers for whom this is enough, shall fail. Where the spirit of self devotion is absent how can the Spirit of Christ exist ?

TEACHING WITH AUTHORITY.

"And they go into Capernaum ; and straightway on the sabbath day He entered into the synagogue and taught. And they were astonished at His teaching : for He taught them as having authority, and not as the scribes."—MARK i. 21, 22 (R.V.).

THE worship of the synagogues, not having been instituted by Moses, but gradually developed by the public need, was comparatively free and unconventional. Sometimes it happened that remarkable and

serious-looking strangers were invited, if they had any
word of exhortation, to say on (Acts xiii. 15). Sometimes one presented himself, as the custom of our Lord
was (Luke iv. 16). Amid the dull mechanical tendencies which were then turning the heart of Judaism
to stone, the synagogue may have been often a centre
of life and rallying-place of freedom. In Galilee, where
such worship predominated over that of the remote
Temple and its hierarchy, Jesus found His trusted
followers and the nucleus of the Church. In foreign
lands, St. Paul bore first to his brethren in their synagogues the strange tidings that their Messiah had
expired upon a cross. And before His rupture with
the chiefs of Judaism, the synagogues were fitting
places for our Lord's early teaching. He made use of
the existing system, and applied it, just as we have
seen Him use the teaching of the Baptist as a starting-
point for His own. And this ought to be observed, that
Jesus revolutionized the world by methods the furthest
from being revolutionary. The institutions of His age
and land were corrupt well-nigh to the core, but He
did not therefore make a clean sweep, and begin again.
He did not turn His back on the Temple and synagogues,
nor outrage sabbaths, nor come to destroy the law and
the prophets. He bade His followers reverence the
seat where the scribes and Pharisees sat, and drew the
line at their false lives and perilous examples. Amid
that evil generation He found soil wherein His seed
might germinate, and was content to hide His leaven
in the lump where it should gradually work out its
destiny. In so doing He was at one with Providence,
which had slowly evolved the convictions of the Old
Testament, spending centuries upon the process. Now
the power which belongs to such moderation has

scarcely been recognised until these latter days. The
political sagacity of Somers and Burke, and the ecclesiastical wisdom of our own reformers, had their occult
and unsuspected fountains in the method by which
Jesus planted the kingdom which came not with observation. But who taught the Carpenter ? It is therefore significant that all the Gospels of the Galilean
ministry connect our Lord's early teaching with the
synagogue.

St. Mark is by no means the evangelist of the discourses. And this adds to the interest with which we
find him indicate, with precise exactitude, the first
great difference that would strike the hearers of Christ
between His teaching and that of others. He taught
with authority, and not **as** the scribes. Their doctrine was built with dreary and irrational ingenuity,
upon perverted views of the old law. The shape
of a Hebrew letter, words whereof the initals would
spell some important name, wire-drawn inferences,
astounding allusions, ingenuity such as men waste now
upon the number of the beast and the measurement of
a pyramid, these were the doctrine of the scribes.

And an acute observer would remark that the authority
of Christ's teaching was peculiar in a farther-reaching
sense. If, as seems clear, Jesus said, " Ye have heard
that it hath been said " (not " by," but) " to them
of old time, but I say unto you," He then claimed the
place, not of Moses who heard the Divine Voice, but of
Him Who spoke. Even if this could be doubted, the
same spirit is elsewhere unmistakable. The tables
which Moses brought were inscribed by the finger of
Another : none could make him the Supreme arbitrator
while overhead the trumpet waxed louder and louder,
while the fiery pillar marshalled their journeying, while

the mysterious Presence consecrated the mysterious shrine. Prophet after prophet opened and closed his message with the words, "Thus saith the Lord." . . . "For the mouth of the Lord hath spoken it." Jesus was content with the attestation, "Verily, I say unto you." Blessed as a wise builder was the hearer and doer of "these words of Mine." Everywhere in His teaching the centre of authority is personal. He distinctly recognises the fact that He is adding to the range of the ancient law of respect for human life, and for purity, veracity and kindness. But He assigns no authority for these additions, beyond His own. Persecution by all men is a blessed thing to endure, if it be for His sake and the gospel's. Now this is unique. Moses or Isaiah never dreamed that devotion to himself took rank with devotion to his message. Nor did St. Paul. But Christ opens His ministry with the same pretensions as at the close, when others may not be called Rabbi, nor Master, because these titles belong to Him.

And the lapse of ages renders this "authority" of Christ more wonderful than at first. The world bows down before something other than His clearness of logic or subtlety of inference. He still announces where others argue, He reveals, imposes on us His supremacy, bids us take His yoke and learn. And we still discover in His teaching a freshness and profundity, a universal reach of application and yet an unearthliness of aspect, which suit so unparalleled a claim. Others have constructed cisterns in which to store truth, or aqueducts to convey it from higher levels. Christ is Himself a fountain; and not only so, but the water which He gives, when received aright, becomes in the faithful heart a well of water springing up in new, inexhaustible developments.

MIRACLES.

" And straightway there was in their synagogue a man with an un‹ clean spirit."—MARK i. 23 (R.V.).

WE have just read that Christ's teaching astonished the hearers. He was about to astonish them yet more, for we have now reached the first miracle which St. Mark records. With what sentiments should such a narrative be approached? The evangelist connects it emphatically with Christ's assertion of authority. Immediately upon the impression which His manner of teaching produced, straightway, there was in the synagogue a man with an unclean spirit. And upon its expulsion, what most impressed the people was, that as He taught with authority, so " with authority He commandeth even the unclean spirits, and they obey Him."

Let us try whether this may not be a providential clue, to guide us amid the embarrassments which beset, in our day, the whole subject of miracles.

A miracle, we are told, is an interference with the laws of nature; and it is impossible, because they are fixed and their operation is uniform. But these bold words need not disconcert any one who has learned to ask, In what sense are the operations of nature uniform? Is the operation of the laws which govern the wind uniform, whether my helm is to port or starboard? Can I not modify the operation of sanitary laws by deodorization, by drainage, by a thousand resources of civilization? The truth is, that while natural laws remain fixed, human intelligence profoundly modifies their operation. How then will the objector prove that no higher Being can as naturally

do the same ? He answers, Because the sum total
of the forces of nature is a fixed quantity : nothing
can be added to that sum, nothing taken from it :
the energy of all our machinery existed ages ago in
the heat of tropical suns, then in vegetation, and ever
since, though latent, in our coal beds ; and the claim
to add anything to that total is subversive of modern
science. But again we ask, If the physician adds
nothing to the sum of forces when he banishes one
disease by inoculation, and another by draining a
marsh, why must Jesus have added to the sum of
forces in order to expel a demon or to cool a fever ?
It will not suffice to answer, because His methods are
contrary to experience. Beyond experience they are.
But so were the marvels of electricity to our parents
and of steam to theirs. The chemistry which analyses
the stars is not incredible, although thirty years ago
its methods were " contrary " to the universal experience of humanity. Man is now doing what he never
did before, because he is a more skilful and better
informed agent than he ever was. Perhaps at this
moment, in the laboratory of some unknown student,
some new force is preparing to amaze the world. But
the sum of the forces of nature will remain unchanged.
Why is it assumed that a miracle must change them ?
Simply because men have already denied God, or at
least denied that He is present within His world, as
truly as the chemist is within it. If we think of Him
as interrupting its processes from without, laying upon
the vast machine so powerful a grasp as to arrest its
working, then indeed the sum of forces is disturbed,
and the complaints of science are justified. This may,
or it may not, have been the case in creative epochs,
of which science knows no more than of the beginning

of life and of consciousness.   But it has nothing to say
against the doctrine of the miracles of Jesus.   For this
doctrine assumes that God is ever present in His universe ; that by Him all things consist ; that He is not
far from any one of us, for in Him we live and move
and have our being, although men may be as unconscious of Him as of gravitation and electricity.   When
these became known to man, the stability of law was unaffected.   And it is a wild assumption that if a supreme
and vital force exist, a living God, He cannot make His
energies visible without affecting the stability of law.

Now Christ Himself appeals expressly and repeatedly
to this immanent presence of God as the explanation
of His " works."

" My Father worketh hitherto, and I work."   " The
Father loveth the Son, and showeth Him all things
that Himself doeth."   " I, by the finger of God, cast out
devils."

Thus a miracle, even in the Old Testament, is not
an interruption of law by God, but a manifestation of
God who is within nature always ; to common events
it is as the lightning to the cloud, a revelation of the
electricity which was already there.   God was made
known, when invoked by His agents, in signs from
heaven, in fire and tempest, in drought and pestilence,
a God who judgeth.   These are the miracles of God
interposing for His people against their foes.   But the
miracles of Christ are those of God carrying forward
to the uttermost His presence in the world, God manifest in the flesh.   They are the works of Him in Whom
dwelleth all the fulness of the Godhead bodily.

And this explains what would otherwise be so perplexing, the essentially different nature of His miracles
from those of the Old Testament.   Infidelity pretends

that those are the models on which myth or legend formed the miracles of Jesus, but the plain answer is that they are built on no model of the kind. The difference is so great as to be startling.

Tremendous convulsions and visitations of wrath are now unknown, because God is now reconciling the world unto Himself, and exhibiting in miracles the presence of Him Who is not far from every one of us, His presence in love to redeem the common life of man, and to bless, by sharing it. Therefore His gifts are homely, they deal with average life and its necessities, bread and wine and fish are more to the purpose than that man should eat angels' food, the rescue of storm-tossed fishermen than the engulfment of pursuing armies, the healing of prevalent disease than the plaguing of Egypt or the destruction of Sennacherib.

Such a Presence thus manifested is the consistent doctrine of the Church. It is a theory which men may reject at their own peril if they please. But they must not pretend to refute it by any appeal to either the uniformity of law or the stability of force.

Men tell us that the divinity of Jesus was an afterthought; what shall we say then to this fact, that men observed from the very first a difference between the manner of His miracles and all that was recorded in their Scriptures, or that they could have deemed fit? It is exactly the same peculiarity, carried to the highest pitch, as they already felt in His discourses. They are wrought without any reference whatever to a superior will. Moses cried unto the Lord, saying, What shall I do? Elijah said, Hear me O Lord, hear me. But Jesus said, I will . . . I charge thee come out . . . I am able to do this. And so marked is the change, that even His followers cast out devils in His name, and

say not, Where is the Lord God of Israel ? but, In the
Name of Jesus Christ of Nazareth. His power is
inherent, it is self-possessed, and His acts in the
synoptics are only explained by His words in St. John,
" What things soever the Father doeth, these the Son
also doeth in like manner."   No wonder that St. Mark
adds to His very first record of a miracle, that the
people were amazed, and asked, What is this ? a new
teaching ! with authority He commandeth even the
unclean spirits and they do obey Him !   It was
divinity which, without recognising, they felt, implicit
in His bearing. No wonder also that His enemies
strove hard to make Him say, Who gave Thee this
authority ?   Nor could they succeed in drawing from
Him any sign from heaven. The centre and source
of the supernatural, for human apprehension, has
shifted itself, and the vision of Jesus is the vision of
the Father also.

THE DEMONIAC.

" And straightway there was in their synagogue a man with an
unclean spirit ; and he cried out, saying, What have we to do with
Thee, Thou Jesus of Nazareth ? art Thou come to destroy us ? I
know Thee Who Thou art, the Holy One of God. And Jesus rebuked
him, saying, Hold thy peace, and come out of him. And the unclean
spirit, tearing him and crying with a loud voice, came out of him. And
they were all amazed, insomuch that they questioned among themselves, saying, What is this ? a new teaching ! with authority He commandeth even the unclean spirits, and they obey Him. And the
report of Him went out straightway everywhere into all the region of
Galilee round about."—MARK i. 23–28 (R.V).

WE have seen that belief in the stability of natural law
does not forbid us to believe in miracles.

Special objections are urged, however, against the
belief in demoniacal possession. The very existence of

demons is declared to be inconsistent with the omnipotence of God, or else with His goodness.

And it may be granted that abstract reasoning in
an ideal world, thought moving in a vacuum, would
scarcely evolve a state of things so far removed from
the ideal. This, however, is an argument against the
existence, not of demons, but of evil in any shape. It
is the familiar insoluble problem of all religions, How
can evil exist in the universe of God? And it is
balanced by the insoluble problem of all irreligious
systems : In a universe without God, how can either
good or evil exist, as distinguished from the advan-
tageous and the unprofitable? Whence comes the unquestionable difference between a lie and a bad bargain?

But the argument against evil spirits professes to be
something more than a disguised reproduction of this
abstract problem. What more is it? What is gained
by denying the fiends, as long as we cannot deny the
fiends incarnate—the men who take pleasure in unrighteousness, in the seduction and ruin of their
fellows, in the infliction of torture and outrage, in the
ravage and desolation of nations? Such freedom has
been granted to the human will, for even these
ghastly issues have not been judged so deadly as
coercion and moral fatalism. What presumption can
possibly remain against the existence of other beings
than men, who have fallen yet farther? If, indeed,
it be certainly so much farther. For we know that
men have lived, not outcasts from society, but boastful
sons of Abraham, who willed to perform the lusts
(τὰς ἐπιθυμίας) of their father the devil. Now since we
are not told that the wickedness of demons is infinite,*

---

* The opposite is asserted by the fact that one demon may ally
himself with seven others worse.

but only that it is abysmal, and since we know that abysses of wickedness do actually exist, what sort of vindication of Deity is this which will believe that such gulfs are yawning only in the bosom of man ?

It alarms and shocks us to think that evil spirits have power over the human mind, and still more that such power should extend, as in cases of possession, even to the body.   Evil men, however, manifestly wield such power.   "They got rid of the wicked one," said Goethe, " but they could not get rid of the wicked ones." Social and intellectual charm, high rank, the mysterious attraction of a strong individuality, all are employed at times to mislead and debase the shuddering, reluctant, mesmerised wills of weaker men and women.   And then the mind acts upon the body, as perhaps it always does.   Drunkenness and debauchery shake the nerves. Paralysis and lunacy tread hard on the footsteps of excess.   Experience knows no reason for denying that when wickedness conquers the soul it will also deal hardly with the body.

But we must not stop here.   For the Gospels do not countenance the popular notion that special wickedness was the cause of the fearful wretchedness of the possessed.   Young children suffered.   Jesus often cautioned a sufferer to sin no more lest worse results should follow than those He had removed ; but He is never known to have addressed this warning to demoniacs.   They suffered from the tyranny of Satan, rather than from his seduction ; and the analogies which make credible so frightful an outrage upon human nature, are the wrongs done by despots and mobs, by invading armies and persecuting religionists.   Yet people who cannot believe that a demon could throw a child upon the fire, are not incredulous of Attila, Napoleon, and the Inquisition.

Thus it appears that such a narrative need startle
no believer in God, and in moral good and evil, who
considers the unquestionable facts of life. And how
often will the observant Christian be startled at the
wild insurrection and surging up of evil thought and
dark suggestions, which he cannot believe to be his own,
which will not be gainsaid nor repulsed. How easily
do such experiences fall in with the plain words of Scripture, by which the veil is drawn aside, and the mystery
of the spiritual world laid bare. Then we learn that
man is not only fallen but assaulted, not only feeble but
enslaved, not only a wandering sheep but led captive
by the devil at his will.

We turn to the narrative before us. They are still
wondering at our Lord's authoritative manner, when
"straightway," for opportunities were countless until
unbelief arose, a man with an unclean spirit attracts
attention. We can only conjecture the special meaning
of this description. A recent commentator assumes
that "like the rest, he had his dwelling among the
tombs : an overpowering influence had driven him
away from the haunts of men." (Canon Luckock, *in
loco*). To others this feature in the wretchedness of the
Gadarene may perhaps seem rather to be exceptional,
the last touch in the appalling picture of his misery.
It may be that nothing more outrageous than morbid
gloom or sullen mutterings had hitherto made it necessary to exclude this sufferer from the synagogue. Or
the language may suggest that he rushed abruptly in,
driven by the frantic hostility of the fiend, or impelled
by some mysterious and lingering hope, as the demoniac of Gadara ran to Christ.

What we know is that the sacred Presence provoked
a crisis. There is an unbelief which never can be

silent, never wearies railing at the faith, and there is a corruption which resents goodness and hates it as a personal wrong. So the demons who possessed men were never able to confront Jesus calmly. They resent His interference ; they cry out ; they disclaim having anything to do with Him ; they seem indignant that He should come to destroy them who have destroyed so many. There is something weird and unearthly in the complaint. But men also are wont to forget their wrong doing when they come to suffer, and it is recorded that even Nero had abundance of compassion for himself. Weird also and terrible is it, that this unclean spirit should choose for his confession that pure and exquisite epithet, the Holy One of God. The phrase only recurs in the words of St. Peter, " We have believed and know that Thou art the Holy One of God " (John vi. 69, R. V.). Was it not a mournful association of ideas which then led Jesus to reply, " Have I not chosen you the Twelve, and one of you is a devil ?*" But although the phrase is beautiful, and possibly " wild with all regret," there is no relenting, no better desire than to be " let alone." And so Jesus, so gentle with sinful men, yet sometime to be their judge also, is stern and cold. " Hold thy peace—be muzzled," He answers, as to a wild beast, " and come out of him." Whereupon the evil spirit exhibits at once his ferocity and his defeat. Tearing and scream ing, he came out, but we read in St. Luke that he did the man no harm.

And the spectators drew the proper inference. A new power implied a new revelation. Something far-

---

* The connection would be almost certain if the word "devil" were alike in both. But in all these narratives it is "demon," there being in Scripture but one devil.

reaching and profound might be expected from Him who commanded even the unclean spirits with authority, and was obeyed.

It is the custom of unbelievers to speak as if the air of Palestine were then surcharged with belief in the supernatural. Miracles were everywhere. Thus they would explain away the significance of the popular belief that our Lord wrought signs and wonders. But in so doing they set themselves a worse problem than they evade. If miracles were so very common, it would be as easy to believe that Jesus wrought them as that He worked at His father's bench. But also it would be as inconclusive. And how then are we to explain the astonishment which all the evangelists so constantly record? On any conceivable theory, these writers shared the beliefs of that age. And so did the readers who accepted their assurance that all were amazed, and that His report " went out straightway everywhere into all the region of Galilee." These are emphatic words, and both the author and his readers must have considered a miracle to be more surprising than modern critics believe they did.

Yet we do not read that any one was converted by this miracle. All were amazed, but wonder is not self-surrender. They were content to let their excitement die out, as every violent emotion must, without any change of life, any permanent devotion to the new Teacher and His doctrine.

A GROUP OF MIRACLES.

" And straightway, when they were come out of the synagogue, they came into the house of Simon and Andrew, with James and John. Now Simon's wife's mother lay sick of a fever; and straightway they tell Him of her: and He came and took her by the hand, and raised her up ; and the fever left her, and she ministered unto them. And at even, when the sun did set, they brought unto Him all that were sick, and them that were possessed with devils. And all the city was gathered together at the door. And He healed many that were sick with divers diseases, and cast out many devils ; and He suffered not the devils to speak, because they knew Him."—MARK i. 29-34 (R.V.).

ST. MATTHEW tells us that on leaving the synagogue they entered into Peter's house. St. Mark, with his peculiar sources of information, is aware that Andrew shared the house with his brother.

Especial interest attaches to the mention of the mother-in-law of Peter, as proving that Jesus chose a married man to be an apostle, the very apostle from whom the celibate ministry of Rome professes to have received the keys. The evidence does not stand alone. When St. Paul's apostolic authority was impugned, he insisted that he had the same right to bring with him in his travels a believing wife, which Peter exercised. And Clement of Alexandria tells us that Peter's wife acted as his coadjutor, ministering to women in their own homes, by which means the gospel of Christ penetrated without scandal the privacy of women's apartments. Thus the notion of a Zenana mission is by no means modern.

The mother of such a wife is afflicted by fever of a kind which still haunts that district. "And they tell Him of her." Doubtless there was solicitude and hope in their voices, even if desire did not take the shape of formal prayer. We are just emerging from that early period when belief in His power to heal might still be united with some doubt whether free application might be made to Him. His disciples might still be as unwise as those modern theologians who are so busy studying the miracles as a sign that they forget to think of them as works of love. Any such hesitation was now to be dispelled for ever.

It is possible that such is the meaning of the expression, and if so, it has a useful lesson. Sometimes there are temporal gifts which we scarce know whether we should pray for, so complex are our feelings, so entangled our interests with those of others, so obscure and dubious the springs which move our desire. Is it presumptuous to ask? Yet can it be right to keep anything back, in our communion with our Father?

Now there is a curious similarity between the expression "they tell Jesus of her" and that phrase which is only applied to prayer when St. Paul bids us pray for all that is in our hearts. "In nothing be anxious, but in everything by prayer and supplication with thanksgiving let your requests be made known unto God." So shall the great benediction be fulfilled: "The peace of God which passeth all understanding, shall guard your hearts and your thoughts" (Phil. iv. 6, 7). All that is unholy shall be purified, all that is unwise subdued, all that is expedient granted.

If this be indeed the force of St. Mark's phrase, Jesus felt their modest reticence to be a strong appeal, for St. Luke says "they besought Him," while St. Matthew merely writes that He saw her lying. The "Interpreter of St. Peter" is most likely to have caught the exact shade of anxiety and appeal by which her friends drew His attention, and which was indeed a prayer.

The gentle courtesy of our Lord's healings cannot be

too much studied by those who would know His mind and love Him. Never does He fling a careless blessing as coarse benefactors fling their alms ; we shall hereafter see how far He was from leaving fallen bread to be snatched as by a dog, even by one who would have welcomed a boon thus contemptuously given to her ; and in the hour of His arrest, when He would heal the ear of a persecutor, His courtesy appeals to those who had laid hold on Him, "Suffer ye thus far." Thus He went to this woman and took her by the hand and raised her up, laying a cool touch upon her fevered palm, bestowing His strength upon her weakness, healing her as He would fain heal humanity. For at His touch the disease was banished; with His impulse her strength returned.

We do not read that she felt bound thereupon to become an obtrusive public witness to His powers : that was not her function ; but in her quiet home she failed not to minister unto Him who had restored her powers. Would that all whose physical powers Jesus renews from sickness, might devote their energies to Him. Would that all for whom He has calmed the fever of earthly passion, might arise and be energetic in His cause.

Think of the wonder, the gladness and gratitude of their humble feast. But if we felt aright the sickness of our souls, and the grace which heals them, equal gratitude would fill our lives as He sups with us and we with Him.

Tidings of the two miracles have quickly gone abroad, and as the sun sets, and the restraint of the sabbath is removed, all the city gathers all the sick around His door.

Now here is a curious example of the peril of pressing too eagerly our inferences from the expressions of an evangelist. St. Mark tells us that they brought "all their sick and them that were possessed with devils. And He healed" (not all, but) "many that were sick, and cast out many devils." How easily we might distinguish between the "all" who came, and the "many" who were healed. Want of faith would explain the difference, and spiritual analogies would be found for those who remained unhealed at the feet of the good Physician. These lessons might be very edifying, but they would be out of place, for St. Matthew tells us that He healed them all.

But who can fail to contrast this universal movement, the urgent quest of bodily health, and the willingness of friends and neighbours to convey their sick to Jesus, with our indifference to the health of the soul, and our neglect to lead others to the Saviour. Disease being the cold shadow of sin, its removal was a kind of sacrament, an outward and visible sign that the Healer of souls was nigh. But the chillness of the shadow afflicts us more than the pollution of the substance, and few professing Christians lament a hot temper as sincerely as a fever.

As Jesus drove out the demons, He suffered them not to speak because they knew Him. We cannot believe that His rejection of their impure testimony was prudential only, whatever possibility there may have been of that charge of complicity which was afterwards actually brought. Any help which might have come to Him from the lips of hell was shocking and revolting to our Lord. And this is a lesson for all religious and political partisans who stop short of doing evil themselves, but reject no advantage which the evil deeds of others may bestow. Not so cold and negative is the

morality of Jesus. He regards as contamination whatever help fraud, suppressions of truth, injustice, by
whomsoever wrought, can yield. He rejects them by
an instinct of abhorrence, and not only because shame
and dishonour have always befallen the purest cause
which stooped to unholy alliances.

Jesus that day showed Himself powerful alike in the
congregation, in the home, and in the streets, and over
evil spirits and physical disease alike.

JESUS IN SOLITUDE.

" And in the morning, a great while before day, He rose up and went
out, and departed into a desert place, and there prayed. And Simon
and they that were with him followed after Him ; and they found Him,
and say unto Him, All are seeking Thee. And He saith unto them,
Let us go elsewhere into the next towns, that I may preach there also ;
for to this end came I forth. And He went into their synagogues
throughout all Galilee, and preaching casting out devils."—MARK i.
35–39 (R. V.).

ST. MARK is pre-eminently the historian of Christ's
activities. From him chiefly we learn to add to
our thought of perfect love and gentleness that of One
whom the zeal of God's house ate up. But this
evangelist does not omit to tell us by what secret
fountains this river of life was fed ; how the active
labours of Jesus were inspired in secret prayers. Too
often we allow to one side of religion a development
which is not excessive, but disproportinate, and we are
punished when contemplation becomes nerveless, or
energy burns itself away.

After feeding the five thousand, St. Mark tells us
that Jesus, while the storm gathered over His disciples
on the lake, went up into a mountain to pray. And St.
Luke tells of a whole night of prayer before choosing

His disciples, and how it was to pray that He climbed the mountain of transfiguration.

And we read of Him going into a desert place with His disciples, and to Olivet, and oft-times resorting to the garden where Judas found Him, where, in the dead of night, the traitor naturally sought Him.

Prayer was the spring of all His energies, and His own saying indicated the habit of His mortal life as truly as the law of His mysterious generation : " I live by the Father."

His prayers impress nothing on us more powerfully than the reality of His manhood.   He, Who possesses all things, bends His knees to crave, and His prayers are definite, no empty form, no homage without sense of need, no firing of blank cartridge without an aim.   He asks that His disciples may be with Him where He is, that Simon's strength may fail not, that He may Himself be saved from a dreadful hour.   " Such touches " said Godet " do not look like an artificial apotheosis of Jesus, and they constitute a striking difference between the gospel portrait and the legendary caricature."

The entire evening had been passed in healing the diseases of the whole town ; not the light and careless bestowal of a boon which cost nothing, but wrought with so much sympathy, such draining of His own vital forces, that St. Matthew found in it a fulfilment of the prophecy that He should Himself bear our sicknesses.   And thus exhausted, the frame might have been forgiven for demanding some indulgence, some prolongation of repose.

But the course of our Lord's ministry was now opening up before Him, and the hindrances becoming visible.   How much was to be hoped from the great impression already made ; how much to be feared from the weakness of His followers, the incipient envy of priest and Pharisee, and the volatile excitability of the crowd. At such a time, to relieve His burdened heart with Divine communion was more to Jesus than repose, as, at another time, to serve Him was meat to eat. And therefore, in the still fresh morning, long before the dawn, while every earthly sight was dim but the abysses of heaven were vivid, declaring without voice, amid the silence of earth's discord, the glory and the handiwork of His Father, Jesus went into a solitary place and prayed.

What is it that makes solitude and darkness dreadful to some, and oppressive to very many ?

Partly the sense of physical danger, born of help-lessness and uncertainty. This He never felt, who knew that He must walk to-day and to-morrow, and on the third day be perfected. And partly it is the weight of unwelcome reflection, the searching and rebukes of memory, fears that come of guilt, and inward dis-tractions of a nature estranged from the true nature of the universe. Jesus was agitated by no inward dis-cords, upbraided by no remorse. And He had probably no reveries; He is never recorded to soliloquise; solitude to Him was but another name for communion with God His Father ; He was never alone, for God was with Him.

This retirement enabled Him to remain undisturbed until His disciples found Him, long after the crowds had besieged their dwelling. They had not yet learned how all true external life must rest upon the hidden life of devotion, and there is an accent of regret in the words, " All are seeking Thee," as if Jesus could neglect in self-culture any true opportunity for service.

The answer, noteworthy in itself, demands especial

attention in these times of missions, demonstrations, Salvation Armies, and other wise and unwise attempts to gather excited crowds around the cross.

Mere sensation actually repelled Jesus. Again and again He charged men not to make Him known, in places where He would stay; while in Gadara, which He had to leave, His command to the demoniac was the reverse. Deep and real convictions are not of kin with sight-seeing and the pursuit of wonders. Capernaum has now heard His message, has received its full share of physical blessing, is exalted unto heaven. Those who were looking for redemption knew the gospel, and Jesus must preach it in other towns also. Therefore, and not to be the centre of admiring multitudes, came He forth from His quiet home.

Such is the sane and tranquil action of Jesus, in face of the excitement caused by His many miracles. Now the miracles themselves, and all that depends on them, are declared to be the creation of the wildest fanaticism, either during His lifetime or developing His legend afterwards. And if so, we have here, in the action of human mind, the marvel of modern physicists, ice from a red-hot retort, absolute moderation from a dream of frenzy. And this paradox is created in the act of "explaining" the miracles. The explanation, even were it sustained by any evidence, would be as difficult as any miracle to believe.

THE LEPER.

"And there cometh to Him a leper, beseeching Him, and kneeling down to Him, and saying unto Him, If Thou wilt, Thou canst make me clean. And being moved with compassion, He stretched forth His hand, and touched him, and saith unto him, I will ; be thou made clean. And straightway the leprosy departed from him, and he was made clean. And He strictly charged him, and straightway sent him out, and saith unto him, See thou say nothing to any man : but go thy way, show thyself to the priest, and offer for thy cleansing the things which Moses commanded, for a testimony unto them. But he went out, and began to publish it much, and to spread abroad the matter, insomuch that Jesus could no more openly enter into a city, but was without in desert places : and they came to Him from every quarter."— MARK i. 40-45 (R. V.).

THE disease of leprosy **was** peculiarly fearful to a Jew. In its stealthy beginning, its irresistible advance, the utter ruin which it wrought from the blood outward until the flesh was corroded and fell away, it was a fit type of sin, at first so trivial in its indications, but gradually usurping all the nature and corrupting it. And the terrible fact, that the children of its victims were also doomed, reminded the Israelite of the transmission of the taint of Adam.

The story of Naaman and that of Gehazi make it almost certain that the leprosy of Scripture was not contagious, for they were intimate with kings. But, apparently to complete the type, the law gave to it the artificial contagion of ceremonial uncleanness, and banished the unhappy sufferer from the dwellings of men. Thus he came to be regarded as under an especial ban, and the prophecy which announced that the illustrious Man of Sorrows would be esteemed "stricken of God," was taken to mean that He should be a leper. This banishment of the leper was indeed a remark-

able exception to the humanity of the ancient law,
but when his distress began to be extreme, and "the
plague was turned into white," he was released from
his uncleanness (Lev. xiii. 17). And this may teach
us that sin is to be dreaded most while it is yet
insidious; when developed it gives a sufficient warning
against itself. And now such a sufferer appeals to
Jesus. The incident is one of the most pathetic in the
Gospel; and its graphic details, and the shining character which it reveals, make it very perplexing to
moderate and thoughtful sceptics.

Those who believe that the charm of His presence
was "worth all the resources of medicine," agree that
Christ may have cured even leprosy, and insist that
this story, as told by St. Mark, "must be genuine."
Others suppose that the leper was already cured, and
Jesus only urged him to fulfil the requirements of the
law. And why not deny the story boldly? Why
linger so longingly over the details, when credence is
refused to what is plainly the mainspring of the whole,
the miraculous power of Jesus? The answer is plain.
Honest minds feel the touch of a great nature; the
misery of the suppliant and the compassion of his
Restorer are so vivid as to prove themselves; no
dreamer of a myth, no process of legend-building, ever
wrought after this fashion. But then, the misery and
compassion being granted, the whole story is practically
conceded. It only remains to ask, whether the "presence of the Saintly Man" could work a chemical
change in tainted blood. For it must be insisted that
the man was "full of leprosy," and not, as one suggests, already far advanced towards cure. The contrast
between his running and kneeling at the very feet
of Jesus, and the conduct of the ten lepers, not yet

released from their exclusion, who stood afar off while they cried out (Luke xvii. 12), is sufficient evidence of this, even if the express statement of St. Luke were not decisive.

Repulsive, and until now despairing, only tolerated among men through the completeness of his plague, this man pushes through the crowd which shrinks from him, kneels in an agony of supplication, and says " If Thou wilt, Thou canst make me clean." If Thou wilt! The cruelty of man has taught him to doubt the heart, even though satisfied of the power of Jesus. In a few years, men came to assume the love, and exult in the reflection that He was " able to keep what ' was ' committed to Him," " able to do exceeding abundantly above all that we ask or think." It did not occur to St. Paul that any mention of His will was needed.

Nor did Jesus Himself ask a later suppliant, " Believest thou that I am willing," but " Believest thou that I am able to do this ? "

But the charm of this delightful incident is the manner in which our Lord grants the impassioned prayer. We might have expected a shudder, a natural recoil from the loathsome spectacle, and then a wonder-working word. But misery which He could relieve did not repel Jesus; it attracted Him. His impulse was to approach. He not only answered " I will,"—and deep is the will to remove all anguish in the wonderful heart of Jesus,—but He stretched forth an unshrinking hand, and touched that death in life. It is a parable of all His course, this laying of a clean hand on the sin of the world to cleanse it. At His touch, how was the morbid frame thrilled with delightful pulses of suddenly renovated health. And how ·vas the despairing, joyless heart, incredulous of any real will to help him, soothed and healed by the pure delight of being loved.

This is the true lesson of the narrative. St. Mark treats the miraculous cure much more lightly than the tender compassion and the swift movement to relieve suffering. And He is right. The warm and generous nature revealed by this fine narrative is what, as we have seen, most impresses the doubter, and ought most to comfort the Church. For He is the same yesterday and to-day. And perhaps, if the divinity of love impressed men as much as that of power, there would be less denial of the true Godhead of our Lord.

The touch of a leper made a Jew unclean. And there is a surprising theory, that when Jesus could no more openly enter into a city, it was because the leper had disobediently published what implied His ceremonial defilement. As if our Lord were one to violate the law by stealth.

But is it very remarkable that Christ, Who was born under the law, never betrayed any anxiety about cleanness. The law of impurity was in fact an expression of human frailty. Sin spreads corruption far more easily than virtue diffuses purity. The touch of goodness fails to reproduce goodness. And the prophet Haggai has laid stress upon this contrast, that bread or pottage or wine or oil or any meat will not become holy at the touch of one who bears holy flesh in the skirt of his garment, but if one that is unclean by a dead body touch any of these, it shall be unclean (ii. 12, 13). Our hearts know full well how true to nature is the ordinance.

But Christ brought among us a virtue more contagious than our vices are, being not only a living soul, but a life-imparting Spirit. And thus He lays His hand upon this leper, upon the bier at Nain, upon the corpse of the daughter of Jairus, and as fire is kindled at the touch of fire, so instead of pollution to Him, the pureness of healthful life is imparted to the defiling and defiled.

And His followers also are to possess a religion that is vitalizing, to be the light of the world, and the salt of the earth.

If we are thus to further His cause, we must not only be zealous but obedient. Jesus strictly charged the leper not to fan the flame of an excitement which already impeded His work. But there was an invaluable service which he might render : the formal registration of his cure, the securing its official recognition by the priests, and their consent to offer the commanded sacrifices. In many a subsequent controversy, that "testimony unto them" might have been embarrassing indeed. But the leper lost his opportunity, and put them upon their guard. And as through his impulsive clamour Jesus could no more openly enter into a city, but even in desert places was beset by excited crowds, so is He deprived to-day of many a tranquil ministration and lowly service, by the zeal which despises order and quiet methods, by the undisciplined and ill-judged demonstrations of men and women whom He has blessed.

CHAPTER II.

THE SICK OF THE PALSY.

"And when He entered again into Capernaum after some days, it was noised that He was in the house."—MARK ii. 1 (R.V.).

JESUS returns to Capernaum, and an eager crowd blocks even the approaches to the house where He is known to be. St. Mark, as we should expect, relates the course of events, the multitudes, the ingenious device by which a miracle is obtained, the claim which Jesus advances to yet greater authority than heretofore, and the impression produced. But St. Luke explains that there were "sitting by," having obtained the foremost places which they loved, Pharisees and doctors of the law from every village of Galilee and Judæa, and from Jerusalem itself. And this concourse, evidently preconcerted and unfriendly, explains the first murmurs of opposition recorded by St. Mark. It was the jealousy of rival teachers which so readily pronounced Him a blasphemer.

The crowds besieged the very passages, there was no room, no, not around the door, and even if one might struggle forward, four men bearing a litter might well despair. But with palsied paralysis at stake, they would not be repulsed. They gained the roof by an outer staircase, such as the fugitives from Jerusalem should hereafter use, not going through the house.

Then they uncovered and broke up the roof, by which
strong phrases St. Mark means that they first lifted
the tiles which lay in a bed of mortar or mud, broke
through this, and then tore up the poles and light
rafters by which all this covering was supported.
Then they lowered the sick man upon his pallet, in
front of the Master as He taught.

It was an unceremonious act. However carefully
performed, the audience below must have been not only
disturbed but inconvenienced, and doubtless among
the precise and unmerciful personages in the chief
seats there was many an angry glance, many a murmur,
many a conjecture of rebukes presently to be inflicted
on the intruders.

But Jesus never in any circumstances rebuked for
intrusion any suppliant. And now He discerned the
central spiritual impulse of these men, which was
not obtrusiveness nor disrespect. They believed that
neither din while He preached, nor rubbish falling
among His audience, nor the strange interruption of a
patient and a litter intruded upon His discourse, could
weigh as much with Jesus as the appeal on a sick
man's face. And this was faith. These peasants may
have been far enough from intellectual discernment of
Christ's Personality and the scheme of salvation.
They had however a strong and practical conviction
that He would make whole their palsied friend.

Now the preaching of faith is suspected of endanger-
ing good works. But was this persuasion likely to
make these men torpid ? Is it not plain that all
spiritual apathy comes not from over-trust but from
unbelief, either doubting that sin is present death, or
else that holiness is life, and that Jesus has a gift to
bestow, not in heaven, but promptly, which is better to

gain than all the world? Therefore salvation is linked with faith, which earns nothing but elicits all, like the touch that evokes electricity, but which no man supposes to have made it.

Because they knew the curse of palsy, and believed in a present remedy, these men broke up the roof to come where Jesus was. They won their blessing, but not the less it was His free gift.

Jesus saw and rewarded the faith of all the group. The principle of mutual support and co-operation is the basis alike of the family, the nation, and the Church. Thus the great Apostle desired obscure and long-forgotten men and women to help together with him in their prayers. And He who visits the sins of the fathers upon the children unto the third and fourth generation, shows mercy unto many more, unto thousands, in them that love Him. What a rebuke is all this to men who think it enough that they should do no harm, and live inoffensive lives. Jesus now bestowed such a blessing as awoke strange misgivings among the bystanders. He divined the true burden of that afflicted heart, the dreary memories and worse fears which haunted that sick bed,—and how many are even now preparing such remorse and gloom for a bed of pain hereafter!—and perhaps He discerned the consciousness of some guilty origin of the disease. Certainly He saw there one whose thoughts went beyond his malady, a yearning soul, with hope glowing like red sparks amid the ashes of his self-reproach, that a teacher so gracious as men reported Jesus, might bring with Him a gospel indeed. We know that he felt thus, for Jesus made him of good cheer by pardon rather than by healing, and spoke of the cure itself as wrought less for his sake than as evidence.

4

Surely that was a great moment when the wistful gaze of eyes which disease had dimmed, met the eyes which were as a flame of fire, and knew that all its sullied past was at once comprehended and forgiven.

Jesus said to him, " Son, thy sins are forgiven thee." The term of endearment was new to his lips, and very emphatic ; the same which Mary used when she found Him in the temple, the same as when He argued that even evil men give good gifts unto their children. Such a relation towards Himself He recognised in this afflicted penitent. On the other hand, the dry argumentative temper of the critics is well expressed by the short crackling unemotional utterances of their orthodoxy : " Why doth this man thus speak ? He blasphemeth. Who can forgive sins but one, God." There is no zeal in it, no passion for God's honour, no spiritual insight, it is as heartless as a syllogism. And in what follows a fine contrast is implied between their perplexed orthodoxy, and Christ's profound discernment. For as He had just read the sick man's heart, so He " perceived in His spirit that they so reasoned within themselves." And He asks them the searching question, " Whether is easier to say, Thy sins be forgiven thee, or to say, Arise and walk ? " Now which is really easier ? It is not enough to lay all the emphasis upon " to say," as if with Jesus the ease of an utterance depended on the difficulty of testing it. There is indeed a certain irony in the question. They doubtless imagined that Jesus was evading their scrutiny by only bestowing what they could not test. To them forgiveness seemed more easily offered than a cure. To the Christian, it is less to heal disease, which is a mere consequence, than sin, which is the source of all our woes. To the power of Jesus they were alike, and connected with each other as the symptom and the true disease. In truth, all the compassion which blesses our daily life is a pledge of grace ; and He Who healeth all our diseases forgiveth also all our iniquities. But since healing was the severer test in their reckoning, Jesus does not evade it. He restores the palsied man to health, that they might know that the Son of man hath authority on earth to forgive sins. So then, pardon does not lie concealed and doubtful in the councils of an unknown world. It is pronounced on earth. The Son of man, wearing our nature and touched with our infirmities, bestows it still, in the Scriptures, in the Sacraments, in the ministrations of His servants. Wherever He discerns faith, He responds with assurance of the absolution and remission of sins.

He claims to do this, as men had so lately observed that He both taught and worked miracles, "with authority." We then saw that this word expressed the direct and personal mastery with which He wrought, and which the apostles never claimed for themselves.

Therefore this text cannot be quoted in defence of priestly absolutions, as long as these are hypothetical, and depend on the recipient's earnestness, or on any supposition, any uncertainty whatever. Christ did not utter a hypothesis.

Fortunately, too, the argument that men, priestly men, must have authority on earth to forgive sins, because the Son of man has such authority, can be brought to an easy test. There is a passage elsewhere, which asserts His authority, and upon which the claim to share it can be tried. The words are, "The Father gave Him authority to execute judgment, because He is the Son of man," and they are immediately followed by an announcement of the resurrection to judgment (John v. 27, 29). Is any one prepared to contend that such authority as that is vested in other sons of men ? And if not that, why this ?

But if priestly absolutions are not here, there remains the certainty that Jesus brought to earth, to man, the gift of prompt effective pardon, to be realized by faith.

The sick man is ordered to depart at once. Further discourse might perhaps be reserved for others, but he may not linger, having received his own bodily and spiritual medicine. The teaching of Christ is not for curiosity. It is good for the greatly blessed to be alone. And it is sometimes dangerous for obscure people to be thrust into the centre of attention.

Hereupon, another touch of nature discovers itself in the narrative, for it is now easy to pass through the crowd. Men who would not in their selfishness give place for palsied misery, readily make room for the distinguished person who has received a miraculous blessing.

THE SON OF MAN.

"The Son of man hath power on earth to forgive sins."—MARK ii. 10.

WHEN asserting His power to forgive sins, Jesus, for the first time in our Gospel, called Himself the Son of man.

It is a remarkable phrase. The profound reverence which He from the first inspired, restrained all other lips from using it, save only when the first martyr felt such a rush of sympathy from above poured into his soul, that the thought of Christ's humanity was more moving than that of His deity. So too it is then alone that He is said to be not enthroned in heaven, but standing, "the Son of man, standing on the right hand of God" (Acts vii. 56).*

---

* The exceptions in the Revelation are only apparent. St. John does not call Jesus the Son of man (i. 13), nor see Him, but only the type of Him, standing (v. 6).

What then does this title imply ? Beyond doubt it is derived from Daniel's vision : " Behold there came with the clouds of heaven one like unto a Son of man, and He came even to the Ancient of Days " (vii. 13). And it was by the bold and unequivocal appropriation of this verse that Jesus brought upon Himself the judgment of the council (Matt. xxvi. 64 ; Mark xiv. 62).

Now the first impression which the phrase in Daniel produces is that of strong and designed contrast between the Son of man and the Eternal God. We wonder at seeing man " brought nigh " to Deity. Nor may we suppose that to be " like unto a Son of man," implies only an appearance of manhood. In Daniel the Messiah can be cut off. When Jesus uses the epithet, and even when He quotes the prophecy, He not only resembles a Son of man, He is truly such ; He is most frequently " *the* Son of man," the pre-eminent, perhaps the only one.*

But while the expression intimates a share in the lowliness of human nature, it does not imply a lowly rank among men.

Our Lord often suggested by its use the difference between His circumstances and His dignity. " The Son of man hath not where to lay His head :" " Betrayest thou the Son of man with a kiss," in each of these we feel that the title asserts a claim to different treatment. And in the great verse, God " hath given Him authority to execute judgment, because He is the Son of man," we discern that although human hands are chosen as fittest to do judgment upon humanity, yet His extraordinary dignity is also taken into account.

---

* And this proves beyond question that He did not merely follow Ezekiel in applying to himself the epithet as if it meant a son among many sons of men, but took the description in Daniel for His own. Ezekiel himself indeed never employs the phrase : he only records it.

The title belongs to our Lord's humiliation, but is far
from an additional abasement ; it asserts His supremacy
over those whom He is not ashamed to call brethren.

We all are sons of men ; and Jesus used the phrase
when He promised that all manner of sins and blasphemies shall be forgiven to us. But there is a higher
sense in which, among thousands of the ignoble, we
single out one "real man ;" and in this sense, as fulfilling
the idea, Jesus was the Second Man. What a difference
exists between the loftiest sons of vulgar men, and the
Son of our complete humanity, of the race, " of Man."
The pre-eminence even of our best and greatest is
fragmentary and incomplete. In their veins runs but a
portion of the rich life-blood of the race : but a share of
its energy throbs in the greatest bosom. We seldom
find the typical thinker in the typical man of action.
Originality of purpose and of means are not commonly
united. To know all that holiness embraces, we must
combine the energies of one saint with the gentler graces
of a second and the spiritual insight of a third. There
is no man of genius who fails to make himself the child
of his nation and his age, so that Shakespeare would be
impossible in France, Hugo in Germany, Goethe in Eng-
land. Two great nations slay their kings and surrender
their liberties to military dictators, but Napoleon would
have been unendurable to us, and Cromwell ridiculous
across the channel.

Large allowances are to be made for the Greek in
Plato, the Roman in Epictetus, before we can learn of
them. Each and all are the sons of their tribe and
century, not of all mankind and all time. But who
will point out the Jewish warp in any word or institution of Jesus? In the new man which is after His
image there cannot be Greek and Jew, circumcision and

uncircumcision, barbarian, Scythian, bondman, freeman, but Christ is all and in all, something of Him represented by each, all of them concentrated in Him. He alone speaks to all men without any foreign accent, and He alone is recognised and understood as widely as the voices of nature, as the sigh of waves and breezes, and the still endurance of the stars. Reading the Gospels, we become aware that four writers of widely different bias and temperament have all found an equally congenial subject, so that each has given a portrait harmonious with the others, and yet unique. It is because the sum total of humanity is in Christ, that no single writer could have told His story.

But now consider what this implies. It demands an example from which lonely women and heroic leaders of action should alike take fire. It demands that He should furnish meditation for sages in the closet, and should found a kingdom more brilliant than those of conquerors. It demands that He should strike out new paths towards new objects, and be supremely original without deviating from what is truly sane and human, for any selfish or cruel or unwholesome joy. It demands the gentleness of a sheep before her shearers, and such burning wrath as seven times over denounced against the hypocrites of Jerusalem woe and the damnation of hell. It demands the sensibilities which made Gethsemane dreadful, and the strength which made Calvary sublime. It demands that when we approach Him we should learn to feel the awe of other worlds, the nearness of God, the sinfulness of sin, the folly of laying up much goods for many years; that life should be made solemn and profound, but yet that it should not be darkened nor depressed unduly; that nature and man should be made dear to us, little children, and sinners who are scorned yet who love much, and lepers who stand afar off—yes, and even the lilies of the field, and the fowls of the air; that He should not be unaware of the silent processes of nature which bears fruit of itself, of sunshine and rain, and the fury of storms and torrents, and the leap of the lightning across all the sky. Thus we can bring to Jesus every anxiety and every hope, for He, and only He, was tempted in all points like unto us. Universality of power, of sympathy, and of influence, is the import of this title which Jesus claims. And that demand Jesus only has satisfied, Who is the Master of Sages, the Friend of sinners, the Man of Sorrows, and the King of kings, the one perfect blossom on the tree of our humanity, the ideal of our nature incarnate, the Second Adam in Whom the fulness of the race is visible. The Second Man is the Lord from Heaven. And this strange and solitary grandeur He foretold, when He took to Himself this title, itself equally strange and solitary, the Son of man.

THE CALL AND FEAST OF LEVI.

"And He went forth again by the sea side; and all the multitude resorted unto Him, and He taught them. And as He passed by, He saw Levi the *son* of Alphæus sitting at the place of toll, and He saith unto him, Follow Me. And he arose and followed Him. And it came to pass, that He was sitting at meat in his house, and many publicans and sinners sat down with Jesus and His disciples: for there were many, and they followed Him. And the scribes of the Pharisees, when they saw that He was eating with the sinners and publicans, said unto His disciples, He eateth and drinketh with publicans and sinners. And when Jesus heard it, He saith unto them, They that are whole have no need of a physician, but they that are sick: I came not to call the righteous, but sinners."—MARK ii. 13-17 (R.V.).

JESUS loved the open air. His custom when teaching was to point to the sower, the lily, and the bird. He is no pale recluse emerging from a library to instruct, in the dim religious light of cloisters, a world unknown except by books. Accordingly we find Him "again by the sea-side." And however the scribes and Pharisees may have continued to murmur, the multitudes resorted to Him, confiding in the evidence of their experience, which never saw it on this fashion.

That argument was perfectly logical; it was an induction, yet it led them to a result curiously the reverse of theirs who reject miracles for being contrary to experience. "Yes," they said, "we appeal to experience, but the conclusion is that good deeds which it cannot parallel must come directly from the Giver of all good."

Such good deeds continue. The creed of Christ has re-formed Europe, it is awakening Asia, it has transformed morality, and imposed new virtues on the conscience. It is the one religion for the masses, the lapsed, and indeed for the sick in body as truly as in soul; for while science discourses with enthusiasm upon progress by the rejection of the less fit, our faith cherishes these in hospitals, asylums, and retreats, and prospers by lavishing care upon the outcast and rejected of the world. Now this transcends experience: we never saw it on this fashion; it is supernatural. Or else let scientific atheism produce its reformed magdalens, and its homes for the hopelessly diseased and imbecile, and all "the weakest" who go, as she tenderly assures us, "to the wall."

Jesus now gave a signal proof of His independence of human judgment, His care for the despised and rejected. For such a one He completed the rupture between Himself and the rulers of the people.

Sitting at the receipt of toll, in the act of levying from his own nation the dues of the conqueror, Levi the publican received the call to become an Apostle and Evangelist. It was a resolute defiance of the pharisaic judgment. It was a memorable rebuke for those timid slaves of expediency who nurse their influence, refuse to give offence, fear to "mar their usefulness" by "compromising themselves," and so make their whole life one abject compromise, and let all emphatic usefulness go by.

Here is one upon whom the bigot scowls more darkly still than upon Jesus Himself, by whom the Roman yoke is pressed upon Hebrew necks, an apostate in men's judgment from the national faith and hope. And such judgments sadly verify themselves; a despised man easily becomes despicable.

But however Levi came by so strange and hateful an office, Jesus saw in him no slavish earner of vile bread by doing the foreigner's hateful work. He was more willing than they who scorned him to follow the true King of Israel. It is even possible that the national humiliations to which his very office testified led him to other aspirations, longings after a spiritual kingdom beyond reach of the sword or the exactions of Rome. For his Gospel is full of the true kingdom of heaven, the spiritual fulfilments of prophecy, and the relations between the Old Testament and the Messiah.

Here then is an opportunity to show the sneering scribe and carping Pharisee how little their cynical criticism weighs with Jesus. He calls the despised agent of the heathen to His side, and is obeyed. And now the name of the publican is engraven upon one of the foundations of the city of God.

Nor did Jesus refuse to carry such condescension to its utmost limit, eating and drinking in Levi's house with many publicans and sinners, who were already attracted by His teaching, and now rejoiced in His familiarity. Just in proportion as He offended the pharisaic scribes, so did He inspire with new hope the unhappy classes who were taught to consider themselves castaway. His very presence was medicinal, a rebuke to foul words and thoughts, an outward and visible sign of grace. It brought pure air and sunshine into a fever-stricken chamber.

And this was His justification when assailed. He had borne healing to the sick. He had called sinners to repentance. And therefore His example has a double message. It rebukes those who look curiously on the intercourse of religious people with the world, who are plainly of opinion that the leaven should be hid anywhere but in the meal, who can never fairly understand St. Paul's permission to go to an idolater's feast. But it gives no licence to go where we cannot be a healing influence, where the light must be kept in a dark lantern if not under a bushel, where, instead of drawing men upward, we shall only confirm their indolent self-satisfaction.

Christ's reason for seeking out the sick, the lost, is ominous indeed for the self-satisfied. The whole have no need of a physician; He came not to call the righteous. Such persons, whatever else they be, are not Christians until they come to a different mind.

In calling Himself the Physician of sick souls, Jesus made a startling claim, which becomes more emphatic when we observe that He also quoted the words of Hosea, "I will have mercy and not sacrifice" (Matt. ix. 13; Hos. vi. 6). For this expression occurs in that chapter which tells how the Lord Himself hath smitten and will bind us up. And the complaint is just before it that when Ephraim saw his sickness and Judah saw his wound, then went Ephraim to Assyria and sent to king Jareb, but he is not able to heal you, neither shall he cure you of your wound (Hos. v. 13–vi. 1). As the Lord Himself hath torn, so He must heal.

Now Jesus comes to that part of Israel which the Pharisees despise for being wounded and diseased, and justifies Himself by words which must, from their context, have reminded every Jew of the declaration that God is the physician, and it is vain to seek healing elsewhere. And immediately afterwards, He claims to be the Bridegroom, whom also Hosea spoke of as divine. Yet men profess that only in St. John does He advance such claims that we should ask, Whom makest Thou Thyself? Let them try the experiment, then, of putting such words into the lips of any mortal.

The choice of the apostles, and most of all that of Levi, illustrates the power of the cross to elevate obscure and commonplace lives. He was born, to all appearance, to an uneventful, unobserved existence. We read no remarkable action of the Apostle Matthew; as an Evangelist he is simple, orderly and accurate, as becomes a man of business, but the graphic energy of St. Mark, the pathos of St. Luke, the profundity of St. John are absent. Yet his greatness will outlive the world.

Now as Christ provided nobility and a career for this man of the people, so He does for all. " Are all apostles ? " Nay, but all may become pillars in the temple of eternity. The gospel finds men plunged in monotony, in the routine of callings which machinery and the subdivision of labour make ever more colour-less, spiritless, and dull. It is a small thing that it introduces them to a literature more sublime than Milton, more sincere and direct than Shakespere. It brings their little lives into relationship with eternity. It braces them for a vast struggle, watched by a great cloud of witnesses. It gives meaning and beauty to the sordid present, and to the future a hope full of immortality. It brings the Christ of God nearer to the humblest than when of old He ate and drank with publicans and sinners.

THE CONTROVERSY CONCERNING FASTING.

" And John's disciples and the Pharisees were fasting : and they come and say unto Him, Why do John's disciples and the disciples of the Pharisees fast, but Thy disciples fast not ? "—MARK ii. 18 (R.V.).

THE Pharisees had just complained to the disciples that Jesus ate and drank in questionable company. Now they join with the followers of the ascetic Baptist in complaining to Jesus that His disciples eat and drink at improper seasons, when others fast. And as Jesus had then replied, that being a Physician, He was naturally found among the sick, so He now answered, that being the Bridegroom, fasting in His presence is impossible : " Can the sons of the bridechamber fast while the Bridegroom is with them ? " A new spirit is working in Christianity, far too mightily to be restrained by ancient usages; if the new wine be put into such wineskins it will spoil them, and itself be lost.

Hereupon three remarkable subjects call for attention : the immense personal claim advanced ; the view which Christ takes of fasting ; and, arising out of this, the principle which He applies to all external rites and ceremonies.

I. Jesus does not inquire whether the fasts of other men were unreasonable or not. In any case, He declares that His mere presence put everything on a new footing for His followers who could not fast simply

because He was by.   Thus He assumes a function high
above that of any prophet or teacher : He not only
reveals duty, as a lamp casts light upon the compass
by which men steer ; but He modifies duty itself, as
iron deflects the needle.

This is because He is the Bridegroom.

The disciples of John would hereupon recall his
words of self-effacement ; that He was only the friend
of the Bridegroom, whose fullest joy was to hear the
Bridegroom's exultant voice.

But no Jew could forget the Old Testament use of
the phrase. It is clear from St. Matthew that this
controversy followed immediately upon the last, when
Jesus assumed a function ascribed to God Himself by
the very passage from Hosea which He then quoted.
Then He was the Physician for the soul's diseases ;
now He is the Bridegroom, in Whom centre its hopes, its
joys, its affections, its new life.   That position in the
spiritual existence cannot be given away from God
without idolatry.   The same Hosea who makes God the
Healer, gives to Him also, in the most explicit words,
what Jesus now claims for Himself.   " I will betroth
thee unto Me for ever . . . I will even betroth thee
unto Me in faithfulness, and thou shalt know the Lord '
(ii. 19, 20).   Isaiah too declares "thy Maker is thy
husband," and " as the bridegroom rejoiceth over the
bride, so shall thy God rejoice over thee" (liv. 5 ; lxii.
5).   And in Jeremiah, God remembers the love of
Israel's espousals, who went after Him in the wilderness,
in a land that was not sown (ii. 2).   Now all this is
transferred throughout the New Testament to Jesus.
The Baptist is not alone in this respect.   St. John regards the Bride as the wife of the Lamb (Rev. xxi. 9).
St. Paul would fain present his Corinthian Church as

a pure virgin to Christ, as to one husband (2 Cor. xi. 2). For him, the absolute oneness of marriage is a mystery of the union betwixt Christ and His Church (Eph. v 32). If Jesus be not God, then a relation hitherto exclusively belonging to Jehovah, to rob Him of which is the adultery of the soul, has been systematically transferred by the New Testament to a creature. His glory has been given to another.

This remarkable change is clearly the work of Jesus Himself. The marriage supper of which He spoke is for the King's son. At His return the cry will be heard, Behold the Bridegroom cometh. In this earliest passage His presence causes the joy of the Bride, who said to the Lord in the Old Testament, Thou art my Husband (Hosea ii. 16).

There is not to be found in the Gospel of St. John a passage more certainly calculated to inspire, when Christ's dignity was assured by His resurrection and ascension, the adoration which His Church has always paid to the Lamb in the midst of the throne.

II. The presence of the Bridegroom dispenses with the obligation to fast. Yet it is beyond denial that fasting as a religious exercise comes within the circle of New Testament sanctions. Jesus Himself, when taking our burdens upon Him, as He had stooped to the baptism of repentance, condescended also to fast. He taught His disciples when they fasted to anoint their head and wash their face. The mention of fasting is indeed a later addition to the words " this kind (of demon) goeth not out but by prayer" (Mark ix. 29), but we know that the prophets and teachers of Antioch were fasting when bidden to consecrate Barnabas and Saul, and they fasted again and prayed before they laid their hands upon them (Acts xiii. 2, 3).

Thus it is right to fast, at times and from one point of view ; but at other times, and from Jewish and formal motives, it is unnatural and mischievous. It is right when the Bridegroom is taken away, a phrase which certainly does not cover all this space between the Ascension and the Second Advent, since Jesus still reveals Himself to His own though not unto the world, and is with His Church all the days. Scripture has no countenance for the notion that we lost by the Ascension in privilege or joy. But when the body would fain rise up against the spirit, it must be kept under and brought into subjection (1 Cor. ix. 27). When the closest domestic joys would interrupt the seclusion of the soul with God, they may be suspended, though but for a time (1 Cor. vii. 5). And when the supreme blessing of intercourse with God, the presence of the Bridegroom, is obscured or forfeited through sin, it will then be as inevitable that the loyal heart should turn away from worldly pleasures, as that the first disciples should reject these in the dread hours of their bereavement.

Thus Jesus abolished the superstition that grace may be had by a mechanical observance of a prescribed regimen at an appointed time. He did not deny, but rather implied the truth, that body and soul act and counteract so that spiritual impressions may be weakened and forfeited by untimely indulgence of the flesh.

By such teaching, Jesus carried forward the doctrine already known to the Old Testament. There it was distinctly announced that the return from exile abrogated those fasts which commemorated national calamities, so that "the fast of the fourth month, and of the fifth, and of the seventh and of the tenth shall be to the house of Israel joy and gladness, cheerful feasts " (Zech.

vii. 3, viii. 19). Even while these fasts had lasted they had been futile, because they were only formal. " When ye fasted and mourned, did ye at all fast unto me ? And when ye eat, and when ye drink, do ye not eat for yourselves, and drink for yourselves?" (Zech. vii. 5, 6). And Isaiah had plainly laid down the great rule, that a fast and an acceptable day unto the Lord was not a day to afflict the soul and bow the head, but to deny and discipline our selfishness for some good end, to loose the bonds of wickedness, to undo the bands of the yoke, and to let the oppressed go free, to deal bread to the hungry, and to bring home the poor that is cast out (Isa. lviii. 5–7).

The true spirit of fasting breathes an ampler breath in any of the thousand forms of Christian self-denial, than in those petty abstinences, those microscopic observances, which move our wonder less by the superstition which expects them to bring grace than by the childishness which expects them to have any effect whatever.

III. Jesus now applies a great principle to all external rites and ceremonies. They have their value. As the wineskin retains the wine, so are feelings and aspirations aided, and even preserved, by suitable external forms. Without these, emotion would lose itself for want of restraint, wasted, like spilt wine, by diffuseness. And if the forms are unsuitable and outworn, the same calamity happens, the strong new feelings break through them, "and the wine perisheth, and the skins." In this respect, how many a sad experience of the Church attests the wisdom of her Lord ; what losses have been suffered in the struggle between forms that had stiffened into archaic ceremonialism and new zeal demanding scope for its energy, between the antiquated phrases of a bygone age and the new experience, knowledge and requirements of the next, between the frosty precisions of unsympathetic age and the innocent warmth and freshness of the young, too often, alas, lost to their Master in passionate revolt against restraints which He neither imposed nor smiled upon.

Therefore the coming of a new revelation meant the repeal of old observances, and Christ refused to sew His new faith like a patchwork upon ancient institutions, of which it would only complete the ruin. Thus He anticipated the decision of His apostles releasing the Gentiles from the law of Moses. And He bestowed on His Church an adaptiveness to various times and places, not always remembered by missionaries among the heathen, by fastidious critics of new movements at home, nor by men who would reduce the lawfulness of modern agencies to a question of precedent and archæology.

THE SABBATH.

"And it came to pass, that He was going on the sabbath day through the cornfields; and His disciples began, as they went, to pluck the ears of corn. And the Pharisees said unto Him, Behold, why do they on the sabbath day that which is not lawful? And He said unto them, Did ye never read what David did, when he had need, and was an hungred, he, and they that were with him? How he entered into the house of God when Abiathar was high priest, and did eat the shewbread, which it is not lawful to eat save for the priests, and gave also to them that were with him? And He said unto them, The sabbath was made for man, and not man for the sabbath: so that the Son of man is Lord even of the sabbath."—MARK ii. 23-28 (R.V.).

TWICE in succession Christ had now asserted the freedom of the soul against His Jewish antagonists. He was free to eat with sinners, for their good, and His followers were free to disregard fasts, because the

Bridegroom was with them. A third attack in the
same series is prepared. The Pharisees now take
stronger ground, since the law itself enforced the
obligation of the Sabbath. Even Isaiah, the most
free-spirited of all the prophets, in the same passage
where he denounced the fasts of the self-righteous,
bade men to keep their foot from the Sabbath (Isa.
lviii. 13, 14). Here they felt sure of their position ; and
when they found the disciples, in a cornfield where the
long stems had closed over the path, " making a way,"
which was surely forbidden labour, and this by
" plucking the ears," which was reaping, and then
rubbing these in their hands to reject the chaff, which
was winnowing, they cried out in affected horror,
Behold, why do they that which is not lawful ? To
them it mattered nothing that the disciples really
hungered, and that abstinence, rather than the slight
exertion which they condemned, would cause real inconvenience and unrest.

Perhaps the answer of our Lord has been as much
misunderstood as any other words He ever spoke. It
has been assumed that He spoke across the boundary
between the new dispensation and the old, as One
from whose movements the restraints of Judaism had
entirely fallen away, to those who were still entangled
And it has been inferred that the Fourth Commandment was no more than such a restraint, now thrown
off among the rest. But this is quite a misapprehen-
sion both of His position and theirs. On earth He
was a minister of the circumcision. He bade His
disciples to observe and do all that was commanded
from the seat of Moses. And it is by Old Testament
precedent, and from Old Testament principles, that He
now refutes the objection of the Pharisees. This is

what gives the passage half its charm, this discovery
of freedom like our own in the heart of the stern old
Hebrew discipline, as a fountain and flowers on the face
of a granite crag, this demonstration that all we now
enjoy is developed from what already lay in germ
enfolded in the law.

David and his followers, when at extremity, had
eaten the shewbread which it was not lawful for them
to eat.   It is a striking assertion.   We should probably have sought a softer phrase.   We should have said
that in other circumstances it would have been unlawful, that only necessity made it lawful ; we should have
refused to look straight in the face the naked ugly fact
that David broke the law.   But Jesus was not afraid
of any fact.   He saw and declared that the priests in
the Temple itself profaned the Sabbath when they
baked the shewbread and when they circumcised children.   They were blameless, not because the Fourth
Commandment remained inviolate, but because circumstances made it right for them to profane the Sabbath.
And His disciples were blameless also, upon the same
principle, that the larger obligation overruled the
lesser, that all ceremonial observance gave way to
human need, that mercy is a better thing than sacrifice.

And thus it appeared that the objectors were themselves the transgressors ; they had condemned the
guiltless.

A little reflection will show that our Lord's bold
method, His startling admission that David and the
priests alike did that which was not lawful, is much
more truly reverential than our soft modern compro-
mises, our shifty devices for persuading ourselves that
in various permissible and even necessary deviations

from prescribed observances, there is no real infraction of any law whatever.

To do this, we reduce to a minimum the demands of the precept. We train ourselves to think, not of its full extension, but of what we can compress it into. Therefore, in future, even when no urgency exists, the precept has lost all beyond this minimum; its sharp edges are filed away. Jesus leaves it to resume all its energy, when mercy no longer forbids the sacrifice.

The text, then, says nothing about the abolition of a Day of Rest. On the contrary, it declares that this day is not a Jewish but a universal ordinance, it is made for man. At the same time, it refuses to place the Sabbath among the essential and inflexible laws of right and wrong. It is made for man, for his physical repose and spiritual culture; man was not made for it, as he is for purity, truth, and godliness. Better for him to die than outrage these; they are the laws of his very being; he is royal by serving them; in obeying them he obeys his God. It is not thus with anything external, ceremonial, any ritual, any rule of conduct, however universal be its range, however permanent its sanctions. The Sabbath is such a rule, permanent, far-reaching as humanity, made "for man." But this very fact, Jesus tells us, is the reason why He Who represented the race and its interests, was "Lord even of the Sabbath."

Let those who deny the Divine authority of this great institution ponder well the phrase which asserts its universal range, and which finds it a large assertion of the mastery of Christ that He is Lord "even of the Sabbath." But those who have scruples about the change of day by which honour is paid to Christ's

resurrection, and those who would make burdensome
and dreary, a horror to the young and a torpor to the
old, what should be called a delight and honourable,
these should remember that the ordinance is blighted,
root and branch, when it is forbidden to minister to
the physical or spiritual welfare of the human race.

CHAPTER III.

THE WITHERED HAND.

"And He entered again into the synagogue ; and there was a man there which had his hand withered. And they watched Him, whether He would heal him on the sabbath day ; that they might accuse Him. And He saith unto the man that had his hand withered, Stand forth. And He saith unto them, Is it lawful on the sabbath day to do good or to do harm? to save a life, or to kill? But they held their peace. And when He had looked round about on them with anger, being grieved at the hardening of their heart, He saith unto the man, Stretch forth thy hand. And he stretched it forth : and his hand was restored. And the Pharisees went out, and straightway with the Herodians took counsel against Him, how they might destroy Him."— MARK iii. 1-6 (R.V.).

IN the controversies just recorded, we have recognised the ideal Teacher, clear to discern and quick to exhibit the decisive point at issue, careless of small pedantries, armed with principles and precedents which go to the heart of the dispute.

But the perfect man must be competent in more than theory ; and we have now a marvellous example of tact, decision and self-control in action. When Sabbath observance is again discussed, his enemies have resolved to push matters to extremity. They watch, no longer to cavil, but that they may accuse Him. It is in the synagogue; and their expectations are sharpened by the presence of a pitiable object, a man whose hand is not only paralyzed in the sinews, but withered up and hopeless. St. Luke tells us that it was the right

hand, which deepened his misery. And St. Matthew
records that they asked Christ, Is it lawful to heal on
the Sabbath day ? thus urging Him by a challenge to
the deed which they condemned. What a miserable
state of mind ! They believe that Jesus can work the
cure, since this is the very basis of their plot ; and yet
their hostility is not shaken, for belief in a miracle is
not conversion ; to acknowledge a prodigy is one thing,
and to surrender the will is quite another. Or how
should we see around us so many Christians in theory,
reprobates in life ? They long to see the man healed,
yet there is no compassion in this desire, hatred urges
them to wish what mercy impels Christ to grant. But
while He relieves the sufferer, He will also expose their
malice. Therefore He makes His intention public, and
whets their expectation, by calling the man forth into
the midst. And then He meets their question with
another : Is it lawful to do good on the Sabbath day or
evil, to save life or to kill ? And when they preserved
their calculated silence, we know how He pressed the
question home, reminding them that not one of them
would fail to draw His own sheep out of a pit upon
the Sabbath day. Selfishness made the difference, for
a man was better than a sheep, but did not, like the
sheep, belong to them. They do not answer : instead
of warning Him away from guilt, they eagerly await
the incriminating act : we can almost see the spiteful
subtle smile playing about their bloodless lips ; and
Jesus marks them well. He looked round about them
in anger, but not in bitter personal resentment, for He
was grieved at the hardness of their hearts, and pitied
them also, even while enduring such contradiction of
sinners against Himself. This is the first mention by
St. Mark of that impressive gaze, afterwards so frequent

in every Gospel, which searched the scribe who answered well, and melted the heart of Peter.

And now, by one brief utterance, their prey breaks through their meshes. Any touch would have been a work, a formal infraction of the law. Therefore there is no touch, neither is the helpless man bidden to take up any burden, or instigated to the slightest ritual irregularity. Jesus only bids him do what was forbidden to none, but what had been impossible for him to perform; and the man succeeds, he does stretch forth his hand: he is healed: the work is done. Yet nothing has been done; as a work of healing not even a word has been said. For He who would so often defy their malice has chosen to show once how easily He can evade it, and not one of them is more free from any blame, however technical, than He. The Pharisees are so utterly baffled, so helpless in His hands, so "filled with madness" that they invoke against this new foe the help of their natural enemies, the Herodians. These appear on the stage because the immense spread of the Messianic movement endangers the Idumæan dynasty. When first the wise men sought an infant King of the Jews, the Herod of that day was troubled. That instinct which struck at His cradle is now reawakened, and will not slumber again until the fatal day when the new Herod shall set Him at nought and mock Him. In the meanwhile these strange allies perplex themselves with the hard question, How is it possible to destroy so acute a foe.

While observing their malice, and the exquisite skill which baffles it, we must not lose sight of other lessons. It is to be observed that no offence to hypocrites, no danger to Himself, prevented Jesus from removing human suffering. And also that He expects from the

man a certain co-operation involving faith: he must
stand forth in the midst; every one must see his un-
happiness; he is to assume a position which will
become ridiculous unless a miracle is wrought.   Then
he must make an effort.   In the act of stretching forth
his hand the strength to stretch it forth is given ; but
he would not have tried the experiment unless he
trusted before he discovered the power.   Such is the
faith demanded of our sin-stricken and helpless souls;
a faith which confesses its wretchedness, believes in
the good will of God and the promises of Christ, and
receives the experience of blessing through having acted
on the belief that already the blessing is a fact in the
Divine volition.

Nor may we overlook the mysterious impalpable
spiritual power which effects its purposes without a
touch, or even an explicit word of healing import.
What is it but the power of Him Who spake and it
was done, Who commanded and it stood fast ?

And all this vividness of look and bearing, this
innocent subtlety of device combined with a boldness
which stung His foes to madness, all this richness and
verisimilitude of detail, this truth to the character of
Jesus, this spiritual freedom from the trammels of a
system petrified and grown rigid, this observance in a
secular act of the requirements of the spiritual kingdom,
all this wealth of internal evidence goes to attest one
of the minor miracles which sceptics declare to be
incredible.

THE CHOICE OF THE TWELVE.

"And Jesus with His disciples withdrew to the sea: and a great multitude from Galilee followed: and from Judæa, and from Jerusalem, and from Idumæa, and beyond Jordan, and about Tyre and Sidon, a great multitude, hearing what great things He did, came unto Him. And He spake to His disciples, that a little boat should wait on Him because of the crowd, lest they should throng Him: for He had healed many; insomuch that as many as had plagues pressed upon Him that they might touch Him. And the unclean spirits, whensoever they beheld Him, fell down before Him, and cried, saying, Thou art the Son of God. And He charged them much that they should not make Him known. And He goeth up into the mountain, and calleth unto Him whom He Himself would: and they went unto Him. And He appointed twelve, that they might be with Him, and that He might send them forth to preach, and to have authority to cast out devils: and Simon he surnamed Peter; and James the *son* of Zebedee, and John the brother of James; and them He surnamed Boanerges, which is, Sons of thunder: and Andrew, and Philip, and Bartholomew, and Matthew, and Thomas, and James the *son* of Alphæus, and Thaddæus, and Simon the Cananæan, and Judas Iscariot, which also betrayed Him."— MARK iii. 7–19 (R.V.).

WE have reached a crisis in the labours of the Lord, when hatred which has become deadly is preparing a blow. The Pharisees are aware, by a series of experiences, that His method is destructive to their system, that He is too fearless to make terms with them, that He will strip the mask off their faces. Their rage was presently intensified by an immense extension of His fame. And therefore He withdrew from the plots which ripen most easily in cities, the hotbeds of intrigue, to the open coast. It is His first retreat before opposition, and careful readers of the Gospels must observe that whenever the pressure of His enemies became extreme, He turned for safety to the simple fishermen, among whom they had no party, since they had preached no gospel to the poor, and that He was frequently conveyed by water from point to point, easily reached by followers, who sometimes indeed outran Him upon foot, but where treason had to begin its wiles afresh. Hither, perhaps camping along the beach, came a great multitude not only from Galilee but also from Judæa, and even from the capital, the headquarters of the priesthood, and by a journey of several days from Idumæa, and from Tyre and Sidon, so that afterwards, even there, He could not be hid. Many came to see what great things He did, but others bore with them some afflicted friend, or were themselves sore stricken by disease. And Jesus gave like a God, opening His hand and satisfying their desires, " for power went out of Him, and healed them all." Not yet had the unbelief of man restrained the compassion of His heart, and forced Him to exhibit another phase of the mind of God, by refusing to give that which is holy to the dogs. As yet, therefore, He healeth all their diseases. Then arose an unbecoming and irreverent rush of as many as had plagues to touch Him. A more subtle danger mingled itself with this peril from undue eagerness. For unclean spirits, who knew His mysterious personality, observed that this was still a secret, and was no part of His teaching, since His disciples could not bear it yet. Many months afterwards, flesh and blood had not revealed it even to Peter. And therefore the demons made malicious haste to proclaim Him the Son of God, and Jesus was obliged to charge them much that they should not make Him known. This action of His may teach His followers to be discreet. Falsehood indeed is always evil, but at times reticence is a duty, because certain truths are a medicine too powerful for some stages of spiritual disease. The strong sun which ripens the grain in autumn, would burn up the tender germs of spring.

But it was necessary to teach as well as to heal. And Jesus showed his ready practical ingenuity, by arranging that a little boat should wait on Him, and furnish at once a pulpit and a retreat.

And now Jesus took action distinctly Messianic. The harvest of souls was plenteous, but the appointed labourers were unfaithful, and a new organisation was to take their place. The sacraments and the apostolate are indeed the only two institutions bestowed upon His Church by Christ Himself; but the latter is enough to show that, so early in His course, He saw His way to a revolution. He appointed twelve apostles, in clear allusion to the tribes of a new Israel, a spiritual circumcision, another peculiar people. A new Jerusalem should arise, with their names engraven upon its twelve foundation stones. But since all great changes arrive, not by manufacture but by growth, and in co-operation with existing circumstances, since nations and constitutions are not made but evolved, so was it also with the Church of Christ. The first distinct and formal announcement of a new sheepfold, entered by a new and living Way, only came when evoked by the action of His enemies in casting out the man who was born blind. By that time, the apostles were almost ready to take their place in it. They had learned much. They had watched the marvellous career to which their testimony should be rendered. By exercise they had learned the reality, and by failure the condition of the miraculous powers which they should transmit. But long before, at the period we have now reached, the apostles had been chosen under pressure of the necessity to meet the hostility of the Pharisees with a counter-agency, and to spread the knowledge of His power and doctrine farther than One Teacher, however endowed, could reach. They were to be workers together with Him.

St. Mark tells us that He went up into the mountain, the well known hill of the neighbourhood, as St. Luke also implies, and there called unto Him whom He Himself would. The emphasis refutes a curious conjecture, that Judas may have been urged upon Him with such importunity by the rest that to reject became a worse evil than to receive him.* The choice was all His own, and in their early enthusiasm not one whom He summoned refused the call. Out of these He chose the Twelve, elect of the election.

We learn from St. Luke (v. 12) that His choice, fraught with such momentous issues, was made after a whole night of prayer, and from St. Matthew that He also commanded the whole body of His disciples to pray the Lord of the Harvest, not that they themselves should be chosen, but that He would send forth labourers into His harvest.

Now who were these by whose agency the downward course of humanity was reversed, and the traditions of a Divine faith were poured into a new mould ?

It must not be forgotten that their ranks were afterwards recruited from the purest Hebrew blood and ripest culture of the time, The addition of Saul of Tarsus proved that knowledge and position were no more proscribed than indispensable. Yet is it in the last degree suggestive, that Jesus drew His personal followers from classes, not indeed oppressed by want,

---

* Lange. *Life of Christ*, ii. p. 179,

bu⁺ lowly, unwarped by the prejudicies of the time, living in close contact with nature and with unsophisticated men, speaking and thinking the words and thoughts of the race and not of its coteries, and face to face with the great primitive wants and sorrows over which artificial refinement spreads a thin, but often a baffling veil.

With one exception the Nazarene called Galileans to His ministry; and the Carpenter was followed by a group of fishermen, by a despised publican, by a zealot whose love of Israel had betrayed him into wild and lawless theories at least, perhaps into evil deeds, and by several whose previous life and subsequent labours are unknown to earthly fame. Such are the Judges enthroned over the twelve tribes of Israel.

A mere comparison of the lists refutes the notion that any one Evangelist has worked up the materials of another, so diverse are they, and yet so easily reconciled. Matthew in one is Levi in another. Thaddæus, Jude, and Lebbæus, are interchangeable. The order of the Twelve differs in all the four lists, and yet there are such agreements, even in this respect, as to prove that all the Evangelists were writing about what they understood. Divide the Twelve into three ranks of four, and in none of the four catalogues will any name, or its equivalent, be found to have wandered out of its subdivision, out of the first, second, or third rank, in which doubtless that apostle habitually followed Jesus. Within each rank there is the utmost diversity of place, except that the foremost name in each is never varied; Peter, Philip, and the Lesser James, hold the first, fifth, and ninth place in every catalogue. And the traitor is always last. These are coïncidences too slight for design and too striking for accident, they are the natural signs of truth.   For they indicate, without obtruding or explaining, some arrangement of the ranks, and some leadership of an individual in each.

Moreover, the group of the apostles presents a wonderfully lifelike aspect.   Fear, ambition, rivalry, perplexity, silence when speech is called for, and speech when silence is befitting, vows, failures, and yet real loyalty, alas ! we know them all.   The incidents which are recorded of the chosen of Christ no inventor of the second century would have dared to devise ; and as we study them, we feel the touch of genuine life ; not of colossal statues such as repose beneath the dome of St. Peter's, but of men, genuine, simple and even somewhat childlike, yet full of strong, fresh, unsophisticated feeling, fit therefore to become a great power, and especially so in the capacity of witnesses for an ennobling yet controverted fact.

CHARACTERISTICS OF THE TWELVE.

"And He appointed twelve, that they might be with Him, and that He might send them forth to preach, and to have authority to cast out devils : and Simon He surnamed Peter ; and James the *son* of Zebedee, and John the brother of James ; and them He surnamed Boanerges, which is, Sons of thunder : and Andrew, and Philip, and Bartholomew, and Matthew, and Thomas, and James the *son* of Alphæus, and Thaddæus, and Simon the Cananæan, and Judas Iscariot, which also betrayed Him."—MARK iii. 14–19 (R.V.).

THE pictures of the Twelve, then, are drawn from a living group.   And when they are examined in detail, this appearance of vitality is strengthened, by the richest and most vivid indications of individual character, such indeed as in several cases to throw light upon the choice of Jesus.   To invent such touches is the last attainment of dramatic genius, and the artist rarely succeeds except by deliberate and palpable character-painting. The whole story of Hamlet and of Lear is constructed with this end in view, but no one has ever conjectured that the Gospels were psychological studies. If, then, we can discover several well-defined characters, harmoniously drawn by various writers, as natural as the central figure is supernatural, and to be recognised equally in the common and the miraculous narratives, this will be an evidence of the utmost value.

We are all familiar with the impetuous vigour of St. Peter, a quality which betrayed him into grave and well-nigh fatal errors, but when chastened by suffering made him a noble and formidable leader of the Twelve. We recognise it when He says, "Thou shalt never wash my feet," "Though all men should deny Thee, yet will I never deny Thee," "Lord, to whom should we go? Thou hast the words of everlasting life," "Thou art the Christ, the Son of the living God," and in his rebuke of Jesus for self-sacrifice, and in his rash blow in the garden. Does this, the best established mental quality of any apostle, fail or grow faint in the miraculous stories which are condemned as the accretions of a later time? In such stories he is related to have cried out, "Depart from me, for I am a sinful man, O Lord," he would walk upon the sea to Jesus, he proposed to shelter Moses and Elijah from the night air in booths (a notion so natural to a bewildered man, so exquisite in its officious well-meaning absurdity as to prove itself, for who could have invented it?), he ventured into the empty sepulchre while John stood awe-stricken at the portal, he plunged into the lake to seek his risen Master on the shore, and he was presently the first to draw the net to land. Observe the restless curiosity

6

which beckoned to John to ask who was the traitor,
and compare it with his question, "Lord, and what shall
this man do?" But the second of these was after the
resurrection, and in answer to a prophecy. Everywhere we find a real person and the same, and the
vehemence is everywhere that of a warm heart, which
could fail signally but could weep bitterly as well,
which could learn not to claim, though twice invited,
greater love than that of others, but when asked
"Lovest thou Me" at all, broke out into the passionate
appeal, "Lord, Thou knowest all things, Thou knowest
that I love Thee." Dull is the ear of the critic which
fails to recognise here the voice of Simon. Yet the
story implies the resurrection.

The mind of Jesus was too lofty and grave for
epigram; but He put the wilful self-reliance which
Peter had to subdue even to crucifixion, into one delicate and subtle phrase: "When thou wast young, thou
girdedst thyself, and walkedst whither thou wouldest."
That self-willed stride, with the loins girded, is the
natural gait of Peter, when he was young.

St. James, the first apostolic martyr, seems to have
over-topped for a while his greater brother St. John,
before whom he is usually named, and who is once distinguished as "the brother of James." He shares with
him the title of a Son of Thunder (Mark iii. 17). They
were together in desiring to rival the fiery and aveng-
ing miracle of Elijah, and to partake of the profound
baptism and bitter cup of Christ. It is an undesigned
coincidence in character, that while the latter of these
events is recorded by St. Matthew and St. Mark, the
former, which, it will be observed implies perfect confidence in the supernatural power of Christ, is found in
St. Luke alone, who has not mentioned the title it

justifies so curiously (Matt. xx. 20; Mark x. 35; Luke
ix. 54). It is more remarkable that he whom Christ
bade to share his distinctive title with another, should
not once be named as having acted or spoken by himself. With a fire like that of Peter, but no such power
of initiative and of chieftainship, how natural it is that
his appointed task was martyrdom. Is it objected that
his brother also, the great apostle St. John, received only
a share in that divided title ? But the family trait is
quite as palpable in him. The deeds of John were
seldom wrought upon his own responsibility, never if
we except the bringing of Peter into the palace of the
high priest. He is a keen observer and a deep thinker.
But he cannot, like his Master, combine the quality of
leader with those of student and sage. In company with
Andrew he found the Messiah. We have seen James
leading him for a time. It was in obedience to a sign
from Peter that He asked who was the traitor. With
Peter, when Jesus was arrested, he followed afar off.
It is very characteristic that he shrank from entering
the sepulchre until Peter, coming up behind, went in
first, although it was John who thereupon "saw and
believed." *

With like discernment, he was the first to recognise
Jesus beside the lake, but then it was equally natural
that he should tell Peter, and follow in the ship,
dragging the net to land, as that Peter should gird
himself and plunge into the lake. Peter, when Jesus
drew him aside, turned and saw the disciple whom
Jesus loved following, with the same silent, gentle, and
sociable affection, which had so recently joined him with

---

* It is also very natural that, in telling the story, he should remember how, while hesitating to enter, he "stooped down " to gaze, in the
wild dawn of his new hope.

the saddest and tenderest of all companions underneath
the cross. At this point there is a delicate and suggestive turn of phrase. By what incident would any pen
except his own have chosen to describe the beloved
disciple as Peter then beheld him? Assuredly we
should have written, The disciple whom Jesus loved,
who also followed Him to Calvary, and to whom He
confided His mother. But from St. John himself there
would have been a trace of boastfulness in such a
phrase. Now the author of the Fourth Gospel,
choosing rather to speak of privilege than service,
wrote "The disciple whom Jesus loved, which also
leaned back on His breast at the supper, and said,
Lord, who is he that betrayeth Thee?"

St. John was again with St. Peter at the Beautiful
Gate, and although it was not he who healed the cripple,
yet his co-operation is implied in the words, "Peter,
fastening his eyes on him, *with John.*" And when the
Council would fain have silenced them, the boldness
which spoke in Peter's reply was "the boldness of
Peter and John."

Could any series of events justify more perfectly
a title which implied much zeal, yet zeal that did not
demand a specific unshared epithet? But these events
are interwoven with the miraculous narratives.

Add to this the keenness and deliberation which so
much of his story exhibits, which at the beginning
tendered no hasty homage, but followed Jesus to
examine and to learn, which saw the meaning of the
orderly arrangment of the graveclothes in the empty
tomb, which was first to recognise the Lord upon the
beach, which before this had felt something in Christ's
regard for the least and weakest, inconsistent with
the forbidding of any one to cast out devils, and we

have the very qualities required to supplement those of Peter, without being discordant or uncongenial. And therefore it is with Peter, even more than with his brother, that we have seen John associated. In fact Christ, who sent out His apostles by two and two, joins these in such small matters as the tracking a man with a pitcher into the house where He would keep the Passover. And so, when Mary of Magdala would announce the resurrection, she found the penitent Simon in company with this loving John, comforted, and ready to seek the tomb where he met the Lord of all Pardons.

All this is not only coherent, and full of vital force, but it also strengthens powerfully the evidence for his authorship of the Gospel, written the last, looking deepest into sacred mysteries, and comparatively unconcerned for the mere flow of narrative, but tender with private and loving discourse, with thoughts of the protecting Shepherd, the sustaining Vine, the Friend Who wept by a grave, Who loved John, Who provided amid tortures for His mother, Who knew that Peter loved Him, and bade him feed the lambs—and yet thunderous as becomes a Boanerges, with indignation half suppressed against "the Jews" (so called as if he had renounced his murderous nation), against the selfish high-priest of " that same year," and against the son of perdition, for whom certain astute worldlings have surmised that his wrath was such as they best understand, personal, and perhaps a little spiteful. The temperament of John, revealed throughout, was that of August, brooding and warm and hushed and fruitful, with low rumblings of tempest in the night.

It is remarkable that such another family resemblance as between James and John exists between Peter and

Andrew. The directness and self-reliance of his greater brother may be discovered in the few incidents recorded of Andrew also. At the beginning, and after one interview with Jesus, when he finds his brother, and becomes the first of the Twelve to spread the gospel, he utters the short unhesitating announcement, " We have found the Messiah." When Philip is uncertain about introducing the Greeks who would see Jesus, he consults Andrew, and there is no more hesitation, Andrew and Philip tell Jesus. And in just the same way, when Philip argues that two hundred pennyworth of bread are not enough for the multitude, Andrew intervenes with practical information about the five barley loaves and the two small fishes, insufficient although they seem. A man prompt and ready, and not blind to the resources that exist because they appear scanty.

Twice we have found Philip mentioned in conjunction with him. It was Philip, apparently accosted by the Greeks because of his Gentile name, who could not take upon himself the responsibility of telling Jesus of their wish. And it was he, when consulted about the feeding of the five thousand, who went off into a calculation of the price of the food required—two hundred pennyworth, he says, would not suffice. Is it not highly consistent with this slow deliberation, that he should have accosted Nathanael with a statement so measured and explicit : " We have found Him, of whom Moses in the law, and the prophets did write, Jesus of Nazareth, the Son of Joseph." What a contrast to Andrew's terse announcement, " We have found the Messiah." And how natural that Philip should answer the objection, " Can any good thing come out of Nazareth ? " with the passionless reasonable invitation, "Come and see." It was in the same unimaginative prosaic way that he said long after, "Lord, show us the Father, and it sufficeth us." To this comparatively sluggish temperament, therefore, Jesus Himself had to address the first demand He made on any. "Follow me," He said, and was obeyed. It would not be easy to compress into such brief and incidental notices a more graphic indication of character.

Of the others we know little except the names. The choice of Matthew, the man of business, is chiefly explained by the nature of his Gospel, so explicit, orderly, and methodical, and until it approaches the crucifixion, so devoid of fire.

But when we come to Thomas, we are once more aware of a defined and vivid personality, somewhat perplexed and melancholy, of little hope but settled loyalty.

All the three sayings reported of him belong to a dejected temperament: "Let us also go, that we may die with Him"—as if there could be no brighter meaning than death in Christ's proposal to interrupt a dead man's sleep. "Lord, we know not whither Thou goest, and how can we know the way?"—these words express exactly the same despondent failure to apprehend. And so it comes to pass that nothing short of tangible experience will convince him of the resurrection. And yet there is a warm and devoted heart to be recognised in the proposal to share Christ's death, in the yearning to know whither He went, and even in that agony of unbelief, which dwelt upon the cruel details of suffering, until it gave way to one glad cry of recognition and of worship; therefore his demand was granted, although a richer blessing was reserved for those who, not having seen, believed.

THE APOSTLE JUDAS.

"And Judas Iscariot, which also betrayed Him."—MARK iii. 19.

THE evidential value of what has been written about the apostles will, to some minds, seem to be overborne by the difficulties which start up at the name of Judas. And yet the fact that Jesus chose him—that awful fact which has offended many—is in harmony with all that we see around us, with the prodigious powers bestowed upon Napoleon and Voltaire, bestowed in full knowledge of the dark results, yet given because the issues of human freewill never cancel the trusts imposed on human responsibility. Therefore the issues of the freewill of Judas did not cancel the trust imposed upon his responsibility; and Jesus acted not on His fore-knowledge of the future, but on the mighty possibilities, for good as for evil, which heaved in the bosom of the fated man as he stood upon the mountain sward.

In the story of Judas, the principles which rule the world are made visible. From Adam to this day men have been trusted who failed and fell, and out of their very downfall, but not by precipitating it, the plans of God have evolved themselves.

It is not possible to make such a study of the character of Judas as of some others of the Twelve. A traitor is naturally taciturn. No word of his draws our attention to the fact that he had gained possession of the bag, even though one who had sat at the receipt of custom might more naturally have become the treasurer. We do not hear his voice above the rest, until St. John explains the source of the general discontent, which remonstrated against the waste of ointment. He is silent even at the feast, in despite of the words which revealed his guilty secret, until a slow and tardy question is wrung from him, not "Is it I, Lord?" but "Rabbi, is it I?" His influence is like that of a subtle poison, not discerned until its effects betray it.

But many words of Jesus acquire new force and energy when we observe that, whatever their drift beside, they were plainly calculated to influence and warn Iscariot. Such are the repeated and urgent warnings against covetousness, from the first parable, spoken so shortly after his vocation, which reckons the deceitfulness of riches and the lust of other things among the tares that choke the seed, down to the declaration that they who trust in riches shall hardly enter the kingdom. Such are the denunciations against hypocrisy, spoken openly, as in the Sermon on the Mount, or to His own apart, as when He warned them of the leaven of the Pharisees which is hypocrisy, that secret vice which was eating out the soul of one among them. Such were the opportunities given to retreat without utter dishonour, as when He said, "Do ye also will to go away? . . . Did I not choose you the Twelve, and one of you is a devil?" (John vi. 67, 70). And such also were the awful warnings given of the solemn responsibilities of special privileges. The exalted city which is brought down to hell, the salt which is trodden under foot, the men whose sin remained because they can claim to see, and still more plainly, the first that shall be last, and the man for whom it were good that he had not been born. In many besides the last of these, Judas must have felt himself sternly because faithfully dealt with. And the exasperation which always results from rejected warnings, the sense of a presence utterly repugnant to his nature, may

have largely contributed to his final and disastrous
collapse.

In the life of Judas there was a mysterious imperson-
ation of all the tendencies of godless Judaism, and his
dreadful personality seems to express the whole movement of the nation which rejected Christ.   We see this
in the powerful attraction felt toward Messiah before
His aims were understood, in the deadly estrangement
and hostility which were kindled by the gentle and
self-effacing ways of Jesus, in the treachery of Judas
in the garden and the unscrupulous wiliness of the
priests accusing Christ before the governor, in the
fierce intensity of rage which turned his hands against
himself and which destroyed the nation under Titus.
Nay the very sordidness which made a bargain for
thirty pieces of silver has ever since been a part of the
popular conception of the race.   We are apt to think
of a gross love of money as inconsistent with intense
passion, but in Shylock, the compatriot of Judas,
Shakespeare combines the two.

Contemplating this blighted and sinister career, the
lesson is burnt in upon the conscience, that since Judas
by transgression fell, no place in the Church of Christ
can render any man secure.   And since, falling, he was
openly exposed, none may flatter himself that the cause
of Christ is bound up with his reputation, that the
mischief must needs be averted which his downfall
would entail, that Providence must needs avert from
him the natural penalties of evil-doing.   Though one
was as the signet upon the Lord's hand, yet was he
plucked thence.   There is no security for any soul
anywhere except where love and trust repose, upon the
bosom of Christ.

Now if this be true, and if sin and scandal may conceivably penetrate even the inmost circle of the chosen, how great an error is it to break, because of these offences, the unity of the Church, and institute some new communion, purer far than the Churches of Corinth and Galatia, which were not abandoned but reformed, and more impenetrable to corruption than the little group of those who ate and drank with Jesus.

CHRIST AND BEELZEBUB.

" And the multitude cometh together again, so that they could not so much as eat bread. And when his friends heard it, they went out to lay hold on Him : for they said, He is beside Himself. And the scribes which came down from Jerusalem said, He hath Beelzebub, and, By the prince of the devils casteth He out the devils. And He called them unto Him, and said unto them in parables, How can Satan cast out Satan? And if a kingdom be divided against itself, that kingdom cannot stand. And if an house be divided against itself, that house will not be able to stand. And if Satan hath risen up against himself, and is divided, he cannot stand, but hath an end. But no one can enter into the house of the strong *man*, and spoil his goods, except he first bind the strong *man ;* and then he will spoil his house."—MARK iii. 20–27 (R.V.).

WHILE Christ was upon the mountain with His more immediate followers, the excitement in the plain did not exhaust itself; for even when He entered into a house, the crowds prevented Him and His followers from taking necessary food. And when His friends heard of this, they judged Him as men who profess to have learned the lesson of His life still judge, too often, all whose devotion carries them beyond the boundaries of convention and of convenience. For there is a curious betrayal of the popular estimate of this world and the world to come, in the honour paid to those who cast away life in battle, or sap it slowly in pursuit of wealth or honours, and the contempt expressed for those who compromise it on behalf of souls, for which Christ died.

Whenever by exertion in any unselfish cause health is broken, or fortune impaired, or influential friends estranged, the follower of Christ is called an enthusiast, a fanatic, or even more plainly a man of unsettled mind. He may be comforted by remembering that Jesus was said to be beside Himself when teaching and healing left Him not leisure even to eat.

To this incessant and exhausting strain upon His energies and sympathies, St. Matthew applies the prophetic words, " Himself took our infirmities and bare our diseases " (viii. 17). And it is worth while to compare with that passage and the one before us, Renan's assertion, that He traversed Galilee " in the midst of a perpetual fête," and that "joyous Galilee celebrated in fêtes the approach of the well-beloved." (*Vie de J.*, pp. 197, 202). The contrast gives a fine illustration of the inaccurate shallowness of the Frenchman's whole conception of the sacred life.

But it is remarkable that while His friends could not yet believe His claims, and even strove to lay hold on Him, no worse suspicion ever darkened the mind of those who knew Him best than that His reason had been disturbed. Not these called Him gluttonous and a winebibber. Not these blasphemed His motives. But the envoys of the priestly faction, partisans from Jerusalem, were ready with an atrocious suggestion. He was Himself possessed with a worse devil, before whom the lesser ones retired. By the prince of the devils He cast out the devils. To this desperate evasion, St. Matthew tells us, they were driven by a remarkable miracle, the expulsion of a blind and dumb spirit, and the perfect healing of his victim. Now the literature of the world cannot produce invective more terrible than Jesus had at His command for these very scribes and Pharisees, hypocrites. This is what gives majesty to His endurance. No personal insult, no resentment at His own wrong, could ruffle the sublime composure which, upon occasion, gave way to a moral indignation equally sublime. Calmly He calls His traducers to look Him in the face, and appeals to their own reason against their blasphemy. Neither kingdom nor house divided against itself can stand. And if Satan be divided against himself and his evil works, undoing the miseries and opening the eyes of men, his kingdom has an end. All the experience of the world since the beginning was proof enough that such a suicide of evil was beyond hope. The best refutation of the notion that Satan had risen up against himself and was divided was its clear expression. But what was the alternative? If Satan were not committing suicide, he was overpowered. There is indeed a fitful temporary reformation, followed by a deeper fall, which St. Matthew tells us that Christ compared to the cleansing of a house from whence the evil tenant has capriciously wandered forth, confident that it is still his own, and prepared to return to it with seven other and worse fiends. A little observation would detect such illusory improvement. But the case before them was that of an external summons reluctantly obeyed. It required the interference of a stronger power, which could only be the power of God. None could enter into the strong man's house, and spoil his goods, unless the strong man were first bound, " and then he will spoil his house." No more distinct assertion of the personality of evil spirits than this could be devised. Jesus and the Pharisees are not at all at issue upon this point. He does not scout as a baseless superstition their belief that evil spirits are at work in the world.

But He declares that His own work is the reversal of theirs. He is spoiling the strong man, whose terrible ascendancy over the possessed resembles the dominion of a man in his own house, among chattels without a will.

That dominion Christ declares that only a stronger can overcome, and His argument assumes that the stronger must needs be the finger of God, the power of God, come unto them. The supernatural exists only above us and below.

Ages have passed away since then. Innumerable schemes have been devised for the expulsion of the evils under which the world is groaning, and if they are evils of merely human origin, human power should suffice for their removal. The march of civilisation is sometimes appealed to. But what blessings has civilisation without Christ ever borne to savage men? The answer is painful: rum, gunpowder, slavery, massacre, small-pox, pulmonary consumption, and the extinction of their races, these are all it has been able to bestow. Education is sometimes spoken of, as if it would gradually heal our passions and expel vice and misery from the world, as if the worst crimes and most flagrant vices of our time were peculiar to the ignorant and the untaught, as if no forger had ever learned to write. And sometimes great things are promised from the advance of science, as if all the works of dynamite and nitro-glycerine, were, like those of the Creator, very good.

No man can be deceived by such flattering hopes, who rightly considers the volcanic energies, the frantic rage, the unreasoning all-sacrificing recklessness of human passions and desires. Surely they are set on fire of hell, and only heaven can quench the conflagration. Jesus has undertaken to do this. His religion has been a spell of power among the degraded and the lost ; and when we come to consider mankind in bulk, it is plain enough that no other power has had a really reclaiming, elevating effect upon tribes and races. In our own land, what great or lasting work of refcrmation, or even of temporal benevolence, has ever gone forward without the blessing of religion to sustain it ? Nowhere is Satan cast out but by the Stronger than he, binding him, overmastering the evil principle which tramples human nature down, as the very first step towards spoiling his goods. The spiritual victory must precede the removal of misery, convulsion and disease. There is no golden age for the world, except the reign of Christ.

"ETERNAL SIN."

" Verily I say unto you, All their sins shall be forgiven unto the sons of men, and their blasphemies wherewith soever they shall blaspheme : but whosoever shall blaspheme against the Holy Spirit hath never forgiveness, but is guilty of an eternal sin."—MARK iii. 28, 29 (R.V.).

HAVING first shown that His works cannot be ascribed to Satan, Jesus proceeds to utter the most terrible of warnings, because they said, He hath an unclean spirit.

"All their sins shall be forgiven unto the sons of men, and their blasphemies wherewith soever they shall blaspheme, but whosoever shall blaspheme against the Holy Spirit hath never forgiveness, but is guilty of an eternal sin."

What is the nature of this terrible offence ? It is plain that their slanderous attack lay in the direction of it, since they needed warning ; and probable that they had not yet fallen into the abyss, because they could still be warned against it. At least, if the guilt of some had

reached that depth, there must have been others involved in their offence who were still within reach of
Christ's solemn admonition.   It would seem therefore
that in saying, "He casteth out devils by Beelzebub
... He hath an unclean spirit," they approached the
confines and doubtful boundaries between that blasphemy against the Son of man which shall be forgiven,
and the blasphemy against the Holy Spirit which hath
never forgiveness.

It is evident also that any crime declared by Scripture elsewhere to be incurable, must be identical with
this, however different its guise, since Jesus plainly and
indisputably announces that all other sins but this
shall be forgiven.

Now there are several other passages of the kind.
St. John bade his disciples to pray, when any saw a
brother sinning a sin not unto death, "and God will
give him life for them that sin not unto death.   There
is a sin unto death : not concerning this do I say that
he should make request " (I John v. 16).   It is idle to
suppose that, in the case of this sin unto death, the
Apostle only meant to leave his disciples free to pray
or not to pray.   If death were not certain, it would
be their duty, in common charity, to pray.   But the
sin is so vaguely and even mysteriously referred to,
that we learn little more from that passage than that it
was an overt public act, of which other men could so
distinctly judge the flagrancy that from it they should
withhold their prayers.   It has nothing in common
with those unhappy wanderings of thought or affection
which morbid introspection broods upon, until it pleads
guilty to the unpardonable sin, for lapses of which no
other could take cognizance.   And in Christ's words,
the very epithet, blasphemy, involves the same public,

open revolt against good.* And let it be remembered
that every other sin shall be forgiven.

There are also two solemn passages in the Epistle to
the Hebrews (vi. 4-6 ; x. 26-31). The first of these
declares that it is impossible for men who once ex-
perienced all the enlightening and sweet influences of
God, "and then fell away," to be renewed again
unto repentance. But falling upon the road is very
different from thus falling away, or how could Peter
have been recovered ? Their fall is total apostasy,
"they crucify to themselves the Son of God afresh, and
put Him to an open shame." They are not fruitful
land in which tares are mingled ; they bear only thorns
and thistles, and are utterly rejected. And so in the
tenth chapter, they who sin wilfully are men who
tread under foot the Son of God, and count the blood
of the covenant an unholy thing, and do despite
(insult) unto the Spirit of grace.

Again we read that in the last time there will arise
an enemy of God so unparalleled that his movement
will outstrip all others, and be *"the* falling away," and
he himself will be "the man of sin" and "the son
of perdition," which latter title he only shares with Iscariot. Now the essence of his portentous guilt is that
"he opposeth and exalteth himself against all that is
called God or that is worshipped" : it is a monstrous
egotism, "setting himself forth as God," and such a
hatred of restraint as makes him "the lawless one"
(2 Thess. ii. 3-10).

---

* "Theology would have been spared much trouble concerning this
passage, and anxious timid souls unspeakable anguish, if men had
adhered strictly to Christ's own expression. For it is not *a sin* against
the Holy Ghost which is here spoken of, but *blasphemy* against the
Holy Ghost."—Lange "*Life of Christ*," vol. ii. p. 269.

So far as these passages are at all definite in their descriptions, they are entirely harmonious. They describe no sin of the flesh, of impulse, frailty or passion, nor yet a spiritual lapse of an unguarded hour, of rash speculation, of erring or misled opinion. They speak not of sincere failure to accept Christ's doctrine or to recognise His commission, even though it breathe out threats and slaughters. They do not even apply to the dreadful sin of denying Christ in terror, though one should curse and swear, saying, I know not the man. They speak of a deliberate and conscious rejection of good and choice of evil, of the wilful aversion of the soul from sacred influences, the public denial and trampling under foot of Christ, the opposing of all that is called God.

And a comparison of these passages enables us to understand why this sin never can be pardoned. It is because good itself has become the food and fuel of its wickedness, stirring up its opposition, calling out its rage, that the apostate cannot be renewed again unto repentance. The sin is rather indomitable than unpardonable : it has become part of the sinner's personality ; it is incurable, an eternal sin.

Here is nothing to alarm any mourner whose contrition proves that it has actually been possible to enew him unto repentance. No penitent has ever yet been rejected for this guilt, for no penitent has ever been thus guilty.

And this being so, here is the strongest possible encouragement for all who desire mercy. Every other sin, every other blasphemy shall be forgiven. Heaven does not reject the vilest whom the world hisses at, the most desperate and bloodstained whose life the world exacts in vengeance for his outrages. None is lost but the hard and impenitent heart which treasures up for itself wrath against the day of wrath.

THE FRIENDS OF JESUS.

" And there come His mother and His brethren ; and, standing with-out, they sent unto Him, calling Him.   And a multitude was sitting about Him ; and they say unto Him, Behold, Thy mother and Thy brethren without seek for Thee.   And He answereth them, and saith, Who is My mother and My brethren?   And looking round on them which sat round about Him He saith, Behold My mother and My brethren !   For whosoever shall do the will of God, the same is My brother, and sister, and mother."—MARK iii. 31–35 (R. V.).

WE have lately read that the relatives of Jesus, hearing of His self-sacrificing devotion, sought to lay hold on Him, because they said, He is beside Himself.   Their concern would not be lightened upon hearing of His rupture with the chiefs of their religion and their nation. And so it was, that while a multitude hung upon His lips, some unsympathizing critic, or perhaps some hostile scribe, interrupted Him with their message.   They desired to speak with Him, possibly with rude inten-tions, while in any case, to grant their wish might easily have led to a painful altercation, offending weak disciples, and furnishing a scandal to His eager foes.

Their interference must have caused the Lord a bitter pang.   It was sad that they were not among His hearers, but worse that they should seek to mar His work.   To Jesus, endowed with every innocent human instinct, worn with labour and aware of gathering perils, they were an offence of the same kind as Peter made himself when he became the mouthpiece of the tempter.   For their own sakes, whose faith He was yet to win, it was needful to be very firm.   Moreover, He was soon to make it a law of the kingdom that men

should be ready for His sake to leave brethren, or
sisters, or mother, and in so doing should receive back
all these a hundredfold in the present time (x. 29, 30).
To this law it was now His own duty to conform.
Yet it was impossible for Jesus to be harsh and stern
to a group of relatives with His mother in the midst of
them; and it would be a hard problem for the finest
dramatic genius to reconcile the conflicting claims of
the emergency, fidelity to God and the cause, a striking
rebuke to the officious interference of His kinsfolk, and
a full and affectionate recognition of the relationship
which could not make Him swerve.   How shall He
"leave" His mother and his brethren, and yet not
deny His heart?   How shall He be strong without
being harsh?

Jesus reconciles all the conditions of the problem,
as pointing to His attentive hearers, He pronounces
these to be His true relatives, but yet finds no warmer
term to express what He feels for them than the dear
names of mother, sisters, brethren.

Observers whose souls were not warmed as He
spoke, may have supposed that it was cold indifference
to the calls of nature which allowed His mother and
brethren to stand without.   In truth, it was not that
He denied the claims of the flesh, but that He was
sensitive to other, subtler, profounder claims of the
spirit and spiritual kinship.   He would not carelessly
wound a mother's or a brother's heart, but the life
Divine had also its fellowships and its affinities, and
still less could He throw these aside.   No cold sense of
duty detains Him with His congregation while affection
seeks Him in the vestibule; no, it is a burning love,
the love of a brother or even of a son, which binds
Him to His people.

Happy are they who are in such a case. And Jesus gives us a ready means of knowing whether we are among those whom He so wonderfully condescends to love. "Whosoever shall do the will of My Father which is in heaven." Feelings may ebb, and self-confidence may be shaken, but obedience depends not upon excitement, and may be rendered by a breaking heart.

It is important to observe that this saying declares that obedience does not earn kinship; but only proves it, as the fruit proves the tree. Kinship must go before acceptable service; none can do the will of the Father who is not already the kinsman of Jesus, for He says, Whosoever shall (*hereafter*) do the will of My Father, the same is (*already*) My brother and sister and mother. There are men who would fain reverse the process, and do God's will in order to merit the brotherhood of Jesus. They would drill themselves and win battles for Him, in order to be enrolled among His soldiers. They would accept the gospel invitation as soon as they refute the gospel warnings that without Him they can do nothing, and that they need the creation of a new heart and the renewal of a right spirit within them. But when homage was offered to Jesus as a Divine teacher and no more, He rejoined, Teaching is not what is required: holiness does not result from mere enlightenment: Verily, verily, I say unto thee, except a man be born again, he cannot see the kingdom of God. Because the new birth is the condition of all spiritual power and energy, it follows that if any man shall henceforth do God's will, he must already be of the family of Christ.

Men may avoid evil through self-respect, from early training and restraints of conscience, from temporal

prudence or dread of the future. And this is virtuous
only as the paying of a fire-insurance is so. But
secondary motives will never lift any man so high as
to satisfy this sublime standard, the doing of the will
of the Father. That can only be attained, like all true
and glorious service in every cause, by the heart, by
enthusiasm, by love. And Jesus was bound to all who
loved His Father by as strong a cord as united His
perfect heart with brother and sister and mother.

But as there is no true obedience without relationship,
so is there no true relationship unfollowed by obedience. Christ was not content to say, Whoso doeth
God's will is My kinsman: He asked, Who is My
kinsman? and gave this as an exhaustive reply. He
has none other. Every sheep in His fold hears His
voice and follows Him. We may feel keen emotions as
we listen to passionate declamations, or kneel in an
excited prayer-meeting, or bear our part in an imposing
ritual; we may be moved to tears by thinking of the
dupes of whatever heterodoxy we most condemn;
tender and soft emotions may be stirred in our bosom
by the story of the perfect life and Divine death of
Jesus; and yet we may be as far from a renewed
heart as was that ancient tyrant from genuine compassion, who wept over the brevity of the lives of the
soldiers whom he sent into a wanton war.

Mere feeling is not life. It moves truly; but only
as a balloon moves, rising by virtue of its emptiness,
driven about by every blast that veers, and sinking
when its inflation is at an end. But mark the living
creature poised on widespread wings; it has a will, an
intention, and an initiative, and as long as its life is
healthy and unenslaved, it moves at its own good
pleasure. How shall I know whether or not I am

a true kinsman of the Lord ? By seeing whether
I advance, whether I work, whether I have real and
practical zeal and love, or whether I have grown cold,
and make more allowance for the flesh than I used to
do, and expect less from the spirit. Obedience does
not produce grace. But it proves it, for we can no
more bear fruit except we abide in Christ, than the
branch that does not abide in the vine.

Lastly, we observe the individual love, the personal
affection of Christ for each of His people. There is
a love for masses of men and philanthropic causes,
which does not much observe the men who compose
the masses, and upon whom the causes depend. Thus,
one may love his country, and rejoice when her
flag advances, without much care for any soldier who
has been shot down, or has won promotion. And so
we think of Africa or India, without really feeling
much about the individual Egyptian or Hindoo. Who
can discriminate and feel for each one of the multitudes included in such a word as Want, or Sickness,
or Heathenism ? And judging by our own frailty, we
are led to think that Christ's love can mean but little
beyond this. As a statesman who loves the nation
may be said, in some vague way, to love and care for
me, so people think of Christ as loving and pitying
us because we are items in the race He loves. But
He has eyes and a heart, not only for all, but for
each one. Looking down the shadowy vista of the
generations, every sigh, every broken heart, every
blasphemy, is a separate pang to His all-embracing
heart. " Before that Philip called thee, when thou
wast under the fig-tree, I saw *thee*," lonely, unconscious,
undistinguished drop in the tide of life, one leaf among
the myriads which rustle and fall in the vast forest of

existence.   St. Paul speaks truly of Christ " Who loved
me, and gave Himself for me."   He shall bring every
secret sin to judgment, and shall we so far wrong Him
as to think His justice more searching, more penetrating, more individualizing than His love, His memory
than His heart ?   It is not so.   The love He offers
adapts itself to every age and sex : it distinguishes
brother from sister, and sister again from mother.   It
is mindful of " the least of these My brethren."   But
it names no Father except One.

CHAPTER IV.

THE PARABLES.

"And again He began to teach by the sea side. And there is gathered unto Him a very great multitude, so that He entered into a boat, and sat in the sea ; and all the multitude were by the sea on the land. And He taught them many things in parables, and said unto them in His teaching. . . .

"And when He was alone, they that were about Him with the twelve asked of Him the parables. And He said unto them, Unto you is given the mystery of the kingdom of God : but unto them that are without, all things are done in parables : that seeing they may see, and not perceive ; and hearing they may hear, and not understand ; lest haply they should turn again, and it should be forgiven them. And He saith unto them, Know ye not this parable? and how shall ye know all the parables ? "—MARK iv. 1, 2, 10–13 (R.V.).

AS opposition deepened, and to a vulgar ambition, the temptation to retain disciples by all means would have become greater, Jesus began to teach in parables. We know that He had not hitherto done so, both by the surprise of the Twelve, and by the necessity which He found, of giving them a clue to the meaning of such teachings, and so to "all the parables." His own ought to have understood. But He was merciful to the weakness which confessed its failure and asked for instruction.

And yet He foresaw that they which were without would discern no spiritual meaning in such discourse. It was to have, at the same time, a revealing and a

baffling effect, and therefore it was peculiarly suitable
for the purposes of a Teacher watched by vindictive
foes. Thus, when cross-examined about His authority by men who themselves professed to know not
whence John's baptism was, He could refuse to be
entrapped, and yet tell of One Who sent His own
Son, His Beloved, to receive the fruit of the vineyard.

This diverse effect is derived from the very nature of
the parables of Jesus. They are not, like some in the
Old Testament, mere fables, in which things occur that
never happen in real life. Jotham's trees seeking a
king, are as incredible as Æsop's fox leaping for grapes.
But Jesus never uttered a parable which was not true
to nature, the kind of thing which one expects to
happen. We cannot say that a rich man in hell actually
spoke to Abraham in heaven. But if he could do so, of
which we are not competent to judge, we can well believe that he would have spoken just what we read, and
that his pathetic cry, " Father Abraham," would have
been as gently answered, " Son, remember." There is
no ferocity in the skies ; neither has the lost soul
become a fiend. Everything commends itself to our
judgment. And therefore the story not only illustrates,
but appeals, enforces, almost proves.

God in nature does not arrange that all seeds should
grow : men have patience while the germ slowly fructi-
fies, they know not how ; in all things but religion such
sacrifices are made, that the merchant sells all to buy
one goodly pearl ; an earthly father kisses his repentant
prodigal ; and even a Samaritan can be neighbour to a
Jew in his extremity. So the world is constructed :
such is even the fallen human heart. Is it not reasonable to believe that the same principles will extend

farther ; that as God governs the world of matter so He may govern the world of spirits, and that human helpfulness and clemency will not outrun the graces of the Giver of all good ?

This is the famous argument from analogy, applied long before the time of Butler, to purposes fartherreaching than his. But there is this remarkable difference, that the analogy is never pressed, men are left to discover it for themselves, or at least, to ask for an explanation, because they are conscious of something beyond the tale, something spiritual, something which they fain would understand.

Now this difference is not a mannerism ; it is intended. Butler pressed home his analogies because he was striving to silence gainsayers. His Lord and ours left men to discern or to be blind, because they had already opportunity to become His disciples if they would. The faithful among them ought to be conscious, or at least they should now become conscious, of the God of grace in the God of nature. To them the world should be eloquent of the Father's mind. They should indeed find tongues in trees, books in the running brooks, sermons in stones. He spoke to the sensitive mind, which would understand Him, as a wife reads her husband's secret joys and sorrows by signs no stranger can understand. Even if she fails to comprehend, she knows there is something to ask about. And thus, when they were alone, the Twelve asked Him of the parables. When they were instructed, they gained not only the moral lesson, and the sweet pastoral narrative, the idyllic picture which conveyed it, but also the assurance imparted by recognizing the same mind of God which is revealed in His world, or justified by the best impulses of humanity. Therefore, no parable is sensational.

It cannot root itself in the exceptional, the abnormal events on which men do not reckon, which come upon us with a shock. For we do not argue from these to daily life.

But while this mode of teaching was profitable to His disciples, and protected Him against His foes, it had formidable consequences for the frivolous empty followers after a sign. Because they were such they could only find frivolity and lightness in these stories; the deeper meaning lay farther below the surface than such eyes could pierce. Thus the light they had abused was taken from them. And Jesus explained to His disciples that, in acting thus, He pursued the fixed rule of God. The worst penalty of vice is that it loses the knowledge of virtue, and of levity that it cannot appreciate seriousness. He taught in parables, as Isaiah prophesied, "that seeing they may see, and not perceive, and hearing they may hear, and not understand; lest haply they should turn again and it should be forgiven them." These last words prove how completely penal, how free from all caprice, was this terrible decision of our gentle Lord, that precautions must be taken against evasion of the consequences of crime. But it is a warning by no means unique. He said, "The things which make for thy peace . . . are hid from thine eyes" (Luke xix. 42). And St. Paul said, "If our gospel is veiled, it is veiled in them that are perishing"; and still more to the point, "The natural man receiveth not the things of the Spirit of God, for they are foolishness unto him; and he cannot know them, because they are spiritually discerned" (2 Cor. iv. 3; 1 Cor. ii. 14). To this law Christ, in speaking by parables, was conscious that He conformed.

But now let it be observed how completely this

mode of teaching suited our Lord's habit of mind. If men could finally rid themselves of His Divine claim, they would at once recognise the greatest of the sages; and they would also find in Him the sunniest, sweetest and most accurate discernment of nature, and its more quiet beauties, that ever became a vehicle for moral teaching. The sun and rain bestowed on the evil and the good, the fountain and the trees which regulate the waters and the fruit, the death of the seed by which it buys its increase, the provision for bird and blossom without anxiety of theirs, the preference for a lily over Solomon's gorgeous robes, the meaning of a red sky at sunrise and sunset, the hen gathering her chickens under her wing, the vine and its branches, the sheep and their shepherd, the lightning seen over all the sky, every one of these needed only to be re-set and it would have become a parable.

All the Gospels, including the fourth, are full of proofs of this rich and attractive endowment, this warm sympathy with nature; and this fact is among the evidences that they all drew the same character, and drew it faithfully.

THE SOWER.

"Hearken: Behold the sower went forth to sow: and it came to pass, as he sowed, some *seed* fell by the way side, and the birds came and devoured it. And other fell on the rocky *ground*, where it had not much earth; and straightway it sprang up, because it had no deepness of earth: and when the sun was risen, it was scorched; and because it had no root, it withered away. And other fell among the thorns, and the thorns grew up, and choked it, and it yielded no fruit. And others fell into the good ground, and yielded fruit, growing up and increasing; and brought forth, thirtyfold, and sixtyfold, and a hundredfold. And He said, Who hath ears to hear, let him hear. . . .

"The sower soweth the word. And these are they by the way side, where the word is sown ; and when they have heard, straightway cometh Satan, and taketh away the word which hath been sown in them. And these in like manner are they that are sown upon the rocky *places*, who, when they have heard the word, straightway receive it with joy ; and they have no root in themselves, but endure for a while ; then, when tribulation or persecution ariseth because of the word, straightway they stumble. And others are they that are sown among the thorns ; these are they that have heard the word, and the cares of the world, and the deceitfulness of riches, and the lusts of other things entering in, choke the word, and it becometh unfruitful. And those are they that were sown upon the good ground ; such as hear the word, and accept it, and bear fruit, thirtyfold, and sixtyfold, and a hundredfold."—MARK iv. 3–9, 14–20 (R.V.).

"HEARKEN" Jesus said; willing to caution men against the danger of slighting His simple story, and to impress on them that it conveyed more than met their ears. In so doing He protested in advance against fatalistic abuses of the parable, as if we were already doomed to be hard, or shallow, or thorny, or fruitful soil. And at the close He brought out still more clearly His protest against such doctrine, by impressing upon all, that if the vitalising seed were the imparted word, it was their part to receive and treasure it. Indolence and shallowness *must* fail to bear fruit : that is the essential doctrine of the parable ; but it is not necessary that we should remain indolent or shallow : " He that hath ears to hear, let him hear."

And when the Epistle to the Hebrews reproduces the image of land which bringeth forth thorns and thistles, our Revised Version rightly brings out the fact, on which indeed the whole exhortation depends, that the same piece of land might have borne herbs meet for those for whose sake it is tilled (vi. 7).

Having said " Hearken," Jesus added, " Behold." It has been rightly inferred that the scene was before their eyes.   Very possibly some such process was within sight of the shore on which they were gathered; but in any case, a process was visible, if they would but see, of which the tilling of the ground was only a type.   A nobler seed was being scattered for a vaster harvest, and it was no common labourer, but the true sower, who went forth to sow.   "The sower soweth the word."   But who was he?   St. Matthew tells us "the sower is the Son of man," and whether the words were expressly uttered, or only implied, as the silence of St. Mark and St. Luke might possibly suggest, it is clear that none of His disciples could mistake His meaning.   Ages have passed and He is the sower still, by whatever instrument He works, for we are God's husbandry as well as God's building.   And the seed is the Word of God, so strangely able to work below the surface of human life, invisible at first, yet vital, and grasping from within and without, from secret thoughts and from circumstances, as from the chemical ingredients of the soil and from the sunshine and the shower, all that will contribute to its growth, until the field itself is assimilated, spread from end to end with waving ears, a corn-field now.   This is why Jesus in His second parable did not any longer say "the seed is the word," but "the good seed are the sons of the kingdom" (Matt. xiii. 38).   The word planted was able to identify itself with the heart.

And this seed, the Word of God, is sown broadcast as all our opportunities are given.   A talent was not refused to him who buried it.   Judas was an apostle. Men may receive the grace of God in vain, and this in more ways than one.   On some it produces no vital impression whatever; it lies on the surface of a mind which the feet of earthly interests have trodden hard.

There is no chance for it to expand, to begin its operation by sending out the smallest tendrils to grasp, to appropriate anything, to take root. And it may well be doubted whether any soul, wholly indifferent to religious truth, ever retained even its theoretic knowledge long. The foolish heart is darkened. The fowls of the air catch away for ever the priceless seed of eternity. Now it is of great importance to observe how Jesus explained this calamity. We should probably have spoken of forgetfulness, the fading away of neglected impressions, or at most of some judicial act of providence hiding the truth from the careless. But Jesus said, " straightway cometh Satan and taketh away the word which hath been sown in them." No person can fairly explain this text away, as men have striven to explain Christ's language to the demoniacs, by any theory of the use of popular language, or the toleration of harmless notions. The introduction of Satan into this parable is unexpected and uncalled for by any demand save one, the necessity of telling all the truth. It is true therefore that an active and deadly enemy of souls is at work to quicken the mischief which neglect and indifference would themselves produce, that evil processes are helped from beneath as truly as good ones from above; that the seed which is left to-day upon the surface may be maliciously taken thence long before it would have perished by natural decay; that men cannot reckon upon stopping short in their contempt of grace, since what they neglect the devil snatches quite away from them. And as seed is only safe from fowls when buried in the soil, so is the word of life only safe against the rapacity of hell when it has sunk down into our hearts.

In the story of the early Church, St. Paul sowed
upon such ground as this in Athens. Men who
spent their time in the pursuit of artistic and cultivated
novelties, in hearing and telling some new thing,
mocked the gospel, or at best proposed to hear its
preacher yet again. How long did such a purpose
last ?

But there are other dangers to dread, besides absolute indifference to truth. And the first of these is a
too shallow and easy acquiescence. The message of
salvation is designed to affect the whole of human life
profoundly. It comes to bind a strong man armed, it
summons easy and indifferent hearts to wrestle against
spiritual foes, to crucify the flesh, to die daily. On
these conditions it offers the noblest blessings. But
the conditions are grave and sobering. If one hears
them without solemn and earnest searching of heart,
he has only, at the best, apprehended half the message.
Christ has warned us that we cannot build a tower
without sitting down to count our means, nor fight
a hostile king without reckoning the prospects of
invasion. And it is very striking to compare the
gushing and impulsive sensationalism of some modern
schools, with the deliberate and circumspect action of
St. Paul, even after God had been pleased miraculously
to reveal His Son in him. He went into seclusion.
He returned to Damascus to his first instructor. Four-
een years afterwards he deliberately laid his gospel
before the Apostles, lest by any means he should be
running or had run in vain. Such is the action of one
penetrated with a sense of reality and responsibility in
his decision ; it is not the action likely to result from
teaching men that it suffices to " say you believe " and
to be " made happy." And in this parable, our Saviour

8

has given striking expression to His judgment of the school which relies upon mere happiness. Next to those who leave the seed for Satan to snatch away, He places them "who, when they have heard the word, straightway receive it with joy." They have taken the promises without the precepts, they have hoped for the crown without the cross. Their type is the thin layer of earth spread over a shelf of rock. The water, which cannot sink down, and the heat reflected up from the stone, make it for a time almost a hot bed. Straightway the seed sprang up, because it had no deepness of earth. But the moisture thus detained upon the surface vanished utterly in time of drought; the young roots, unable to penetrate to any deeper supplies, were scorched; and it withered away. That superficial heat and moisture was impulsive emotion, glad to hear of heaven, and love, and privilege, but forgetful to mortify the flesh, and to be partaker with Christ in His death. The roots of a real Christian life must strike deeper down. Consciousness of sin and its penalty and of the awful price by which that penalty has been paid, consciousness of what life should have been and how we have degraded it, consciousness of what it must yet be made by grace —these do not lead to joy so immediate, so impulsive, as the growth of this shallow vegetation. A mature and settled joy is among "the fruits of the spirit:" it is not the first blade that shoots up.

Now because the sense of sin and duty and atonement have not done their sobering work, the feelings, so easily quickened, are also easily perverted: "When tribulation or persecution ariseth because of the word, straightway they stumble." These were not counted upon. Neither trouble of mind nor opposition of wicked men was

included in the holiday scheme of the life Divine.   And
their pressure is not counter-weighted by that of any
deep convictions.   The roots have never penetrated
farther than temporal calamities and trials can reach.
In the time of drought they have *not* enough.   They
endure, but only for a while.

St. Paul sowed upon just such soil in Galatia.   There
his hearers spoke of such blessedness that they would
have plucked out their eyes for him.   But he became
their enemy because he told them all the truth, when
only a part was welcome.   And as Christ said, Straightway they stumble, so St. Paul had to marvel that they
were so soon subverted.

If indifference be the first danger, and shallowness
the second, mixed motive is the third.   Men there are
who are very earnest, and far indeed from slight views
of truth, who are nevertheless in sore danger, because
they are equally earnest about other things ; because
they cannot resign this world, whatever be their
concern about the next ; because the soil of their life
would fain grow two inconsistent harvests.   Like seed
sown among thorns, "choked" by their entangling
roots and light-excluding growths, the word in such
hearts, though neither left upon a hard surface nor
forbidden by rock to strike deep into the earth,
is overmastered by an unworthy rivalry.   A kind
of vegetation it does produce, but not such as the
tiller seeks : the word becometh unfruitful.   It is
the same lesson as when Jesus said, " No man can
serve two masters.   Ye cannot serve God and
mammon."

Perhaps it is the one most needed in our time of
feverish religious controversy and heated party spirit,
when every one hath a teaching, hath a revelation,

hath a tongue, hath an interpretation, but scarcely any have denied the world and taken in exchange a cross.

St. Paul found a thorny soil in Corinth which came behind in no gift, if only gifts had been graces, but was indulgent, factious and selfish, puffed up amid flagrant vices, one hungry and another drunken, while wrangling about the doctrine of the resurrection.

The various evils of this parable are all of them worldliness, differently manifested. The deadening effect of habitual forgetfulness of God, treading the soil so hard that no seed can enter it ; the treacherous effect of secret love of earth, a buried obstruction refusing to admit the gospel into the recesses of the life, however it may reach the feelings ; and the fierce and stubborn competition of worldly interests, wherever they are not resolutely weeded out, against these Jesus spoke His earliest parable. And it is instructive to review the foes by which He represented His Gospel as warred upon. The personal activity of Satan ; "tribulation or persecution" from without, and within the heart "cares" rather for self than for the dependent and the poor, "deceitfulness of riches" for those who possess enough to trust in, or to replace with a fictitious importance the only genuine value, which is that of character (although men are still esteemed for being "worth" a round sum, a strange estimate, to be made by Christians, of a being with a soul burning in him); and alike for rich and poor, "the lusts of other things," since none is too poor to covet, and none so rich that his desires shall not increase, like some diseases, by being fed.

Lastly, we have those on the good ground, who are not described by their sensibilities or their enjoyments,

but by their loyalty.   They " hear the word and accept
it and bear fruit."   To accept is what distinguishes
them alike from the wayside hearers into whose attention the word never sinks, from the rocky hearers
who only receive it with a superficial welcome, and
from the thorny hearers who only give it a divided
welcome.   It is not said, as if the word were merely
the precepts, that they obey it.   The sower of this
seed is not he who bade the soldier not to do violence, and the publican not to extort : it is He who
said, Repent, and believe the gospel.   He implanted
new hopes, convictions, and affections, as the germ
which should unfold in a new life.   And the good
fruit is borne by those who honestly "accept" His
word.

Fruitfulness is never in the gospel the condition by
which life is earned, but it is always the test by which
to prove it.   In all the accounts of the final judgment,
we catch the principle of the bold challenge of St.
James, "Show me thy faith without thy works, and I
will show thee my faith by my works."   The talent
must produce more talents, and the pound more
pounds ; the servant must have his loins girt and a
light in his hand ; the blessed are they who did unto
Jesus the kindness they did unto the least of His
brethren, and the accursed are they who did it not to
Jesus in His people.

We are not wrong in preaching that honest faith in
Christ is the only condition of acceptance, and the way
to obtain strength for good works.   But perhaps we
fail to add, with sufficient emphasis, that good works
are the only sufficient evidence of real faith, of genuine
conversion.   Lydia, whose heart the Lord opened and
who constrained the Apostle to abide in her house, was

converted as truly as the gaoler who passed through all the vicissitudes of despair, trembling and astonishment, and belief.

"They bear fruit, thirtyfold and sixtyfold and an hundredfold." And all are alike accepted. But the parable of the pounds shows that all are not alike rewarded, and in equal circumstances superior efficiency wins a superior prize. One star differeth from another star in glory, and they who turn many to righteousness shall shine as the sun for ever.

LAMP AND STAND.

"And He said unto them, Is the lamp brought to be put under the bushel, or under the bed? and not to be put on the stand? For there is nothing hid, save that it should be manifested; neither was anything made secret, but that it should come to light. If any man hath ears to hear, let him hear. And He said unto them, Take heed what ye hear: with what measure ye mete it shall be measured unto you: and more shall be given unto you. For he that hath, to him shall be given: and he that hath not, from him shall be taken away even that which he hath."—MARK iv. 21–25 (R. V.).

JESUS had now taught that the only good ground was that in which the good seed bore fruit. And He adds explicitly, that men receive the truth in order to spread it, and are given grace that they may become, in turn, good stewards of the manifold grace of God.

"Is the lamp brought to be put under the bushel or under the bed, and not to be put on the stand?" The language may possibly be due, as men have argued, to the simple conditions of life among the Hebrew peasantry, who possessed only one lamp, one corn-measure, and perhaps one bed. All the greater marvel is it that amid such surroundings He should have announced, and not in vain, that His disciples, His

Church, should become the light of all humanity, "the lamp." Already He had put forward the same claim even more explicitly, saying, "Ye are the light of the world." And in each case, He spoke not in the intoxication of pride or self-assertion, but in all gravity, and as a solemn warning. The city on the hill could not be hid. The lamp would burn dimly under the bed; it would be extinguished entirely by the bushel. Publicity is the soul of religion, since religion is light. It is meant to diffuse itself, to be, as He expressed it, like leaven which may be hid at first, but cannot be concealed, since it will leaven all the lump. And so, if He spoke in parables, and consciously hid His meaning by so doing, this was not to withdraw His teaching from the masses, it was to shelter the flame which should presently illuminate all the house. Nothing was hid, save that it should be manifested, nor made secret, but that it should come to light. And it has never been otherwise. Our religion has no privileged inner circle, no esoteric doctrine; and its chiefs, when men glorified one or another, asked, What then is Apollos? And what is Paul? Ministers through whom ye believed. Agents only, for conveying to others what they had received from God. And thus He Who now spoke in parables, and again charged them not to make Him known, was able at the end to say, In secret have I spoken nothing. Therefore He repeats with emphasis His former words, frequent on His lips henceforward, and ringing through the messages He spoke in glory to His Churches. If any man hath ears to hear, let him hear. None is excluded but by himself.

Yet another caution follows. If the seed be the Word, there is sore danger from false teaching; from strewing

the ground with adulterated grain. St. Mark, indeed,
has not recorded the Parable of the Tares. But there
are indications of it, and the same thought is audible
in this saying, " Take heed what ye hear." The added
words are a little surprising : " With what measure ye
mete it shall be measured unto you, and more shall be
given unto you." The last clause expresses exactly
the principle on which the forfeited pound was given to
Him who had ten pounds already, the open hand of
God lavishing additional gifts upon him who was
capable of using them. But does not the whole statement seem to follow more suitably upon a command to
beware what we teach, and thus "mete" to others, than
what we hear ? A closer examination finds in this
apparent unfitness, a deeper harmony of thought. To
"accept" the genuine word is the same as to bring
forth fruit for God; it is to reckon with the Lord of
the talents, and to yield the fruit of the vineyard. And
this is to "mete," not indeed unto man, but unto God,
Who shows Himself froward with the froward, and
from him that hath not, whose possession is below his
accountability, takes away even that he hath, but gives
exceeding abundantly above all they ask or think to
those who have, who are not disobedient to the heavenly
calling.

All this is most delicately connected with what precedes it; and the parables, hiding the truth from
some, giving it authority, and colour, and effect to
others, were a striking example of the process here
announced.

Never was the warning to be heedful what we hear,
more needed than at present. Men think themselves
free to follow any teacher, especially if he be eloquent,
to read any book, if only it be in demand, and to dis-

cuss any theory, provided it be fashionable, while
perfectly well aware that they are neither earnest
inquirers after truth, nor qualified champions against
its assailants.   For what then do they read and
hear ?   For the pleasure of a rounded phrase, or to
augment the prattle of conceited ignorance in a
drawing-room.

De we wonder when these players with edged tools
injure .hemselves, and become perverts or agnostics ?
It would be more wonderful if they remained unhurt,
since Jesus said, " Take heed what ye hear . . . from
him that hath not shall be taken even that he hath."
A rash and uninstructed exposure of our intellects to
evil influences, is meting to God with an unjust measure,
as really as a wilful plunge into any other temptation,
since we are bidden to cleanse ourselves from all defilement of the spirit as well as of the flesh.

THE SEED GROWING SECRETLY.

" And He said, So is the kingdom of God, as if a man should cast
seed upon the earth ; and should sleep and rise night and day, and the
seed should spring up and grow, he knoweth not how.   The earth
beareth fruit of herself ; first the blade, then the ear, then the full corn
in the ear.   But when the fruit is ripe, straightway he putteth forth the
sickle, because the harvest is come."—MARK iv. 26-29 (R.V.).

ST. MARK alone records this parable of a sower who
sleeps by night, and rises for other business by day,
and knows not how the seed springs up.   That is not
the sower's concern : all that remains for him is to put
forth the sickle when the harvest is come.

It is a startling parable for us who believe in the
fostering care of the Divine Spirit.   And the paradox
is forced on our attention by the words "the earth
beareth fruit of herself," contrasting strangely as it

does with such other assertions, as that the branch cannot bear fruit of itself, that without Christ we can do nothing, and that when we live it is not we but Christ who liveth in us.

It will often help us to understand a paradox if we can discover another like it. And exactly such an one as this will be found in the record of creation. God rested on the seventh day from all His work, yet we know that His providence never slumbers, that by Him all things consist, and that Jesus defended His own work of healing on a Sabbath day by urging that the Sabbath of God was occupied in gracious provision for His world. " My Father worketh hitherto, and I work." Thus the rest of God from creative work says nothing about His energies in that other field of providential care. Exactly so Jesus here treats only of what may be called the creative spiritual work, the deposit of the seed of life. And the essence of this remarkable parable is the assertion that we are to expect an orderly, quiet and gradual development from this principle of life, not a series of communications from without, of additional revelations, of semi-miraculous interferences. The life of grace is a natural process in the supernatural sphere. In one sense it is all of God, who maketh His sun to rise, and sendeth rain, without which the earth could bear no fruit of herself. In another sense we must work out our own salvation all the more earnestly because it is God that worketh in us.

Now this parable, thus explained, has been proved true in the wonderful history of the Church. She has grown, not only in extent but by development, as marvellously as a corn of wheat which is now a waving wheat-stem with its ripening ear. When Cardinal

Newman urged that an ancient Christian, returning to earth, would recognise the services and the Church of Rome, and would fail to recognise ours, he was probably mistaken. To go no farther, there is no Church on earth so unlike the Churches of the New Testament as that which offers praise to God in a strange tongue. St. Paul apprehended that a stranger in such an assembly would reckon the worshippers mad. But in any case the argument forgets that the whole kingdom of God is to resemble seed, not in a drawer, but in the earth, and advancing towards the harvest. It must "die" to much if it will bring forth fruit. It must acquire strange bulk, strange forms, strange organisms. It must become, to those who only knew it as it was, quite as unrecognisable as our Churches are said to be. And yet the changes must be those of logical growth, not of corruption. And this parable tells us they must be accomplished without any special interference such as marked the sowing time. Well then, the parable is a prophecy. Movement after movement has modified the life of the Church. Even its structure is not all it was. But these changes have every one been wrought by human agency, they have come from within it, like the force which pushes the germ out of the soil, and expands the bud into the full corn in the ear. There has been no grafting knife to insert a new principle of richer life ; the gospel and the sacraments of our Lord have contained in them the promise and potency of all that was yet to be unfolded, all the gracefulness and all the fruit. And these words, "the earth beareth fruit of herself, first the blade, then the ear, then the full corn in the ear," each so different, and yet so dependent on what preceded, teach us two great ecclesiastical lessons.

They condemn the violent and revolutionary changes, which would not develop old germs but tear them open or perhaps pull them up. Much may be distasteful to the spirit of sordid utilitarianism; a mere husk, which nevertheless within it shelters precious grain, otherwise sure to perish. If thus we learn to respect the old, still more do we learn that what is new has also its all-important part to play. The blade and the ear in turn are innovations. We must not condemn those new forms of Christian activity, Christian association, and Christian councils, which new times evoke, until we have considered well whether they are truly expansions, in the light and heat of our century, of the sacred life-germ of the ancient faith and the ancient love.

And what lessons has this parable for the individual? Surely that of active present faith, not waiting for future gifts of light or feeling, but confident that the seed already sown, the seed of the word, has power to develop into the rich fruit of Christian character. In this respect the parable supplements the first one. From that we learned that if the soil were not in fault, if the heart were honest and good, the seed would fructify. From this we learn that these conditions suffice for a perfect harvest. The incessant, all-important help of God, we have seen, is not denied; it is taken for granted, as the atmospheric and magnetic influences upon the grain. So should we reverentially and thankfully rely upon the aid of God, and then, instead of waiting for strange visitations and special stirrings of grace, account that we already possess enough to make us responsible for the harvest of the soul. Multitudes of souls, whose true calling is, in obedient trust, to arise and walk, are at this moment lying impotent beside some pool which they expect an angel to stir, and into which they fain would then be put by some one, they know not whom—multitudes of expectant, inert, inactive souls, who know not that the text they have most need to ponder is this : "the earth beareth fruit of itself." For want of this they are actually, day by day, receiving the grace of God in vain.

We learn also to be content with gradual progress. St. John did not blame the children and young men to whom he wrote, because they were not mature in wisdom and experience. St. Paul exhorts us to grow up in all things into Him which is the Head, even Christ. They do not ask for more than steady growth; and their Master, as He distrusted the fleeting joy of hearers whose hearts were shallow, now explicitly bids us not to be content with any first attainment, not to count all done if we are converted, but to develop first the blade, then the ear, and lastly the full corn in the ear.

Does it seem a tedious weary sentence ? Are we discontent for want of conscious interferences of heaven ? Do we complain that, to human consciousness, the great Sower sleeps and rises up and leaves the grain to fare He knows not how ? It is only for a little while. When the fruit is ripe, He will Himself gather it into His eternal garner.

THE MUSTARD SEED.

" And He said, How shall we liken the kingdom of God ? or in what parable shall we set it forth ? It is like a grain of mustard seed, which, when it is sown upon the earth, though it be less than all the seeds that are upon the earth, yet when it is sown, groweth up, and becometh greater than all the herbs, and putteth out great branches ; so that the birds of the heaven can lodge under the shadow thereof. And with many such parables spake He the word unto them, as they were able to hear it : and without a parable spake He not unto them : but privately to His own disciples He expounded all things."—MARK iv. 30–34 (R.V.).

ST. MARK has recorded one other parable of this great cycle. Jesus now invites the disciples to let their own minds play upon the subject. Each is to ask himself a question : How shall we liken the kingdom of God ? or in what parable shall we set it forth ?

A gentle pause, time for them to form some splendid and ambitious image in their minds, and then we can suppose with what surprise they heard His own answer, " It is like a grain of mustard seed." And truly some Christians of a later day might be astonished also, if they could call up a fair image of their own conceptions of the kingdom of God, and compare it with this figure, employed by Jesus.

But here one must observe a peculiarity in our Saviour's use of images. His illustrations of His first coming, and of His work of grace, which are many, are all of the homeliest kind. He is a shepherd who seeks one sheep. He is not an eagle that fluttereth over her young and beareth them on her pinions, but a hen who gathereth her chickens under her wings. Never once does He rise into that high and poetic strain with which His followers have loved to sing of the Star of Bethlehem, and which Isaiah lavished beforehand

upon the birth of the Prince of Peace. There is no
language more intensely concentrated and glowing than
He has employed to describe the judgment of the
hypocrites who rejected Him, of Jerusalem, and of the
world at last. But when He speaks of His first coming
and its effects, it is not of that sunrise to which all
kings and nations shall hasten, but of a little grain of
mustard seed, which is to become "greater than all
the herbs," and put forth great branches, "so that the
birds of the heaven can lodge under the shadow of
them." When one thinks of such an image for such
an event, of the founding of the kingdom of God,
and its advance to universal supremacy, represented by
the small seed of a shrub which grows to the height
of a tree, and even harbours birds, he is conscious
almost of incongruity. But when one reconsiders it,
he is filled with awe and reverence. For this exactly
expresses the way of thinking natural to One who has
stooped immeasurably down to the task which all
others feel to be so lofty. There is a poem of Shelley,
which expresses the relative greatness of three spirits
by the less and less value which they set on the
splendours of the material heavens. To the first they
are a palace-roof of golden lights, to the second but
the mind's first chamber, to the last only drops which
Nature's mighty heart drives through thinnest veins.
Now that which was to Isaiah the exalting of every
valley and the bringing low of every mountain, and to
Daniel the overthrow of a mighty image whose aspect
was terrible, by a stone cut out without hands, was to
Jesus but the sowing of a grain of mustard seed.
Could any other have spoken thus of the founding of
the kingdom of God? An enthusiast over-values his
work, he can think of nothing else; and he expects

immediate revolutions. Jesus was keenly aware that His work in itself was very small, no more than the sowing of a seed, and even of the least, popularly speaking, among all seeds. Clearly He did not over-rate the apparent effect of His work on earth. And indeed, what germ of religious teaching could be less promising than the doctrine of the cross, held by a few peasants in a despised province of a nation already subjugated and soon to be overwhelmed?

The image expresses more than the feeble beginning and victorious issue of His work, more than even the gradual and logical process by which this final triumph should be attained. All this we found in the preceding parable. But here the emphasis is laid on the develop-ment of Christ's influence in unexpected spheres. Un-like other herbs, the mustard in Eastern climates does grow into a tree, shoot out great branches from the main stem, and give shelter to the birds of the air. So has the Christian faith developed ever new collateral agencies, charitable, educational, and social : so have architecture, music, literature, flourished under its shade, and there is not one truly human interest which would not be deprived of its best shelter if the rod of Jesse were hewn down. Nay, we may urge that the Church itself has become the most potent force in direc-tions not its own : it broke the chains of the negro ; it asserts the rights of woman and of the poor ; its noble literature is finding a response in the breast of a hundred degraded races ; the herb has become a tree.

And so in the life of individuals, if the seed be allowed its due scope and place to grow, it gives shelter and blessing to whatsoever things are honest and lovely, not only if there be any virtue, but also if there be any praise.

Well is it with the nation, and well with the soul, when the faith of Jesus is not rigidly restricted to a prescribed sphere, when the leaves which are for the healing of the nations cast their shadow broad and cool over all the spaces in which all its birds of song are nestling.

A remarkable assertion is added. Although the parabolic mode of teaching was adopted in judgment, yet its severe effect was confined within the narrowest limits. His many parables were spoken " as they were able to hear," but only to His own disciples privately was all their meaning expounded.

FOUR MIRACLES.

" And there was a great calm."—MARK iv. 39 (R.V.).

" Behold, him that was possessed with devils, sitting, clothed and in his right mind, *even* him that had the legion."—v. 15 (R.V.).

" Who touched Me ? "—v. 31 (R.V.).

" Talitha cumi."—v. 41 (R.V.).

THERE are two ways, equally useful, of studying Scripture, as there are of regarding the other book of God, the face of Nature. We may bend over a wild flower, or gaze across a landscape ; and it will happen that a naturalist, pursuing a moth, loses sight of a mountain-range. It is a well-known proverb, that one may fail to see the wood for the trees, losing in details the general effect. And so the careful student of isolated texts may never perceive the force and cohesion of a connected passage.

The reader of a Gospel narrative thinks, that by pondering it as a whole, he secures himself against any such misfortune. But a narrative dislocated, often loses as much as a detached verse. The actions of our Lord are often exquisitely grouped, as becometh Him

9

Who hath made everything not beautiful only, but especially beautiful in its season. And we should not be content without combining the two ways of reading Scripture, the detailed and the rapid,—lingering at times to apprehend the marvellous force of a solitary verse, and again sweeping over a broad expanse, like a surveyor, who, to map a country, stretches his triangles from mountain peak to peak.

We have reached a point at which St. Mark records a special outshining of miraculous power. Four striking works follow each other without a break, and it must not for a moment be supposed that the narrative is thus constructed, certain intermediate discourses and events being sacrificed for the purpose, without a deliberate and a truthful intention. That intention is to represent the effect, intense and exalting, produced by such a cycle of wonders on the minds of His disciples. They saw them come close upon each other : we should lose the impression as we read, if other incidents were allowed to interpose themselves. It is one more example of St. Mark's desire to throw light, above all things, upon the energy and power of the sacred life.

We have to observe therefore the bearing of these four miracles on each other, and upon what precedes, before studying them one by one.

It was a time of trial. The Pharisees had decided that He had a devil. His relatives had said He was beside Himself. His manner of teaching had changed, because the people should see without perceiving, and hear without understanding. They who understood His parables heard much of seed that failed, of success a great way off, of a kingdom which would indeed be great at last, but for the present weak and small. And it is certain that there must have been heavy hearts

among those who left, with Him, the populous side of
the lake, to cross over into remote and semi-pagan
retirement. To encourage them, and as if in protest
against His rejection by the authorities, Jesus enters
upon this great cycle of miracles.

They find themselves, as the Church has often since
been placed, and as every human soul has had to feel
itself, far from shore, and tempest-beaten. The rage
of human foes is not so deaf, so implacable, as that of
wind and wave. It is the stress of adverse circumstances in the direst form. But Jesus proves Himself
to be Master of the forces of nature which would over-
whelm them.

Nay, they learn that His seeming indifference is no
proof that they are neglected, by the rebuke He speaks
to their over-importunate appeals, Why are ye so fearful ? have ye not yet faith ? And they, who might
have been shaken by the infidelity of other men, fear
exceedingly as they behold the obedience of the wind
and the sea, and ask, Who then is this ?

But in their mission as His disciples, a worse danger
than the enmity of man or convulsions of nature awaits
them. On landing, they are at once confronted by one
whom an evil spirit has made exceeding fierce, so that
no man could pass by that way. It is their way
nevertheless, and they must tread it. And the demoniac adores, and the evil spirits themselves are
abject in supplication, and at the word of Jesus are
expelled. Even the inhabitants, who will not receive
Him, are awe-struck and deprecatory, and if at their
bidding Jesus turns away again, His followers may
judge whether the habitual meekness of such a one
is due to feebleness or to a noble self-command.

Landing once more, they are soon accosted by a

ruler of the synagogue, whom sorrow has purified from the prejudices of his class. And Jesus is about to heal the daughter of Jairus, when another form of need is brought to light. A slow and secret decline, wasting the vital powers, a silent woe, speechless, stealthily approaching the Healer—over this grief also He is Lord. And it is seen that neither the visible actions of Jesus nor the audible praises of His petitioners can measure the power that goes out of Him, the physical benefits which encompass the Teacher as a halo envelopes flame.

Circumstances, and the fiends of the pit, and the woes that waste the lives of men, over these He has been seen to triumph. But behind all that we strive with here, there lurks the last enemy, and he also shall be subdued. And now first an example is recorded of what we know to have already taken place, the conquest of death by his predicted Spoiler. Youth and gentle maidenhood, high hope and prosperous circumstances have been wasted, but the call of Jesus is heard by the ear that was stopped with dust, and the spirit obeys Him in the far off realm of the departed, and they who have just seen such other marvels, are nevertheless amazed with a great amazement.

No cycle of miracles could be more rounded, symmetrical and exhaustive; none could better vindicate to His disciples His impugned authority, or brace their endangered faith, or fit them for what almost immediately followed, their own commission, and the first journey upon which they too cast out many devils, and anointed with oil many that were sick, and healed them.

THE TWO STORMS.

" And on that day, when even was come, He saith unto them, Let us go over unto the other side. And leaving the multitude, they take Him with them, even as He was, in the boat. And other boats were with Him. And there ariseth a great storm of wind, and the waves beat into the boat, insomuch that the boat was now filling. And He Himself was in the stern, asleep on the cushion : and they awake Him, and say unto Him, Master, carest Thou not that we perish ? And He awoke, and rebuked the wind, and said unto the sea, Peace, be still. And the wind ceased, and there was a great calm. And He said unto them, Why are ye fearful ? have ye not yet faith ? And they feared exceedingly, and said one to another, Who then is this, that even the wind and the sea obey him ? "—MARK iv. 35-41 (R.V.).

" And when even was come, the boat was in the midst of the sea, and He alone on the land. And seeing them distressed in rowing, for the wind was contrary unto them, about the fourth watch of the night He cometh unto them, walking on the sea ; and He would have passed by them : but they, when they saw Him walking on the sea, supposed that it was an apparition, and cried out : for they all saw Him, and were troubled. But He straightway spake with them, and saith unto them, Be of good cheer : it is I ; be not afraid. And He went up unto them into the boat ; and the wind ceased : and they were sore amazed in themselves. For they understood not concerning the loaves, but their hearts were hardened."—MARK vi. 47-52 (R.V.).

FEW readers are insensible to the wonderful power with which the Gospels tell the story of the two storms upon the lake. The narratives are favourites in every Sunday school ; they form the basis of countless hymns and poems ; and we always recur to them with fresh delight.

In the first account we see as in a picture the weariness of the great Teacher, when, the long day being over and the multitude dismissed, He retreats across the sea without preparation, and "as He was," and sinks to sleep on the one cushion in the stern, undisturbed by the raging tempest or by the waves which beat into the boat. We observe the reluctance of the disciples to arouse Him until the peril is extreme, and the boat is "now" filling. We hear from St. Mark, the associate of St. Peter, the presumptuous and characteristic cry which expresses terror, and perhaps dread lest His tranquil slumbers may indicate a separation between His cause and theirs, who perish while He is unconcerned. We admire equally the calm and masterful words which quell the tempest, and those which enjoin a faith so lofty as to endure the last extremities of peril without dismay, without agitation in its prayers. We observe the strange incident, that no sooner does the storm cease than the waters, commonly seething for many hours afterwards, grow calm. And the picture is completed by the mention of their new dread (fear of the supernatural Man replacing their terror amid the convulsions of nature), and of their awestruck questioning among themselves.

In the second narrative we see the ship far out in the lake, but watched by One, Who is alone upon the land. Through the gloom He sees them "tormented" by fruitless rowing; but though this is the reason why He comes, He is about to pass them by. The watch of the night is remembered; it is the fourth. The cry of their alarm is universal, for they all saw Him and were troubled. We are told of the promptitude with which He thereupon relieved their fears; we see Him climb up into the boat, and the sudden ceasing of the storm, and their amazement. Nor is that after-thought omitted in which they blamed themselves for their astonishment. If their hearts had not been hardened, the miracle of the loaves would have taught them that Jesus was the master of the physical world.

Now all this picturesque detail belongs to a single Gospel. And it is exactly what a believer would

expect. How much soever the healing of disease
might interest St. Luke the physician, who relates all
such events so vividly, it would have impressed the
patient himself yet more, and an account of it by him,
if we had it, would be full of graphic touches. Now
these two miracles were wrought for the rescue of the
apostles themselves. The Twelve took the place held
in others by the lame, the halt and the blind: the
suspense, the appeal, and the joy of deliverance were
all their own. It is therefore no wonder that we find
their accounts of these especial miracles so picturesque.
But this is a solid evidence of the truth of the narratives; for while the remembrance of such actual events
should thrill with agitated life, there is no reason why
a legend of the kind should be especially clear and
vivid. The same argument might easily be carried
farther. When the disciples began to reproach themselves for their unbelieving astonishment, they were
naturally conscious of having failed to learn the lesson
which had been taught them just before. Later students
and moralists would have observed that another miracle,
a little earlier, was a still closer precedent, but they
naturally blamed themselves most for being blind to
what was immediately before their eyes. Now when
Jesus walked upon the waters and the disciples were
amazed, it is not said that they forgot how He had
already stilled a tempest, but they considered not the
miracle of the loaves, for their heart was hardened.
In touches like this we find the influence of a bystander beyond denial.

Every student of Scripture must have observed the
special significance of those parables and miracles
which recur a second time with certain designed variations. In the miraculous draughts of fishes, Christ

Himself avowed an allusion to the catching of men. And the Church has always discerned a spiritual intention in these two storms, in one of which Christ slept, while in the other His disciples toiled alone, and which express, between them, the whole strain exercised upon a devout spirit by adverse circumstances. Dangers never alarmed one who realized both the presence of Jesus and His vigilant care. Temptation enters only because this is veiled. Why do adversities press hard upon me, if indeed I belong to Christ ? He must either be indifferent and sleeping, or else absent altogether from my frail and foundering bark. It is thus that we let go our confidence, and incur agonies of mental suffering, and the rebuke of our Master, even though He continues to be the Protector of His unworthy people.

On the voyage of life we may conceive of Jesus as our Companion, for He is with us always, or as watching us from the everlasting hills, whither it was expedient for us that He should go. Nevertheless, we are storm-tossed and in danger. Although we are His, and not separated from Him by any conscious disobedience, yet the conditions of life are unmitigated, the winds as wild, the waves as merciless, the boat as cruelly "tormented" as ever. And no rescue comes : Jesus is asleep : He cares not that we perish. Then we pray after a fashion so clamorous, and with supplication so like demands, that we too appear to have undertaken to awake our Lord. Then we have to learn from the first of these miracles, and especially from its delay. The disciples were safe, had they only known it, whether Jesus would have interposed of His own accord, or whether they might still have needed to appeal to Him, but in a gentler fashion. We may ask

help, provided that we do so in a serene and trustful
spirit, anxious for nothing, not seeking to extort a concession, but approaching with boldness the throne of
grace, on which our Father sits.   It is thus that the
peace of God shall rule our hearts and minds, for want
of which the apostles were asked, Where is your faith?
Comparing the narratives, we learn that Jesus reassured
their hearts even before He arose, and then, having
first silenced by His calmness the storm within them,
He stood up and rebuked the storm around.

St. Augustine gave a false turn to the application,
when he said, " If Jesus were not asleep within thee,
thou wouldst be calm and at rest.   But why is He
asleep?   Because thy faith is asleep," etc. (Sermon lxiii.)
The sleep of Jesus was natural and right; and it
answers not to our spiritual torpor, but to His apparent
indifference and non-intervention in our time of distress.
And the true lesson of the miracle is that we should
trust Him Whose care fails not when it seems to fail,
Who is able to save to the uttermost, and Whom we
should approach in the direst peril without panic.   It
was fitly taught them first when all the powers of the
State and the Church were leagued against Him, and
He as a blind man saw not and as a dumb man opened
not His mouth.

The second storm should have found them braver by
the experience of the first; but spiritually as well as
bodily they were farther removed from Christ.   The
people, profoundly moved by the murder of the Baptist,
wished to set Jesus on the throne, and the disciples were
too ambitious to be allowed to be present while He dismissed the multitudes.   They had to be sent away, and
it was from the distant hillside that Jesus saw their
danger.   Surely it is instructive, that neither the shades

of night, nor the abstracted fervour of His prayers, prevented him from seeing it, nor the stormlashed waters
from bringing aid. And significant also, that the experience of remoteness, though not sinful, since He had
sent them away, was yet the result of their own worldliness. It is when we are out of sympathy with Jesus
that we are most likely to be alone in trouble. None
was in their boat to save them, and in heart also they
had gone out from the presence of their God. Therefore
they failed to trust in His guidance Who had sent
them into the ship : they had no sense of protection or
of supervision ; and it was a terrible moment when a
form was vaguely seen to glide over the waves. Christ,
it would seem, would have gone before and led them
to the haven where they would be. Or perhaps He
"would have passed by them," as He would afterwards have gone further than Emmaus, to elicit any
trustful half-recognition which might call to Him and
be rewarded. But they cried out for fear. And so it
is continually with God in His world, men are terrified
at the presence of the supernatural, because they fail
to apprehend the abiding presence of the supernatural
Christ. And yet there is one point at least in every
life, the final moment, in which all else must recede,
and the soul be left alone with the beings of another
world. Then, and in every trial, and especially in all
trials which press in upon us the consciousness of the
spiritual universe, well is it for him who hears the
voice of Jesus saying, It is I, be not afraid.

For only through Jesus, only in His person, has
that unknown universe ceased to be dreadful and
mysterious. Only when He is welcomed does the
storm cease to rage around us.

It was the earlier of these miracles which first taught

the disciples that not only were human disorders under His control, and gifts and blessings at His disposal, but also the whole range of nature was subject to Him, and the winds and the sea obey Him.

Shall we say that His rebuke addressed to these was a mere figure of speech ? Some have inferred that natural convulsions are so directly the work of evil angels that the words of Jesus were really spoken to them. But the plain assertion is that He rebuked the winds and the waves, and these would not become identical with Satan even upon the supposition that he excites them. We ourselves continually personify the course of nature, and even complain of it, wantonly enough, and Scripture does not deny itself the use of ordinary human forms of speech. Yet the very peculiar word employed by Jesus cannot be without significance. It is the same with which He had already confronted the violence of the demoniac in the synagogue, Be muzzled. At the least it expresses stern repression, and thus it reminds us that creation itself is made subject to vanity, the world deranged by sin, so that all around us requires readjustment as truly as all within, and Christ shall at last create a new earth as well as a new heaven.

Some pious people resign themselves much too passively to the mischiefs of the material universe, supposing that troubles which are not of their own making, must needs be a Divine infliction, calling only for submission. But God sends oppositions to be conquered as well as burdens to be borne ; and even before the fall the world had to be subdued. And our final mastery over the surrounding universe was expressed, when Jesus our Head rebuked the winds, and stilled the waves when they arose.

As they beheld, a new sense fell upon His disciples of a more awful presence than they had yet discerned. They asked not only what manner of man is this ? but, with surmises which went out beyond the limits of human greatness, Who then is this, that even the winds and the sea obey Him ?

CHAPTER V.

THE DEMONIAC OF GADARA.

" And they came to the other side of the sea, into the country of the Gerasenes. And when He was come out of the boat, straightway there met Him out of the tombs a man with an unclean spirit, who had his dwelling in the tombs : and no man could any more bind him, no, not with a chain ; because that he had been often bound with fetters and chains, and the chains had been rent asunder by him, and the fetters broken in pieces : and no man had strength to tame him. And always, night and day, in the tombs and in the mountains, he was crying out, and cutting himself with stones. And when he saw Jesus from afar, he ran and worshipped Him ; and crying out with a loud voice, he saith, What have I to do with Thee, Jesus, Thou Son of the Most High God ? I adjure Thee by God, torment me not. For He said unto him, Come forth, thou unclean spirit, out of the man. And He asked him, What is thy name? And he saith unto Him, My name is Legion ; for we are many. And he besought Him much that He would not send them away out of the country. Now there was there on the mountain side a great herd of swine feeding. And they besought Him, saying, Send us into the swine, that we may enter into them. And He gave them leave. And the unclean spirits came out, and entered into the swine : and the herd rushed down the steep into the sea, *in number* about two thousand ; and they were choked in the sea. And they that fed them fled, and told it in the city, and in the country. And they came to see what it was that had come to pass. And they come to Jesus, and behold him that was possessed with devils sitting, clothed and in his right mind, *even* him that had the legion : and they were afraid. And they that saw it declared unto them how it befell him that was possessed with devils, and concerning the swine. And they began to beseech Him to depart from their borders. And as He was entering into the boat, he that had been possessed with devils besought Him that he might be with Him. And He suffered him not, but saith unto him, Go to thy house unto thy friends, and tell them how great things the Lord hath done for thee, and *how* He had mercy on thee. And he went his way, and began to publish in Decapolis how great things Jesus had done for him : and all men did marvel."—MARK v. 1–20 (R.V.).

FRESH from asserting His mastery over winds and waves, the Lord was met by a more terrible enemy, the rage of human nature enslaved and impelled by the cruelty of hell. The place where He landed was a theatre not unfit for the tragedy which it revealed. A mixed race was there, indifferent to religion, rearing great herds of swine, upon which the law looked askance, but the profits of which they held so dear that they would choose to banish a Divine ambassador, and one who had released them from an incessant peril, rather than be deprived of these. Now it has already been shown that the wretches possessed by devils were not of necessity stained with special guilt. Even children fell into this misery. But yet we should expect to find it most rampant in places where God was dishonoured, in Gerasa and in the coasts of Tyre and Sidon. And it is so. All misery is the consequence of sin, although individual misery does not measure individual guilt. And the places where the shadow of sin has fallen heaviest are always the haunts of direst wretchedness.

The first Gospel mentions two demoniacs, but one was doubtless so pre-eminently fierce, and possibly so zealous afterward in proclaiming his deliverance, that only St. Matthew learned the existence of another, upon whom also Satan had wrought, if not his worst, enough to show his hatred, and the woes he would fain bring upon humanity.

Among the few terrible glimpses given us of the mind of the fallen angels, one is most significant and sinister.   When the unclean spirit is gone out of a man, to what haunts does he turn ?   He has no sympathy with what is lovely or sublime : in search of rest he wanders through dry places, deserts of arid sand in which his misery may be soothed by congenial desolation.   Thus the ruins of the mystic Babylon become an abode of devils.   And thus the unclean spirit, when he mastered this demoniac, drove him to a foul and dreary abode among the tombs.   One can picture the victim in some lucid moment, awakening to consciousness only to shudder in his dreadful home, and scared back again into that ferocity which is the child of terror.

> " Is it not very like,
> The horrible conceit of death and night,
> Together with the terror of the place
> .   .   .   .   .   .
> Oh ! if I wake, shall I not be distraught,
> Environéd with all these hideous fears ? "
>
> *Romeo and Juliet,* **iv. 3.**

There was a time when he had been under restraint, but " now no man could any more bind him " even with iron upon feet and wrists.   The ferocity of his cruel subjugator turned his own strength against himself, so that night and day his howling was heard, as he cut himself with stones, and his haunts in the tombs and in the mountains were as dangerous as the lair of a wild breast, which no man dared pass by.   What strange impulse drove him thence to the feet of Jesus ? Very dreadful is the picture of his conflicting tendencies ; the fiend within him struggling against something still human and attracted by the Divine, so that he runs from afar, yet cries aloud, and worships yet disowns having anything to do with Him; and as if the fiend

had subverted the true personality, and become tl.e very
man, when ordered to come out he adjures Jesus to
torment him not.

And here we observe the knowledge of Christ's rank
possessed by the evil ones.   Long before Peter won a
special blessing for acknowledging the Son of the
living God, the demoniac called Him by the very name
which flesh and blood did not reveal to Cephas.   For
their chief had tested and discovered Him in the
wilderness, saying twice with dread surmise, If Thou
be the Son of God. It is also noteworthy that the
phrase, the most High God, is the name of Jehovah
among the non-Jewish races.   It occurs in both Testaments in connection with Melchizedek the Canaanite.
It is used throughout the Babylonian proclamations in
the book of Daniel.   Micah puts it into the lips of
Balaam.   And the damsel with a spirit of divination
employed it in Philippi. Except once, in a Psalm which
tells of the return of apostate Israel to the Most High
God (lxxviii. 35), the epithet is used only in relation
with the nations outside the covenant.   Its occurrence
here is probably a sign of the pagan influences by which
Gadara was infected, and for which it was plagued.   By
the name of God then, whose Son He loudly confessed
that Jesus was, the fiend within the man adjures Him
to torment Him not.   But Jesus had not asked to be
acknowledged ; He had bidden the devil to come out.
And persons who substitute loud confessions and
clamorous orthodoxies for obedience should remember
that so did the fiend of Gadara.   Jesus replied by
asking, What is thy name ?   The question was not an
idle one, but had a healing tendency.   For the man
was beside himself : it was part of his cure that he was
found "in his right mind ;" and meanwhile his very

consciousness was merged in that of the fiends who tortured him, so that his voice was their voice, and they returned a vaunting answer through His lips. Our Lord sought therefore both to calm His excitement and to remind him of himself, and of what he once had been before evil beings dethroned his will. These were not the man, but his enemies by whom he was " carried about," and " led captive at their will." And it is always sobering to think of " Myself," the lonely individual, apart from even those who most influence me, with a soul to lose or save. With this very question the Church Catechism begins its work of arousing and instructing the conscience of each child, separating him from his fellows in order to lead him on to the knowledge of the individualising grace of God.

It may be that the fiends within him dictated his reply, or that he himself, conscious of their tyranny, cried out in agony, We are many ; a regiment like those of conquering Rome, drilled and armed to trample and destroy, a legion. This answer distinctly contravened what Christ had just implied, that he was one, an individual, and precious in his Maker's eyes. But there are men and women in every Christian land, whom it might startle to look within, and see how far their individuality is oppressed and overlaid by a legion of impulses, appetites, and conventionalities, which leave them nothing personal, nothing essential and characteristic, nothing that deserves a name. The demons, now conscious of the power which calls them forth, besought Him to leave them a refuge in that country. St. Luke throws light upon this petition, as well as their former complaint, when he tells us they feared to be sent to " the abyss " of their final retribution. And as we read of men who are haunted by a fearful looking

10

for of judgment and a fierceness of fire, so they had no hope of escape, except until "the time." For a little respite they prayed to be sent even into the swine, and Jesus gave them leave.

What a difference there is between the proud and heroic spirits whom Milton celebrated, and these malignant but miserable beings, haunting the sepulchres like ghosts, truculent and yet dastardly, as ready to supplicate as to rend, filled with dread of the appointed time and of the abyss, clinging to that outlying country as a congenial haunt, and devising for themselves a last asylum among the brutes. And yet they are equally far from the materialistic superstitions of that age and place ; they are not amenable to fumigations or exorcisms, and they do not upset the furniture in rushing out. Many questions have been asked about the petition of the demons and our Lord's consent. But none of them need much distress the reverential enquirer, who remembers by what misty horizons all our knowledge is enclosed. Most absurd is the charge that Jesus acted indefensibly in destroying property. Is it then so clear that the owners did not deserve their loss through the nature of their investments ? Was it merely as a man, or as the Son of the living God, that His consent was felt to be necessary ? And was it any part of His mission to protect brutes from death ?

The loss endured was no greater than when a crop is beaten down by hail, or a vineyard devastated by insects, and in these cases an agency beyond the control of man is sent or permitted by God, Who was in Christ.

A far harder question it is, How could devils enter into brute creatures? and again, Why did they desire to do so? But the first of these is only a subdivision of the vaster problem, at once inevitable and insoluble, How does spirit in any of its forms animate matter, or even manipulate it ? We know not by what strange link a thought contracts a sinew, and transmutes itself into words or deeds.   And if we believe the dread and melancholy fact of the possession of a child by a fiend, what reason have we, beyond prejudice, for doubting the possession of swine ?   It must be observed also, that no such possession is proved by this narrative to be a common event, but the reverse.   The notion is a last and wild expedient of despair, proposing to content itself with the uttermost abasement, if only the demons might still haunt the region where they had thriven so well.   And the consent of Jesus does not commit Him to any judgment upon the merit or the possibility of the project.   He leaves the experiment to prove itself, exactly as when Peter would walk upon the water ; and a laconic " Go" in this case recalls the "Come" in that ; an assent, without approval, to an attempt which was about to fail.   Not in the world of brutes could they find shelter from the banishment they dreaded ; for the whole herd, frantic and un-governed, rushed headlong into the sea and was destroyed.   The second victory of the series was thus completed.   Jesus was Master over the evil spirits which afflict humanity, as well as over the fierceness of the elements which rise against us.

THE MEN OF GADARA.

"And they that fed them fled, and told it in the city, and in the country. And they came to see what it was that had come to pass, And they come to Jesus, and behold him that was possessed with devils sitting, clothed and in his right mind, *even* him that had the legion : and they were afraid. And they that saw it declared unto them how it befell him that was possessed with devils, and concerning the swine. And they began to beseech him to depart from their borders. And as He was entering into the boat, he that had been possessed with devils besought Him that he might be with Him. And He suffered him not, but saith unto him, Go to thy house unto thy friends, and tell them how great things the Lord hath done for thee, and *how* He had mercy on thee. And he went his way, and began to publish in Decapolis how great things Jesus had done for him : and all men did marvel."— MARK v. 14–20 (R.V.).

THE expulsion of the demons from the possessed, their entrance into the herd, and the destruction of the two thousand swine, were virtually one transaction, and must have impressed the swineherds in its totality. They saw on the one hand the restoration of a dangerous and raging madman, known to be actuated by evil spirits, the removal of a standing peril which had already made one tract of country impassable, and (if they considered such a thing at all) the calming of a human soul, and its advent within the reach of all sacred influences. On the other side what was there ? The loss of two thousand swine ; and the consciousness that the kingdom of God was come nigh unto them. This was always an alarming discovery. Isaiah said, Woe is me ! when his eyes beheld God high and lifted up. And Peter said, Depart from me, when he learned by the miraculous draught of fish that the Lord was there. But Isaiah's concern was because he was a man of unclean lips, and Peter's was because he was a sinful man. Their alarm was that of an awakened conscience, and therefore they became the heralds of Him Whom they feared. But these men were simply scared at what they instinctively felt to be dangerous; and so they took refuge in a crowd, that frequent resort of the frivolous and conscience-stricken, and told in the city what they had seen. And when the inhabitants came forth, a sight met them which might have won the sternest, the man sitting, clothed (a nice coincidence, since St. Mark had not mentioned that he "ware no clothes,") and in his right mind, even him that had the legion, as the narrative emphatically adds. And doubtless the much debated incident of the swine had greatly helped to reassure this afflicted soul; the demons were palpably gone, visibly enough they were overmastered. But the citizens, like the swineherds, were merely terrified, neither grateful nor sympathetic; uninspired with hope of pure teaching, of rescue from other influences of the evil one, or of any unearthly kingdom. Their formidable visitant was one to treat with all respect, but to remove with all speed, " and they began to beseech Him to depart from their borders." They began, for it did not require long entreaty; the gospel which was free to all was not to be forced upon any. But how much did they blindly fling away, who refused the presence of the meek and lowly Giver of rest unto souls; and chose to be denied, as strangers whom He never knew, in the day when every eye shall see Him.

With how sad a heart must Jesus have turned away. Yet one soul at least was won, for as He was entering into the boat, the man who owed all to Him prayed Him that he might be with Him. Why was the prayer refused? Doubtless it sprang chiefly from gratitude and love, thinking it hard to lose so soon the

wondrous benefactor, the Man at whose feet he had
sat down, Who alone had looked with pitiful and
helpful eyes on one whom others only sought to
"tame." Such feelings are admirable, but they must
be disciplined so as to seek, not their own indulgence,
but their Master's real service. Now a reclaimed demoniac would have been a suspected companion for
One who was accused of league with the Prince of the
devils. There is no reason to suppose that he had
any fitness whatever to enter the immediate circle of
our Lord's intimate disciples. His special testimony
would lose all its force when he left the district where
he was known; but there, on the contrary, the miracle
could not fail to be impressive, as its extent and permanence were seen. This man was perhaps the only
missionary who could reckon upon a hearing from
those who banished Jesus from their coasts. And
Christ's loving and unresentful heart would give this
testimony to them in its fulness. It should begin at
his own house and among his friends, who would
surely listen. They should be told how great things
the Lord had done for him, and Jesus expressly added,
how He had mercy upon thee, that so they might learn
their mistake, who feared and shrank from such a kindly
visitant. Here is a lesson for these modern days, when
the conversion of any noted profligate is sure to be
followed by attempts to push him into a vagrant
publicity, not only full of peril in itself, but also removing him from the familiar sphere in which his consistent life would be more convincing than all sermons,
and where no suspicion of self-interest could overcloud
the brightness of his testimony.

Possibly there was yet another reason for leaving
him in his home. He may have desired to remain close

to Jesus, lest, when the Saviour was absent, the evil
spirits should resume their sway. In that case it
would be necessary to exercise his faith and convince
him that the words of Jesus were far-reaching and
effectual, even when He was Himself remote. If so,
he learned the lesson well, and became an evangelist
through all the region of Decapolis. And where all
did marvel, we may hope that some were won. What
a revelation of mastery over the darkest and most
dreadful forces of evil, and of respect for the human
will (which Jesus never once coerced by miracle, even
when it rejected Him), what unwearied care for the
rebellious, and what a sense of sacredness in lowly
duties, better for the demoniac than the physical nearness of his Lord, are combined in this astonishing
narrative, which to invent in the second century would
itself have required miraculous powers.

WITH JAIRUS.

"And when Jesus had crossed over again in the boat unto the other
side, a great multitude was gathered unto Him : and He was by the
sea. And there cometh one of the rulers of the synagogue, Jaïrus by
name ; and seeing Him, he falleth at His feet, and beseecheth Him
much, saying, My little daughter is at the point of death : *I pray Thee*
that Thou come and lay Thy hands on her, that she may be made
whole, and live. And He went with him ; and a great multitude
followed Him, and they thronged Him. And a woman, which had an
issue of blood twelve years, and had suffered many things of many
physicians, and had spent all that she had, and was nothing bettered,
but rather grew worse, having heard the things concerning Jesus, came
in the crowd behind, and touched His garment. For she said, If I
touch but His garments, I shall be made whole. And straightway the
fountain of her blood was dried up; and she felt in her body that she
was healed of her plague. And straightway Jesus, perceiving in Himself that the power *proceeding* from Him had gone forth, turned Him
about in the crowd, and said, Who touched My garments ? And His
disciples said unto Him, Thou seest the multitude thronging Thee,

and sayest Thou, Who touched Me? And He looked round about to see her that had done this thing. But the woman fearing and trembling, knowing what had been done to her, came and fell down before Him, and told Him all the truth. And He said unto her, Daughter, thy faith hath made thee whole; go in peace, and be whole of thy plague. While He yet spake, they come from the ruler of the synagogue's *house*, saying, Thy daughter is dead: why troublest thou the Master any further? But Jesus not heeding the word spoken, saith unto the ruler of the synagogue, Fear not, only believe. And He suffered no man to follow with Him, save Peter, and James, and John the brother of James. And they come to the house of the ruler of the synagogue; and He beholdeth a tumult, and *many* weeping and wailing greatly. And when He was entered in, He saith unto them, Why make ye a tumult, and weep? the child is not dead, but sleepeth. And they laughed Him to scorn. But He, having put them all forth, taketh the father of the child and her mother and them that were with Him, and goeth in where the child was. And taking the child by the hand, He saith unto her, Talitha cumi; which is, being interpreted, Damsel, I say unto thee, Arise. And straightway the damsel rose up, and walked; for she was twelve years old. And they were amazed straightway with a great amazement. And He charged them much that no man should know this; and He commanded that *something* should be given her to eat."—MARK v. 21–43 (R.V.).

REPULSED from Decapolis, but consoled by the rescue and zeal of the demoniac, Jesus returned to the western shore, and a great multitude assembled. The other boats which were with Him had doubtless spread the tidings of the preternatural calm which rescued them from deadly peril, and it may be that news of the event of Gadara arrived almost as soon as He Whom they celebrated. We have seen that St. Mark aims at bringing the four great miracles of this period into the closest sequence. And so he passes over a certain brief period with the words "He was by the sea." But in fact Jesus was reasoning with the Pharisees, and with the disciples of John, who had assailed Him and His followers, when one of their natural leaders threw himself at His feet.

The contrast is sharp enough, as He rises from a feast to go to the house of mourning, from eating with publicans and sinners to accompany a ruler of the synagogue. These unexpected calls, these sudden alternations all found Him equally ready to bear the same noble part, in the most dissimilar scenes, and in treating temperaments the most unlike. But the contrast should also be observed between those harsh and hostile critics who hated Him in the interests of dogma and of ceremonial, and Jairus, whose views were theirs, but whose heart was softened by trouble. The danger of his child was what drove him, perhaps reluctantly enough, to beseech Jesus much. And nothing could be more touching than his prayer for his " little daughter," its sequence broken as if with a sob ; wistfully pictorial as to the process, " that Thou come and lay Thy hands upon her," and dilating wistfully too upon the effect, " that she may be made whole and live." If a miracle were not in question, the dullest critic in Europe would confess that this exquisite supplication was not composed by an evangelist, but a father. And he would understand also why the very words in their native dialect were not forgotten, which men had heard awake the dead.

As Jesus went with him, a great multitude followed Him, and they thronged Him. It is quite evident that Jesus did not love these gatherings of the idly curious. Partly from such movements He had withdrawn Himself to Gadara ; and partly to avoid exciting them He strove to keep many of His miracles a secret. Sensationalism is neither grace nor a means of grace. And it must be considered that the perfect Man, as far from mental apathy or physical insensibility as from morbid fastidiousness, would find much to shrink away from in the pressure of a city crowd.   The contact of inferior organizations, selfishness driving back the weak and gent.e, vulgar scrutiny and audible comment, and the desire for some miracle as an idle show, which He would only work because His gentle heart was full of pity, all these would be utterly distressing to Him who was

" The first true gentleman that ever breathed,"

as well as the revelation of God in flesh.   It is therefore noteworthy that we have many examples of His grace and goodness amid such trying scenes, as when He spoke to Zacchæus, and called Bartimæus to Him to be healed.   Jesus could be wrathful but He was never irritated.   Of these examples one of the most beautiful is here recorded, for as He went with Jairus, amidst the rude and violent thronging of the crowds, moving alone (as men often are in sympathy and in heart alone amid seething thoroughfares), He suddenly became aware of a touch, the timid and stealthy touch of a broken-hearted woman, pale and wasted with disease, but borne through the crowd by the last effort of despair and the first energy of a newborn hope.   She ought not to have come thither, since her touch spread ceremonial uncleanness far and wide.   Nor ought she to have stolen a blessing instead of praying for it.   And if we seek to blame her still further, we may condemn the superstitious notion that Christ's gifts of healing were not conscious and loving actions, but a mere contagion of health, by which one might profit unfelt and undiscovered.   It is urged indeed that hers was not a faith thus clouded, but so majestic as to believe that Christ would know and re-spond to the silent hint of a gentle touch.   And is it supposed that Jesus would have dragged into publicity such a perfect lily of the vale as this ?   and what means her trembling confession, and the discovery that she could not be hid? But when our keener intellects have criticised her errors, and our clearer ethics have frowned upon her misconduct, one fact remains. She is the only woman upon whom Jesus is recorded to have bestowed any epithet but a formal one. Her misery and her faith drew from His guarded lips, the tender and yet lofty word Daughter.

So much better is the faith which seeks for blessing, however erroneous be its means, than the heartless propriety which criticises with most dispassionate clearness, chiefly because it really seeks nothing for itself at all. Such faith is always an appeal, and is responded to, not as she supposed, mechanically, unconsciously, nor, of course, by the *opus operatum* of a garment touched (or of a sacrament formally received), but by the going forth of power from a conscious Giver, in response to the need which has approached His fulness. He knew her secret and fearful approach to Him, as He knew the guileless heart of Nathanael, whom He marked beneath the fig-tree. And He dealt with her very gently. Doubtless there are many such concealed woes, secret, untold miseries which eat deep into gentle hearts, and are never spoken, and cannot, like Bartimæus, cry aloud for public pity. For these also there is balm in Gilead, and if the Lord requires them to confess Him publicly, He will first give them due strength to do so. This enfeebled and emaciated woman was allowed to feel in her body that she was healed of her plague, before she was called upon for her confession. Jesus asked, Who touched my clothes? It was one thing to press Him, driven forward by the multitude around, as circumstances impel so many to become churchgoers, readers of Scripture, interested in

sacred questions and controversies until they are borne
as by physical propulsion into the closest contact with
our Lord, but not drawn thither by any personal craving or sense of want, nor expecting any blessed reaction
of "the power proceeding from Him." It was another
thing to reach out a timid hand and touch appealingly
even that tasselled fringe of His garment which had
a religious significance, whence perhaps she drew a
semi-superstitious hope. In the face of this incident,
can any orthodoxy forbid us to believe that the grace
of Christ extends, now as of yore, to many a superstitious and erring approach by which souls reach after
Christ ?

The disciples wondered at His question : they knew
not that "the flesh presses but faith touches ;" but as
He continued to look around and seek her that had
done this thing, she fell down and told Him all the
truth. Fearing and trembling she spoke, for indeed
she had been presumptuous, and ventured without
permission. But the chief thing was that she had
ventured, and so He graciously replied, Daughter, thy
faith hath made thee whole, go in peace and be whole
of thy plague. Thus she received more than she had
asked or thought ; not only healing for the body, but
also a victory over that self-effacing, fearful, half morbid diffidence, which long and weakening disease entails.
Thus also, instead of a secret cure, she was given the
open benediction of her Lord, and such confirmation in
her privilege as many more would enjoy if only with
their mouth confession were made unto salvation.

While He yet spoke, and the heart of Jairus was
divided between joy at a new evidence of the power
of Christ, and impatience at every moment of delay,
not knowing that his Benefactor was the Lord of time

itself, the fatal message came, tinged with some little
irony as it asked, Why troublest thou the Teacher
any more? It is quite certain that Jesus had before
now raised the dead, but no miracle of the kind had
acquired such prominence as afterwards to claim a
place in the Gospel narratives.

One is led to suspect that the care of Jesus had prevailed, and they had not been widely published. To
those who brought this message, perhaps no such case
had travelled, certainly none had gained their credence. It was in their eyes a thing incredible that He
should raise the dead, and indeed there is a wide
difference between every other miracle and this. We
struggle against all else, but when death comes we feel
that all is over except to bury out of our sight what
once was beautiful and dear. Death is destiny made
visible; it is the irrevocable. Who shall unsay the
words of a bleeding heart, I shall go to him but he
shall not return to me? But Christ came to destroy
him that had the power of death. Even now, through
Him, we are partakers of a more intense and deeper
life, and have not only the hope but the beginning of
immortality. And it was the natural seal upon His
lofty mission, that He should publicly raise up the dead.
For so great a task, shall we say that Jesus now
gathers all His energies? That would be woefully to
misread the story; for a grand simplicity, the easy
bearing of unstrained and amply adequate resources, is
common to all the narratives of life brought back. We
shall hereafter see good reason why Jesus employed
means for other miracles, and even advanced by stages
in the work. But lest we should suppose that effort
was necessary, and His power but just sufficed to overcome the resistance, none of these supreme miracles

is wrought with the slightest effort. Prophets and
apostles may need to stretch themselves upon the bed or
to embrace the corpse ; Jesus, in His own noble phrase,
awakes it out of sleep. A wonderful ease and quiet-
ness pervade the narratives, expressing exactly the
serene bearing of the Lord of the dead and of the
living. There is no holding back, no toying with the
sorrow of the bereaved, such as even Euripides, the
tenderest of the Greeks, ascribed to the demigod who
tore from the grip of death the heroic wife of Admetus.
Hercules plays with the husband's sorrow, suggests
the consolation of a new bridal, and extorts the angry
cry, "Silence, what have you said ?   I would not have
believed it of you." But what is natural to a hero,
flushed with victory and the sense of patronage, would
have ill become the absolute self-possession and gentle
grace of Jesus. In every case, therefore, He is full of
encouragement and sympathy, even before His work is
wrought. To the widow of Nain He says, "Weep not."
He tells the sister of Lazarus, "If thou wilt believe,
thou shalt see the salvation of God." And when these
disastrous tidings shake all the faith of Jairus, Jesus
loses not a moment in reassuring Him : "Fear not,
only believe," He says, not heeding the word spoken ;
that is to say, Himself unagitated and serene.*

In every case some co-operation was expected from the
bystanders. The bearers of the widow's son halted, expectant, when this majestic and tender Wayfarer touched
the bier. The friends of Lazarus rolled away the stone
from the sepulchre. But the professional mourners in
the house of Jairus were callous and insensible, and

---

* Unless indeed the meaning be rather, "*over* hearing the word,"
which is not its force in the New Testament (Matt. xviii. 17, twice).

when He interrupted their clamorous wailing, with the
question, Why make ye tumult and weep? they laughed
Him to scorn; a fit expression of the world's purblind
incredulity, its reliance upon ordinary "experience" to
disprove all possibilities of the extraordinary and Divine,
and its heartless transition from conventional sorrow
to ghastly laughter, mocking in the presence of death
—which is, in its view, so desperate—the last hope of
humanity. Laughter is not the fitting mood in which
to contradict the Christian hope, that our lost ones are
not dead, but sleep. The new and strange hope for
humanity which Jesus thus asserted, He went on to
prove, but not for them. Exerting that moral ascen-
dency, which sufficed Him twice to cleanse the Temple,
He put them all forth, as already He had shut out the
crowd, and all His disciples but "the elect of His election," the three who now first obtain a special privilege.
The scene was one of surpassing solemnity and awe;
but not more so than that of Nain, or by the tomb of
Lazarus. Why then were not only the idly curious
and the scornful, but nine of His chosen ones excluded?
Surely we may believe, for the sake of the little girl,
whose tender grace of unconscious maidenhood should
not, in its hour of reawakened vitality, be the centre
of a gazing circle. He kept with Him the deeply
reverential and the loving, the ripest apostles and the
parents of the child, since love and reverence are ever
the conditions of real insight. And then, first, was
exhibited the gentle and profound regard of Christ for
children. He did not arouse her, as others, with a call
only, but took her by the hand, while He spoke to her
those Aramaic words, so marvellous in their effect,
which St. Peter did not fail to repeat to St. Mark as he
had heard them, Talitha cumi; Damsel, I say unto thee,

Arise. They have an added sweetness when we reflect
that the former word, though applied to a very young
child, is in its root a variation of the word for a little
lamb. How exquisite from the lips of the Good Shepherd, Who gave His life for the sheep. How strange
to be thus awakened from the mysterious sleep, and to
gaze with a child's fresh eyes into the loving eyes of
Jesus. Let us seek to realise such positions, to comprehend the marvellous heart which they reveal to us,
and we shall derive more love and trust from the effort
than from all such doctrinal inference and allegorizing
as would dry up, into a *hortus siccus*, the sweetest blooms
of the sweetest story ever told.

So shall we understand what happened next in all
three cases. Something preternatural and therefore
dreadful, appeared to hang about the lives so wondrously restored. The widow of Nain did not dare to
embrace her son until Christ "gave him to his mother."
The bystanders did not touch Lazarus, bound hand and
foot, until Jesus bade them "loose him and let him go."
And the five who stood about this child's bed, amazed
straightway with a great amazement, had to be reminded
that being now in perfect health, after an illness which
left her system wholly unsupplied, something should be
given her to eat. This is the point at which Euripides
could find nothing fitter for Hercules to utter than the
awkward boast, "Thou wilt some day say that the
son of Jove was a capital guest to entertain." What a
contrast. For Jesus was utterly unflushed, undazzled,
apparently unconscious of anything to disturb His
composure. And so far was He from the unhappy
modern notion, that every act of grace must be proclaimed on the housetop, and every recipient of grace
however young, however unmatured, paraded and ex-

hibited, that He charged them much that no man should know this.

The story throughout is graphic and full of character, every touch, every word reveals the Divine Man ; and only reluctance to believe a miracle prevents it from proving itself to every candid mind. Whether it be accepted or rejected, it is itself miraculous. It could not have grown up in the soil which generated the early myths and legends, by the working of the ordinary laws of mind. It is beyond their power to invent or to dream, supernatural in the strictest sense.

This miracle completes the cycle. Nature, distracted by the Fall, has revolted against Him in vain. Satan, intrenched in his last stronghold, has resisted, and humbled himself to entreaties and to desperate contrivances, in vain. Secret and unspoken woes, and silent germs of belief, have hidden from Him in vain. Death itself has closed its bony fingers upon its prey, in vain. Nothing can resist the power and love, which are enlisted on behalf of all who put their trust in Jesus.

CHAPTER VI.

REJECTED IN HIS OWN COUNTRY.

" And He went out from thence; and He cometh into His own country; and His disciples follow Him."—MARK vi. 1–6 (R.V.).

WE have seen how St. Mark, to bring out more vividly the connection between four mighty signs, their ideal completeness as a whole, and that mastery over nature and the spiritual world which they reveal, grouped them resolutely together, excluding even significant incidents which would break in upon their sequence. Bearing this in mind, how profoundly instructive it is that our Evangelist shows us this Master over storm and demons, over too-silent disease, and over death, too clamorously bewailed, in the next place teaching His own countrymen in vain, and an offence to them. How startling to read, at this juncture, when legend would surely have thrown all men prostrate at his feet, of His homely family and His trade, and how He Who rebuked the storm " could there do no mighty work."

First of all, it is touching to see Jesus turning once more to " His own country," just at this crisis. They had rejected Him in a frenzy of rage, at the outset of His ministry. And He had very lately repulsed the rude attempt of His immediate relatives to interrupt His mission. But now His heart leads Him thither, once again to appeal to the companions of His youth, with the halo of His recent and surpassing works upon His forehead. He does not abruptly interrupt their vocations, but waits as before for the Sabbath, and the hushed assembly in the sacred place. And as He teaches in the synagogue, they are conscious of His power. Whence could He have these things? His wisdom was an equal wonder with His mighty works, of the reality of which they could not doubt. And what excuse then had they for listening to His wisdom in vain? But they went on to ask, Is not this the carpenter? the Son of Mary? they knew His brothers, and His sisters were living among them. And they were offended in Him, naturally enough. It *is* hard to believe in the supremacy of one, whom circumstances marked as our equal, and to admit the chieftainship of one who started side by side with us. In Palestine it was not disgraceful to be a tradesman, but yet they could fairly claim equality with "the carpenter." And it is plain enough that they found no impressive or significant difference from their neighbours in the "sisters" of Jesus, nor even in her whom all generations call blessed. Why then should they abase themselves before the claims of Jesus?

It is an instructive incident. First of all, it shows us the perfection of our Lord's abasement. He was not only a carpenter's son, but what this passage only declares to us explicitly, He wrought as an artizan, and consecrated for ever a lowly trade, by the toil of those holy limbs whose sufferings should redeem the world.

And we learn the abject folly of judging by mere worldly standards. We are bound to give due honour and precedence to rank and station. Refusing to do this, we virtually undertake to dissolve society, and readjust it upon other principles, or by instincts and intuitions of our own, a grave task, when it is realized. But we are not to be dazzled, much less to be misled, by the advantages of station or of birth. Yet if, as it would seem, Nazareth rejected Christ because He was not a person of quality, this is only the most extreme and ironical exhibition of what happens every day, when a noble character, self-denying, self-controlled and wise, fails to win the respect which is freely and gladly granted to vice and folly in a coronet.

And yet, to one who reflected, the very objection they put forward was an evidence of His mission. His wisdom was confessed, and His miracles were not denied; were they less wonderful or more amazing, more supernatural, as the endowments of the carpenter whom they knew? Whence, they asked, had He derived His learning, as if it were not more noble for being original.

Are we sure that men do not still make the same mistake? The perfect and lowly humanity of Jesus is a stumbling block to some who will freely admit His ideal perfections, and the matchless nobility of His moral teaching. They will grant anything but the supernatural origin of Him to Whom they attribute qualities beyond parallel. But whence had He those qualities? What is there in the Galilee of the first century which prepares one for discovering there and then the revolutionizer of the virtues of the world, the most original, profound, and unique of all teachers, Him Whose example is still mightier than His precepts, and only not more perfect, because these also are without a flaw, Him Whom even unbelief would shrink from saluting by so cold a title as that of the most saintly of the saints. To ask with a clear scrutiny, whence the teaching of Jesus came, to realize the isolation from all centres of thought and movement, of this Hebrew, this provincial among Hebrews, this villager in Galilee, this carpenter in a village, and then to observe His mighty works in every quarter of the globe, is enough to satisfy all candid minds that His earthly circumstances have something totally unlike themselves behind them. And the more men give ear to materialism and to materialistic evolution without an evolving mind, so much the more does the problem press upon them, Whence hath this man this wisdom? and what mean these mighty works?

From our Lord's own commentary upon their rejection we learn to beware of the vulgarising effects of familiarity. They had seen His holy youth, against which no slander was ever breathed. And yet, while His teaching astonished them, He had no honour in his own house. It is the same result which so often seems to follow from a lifelong familiarity with Scripture and the means of grace. We read, almost mechanically, what melts and amazes the pagan to whom it is a new word. We forsake, or submit to the dull routine of, ordinances the most sacred, the most searching, the most invigorating and the most picturesque.

And yet we wonder that the men of Nazareth could not discern the divinity of "the carpenter," whose family lived quiet and unassuming lives in their own village.

It is St. Mark, the historian of the energies of Christ, who tells us that He " could there do no mighty work," with only sufficient exception to prove that neither physical power nor compassion was what failed Him, since "He laid His hands upon a few sick folk and healed them." What then is conveyed by this bold phrase? Surely the fearful power of the human will to resist the will of man's compassionate Redeemer

He would have gathered Jerusalem under His wing, but she would not; and the temporal results of her disobedience had to follow; siege, massacre and ruin. God has no pleasure in the death of him who dieth, yet death follows, as the inevitable wages of sin. Therefore, as surely as the miracles of Jesus typified His gracious purposes for the souls of men, Who forgiveth all our iniquities, Who healeth all our diseases, so surely the rejection and defeat of those loving purposes paralysed the arm stretched out to heal their sick.

Does it seem as if the words "He could not," even thus explained, convey a certain affront, throw a shadow upon the glory of our Master? And the words "they mocked, scourged, crucified Him," do these convey no affront? The suffering of Jesus was not only physical: His heart was wounded; His overtures were rejected; His hands were stretched out in vain; His pity and love were crucified.

But now let this be considered, that men who refuse His Spirit continually presume upon His mercy, and expect not to suffer the penalty of their evil deeds. Alas, that is impossible. Where unbelief rejected His teaching, He "could not" work the marvels of His grace. How shall they escape who reject so great salvation?

THE MISSION OF THE TWELVE.

" And He called unto Him the twelve, and began to send them forth by two and two ; and He gave them authority over the unclean spirits ; and He charged them that they should take nothing for *their* journey, save a staff only ; no bread, no wallet, no money in their purse ; but *to go* shod with sandals : and, *said He,* put not on two coats. And He said unto them, Wheresoever ye enter into a house, there abide till ye depart thence. And whatsoever place shall not receive you, and they hear you not, as ye go forth thence, shake off the dust that is under your feet for a testimony unto them. And they went out, and preached that *men* should repent. And they cast out many devils, and anointed with oil many that were sick, and healed them."—MARK vi. 7-13 (R.V.).

REPULSED a second time from the cradle of His youth, even as lately from Decapolis, with what a heavy heart must the Loving One have turned away. Yet we read of no abatement of His labours. He did not, like the fiery prophet, wander into the desert and make request that He might die. And it helps us to realise the elevation of our Lord, when we reflect how utterly the discouragement with which we sympathise in the great Elijah would ruin our conception of Jesus.

It was now that He set on foot new efforts, and advanced in the training of His elect. For Himself, He went about the villages, whither slander and pre- judice had not yet penetrated, and was content to break new ground among the most untaught and sequestered of the people. The humblest field of labour was not too lowly for the Lord, although we meet, every day, with men who are "thrown away" and "buried" in obscure fields of usefulness. We have not yet learned to follow without a murmur the Carpenter, and the Teacher in villages, even though we are soothed in grief by thinking, because we endure the inevitable, that we are followers of the Man of Sorrows.

At the same moment when democracies and priesthoods are rejecting their Lord, a king had destroyed His forerunner. On every account it was necessary to vary as well as multiply the means for the evangelisation of the country. Thus the movement would be accelerated, and it would no longer present one solitary point of attack to its unscrupulous foes.

Jesus therefore called to Him the Twelve, and began to send them forth. In so doing, His directions revealed at once His wisdom and His fears for them.

Not even for unfallen man was it good to be alone. It was a bitter ingredient in the cup which Christ Himself drank, that His followers should be scattered to their own and leave Him alone. And it was at the last extremity, when he could no longer forbear, that St. Paul thought it good to be at Athens alone. Jesus therefore would not send His inexperienced heralds forth for the first time except by two and two, that each might sustain the courage and wisdom of his comrade. And His example was not forgotten. Peter and John together visited the converts in Samaria. And when Paul and Barnabas, whose first journey was together, could no longer agree, each of them took a new comrade end departed. Perhaps our modern missionaries lose more in energy than is gained in area by neglecting so humane a precedent, and forfeiting the special presence vouchsafed to the common worship of two or three.

St. Mark has not recorded the mission of the seventy evangelists, but this narrative is clearly coloured by his knowledge of that event. Thus He does not mention the gift of miraculous power, which was common to both, but He does tell of the authority over unclean spirits, which was explicitly given to the Twelve, and which the Seventy, returning with joy, related that they also had successfully dared to claim. In conferring such power upon His disciples, Jesus took the first step towards that marvellous identification of Himself and His mastery over evil, with all His followers, that giving of His presence to their assemblies, His honour to their keeping, His victory to their experience, and His lifeblood to their veins, which makes Him the second Adam, represented in all the new-born race, and which finds its most vivid and blessed expression in the sacrament where His flesh is meat indeed and His blood is drink indeed. Now first He is seen to commit His powers and His honour into mortal hands.

In doing this, He impressed on them the fact that they were not sent at first upon a toilsome and protracted journey. Their personal connection with Him was not broken but suspended for a little while. Hereafter, they would need to prepare for hardship, and he that had two coats should take them. It was not so now: sandals would suffice their feet; they should carry no wallet; only a staff was needed for their brief excursion through a hospitable land. But hospitality itself would have its dangers for them, and when warmly received they might be tempted to be fêted by various hosts, enjoying the first enthusiastic welcome of each, and refusing to share afterwards the homely domestic life which would succeed. Yet it was when they ceased to be strangers that their influence would really be strongest; and so there was good reason, both for the sake of the family they might win, and for themselves who should not become self-indulgent, why they should not go from house to house.

These directions were not meant to become universal

rules, and we have seen how Jesus afterwards explicitly varied them. But their spirit is an admonition to all who are tempted to forget their mission in personal advantages which it may offer. Thus commissioned and endowed, they should feel as they went the greatness of the message they conveyed. Wherever they were rejected, no false meekness should forbid their indignant protest, and they should refuse to carry even the dust of that evil and doomed place upon their feet.

And they went forth and preached repentance, casting out many devils, and healing many that were sick. In doing this, they anointed them with oil, as St. James afterwards directed, but as Jesus never did. He used no means, or when faith needed to be helped by a visible application, it was always the touch of His own hand or the moisture of His own lip. The distinction is significant. And also it must be remembered that oil was never used by disciples for the edification of the dying, but for the recovery of the sick.

By this new agency the name of Jesus was more than ever spread abroad, until it reached the ears of a murderous tyrant, and stirred in his bosom not the repentance which they preached, but the horrors of ineffectual remorse.

HEROD.

"And king Herod heard *thereof;* for His name had become known: and he said, John the Baptist is risen from the dead, and therefore do these powers work in him. But others said, It is Elijah. And others said, *It is* a prophet, *even* as one of the prophets. But Herod, when he heard *thereof,* said, John, whom I beheaded, he is risen. For Herod himself had sent forth and laid hold upon John, and bound him in prison for the sake of Herodias, his brother Philip's wife: for he had married her. For John said unto Herod, It is not lawful for thee to have thy brother's wife. And Herodias set herself against him, and desired to kill him; and she could not; for Herod feared John, knowing that he was a righteous man and a holy, and kept him safe. And when he heard him, he was much perplexed; and he heard him gladly. And when a convenient day was come, that Herod on his birthday made a supper to his lords, and the high captains, and the chief men of Galilee; and when the daughter of Herodias herself came in and danced, she pleased Herod and them that sat at meat with him; and the king said unto the damsel, Ask of me whatsoever thou wilt, and I will give it thee. And he sware unto her, Whatsoever thou shalt ask of me, I will give it thee, unto the half of my kingdom. And she went out, and said unto her mother, What shall I ask? And she said, The head of John the Baptist. And she came in straightway with haste unto the king, and asked, saying, I will that thou forthwith give me in a charger the head of John the Baptist. And the king was exceeding sorry; but for the sake of his oaths, and of them that sat at meat, he would not reject her. And straightway the king sent forth a soldier of his guard, and commanded to bring his head: and he went and beheaded him in the prison, and brought his head in a charger, and gave it to the damsel; and the damsel gave it to her mother. And when his disciples heard *thereof*, they came and took up his corpse, and laid it in a tomb."—MARK vi. 14–29 (R.V.).

THE growing influence of Jesus demanded the mission of the Twelve, and this in its turn increased His fame until it alarmed the tetrarch Herod. An Idumæan ruler of Israel was forced to dread every religious movement, for all the waves of Hebrew fanaticism beat against the foreign throne. And Herod Antipas was especially the creature of circumstances, a weak and plastic man. He is the Ahab of the New Testament, and it is a curious coincidence that he should have to do with its Elijah. As Ahab fasted when he heard his doom, and postponed the evil by his submission, so Herod was impressed and agitated by the teaching of the Baptist. But Ahab surrendered his soul to the imperious Jezebel, and Herod was ruined by Herodias. Each is the sport of strong influences from without, and warns us that a man, no more than a ship, can hope by drifting to come safe to haven.

No contrast could be imagined more dramatic than between the sleek seducer of his brother's wife and the imperious reformer, rude in garment and frugal of fare, thundering against the generation of vipers who were the chiefs of his religion.

How were these two brought together? Did the Baptist stride unsummoned into the court? Did his crafty foemen contrive his ruin by inciting the Tetrarch to consult him? Or did that restless religious curiosity, which afterwards desired to see Jesus, lead Herod to consult his forerunner? The abrupt words of John are not unlike an answer to some feeble question of casuistry, some plea of extenuating circumstances such as all can urge in mitigation of their worst deeds. He simply and boldly states the inflexible ordinance of God: It is not lawful for thee to have her.

What follows may teach us much.

1. It warns us that good inclinations, veneration for holiness in others, and ineffectual struggles against our own vices, do not guarantee salvation. He who feels them is not God-forsaken, since every such emotion is a grace. But he must not infer that he never may be forsaken, or that because he is not wholly indifferent or disobedient, God will some day make him all that his better moods desire. Such a man should be warned by Herod Antipas. Ruggedly and abruptly rebuked, his soul recognised and did homage to the truthfulness of his teacher. Admiration replaced the anger in which he cast him into prison. As he stood between him and the relentless Herodias, and "kept him safely," he perhaps believed that the gloomy dungeon, and the utter interruption of a great career, were only for the Baptist's preservation. Alas, there was another cause. He was "much perplexed"; he dared not provoke his

temptress by releasing the man of God. And thus temporizing, and daily weakening the voice of conscience by disobedience, he was lost.

2. It is distinctly a bad omen that he "heard him gladly," since he had no claim to well-founded religious happiness. Our Lord had already observed the shallowness of men who immediately with joy receive the word, yet have no root. But this guilty man, disquieted by the reproaches of memory and the demands of conscience, found it a relief to hear stern truth, and to see from far the beauteous light of righteousness. He would not reform his life, but he would fain keep his sensibilities alive. It was so that Italian brigands used to maintain a priest. And it is so that fraudulent British tradesmen too frequently pass for religious men. People cry shame on their hypocrisy. Yet perhaps they less often wear a mask to deceive others than a cloke to keep their own hearts warm, and should not be quoted to prove that religion is a deceit, but as witnesses that even the most worldly soul craves as much of it as he can assimilate. So it was with Herod Antipas.

3. But no man can serve two masters. He who refuses the command of God to choose whom he will serve, in calmness and meditation, when the means of grace and the guidance of the Spirit are with him, shall hear some day the voice of the Tempter, derisive and triumphant, amid evil companions, when flushed with guilty excitements and with sensual desires, and deeply committed by rash words and "honour rooted in dishonour," bidding him choose now, and choose finally. Salome will tolerate neither weak hesitation nor half measures ; she must herself possess "forthwith" the head of her mother's foe, which is worth more than half the kingdom,

since his influence might rob them of it all. And the king was exceeding sorry, but chose to be a murderer rather than be taken for a perjurer by the bad companions who sat with him. What a picture of a craven soul, enslaved even in the purple. And of the meshes for his own feet which that man weaves, who gathers around him such friends that their influence will surely mislead his lonely soul in its future struggles to be virtuous. What a lurid light does this passage throw upon another and a worse scene, when we meet Herod again, not without tne tyrannous influence of his men of war.

4. We learn the mysterious interconnection of sin with sin. Vicious luxury and self-indulgence, the plastic feebleness of character which half yields to John, yet cannot break with Herodias altogether, these do not seem likely to end in murder. They have scarcely strength enough, we feel, for a great crime. Alas, they have feebleness enough for it, for he who joins in the dance of the graces may give his hand to the furies unawares. Nothing formidable is to be seen in Herod, up to the fatal moment when revelry, and the influence of his associates, and the graceful dancing of a woman whose beauty was pitiless, urged him irresistibly forward to bathe his shrinking hands in blood. And from this time forward he is a lost man. When a greater than John is reported to be working miracles, he has a wild explanation for the new portent, and his agitation is betrayed in his broken words, " John, whom I beheaded, he is risen." " For " St. Mark adds with quiet but grave significance, " Herod himself had sent forth and laid hold upon John, and bound him." Others might speak of a mere teacher, but the conscience of Herod will not si.ffer it to be so ; it is his victim ; he has learnt

the secret of eternity; "and therefore do these powers work in him." Yet Herod was a Sadducee.

5. These words are dramatic enough to prove themselves; it would have tasked Shakespere to invent them. But they involve .he ascription from the first of unearthly powers to Jesus, and they disprove, what sceptics would fain persuade us, that miracles were inevitably ascribed, by the credulity of the age, to all great teachers, since John wrought none, and the astonishing theory that he had graduated in another world, was invented by Herod to account for those of Jesus. How inevitable it was that such a man should set at nought our Lord. Dread, and moral repulsion, and the suspicion that he himself was the mark against which all the powers of the avenger would be directed, these would not produce a mood in which to comprehend One who did not strive nor cry. To them it was a supreme relief to be able to despise Christ.

Elsewhere we can trace the gradual cessation of the alarm of Herod. At first he dreads the presence of the new Teacher, and yet dares not assail Him openly. And so, when Jesus was advised to go thence or Herod would kill Him, He at once knew who had instigated the crafty monition, and sent back his defiance to that fox. But even fear quickly dies in a callous heart, and only curiosity survives. Herod is soon glad to see Jesus, and hopes that He may work a miracle. For religious curiosity and the love of spiritual excitement often survive grace, just as the love of stimulants survives the healthy appetite for bread. But our Lord, Who explained so much for Pilate, spoke not a word to him. And the wretch, whom once the forerunner had all but won, now set the Christ Himself at nought, and mocked Him. So yet does the God of this world blind the eyes of the unbelieving. So great are still the dangers of hesitation, since not to be for Christ is to be against Him.

6. But the blood of the martyr was not shed before his work was done. As the falling blossom admits the sunshine to the fruit, so the herald died when his influence might have clashed with the growing influence of his Lord, Whom the Twelve were at last trained to proclaim far and wide. At a stroke, his best followers were naturally transferred to Jesus, Whose way he had prepared. Rightly, therefore, has St. Mark placed the narrative at this juncture, and very significantly does St. Matthew relate that his disciples, when they had buried him, " came and told Jesus."

Upon the path of our Lord Himself this violent death fell as a heavy shadow. Nor was He unconscious of its menace, for after the transfiguration He distinctly connected with a prediction of His own death, the fact that they had done to Elias also whatsoever they listed. Such connections of thought help us to realise the truth, that not once only, but throughout His ministry, He Who bids us bear our cross while we follow Him, was consciously bearing His own. We must not limit to " three days " the sorrows which redeemed the world.

BREAD IN THE DESERT.

"And the apostles gather themselves together unto Jesus ; and they told Him all things, whatsoever they had done, and whatsoever they had taught. And He saith unto them, Come ye yourselves apart into a desert place, and rest awhile. For there were many coming and going, and they had no leisure so much as to eat. And they went away in the boat to a desert place apart. And *the people* saw them going, and many knew *them*, and they ran there together on foot from all the cities, and outwent them. And He came forth and saw a great multitude, and He had compassion on them, because they were as sheep not having a shepherd : and He began to teach them many things. And when the day was now far spent, His disciples came unto Him, and said, The place is desert, and the day is now far spent : send them away, that they may go into the country and villages round about, and buy themselves somewhat to eat. But He answered and said unto them, Give ye them to eat. And they say unto Him, Shall we go and buy two hundred pennyworth of bread, and give them to eat? And He saith unto them, How many loaves have ye? go *and* see. And when they knew, they say, Five, and two fishes. And He commanded them that all should sit down by companies upon the green grass. And they sat down in ranks, by hundreds, and by fifties. And He took the five loaves and the two fishes, and looking up to heaven, He blessed, and brake the loaves ; and He gave to the disciples to set before them ; and the two fishes divided He among them all. And they did all eat, and were filled. And they took up broken pieces, twelve basketfuls, and also of the fishes. And they that ate the loave were five thousand men. And straightway He constrained His disciples to enter into the boat, and to go before *Him* unto the other side to Bethsaida, while He Himself sendeth the multitude away. And after He had taken leave of them He departed into the mountain to pray."—MARK vi. 30-46 (R.V.).

THE Apostles, now first called by that name, because now first these " Messengers " had carried the message of their Lord, returned and told Him all, the miracles they had performed, and whatever they had taught. From the latter clause it is plain that to preach " that men should repent," involved arguments, motives, promises, and perhaps threatenings which rendered it no meagre announcement. It is in truth a demand which involves free will and responsibility as its bases, and has hell or heaven for the result of disobedience or compliance. Into what controversies may it have led these first preachers of Jesus ! All was now submitted to the judgment of their Master. And happy are they still who do not shrink from the healing pain of bringing all their actions and words to Him, and hearkening what the Lord will speak.

Upon the whole, they brought a record of success,

12

And around Him also were so many coming and going
that they had no leisure so much as to eat. Whereupon Jesus draws them aside to rest awhile. For the
balance must never be forgotten between the outer and
the inner life. The Lord Himself spent the following night in prayer, until He saw the distress of His
disciples, and came to them upon the waves. And the
time was at hand when they, who now rejoiced that
the devils were subject unto them, should learn by
sore humiliation and defeat that this kind goeth not
forth except by prayer. We may be certain that it
was not bodily repose alone that Jesus desired for his
flushed and excited ambassadors, in the hour of their
success. And yet bodily repose also at such a time is
healing, and in the very pause, the silence, the cessation of the rush, pressure, and excitement of every
conspicuous career, there is an opportunity and even a
suggestion of calm and humble recollection of the soul.
Accordingly they crossed in the boat to some quiet spot,
open and unreclaimed, but very far from such dreari-
ness as the mention of a desert suggests to us. But
the people saw Him, and watched His course, while out-
running him along the coast, and their numbers were
augmented from every town as they poured through it,
until He came forth and saw a great multitude, and
knew that His quest of solitude was baffled. Few
things are more trying than the world's remorseless
intrusion upon one's privacy, and subversions of plans
which one has laid, not for himself alone. But Jesus
was as thoughtful for the multitude as He had just
shown Himself to be for His disciples. Not to petu-
lance but to compassion did their urgency excite Him;
for as they streamed across the wilderness, far from
believing upon Him, but yet conscious of sore need,

unsatisfied with the doctrine of their professional teachers, and just bereaved of the Baptist, they seemed in the desert like sheep that had no shepherd. And He patiently taught them many things.

Nor was He careful only for their souls. We have now reached that remarkable miracle which alone is related by all the four Evangelists. And the narratives, while each has its individual and peculiar points, corroborate each other very strikingly. All four mention the same kind of basket, quite different from what appears in the feeding of the four thousand. St. John alone tells us that it was the season of the Passover, the middle of the Galilean spring-time ; but yet this agrees exactly with St. Mark's allusion to the " green grass " which summer has not yet dried up. All four have recorded that Jesus " blessed " or " gave thanks," and three of them that He looked up to heaven while doing so. What was there so remarkable, so intense or pathetic in His expression, that it should have won this three-fold celebration ? If we remember the symbolical meaning of what He did, and that as His hands were laid upon the bread which He would break, so His own body should soon be broken for the relief of the hunger of the world, how can we doubt that absolute self-devotion, infinite love, and pathetic resignation were in that wonderful look, which never could be forgotten ?

There could have been but few women and children among the multitudes who " outran Jesus," and these few would certainly have been trodden down if a rush of strong and hungry men for bread had taken place. Therefore St. John mentions that while Jesus bade " the people " to be seated, it was the men who were actually arranged (vi. 10 R.V.). Groups of fifty were easy to keep in order, and a hundred of these were easily counted. And thus it comes to pass that we know that there were five thousand men, while the women and children remained unreckoned, as St. Matthew asserts, and St. Mark implies. This is a kind of harmony which we do not find in two versions of any legend. Nor could any legendary impulse have imagined the remarkable injuction, which impressed all four Evangelists, to be frugal when it would seem that the utmost lavishness was pardonable. They were not indeed bidden to gather up fragments left behind upon the ground, for thrift is not meanness ; but the " broken pieces " which our Lord had provided over and above should not be lost. " This union of economy with creative power," said Olshausen, " could never have been invented, and yet Nature, that mirror of the Divine perfections, exhibits the same combination of boundless munificence with truest frugality." And Godet adds the excellent remark, that "a gift so obtained was not to be squandered."

There is one apparent discord to set against these remarkable harmonies, and it will at least serve to show that they are not calculated and artificial.

St. John represents Jesus as the first to ask Philip, Whence are we to buy bread ? whereas the others represent the Twelve as urging upon Him the need to dismiss the multitude, at so late an hour, from a place so ill provided. The inconsistency is only an apparent one. It was early in the day, and upon "seeing a great company come unto Him," that Jesus questioned Philip, who might have remembered an Old Testament precedent, when Elisha said "Give unto the people that they may eat. And his servitor said, What ? shall I set this before an hundred men ? He said, again . . .

they shall both eat and shall also leave thereof." But the faith of Philip did not respond, and if any hope of a miracle were excited, it faded as time passed over. Hours later, when the day was far spent, the Twelve, now perhaps excited by Philip's misgiving, and repeating his calculation about the two hundred pence, urge Jesus to dismiss the multitude. They took no action until "the time was already past," but Jesus saw the end from the beginning. And surely the issue taught them not to distrust their Master's power. Now the same power is for ever with the Church; and our heavenly Father knoweth that we have need of food and raiment.

Even in the working of a miracle, the scantiest means vouchsafed by Providence are not despised. Jesus takes the barley-loaves and the fishes, and so teaches all men that true faith is remote indeed from the fanaticism which neglects any resources brought within the reach of our study and our toil. And to show how really these materials were employed, the broken pieces which they gathered are expressly said to have been composed of the barley-loaves and of the fish.

Indeed it must be remarked that in no miracle of the Gospel did Jesus actually create. He makes no new members of the body, but restores old useless ones. "And so, without a substratum to work upon He creates neither bread nor wine." To do this would not have been a whit more difficult, but it would have expressed less aptly His mission, which was not to create a new system of thing, sbut to renew the old, to recover the lost sheep, and to heal the sick at heart.

Every circumstance of this miracle is precious. That vigilant care for the weak which made the people sit down in groups, and await their turn to be supplied, is a fine example of the practical eye for details which was never, before or since, so perfectly united with profound thought, insight into the mind of God and the wants of the human race.

The words, Give ye them to eat, may serve as an eternal rebuke to the helplessness of the Church, face to face with a starving world, and regarding her own scanty resources with dismay. In the presence of heathenism, of dissolute cities, and of semi-pagan peasantries, she is ever looking wistfully to some costly far-off supply. And her Master is ever bidding her believe that the few loaves and fishes in her hand, if blessed and distributed by Him, will satisfy the famine of mankind.

For in truth He is Himself this bread. All that the Gospel of St. John explains, underlies the narratives of the four. And shame on us, with Christ given to us to feed and strengthen us, if we think our resources scanty, if we grudge to share them with mankind, if we let our thoughts wander away to the various palliatives for human misery and salves for human anguish, which from time to time gain the credence of an hour; if we send the hungry to the country and villages round about, when Christ the dispenser of the Bread of souls, for ever present in His Church, is saying, They need not depart, give ye them to eat.

The sceptical explanations of this narrative are exquisitely ludicrous. One tells us how, finding themselves in a desert, "thanks to their extreme frugality they were able to exist, and this was naturally" (what, naturally ?) "regarded as a miracle." This is called the legendary explanation, and every one can judge for himself how much it succeeds in explaining to him.

Another tells us that Jesus being greater than Moses, it was felt that He must have outstripped him in miraculous power. And so the belief grew up that as Moses fed a nation during forty years, with angels' food, He, to exceed this, must have bestowed upon five thousand men one meal of barley bread.

This is called the mythical explanation, and the credulity which accepts it must not despise Christians, who only believe their Bibles.

Jesus had called away His followers to rest. The multitude which beheld this miracle was full of passionate hate against the tyrant, upon whose hands the blood of the Baptist was still warm. All they wanted was a leader. And now they would fain have taken Jesus by force to thrust this perilous honour upon Him. Therefore He sent away His disciples first, that ambition and hope might not agitate and secularise their minds; and when He had dismissed the multitude He Himself ascended the neighbouring mountain, to cool His frame with the pure breezes, and to refresh His Holy Spirit by communion with His Father. Prayer was natural to Jesus; but think how much more needful is it to us. And yet perhaps we have never taken one hour from sleep for God.

———————

'JESUS WALKING ON THE WATER.

Mark vi. 47-52 (R.V.).

(See iv. 36, pp. 133—140.)

UNWASHEN HANDS.

"And when they had crossed over, they came to the land unto Gennesaret, and moored to the shore. . . . Making void the word of God by your tradition, which ye have delivered : and many such like things ye do."—MARK vi. 53–vii. 13 (R.V.).

THERE is a condition of mind which readily accepts the temporal blessings of religion, and yet neglects, and perhaps despises, the spiritual truths which they ratify and seal.   When Jesus landed on Gennesaret, He was straightway known, and as He passed through the district, there was hasty bearing of all the sick to meet Him, laying them in public places, and beseeching Him that they might touch, if no more, the border of His garment.   By the faith which believed in so easy a cure, a timid woman had recently won signal commendation. But the very fact that her cure had become public, while it accounts for the action of these crowds, deprives it of any special merit.   We only read that as many as touched Him were made whole.   And we know that just now He was forsaken by many even of His disciples, and had to ask His very apostles, Will ye also go away ?

Thus we find these two conflicting movements : among the sick and their friends a profound persuasion that He can heal them ; and among those whom He would fain teach, resentment and revolt against His doctrine.   The combination is strange, but we dare not call it unfamiliar.   We see the opposing tendencies even in the same man, for sorrow and pain drive to His knees many a one who will not take upon His neck the easy yoke.   Yet how absurd it is to believe in Christ's goodness and His power, and still to dare to sin against Him, still to reject the inevitable inference that His teaching must bring bliss.   Men ought to ask themselves what is involved when they pray to Christ and yet refuse to serve Him.

As Jesus moved thus around the district, and responded so amply to their supplication that His very raiment was charged with health as if with electricity, which leaps out at a touch, what an effect He must have produced, even upon the ceremonial purity of the district.   Sickness meant defilement, not for the sufferer alone, but for his friends, his nurse, and the bearers of his little pallet.   By the recovery of one sick man, a fountain of Levitical pollution was dried up.   And the harsh and rigid legalist ought to have perceived that from his own point of view the pilgrimage of Jesus was like the breath of spring upon a garden, to restore its freshness and bloom.

It was therefore an act of portentous waywardness when, at this juncture, a complaint was made of His indifference to ceremonial cleanness.   For of course a charge against His disciples was really a complaint against the influence which guided them so ill.

It was not a disinterested complaint.   Jerusalem was alarmed at the new movement resulting from the mission of the Twelve, their miracles, and the mighty works which He Himself had lately wrought.   And a deputation of Pharisees and scribes came from this centre of ecclesiastical prejudice, to bring Him to account.   They do not assail His doctrine, nor charge Him with violating the law itself, for He had put to shame their querulous complaints about the sabbath day.   But tradition was altogether upon their side : it was a weapon ready sharpened for their use against one so free, unconventional and fearless.

The law had imposed certain restrictions upon the

chosen race, restrictions which were admirably sanitary in their nature, while aiming also at preserving the isolation of Israel from the corrupt and foul nations which lay around. All such restrictions were now about to pass away, because religion was to become aggressive, it was henceforth to invade the nations from whose inroads it had heretofore sought a covert. But the Pharisees had not been content even with the severe restrictions of the law. They had not regarded these as a fence for themselves against spiritual impurity, but as an elaborate and artificial substitute for love and trust. And therefore, as love and spiritual religion faded out of their hearts, they were the more jealous and sensitive about the letter of the law. They "fenced" it with elaborate rules, and precautions against accidental transgressions, superstitiously dreading an involuntary infraction of its minutest details. Certain substances were unclean food. But who could tell whether some atom of such substance, blown about in the dust of summer, might adhere to the hand with which he ate, or to the cups and pots whence his food was drawn? Moreover, the Gentile nations were unclean, and it was not possible to avoid all contact with them in the market-places, returning whence, therefore, every devout Jew was careful to wash himself, which washing, though certainly not an immersion, is here plainly called a baptism. Thus an elaborate system of ceremonial washing, not for cleansing, but as a religious precaution, had grown up among the Jews.

But the disciples of Jesus had begun to learn their emancipation. Deeper and more spiritual conceptions of God and man and duty had grown up in them. And the Pharisees saw that they ate their bread with unwashen hands. It availed nothing that half a population owed purity and health to their Divine benevolence, if in the process the letter of a tradition were infringed. It was necessary to expostulate with Jesus, because they walked not according to the tradition of the elders, that dried skin of an old orthodoxy in which prescription and routine would ever fain shut up the seething enthusiasms and insights of the present time.

With such attempts to restrict and cramp the free life of the soul, Jesus could have no sympathy. He knew well that an exaggerated trust in any form, any routine or ritual whatever, was due to the need of some stay and support for hearts which have ceased to trust in a Father of souls. But He chose to leave them without excuse by showing their transgression of actual precepts which real reverence for God would have respected. Like books of etiquette for people who have not the instincts of gentlemen ; so do ceremonial religions spring up where the instinct of respect for the will of God is dull or dead. Accordingly Jesus quotes against these Pharisees a distinct precept, a word not of their fathers, but of God, which their tradition had caused them to trample upon. If any genuine reverence for His commandment had survived, it would have been outraged by such a collision between the text and the gloss, the precept and the precautionary supplement. But they had never felt the incongruity, never been jealous enough for the commandment of God to revolt against the encroaching tradition which insulted it. The case which Jesus gave, only as one of " many such like things," was an abuse of the system of vows, and of dedicated property. It would seem that from the custom of "devoting" a man's property, and thus putting it beyond his further control, had grown up the abuse of consecrating it with such limitations, that it should still be available for the owner, but out of his powei to give to others. And thus, by a spell as abject as the taboo of the South Sea islanders, a man glorified God by refusing help to his father and mother, without being at all the poorer for the so-called consecration of his means. And even if he awoke up to the shameful nature of his deed, it was too late, for "ye no longer suffer him to do ought for his father or his mother." And yet Moses had made it a capital offence to " speak evil of father or mother." Did they then allow such slanders ? Not at all, and so they would have refused to confess any aptness in the quotation. But Jesus was not thinking of the letter of a precept, but of the spirit and tendency of a religion, to which they were blind. With what scorn He regarded their miserable subterfuges, is seen by His vigorous word, " full well do ye make void the commandment of God that ye may keep your traditions."

Now the root of all this evil was unreality. It was not merely because their heart was far from God that they invented hollow formalisms ; indifference leads to neglect, not to a perverted and fastidious earnestness. But while their hearts were earthly, they had learned to honour God with their lips. The judgments which had sent their fathers into exile, the pride of their unique position among the nations, and the self-interest of privileged classes, all forbade them to neglect the worship in which they had no joy, and which, therefore, they were unable to follow as it reached out into infinity, panting after God, a living God. There was no principle of life, growth, aspiration, in their dull obedience. And what could it turn into but a routine, a ritual, a verbal homage, and the honour of the lips only ? And how could such a worship fail to shelter

itself in evasions from the heart-searching earnestness
of a law which was spiritual, while the worshipper was
carnal and sold under sin ?

It was inevitable that collisions should arise. And
the same results will always follow the same causes.
Wherever men bow the knee for the sake of respect-
ability, or because they dare not absent themselves
from the outward haunts of piety, yet fail to love God
and their neighbour, there will the form outrage the
spirit, and in vain will they worship, teaching as their
doctrines the traditions of men.

Very completely indeed was the relative position of
Jesus and His critics reversed, since they had expressed
pain at the fruitless effort of His mother to speak with
Him, and He had seemed to set the meanest disciple
upon a level with her.   But He never really denied the
voice of nature, and they never really heard it.   An
affectation of respect would have satisfied their heartless formality : He thought it the highest reward of
discipleship to share the warmth of His love.   And
therefore, in due time, it was seen that His critics
were all unconscious of the wickedness of filial neglect
which set His heart on fire.

CHAPTER VII.

THINGS WHICH DEFILE.

"And He called to Him the multitude again, and said unto them, Hear Me all of you, and understand : there is nothing from without the man, that going into him can defile him : but the things which proceed out of the man are those that defile the man. And when He was entered into the house from the multitude, His disciples asked of Him the parable. And He saith unto them, Are ye so without understanding also ? Perceive ye not, that whatsoever from without goeth into the man, *it* cannot defile him ; because it goeth not into his heart, but into his belly, and goeth out into the draught ? *This He said*, making all meats clean. And He said, That which proceedeth out of the man, that defileth the man. For from within, out of the heart of men, evil thoughts proceed, fornications, thefts, murders, adulteries, covetings, wickednesses, deceit, lasciviousness, an evil eye, railing, pride, foolishness : all these evil things proceed from within, and defile the man."—MARK vii. 14–23 (R.V.).

WHEN Jesus had exposed the hypocrisy of the Pharisees, He took a bold and significant step. Calling the multitude to Him, He publicly announced that no diet can really pollute the soul ; only its own actions and desires can do that : not that which entereth into the man can defile him, but the things which proceed out of the man.

He does not as yet proclaim the abolition of the law, but He surely declares that it is only temporary, because it is conventional, not rooted in the eternal distinctions between right and wrong, but artificial. And He shows that its time is short indeed, by charging the multitude to understand how limited is its reach, how poor are its effects.

Such teaching, addressed with marked emphasis to the public, the masses, whom the Pharisees despised as ignorant of the law, and cursed, was a defiance indeed. And the natural consequence was an opposition so fierce that He was driven to betake Himself, for the only time, and like Elijah in his extremity, to a Gentile land. And yet there was abundant evidence in the Old Testament itself that the precepts of the law were not the life of souls. David ate the shewbread. The priests profaned the sabbath. Isaiah spiritualized fasting. Zechariah foretold the consecration of the Philistines. Whenever the spiritual energies of the ancient saints received a fresh access, they were seen to strive against and shake off some of the trammels of a literal and servile legalism. The doctrine of Jesus explained and justified what already was felt by the foremost spirits in Israel.

When they were alone, " the disciples asked of Him the parable," that is, in other words, the saying which they felt to be deeper than they understood, and full of far-reaching issues. But Jesus rebuked them for not understanding what uncleanness really meant. For Him, defilement was badness, a condition of the soul. And therefore meats could not defile a man, because they did not reach the heart, but only the bodily organs. In so doing, as St. Mark plainly adds, He made all meats clean, and thus pronounced the doom of Judaism, and the new dispensation of the Spirit. In truth, St. Paul did little more than expand this memorable saying. " Nothing that goeth into a man can defile him," here is the germ of all the decision about idol meats—" neither if 'one' eat is he the better, neither if he eat not is he the worse." " The things which proceed out of the man are those which defile the man," here is the germ of all the demonstration that love fulfils the law, and that our true need is to be renewed inwardly, so that we may bring forth fruit unto God.

But the true pollution of the man comes from within; and the life is stained because the heart is impure. For from within, out of the heart of men, evil thoughts proceed, like the uncharitable and bitter judgments of His accusers—and thence come also the sensual indulgences which men ascribe to the flesh, but which depraved imaginations excite, and love of God and their neighbour would restrain—and thence are the sins of violence which men excuse by pleading sudden provocation, whereas the spark led to a conflagration only because the heart was a dry fuel—and thence, plainly enough, come deceit and railing, pride and folly.

It is a hard saying, but our conscience acknowledges the truth of it. We are not the toy of circumstances, but such as we have made ourselves ; and our lives would have been pure if the stream had flowed from a pure fountain. However modern sentiment may rejoice in highly coloured pictures of the noble profligate and his pure minded and elegant victim; of the brigand or the border ruffian full of kindness, with a heart as gentle as his hands are red ; and however true we may feel it to be that the worst heart may never have betrayed itself by the worst actions, but many that are first shall be last, it still continues to be the fact, and undeniable when we do not sophisticate our judgment, that " all these evil things proceed from within."

It is also true that they "further defile the man." The corruption which already existed in the heart is made

worse by passing into action; shame and fear are
weakened; the will is confirmed in evil; a gap is
opened or widened between the man who commits a
new sin, and the virtue on which he has turned his
back. Few, alas! are ignorant of the defiling power of
a bad action, or even of a sinful thought deliberately
harboured, and the harbouring of which is really an
action, a decision of the will.

This word which makes all meats clean, ought for
ever to decide the question whether certain drinks are
in the abstract unlawful for a Christian.

We must remember that it leaves untouched the
question, what restrictions may be necessary for men
who have depraved and debased their own appetites,
until innocent indulgence *does* reach the heart and
pervert it. Hand and foot are innocent, but men there
are who cannot enter into life otherwise than halt or
maimed. Also it leaves untouched the question, as long
as such men exist, how far may I be privileged to
share and so to lighten the burden imposed on them
by past transgressions? It is surely a noble sign of
religious life in our day, that many thousands can say,
as the Apostle said, of innocent joys, " Have we not a
right? . . . Nevertheless we did not use this right, but
we bear all things, that we may cause no hindrance
to the gospel of Christ."

Nevertheless the rule is absolute : " Whatsoever from
without goeth into the man, it cannot defile him."
And the Church of Christ is bound to maintain, un-
compromised and absolute, the liberty of Christian
souls.

Let us not fail to contrast such teaching as this
of Jesus with that of our modern materialism.

" The value of meat and drink is perfectly trans-

cendental," says one. "Man is what he eats," says
another. But it is enough to make us tremble, to ask
what will issue from such teaching if it ever grasps
firmly the mind of a single generation. What will
become of honesty, when the value of what may be
had by theft is transcendental ? How shall armies be
persuaded to suffer hardness, and populations to famish
within beleaguered walls, when they learn that "man is
what he eats," so that his very essence is visibly enfeebled, his personality starved out, as he grows pale
and wasted underneath his country's flag ? In vain
shall such a generation strive to keep alive the flame
of generous self-devotion. Self-devotion seemed to
their fathers to be the noblest attainment; to them
it can be only a worn-out form of speech to say that
the soul can overcome the flesh. For to them the man
is the flesh; he is the resultant of his nourishment;
what enters into the mouth makes his character, for
it makes him all.

There is that within us all which knows better;
which sets against the aphorism, "Man is what he
eats;" the text "As a man thinketh in his heart so is
he;" which will always spurn the doctrine of the brute,
when it is boldly confronted with the doctrine of the
Crucified.

THE CHILDREN AND THE DOGS.

"And from thence He arose, and went away into the borders of Tyre and Sidon. And He entered into a house, and would have no man know it : and He could not be hid. But straightway a woman, whose little daughter had an unclean spirit, having heard of Him, came and fell down at His feet. Now the woman was a Greek, a Syrophœnician by race. And she besought Him that He would cast forth the devil out of her daughter. And He said unto her, Let the children first be filled : for it is not meet to take the children's bread and cast it to the dogs. But she answered and saith unto Him, Yea, Lord : even the dogs under the table eat of the children's crumbs. And He said unto her, For this saying go thy way ; the devil is gone out of thy daughter. And she went away unto her house, and found the child laid upon the bed, and the devil gone out."—MARK vii. 24-30 (R.V.).

THE ingratitude and perverseness of His countrymen have now driven Jesus into retirement "on the borders" of heathenism. It it is not clear that He has yet crossed the frontier, and some presumption to the contrary is found in the statement that a woman, drawn by a fame which had long since gone throughout all Syria, "came out of those borders" to reach Him. She was not only "a Greek" (by language or by creed as conjecture may decide, though very probably the word means little more than a Gentile), but even of the especially accursed race of Canaan, the reprobate of reprobates. And yet the prophet Zechariah had foreseen a time when the Philistine also should be a remnant for our God, and as a chieftain in Judah, and when the most stubborn race of all the Canaanites should be absorbed in Israel as thoroughly as that which gave Araunah to the kindliest intercourse with David, for Ekron should be as a Jebusite (ix. 7). But the hour for breaking down the middle wall of partition was not yet fully come. Nor did any friend plead for this unhappy woman, that she

loved the nation and had built a synagogue; nothing
as yet lifted her above the dead level of that paganism
to which Christ, in the days of His flesh and upon
earth, had no commission.   Even the great champion
and apostle of the Gentiles confessed that his Lord was
a minister of the circumcision by the grace of God, and
it was by His ministry to the Jews that the Gentiles
were ultimately to be won.   We need not be surprised
therefore at His silence when she pleaded, for this
might well be calculated to elicit some expression of
faith, something to separate her from her fellows, and
so enable Him to bless her without breaking down
prematurely all distinctions.   Also it must be considered that nothing could more offend His countrymen than to grant her prayer, while as yet it was
impossible to hope for any compensating harvest among
her fellows, such as had been reaped in Samaria.
What is surprising is the apparent harshness of expression which follows that silence, when even His disciples
are induced to intercede for her.   But theirs was only
the softness which yields to clamour, as many people give
alms, not to silent worth but to loud and pertinacious
importunity.   And they even presumed to thow their
own discomfort into the scale, and urge as a reason for
this intercession, that she crieth after *us*.   But Jesus
was occupied with His mission, and unwilling to go
farther than He was sent.

In her agony she pressed nearer still to Him when
He refused, and worshipped Him, no longer as the Son
of David, since what was Hebrew in His commission
made against her; but simply appealed to His compassion, calling Him Lord.   The absence of these
details from St. Mark's narrative is interesting, and
shows the mistake of thinking that his Gospel is simply

the most graphic and the fullest. It is such when our Lord Himself is in action ; its information is derived from one who pondered and told all things, not as they were pictorial in themselves, but as they illustrated the one great figure of the Son of man. And so the answer of Jesus is fully given, although it does not appear as if grace were poured into His lips. " Let the children first be filled, for it is not meet to take the children's bread, and to cast it to the dogs." It might seem that sterner words could scarcely have been spoken, and that His kindness was only for the Jews, who even in their ingratitude were to the best of the Gentiles as children compared with dogs. Yet she does not contradict Him. Neither does she argue back,—for the words " Truth, Lord, but . . ." have rightly disappeared from the Revised Version, and with them a certain contentious aspect which they give to her reply. On the contrary she assents, she accepts all the seeming severity of His view, because her penetrating faith has detected its kindly undertone, and the triple opportunity which it offers to a quick and confiding intelligence. It is indeed touching to reflect how impregnable was Jesus in controversy with the keenest intellects of Judaism, with how sharp a weapon He rent their snares, and retorted their arguments to their confusion, and then to observe Him inviting, tempting, preparing the way for an argument which would lead Him, gladly won, captive to a heathen's and a woman's importunate and trustful sagacity. It is the same Divine condescension which gave to Jacob his new name of Israel because he had striven with God and prevailed.

And let us reverently ponder the fact that this pagan mother of a demoniacal child, this woman whose name has perished, is the only person who won a dialectical victory in striving with the Wisdom of God ; such a victory as a father allows to his eager child, when he raises gentle obstacles, and even assumes a transparent mask of harshness, but never passes the limit of the trust and love which he is probing.

The first and most obvious opportunity which He gives to her is nevertheless hard to show in English. He might have used an epithet suitable for those fierce creatures which prowl through Eastern streets at night without any master, living upon refuse, a peril even to men who are unarmed. But Jesus used a diminutive word, not found elsewhere in the New Testament, and quite unsuitable to those fierce beasts, a word "in which the idea of uncleanness gives place to that of dependence, of belonging to man and to the family." No one applies our colloquial epithet "doggie" to a fierce or rabid brute. Thus Jesus really domesticated the Gentile world. And nobly, eagerly, yet very modestly she used this tacit concession, when she repeated His carefully selected word, and inferred from it that her place was not among those vile "dogs" which are "without," but with the domestic dogs, the little dogs underneath the table.

Again, she observed the promise which lurked under seeming refusal, when He said, "Let the children first be filled," and so implied that her turn should come, that it was only a question of time. And so she answers that such dogs as He would make of her and hers do not fast utterly until their mealtime after the children have been satisfied ; they wait under the table, and some ungrudged fragments reach them there, some "crumbs."

Moreover, and perhaps chiefly, the bread she craves

need not be torn from hungry children. Their Benefactor has had to wander off into concealment, they have
let fall, unheeding, not only crumbs, although her noble
tact expresses it thus lightly to their countryman, but
far more than she divined, even the very Bread of Life.
Surely His own illustration has admitted her right to
profit by the heedlessness of "the children." And He
had admitted all this : He had meant to be thus overcome.
One loves to think of the first flush of hope in that
trembling mother's heavy heart, as she discerned His
intention and said within herself, " Oh, surely I am not
mistaken ; He does not really refuse at all; He wills
that I should answer Him and prevail." One supposes
that she looked up, half afraid to utter the great
rejoinder, and took courage when she met His questioning inviting gaze.

And then comes the glad response, no longer spoken
coldly and without an epithet : " O woman, great is thy
faith." He praises not her adroitness nor her humility,
but the faith which would not doubt, in that dark hour,
that light was behind the cloud ; and so He sets no
other limit to His reward than the limit of her desires :
"Be it unto thee even as thou wilt."

Let us learn that no case is too desperate for prayer,
and perseverance will surely find at last that our Lord
delighteth to be gracious. Let us be certain that the
brightest and most confiding view of all His dealings is
the truest, and man, if only he trusts aright, shall live
by every word that proceedeth out of the mouth of God.

Thus did Jesus declare, in action as in word, the
fading out of all distinction between the ceremonially
clean and unclean. He crossed the limits of the Holy
Land : He found great faith in a daughter of the
accursed race ; and He ratified and acted upon her

claim that the bread which fell neglected from the table of the Jew was not forbidden to the hunger of the Gentile. The history of the Acts of the Apostles is already here in spirit.

THE DEAF AND DUMB MAN.

" And again He went out from the borders of Tyre, and came through Sidon unto the sea of Galilee, through the midst of the borders of Decapolis. And they bring unto Him one that was deaf, and had an impediment in his speech; and they beseech Him to lay His hand upon him. And He took him aside from the multitude privately, and put His fingers into his ears, and He spat, and touched His tongue; and looking up to heaven, He sighed, and saith unto him, Ephphatha, that is, Be opened. And his ears were opened, and the bond of his tongue was loosed, and he spake plain. And He charged them that they should tell no man: but the more He charged them, so much the more a great deal they published it. And they were beyond measure astonished, saying, He hath done all things well: He maketh even the deaf to hear, and the dumb to speak."—MARK vii. 31–37 (R.V.).

THERE are curious and significant varieties in the methods by which our Saviour healed. We have seen Him, when watched on the sabbath by eager and expectant foes, baffling all their malice by a miracle without a deed, by refusing to cross the line of the most rigid and ceremonial orthodoxy, by only commanding an innocent gesture, Stretch forth thine hand. In sharp contrast with such a miracle is the one which we have now reached. There is brought to Him a man who is deaf, and whose speech therefore could not have been more than a babble, since it is by hearing that we learn to articulate; but of whom we are plainly told that he suffered from organic inability to utter as well as to hear, for he had an impediment in his speech, the string of his tongue needed to be loosed, and Jesus touched his tongue as well as his ears, to heal him.

It should be observed that no unbelieving theory
can explain the change in our Lord's method. Some
pretend that all the stories of His miracles grew up
afterward, from the sense of awe with which He was
regarded. How does that agree with effort, sighing,
and even gradation in the stages of recovery, following
after the most easy, astonishing and instantaneous
cures? Others believe that the enthusiasm of His
teaching and the charm of His presence conveyed healing efficacy to the impressible and the nervous. How
does this account for the fact that His earliest miracles
were the prompt and effortless ones, and as time passes
on, He secludes the patient and uses agencies, as if
the resistance to His power were more appreciable?
Enthusiasm would gather force with every new success.

All becomes clear when we accept the Christian
doctrine. Jesus came in the fulness of the love of God,
with both hands filled with gifts. On His part there
is no hesitation and no limit. But on the part of
man there is doubt, misconception, and at last open
hostility. A real chasm is opened between man and
the grace He gives, so that, although not straitened in
Him, they are straitened in their own affections. Even
while they believe in Him as a healer, they no longer
accept Him as their Lord.

And Jesus makes it plain to them that the gift is no
longer so easy, spontaneous and of public right as
formerly. In His own country He could not do many
mighty works. And now, returning by indirect routes,
and privately, from the heathen shores whither Jewish
enmity had driven Him, He will make the multitude
feel a kind of exclusion, taking the patient from among
them, as He does again presently in Bethsaida (chap. viii.
23). There is also, in the deliberate act of seclusion

and in the means employed, a stimulus for the faith of the sufferer, which would scarcely have been needed a little while before.

The people were unconscious of any reason why this cure should differ from former ones. And so they besought Jesus to lay His hand on him, the usual and natural expression for a conveyance of invisible power. But even if no other objection had existed, this action would have meant little to the deaf and dumb man, living in a silent world, and needing to have his faith aroused by some yet plainer sign. Jesus therefore removes him from the crowd whose curiosity would distract his attention—even as by affliction and pain He still isolates each of us at times from the world, shutting us up with God.

He speaks the only language intelligible to such a man, the language of signs, putting His fingers into his ears as if to break a seal, conveying the moisture of His own lip to the silent tongue, as if to impart its faculty, and then, at what should have been the exultant moment of conscious and triumphant power, He sighed deeply.

What an unexpected revelation of the man rather than the wonder worker. How unlike anything that theological myth or heroic legend would have invented. Perhaps, as Keble sings, He thought of those moral defects for which, in a responsible universe, no miracle may be wrought, of "the deaf heart, the dumb by choice." Perhaps, according to Stier's ingenious guess, He sighed because, in our sinful world, the gift of hearing is so doubtful a blessing, and the faculty of speech so apt to be perverted. One can almost imagine that no human endowment is ever given by Him Who knows all, without a touch of sadness. But it is more natural to suppose that He Who is touched with the feeling of our infirmities, and Who bare our sickness, thought upon the countless miseries of which this was but a specimen, and sighed for the perverseness by which the fulness of His compassion was being restrained. We are reminded by that sigh, however we explain it, that the only triumphs which made Him rejoice in Spirit were very different from displays of His physical ascendancy.

It is interesting to observe that St. Mark, informed by the most ardent and impressible of the apostles, by him who reverted, long afterwards, to the voice which he heard in the holy mount, has recorded several of the Aramaic words which Jesus uttered at memorable junctures. " Ephphatha, Be opened," He said, and the bond of his tongue was loosed, and his speech, hitherto incoherent, became plain. But the Gospel which tells us the first word he heard is silent about what he said. Only we read, and this is suggestive enough, that the command was at once given to him, as well as to the bystanders, to keep silent. Not copious speech, but wise restraint, is what the tongue needs most to learn. To him, as to so many whom Christ had healed, the injunction came, not to preach without a commission, not to suppose that great blessings require loud announcement, or unfit men for lowly and quiet places. Legend would surely have endowed with special eloquence the lips which Jesus unsealed. He charged them that they should tell no man.

It was a double miracle, and the latent unbelief became clear of the very men who had hoped for some measure of blessing. For they were beyond measure astonished, saying He doeth all things well, celebrating the power which restored the hearing and the speech

together.   Do we blame their previous incredulity?
Perhaps we also expect some blessing from our Lord,
yet fail to bring Him all we have and all we are for
blessing.   Perhaps we should be astonished beyond
measure if we received at the hands of Jesus a sanc-
tification that extended to all our powers.

CHAPTER VIII.

THE FOUR THOUSAND.

"In those days, when there was again a great multitude, and they had nothing to eat, He called unto Him His disciples, and saith unto them, I have compassion on the multitude, because they continue with Me now three days, and have nothing to eat: and if I send them away fasting to their home, they will faint in the way; and some of them are come from far. And His disciples answered Him, Whence shall one be able to fill these men with bread here in a desert place? And He asked them, How many loaves have ye? And they said, Seven. And He commandeth the multitude to sit down on the ground: and He took the seven loaves, and having given thanks, He brake, and gave to His disciples, to set before them; and they set them before the multitude. And they had a few small fishes: and having blessed them, He commanded to set these also before them. And they did eat, and were filled: and they took up, of broken pieces that remained over, seven baskets. And they were about four thousand: and He sent them away. And straightway He entered into the boat with His disciples, and came into the parts of Dalmanutha."—MARK viii. 1–10 (R.V.).

WE now come upon a miracle strangely similar to that of the Feeding of the Five Thousand. And it is worth while to ask what would have been the result, if the Gospels which contain this narrative had omitted the former one. Scepticism would have scrutinized every difference between the two, regarding them as variations of the same story, to discover traces of the growth of the myth or legend, and entirely to discredit it. Now however it is plain that the events are quite distinct; and we cannot doubt but that information as full would clear away as completely many a

perplexity which still entangles us.   Archbishop Trench
has well shown that the later narrative cannot have
grown out of the earlier, because it has not grown at
all, but fallen away.   A new legend always " outstrips
the old, but here . . . the numbers fed are smaller,
the supply of food is greater, and the fragments that
remain are fewer."   The latter point is however doubtful.   It is likely that the baskets, though fewer, were
larger, for in such a one St. Paul was lowered down
over the wall of Damascus (Acts ix. 25).   In all the
Gospels the Greek word for baskets in the former
miracle is different from the latter.   And hence arises
an interesting coincidence ; for when the disciples had
gone into a desert place, and there gathered the fragments into wallets, each of them naturally carried one
of these, and accordingly twelve were filled.   But here
they had recourse apparently to the large baskets of
persons who sold bread, and the number seven remains
unaccounted for.   Scepticism indeed persuades itself
that the whole story is to be spiritualized, the twelve
baskets answering to the twelve apostles who distributed
the Bread of Life, and the seven to the seven deacons.
How came it then that the sorts of baskets are so well
discriminated, that the inferior ministers are represented
by the larger ones, and that the bread is not dealt out
from these baskets but gathered into them ?

The second repetition of such a work is a fine proof
of that genuine kindness of heart, to which a miracle is
not merely an evidence, nor rendered useless as soon
as the power to work it is confessed.   Jesus did not
shrink from thus repeating Himself, even upon a lower
level, because His object was not spectacular but
beneficent.   He sought not to astonish but to bless.

It is plain that Jesus strove to lead His disciples,

aware of the former miracle, up to the notion of its
repetition. With this object He marshalled all the
reasons why the people should be relieved. " I have
compassion on the multitude, because they continue
with Me now three days, and have nothing to eat : and
if I send them away fasting to their home, they will
faint in the way ; and some of them are come from
far." It is the grand argument from human necessity
to the Divine compassion. It is an argument which
ought to weigh equally with the Church. For if it is
promised that " nothing shall be impossible " to faith
and prayer, then the deadly wants of debauched cities,
of ignorant and brutal peasantries, and of heathenisms
festering in their corruptions—all these, by their very
urgency, are vehement appeals instead of the dis-
couragements we take them for. And whenever man
is baffled and in need, there he is entitled to fall back
upon the resources of the Omnipotent.

It may be that the disciples had some glimmering
hope, but they did not venture to suggest anything ;
they only asked, Whence shall one be able to fill these
men with bread here in a desert place ? It is the cry
of unbelief—*our* cry, when we look at our resources,
and declare our helplessness, and conclude that possibly
God may interpose, but otherwise nothing can be done.
We ought to be the priests of a famishing world (so
ignorant of any relief, so miserable), its interpreters and
intercessors, full of hope and energy. But we are
content to look at our empty treasuries, and ineffective
organizations, and to ask, Whence shall a man be able
to fill these men with bread ?

They have ascertained however what resources are
forthcoming, and these He proceeds to use, first demanding the faith which He will afterwards honour,

by bidding the multitudes to sit down. And then His loving heart is gratified by relieving the hunger which it pitied, and He promptly sends the multitude away, refreshed and competent for their journey.

THE LEAVEN OF THE PHARISEES.

"And the Pharisees came forth, and began to question with Him, seeking of Him a sign from heaven, tempting Him. And He sighed deeply in His spirit, and saith, Why doth this generation seek a sign? verily I say unto you, There shall no sign be given unto this generation. And He left them, and again entering into *the boat* departed to the other side. And they forgot to take bread ; and they had not in the boat with them more than one loaf. And He charged them, saying, Take heed, beware of the leaven of the Pharisees and the leaven of Herod. And they reasoned one with another, saying, We have no bread. And Jesus perceiving it saith unto them, Why reason ye, because ye have no bread ? do ye not yet perceive, neither understand ? have y your heart hardened ? Having eyes, see ye not ? and having ears, hea; ye not ? and do ye not remember ? When I brake the five loaves among the five thousand, how many baskets full of broken pieces took ye up? They said unto Him, Twelve. And when the seven among the four thousand, how many basketfuls of broken pieces took ye up? And they said unto Him, Seven. And He said unto them, Do ye not yet understand ?"—MARK viii. 11–21 (R.V.).

WHENEVER a miracle produced a deep and special impression, the Pharisees strove to spoil its effect by some counter-demonstration. By so doing, and at least appearing to hold the field, since Jesus always yielded this to them, they encouraged their own faction, and shook the confidence of the feeble and hesitating multitude. At almost every crisis they might have been crushed by an appeal to the stormy passions of those whom the Lord had blessed. Once He might have been made a king. Again and again His enemies were conscious that an imprudent word would suffice to make the people stone them. But that would have spoiled the real work of Jesus more than to retreat

before them, now across the lake, or, just before,
into the coasts of Tyre and Sidon. Doubtless it was
this constant avoidance of physical conflict, this habitual
repression of the carnal zeal of His supporters, this
refusal to form a party instead of founding a Church,
which renewed incessantly the courage of His often-
baffled foes, and led Him, by the path of steady cease-
less self-depression, to the cross which He foresaw,
even while maintaining His unearthly calm, amid the
contradiction of sinners against Himself.

Upon the feeding of the four thousand, they demand
of Him a sign from heaven. He had wrought for the
public no miracle of this peculiar kind. And yet
Moses had gone up, in the sight of all Israel, to com-
mune with God in the mount that burned ; Samuel had
been answered by thunder and rain in the wheat
harvest ; and Elijah had called down fire both upon his
sacrifice and also upon two captains and their bands of
fifty. Such a miracle was now declared to be the regular
authentication of a messenger from God, and the only
sign which evil spirits could not counterfeit.

Moreover the demand would specially embarrass
Jesus, because He alone was not accustomed to invoke
heaven : His miracles were wrought by the exertion
of His own will. And perhaps the challenge implied
some understanding of what this peculiarity involved,
such as Jesus charged them with, when putting into
their mouth the words, This is the heir, come, let us
kill Him. Certainly the demand ignored much. Conceding the fact of certain miracles, and yet imposing
new conditions of belief, they shut their eyes to the
unique nature of the works already wrought, the glory
as of the Only-begotten of the Father which they
displayed. They held that thunder and lightning re-

14

vealed God more certainly than supernatural victories of compassion, tenderness and love. What could be done for moral blindness such as this? How could any sign be devised which unwilling hearts would not evade? No wonder that hearing this demand, Jesus sighed deeply in His spirit. It revealed their utter hardness; it was a snare by which others would be entangled; and for Himself it foretold the cross.

St. Mark simply tells us that He refused to give them any sign. In St. Matthew He justifies this decision by rebuking the moral blindness which demanded it. They had material enough for judgment. The face of the sky foretold storm and fair weather, and the process of nature could be anticipated without miracles to coerce belief. And thus they should have discerned the import of the prophecies, the course of history, the signs of the times in which they lived, so plainly radiant with Messianic promise, so menacing with storm-clouds of vengeance upon sin. The sign was refused moreover to an evil and adulterous generation, as God, in the Old Testament, would not be inquired of at all by such a people as this. This indignant rejoinder St. Mark has compressed into the words, "There shall no sign be given unto this generation" —this which has proof enough, and which deserves none. Men there were to whom a sign from heaven was not refused. At His baptism, on the Mount of Transfiguration, and when the Voice answered His appeal, "Father, glorify Thy name," while the multitude said only that it thundered—at these times His chosen ones received a sign from heaven. But from those who had not was taken away even that which they seemed to have; and the sign of Jonah availed them not.

Once more Jesus "left them" and crossed the lake.

The disciples found themselves with but one loaf, approaching a wilder district, where the ceremonial purity of food could not easily be ascertained. But they had already acted on the principle which Jesus had formally proclaimed, that all meats were clean. And therefore it was not too much to expect them to penetrate below the letter of the words, " Take heed, beware of the leaven of the Pharisees, and the leaven of Herod." In giving them this enigma to discover, He acted according to His usage, wrapping the spiritual truth in earthly phrases, picturesque and impressive ; and He treated them as life treats every one of us, which keeps our responsibility still upon the strain, by presenting new moral problems, fresh questions and trials of insight, for every added attainment which lays our old tasks aside. But they understood Him not. Some new ceremonial appeared to them to be designed, in which everything would be reversed, and the unclean should be those hypocrites, the strictest observers of the old code. Such a mistake, however blameworthy, reveals the profound sense of an ever-widening chasm, and an expectation of a final and hopeless rupture with the chiefs of their religion. It prepares us for what is soon to come, the contrast between the popular belief and theirs, and the selection of a rock on which a new Church is to be built. In the meantime the dire practical inconvenience of this announcement led to hot discussion, because they had no bread. And Jesus, perceiving this, remonstrated in a series of indignant questions. Personal want should not have disturbed their judgment, remembering that twice over He had fed hungry multitudes, and loaded them with the surplus of His gift. Their eyes and ears should have taught them that He was indifferent to such distinctions, and His doctrine could never result in a new Judaism. How was it that they did not understand ?

Thereupon they perceived that His warning was figurative. He had spoken to them, after feeding the five thousand, of spiritual bread which He would give, even His flesh to be their food. What then could He have meant by the leaven of the Pharisees but the imparting of *their* religious tendencies, their teaching, and their insincerity ?

Was there any real danger that these, His chosen ones, should be shaken by the demand for a sign from heaven ? Did not Philip presently, when Christ spoke of seeing the Father, eagerly cry out that this, if it were granted, would suffice them ? In these words he confessed the misgiving which haunted their minds, and the longing for a heavenly sign. And yet the essence of the vision of God was in the life and the love which they had failed to know. If they could not see Him in these, He must for ever remain invisible to them.

We too require the same caution. When we long for miracles, neglecting those standing miracles of our faith, the gospel and the Church : when our reason is satisfied of a doctrine or a duty, and yet we remain irresolute, sighing for the impulse of some rare spiritual enlightenment or excitement, for a revival, or a mission, or an oration to lift us above ourselves, we are virtually asking to be shown what we already confess, to behold a sign, while we possess the evidence.

And the only wisdom of the languid, irresolute will, which postpones action in hope that feeling may be deepened, is to pray. It is by the effort of communion with the unfelt, but confessed Reality above us, that healthy feeling is to be recovered.

MEN AS TREES.

"And they come unto Bethsaida. And they bring to Him a blind man, and beseech Him to touch him. And He took hold of the blind man by the hand, and brought him out of the village; and when He had spit on his eyes, and laid His hands upon him, He asked him, Seest thou aught? And he looked up, and said, I see men; for I behold *them* as trees, walking. Then again He laid His hands upon his eyes; and he looked stedfastly, and was restored, and saw all things clearly. And He sent him away to his home, saying, Do not even enter into the village."—MARK viii. 22-26 (R.V.).

WHEN the disciples arrived at Bethsaida, they were met by the friends of a blind man, who besought Him to touch him. And this gave occasion to the most remarkable by far of all the progressive and tentative miracles, in which means were employed, and the result was gradually reached. The reasons for advancing to this cure by progressive stages have been much discussed. St. Chrysostom and many others have conjectured that the blind man had but little faith, since he neither found his own way to Jesus, nor pleaded his own cause, like Bartimæus. Others brought him, and interceded for him. This may be so, but since he was clearly a consenting party, we can infer little from details which constitutional timidity would explain, or helplessness (for the resources of the blind are very various), or the zeal of friends or of paid servants, or the mere eagerness of a crowd, pushing him forward in desire to see a marvel.

We cannot expect always to penetrate the motives which varied our Saviour's mode of action; it is enough that we can pretty clearly discern some principles which led to their variety. Many of them, including all the greatest, were wrought without instrumentality and without delay, showing His unrestricted and underived power. Others were gradual, and wrought by means. These connected His "signs" with nature and the God of nature ; and they could be so watched as to silence many a cavil ; and they exhibited, by the very disproportion of the means, the grandeur of the Worker. In this respect the successive stages of a miracle were like the subdivisions by which a skilful architect increases the effect of a *façade* or an interior. In every case the means employed were such as to connect the result most intimately with the person as well as the will of Christ.

It must be repeated also, that the need of secondary agents shows itself, only as the increasing wilfulness of Israel separates between Christ and the people. It is as if the first rush of generous and spontaneous power had been frozen by the chill of their ingratitude.

Jesus again, as when healing the deaf and dumb, withdraws from idle curiosity. And we read, what is very impressive when we remember that any of the disciples could have been bidden to lead the blind man, that Jesus Himself drew Him by the hand out of the village. What would have been affectation in other cases was a graceful courtesy to the blind. And it reveals to us the hearty human benignity and condescension of Him Whom to see was to see the Father, that He should have clasped in His helpful hand the hand of a blind suppliant for His grace. Moistening his eyes from His own lips, and laying His hands upon him, so as to convey the utmost assurance of power actually exerted, He asked, Seest thou aught ?

The answer is very striking : it is such as the knowledge of that day could scarcely have imagined ; and yet it is in the closest accord with later scientific discovery. What we call the act of vision is really a two-fold process; there is in it the report of the nerves to the brain, and also an inference, drawn by the mind, which previous experience has educated to understand what that report implies. For want of such experience, an infant thinks the moon as near him as the lamp, and reaches out for it. And when Christian science does its Master's work by opening the eyes of men who have been born blind, they do not know at first what appearances belong to globes and what to flat and square objects. It is certain that every image conveyed to the brain reaches it upside down, and is corrected there. When Jesus then restored a blind man to the perfect enjoyment of effective intelligent vision, He wrought a double miracle; one which instructed the intelligence of the blind man as well as opened his eyes. This was utterly unknown to that age. But the scepticism of our century would complain that to open the eyes was not enough, and that such a miracle would have left the man perplexed; and it would refuse to accept narratives which took no account of this difficulty, but that the cavil is anticipated. The miracle now before us refutes it in advance, for it recognises, what no spectator and no early reader of the marvel could have understood, the middle stage, when sight is gained but is still uncomprehended and ineffective. The process is shown as well as the completed work. Only by their motion could he at first distinguish living creatures from lifeless things of far greater bulk. "He looked up," (mark this picturesque detail,) "and said, I see men; for I behold them as trees, walking."

But Jesus leaves no unfinished work: "Then again laid He His hands upon his eyes, and he looked stedfastly, and was restored, and saw all things clearly."

In this narrative there is a deep significance. That

vision, forfeited until grace restores it, by which we look at the things which are not seen, is not always quite restored at once. We are conscious of great perplexity, obscurity and confusion. But a real work of Christ may have begun amid much that is imperfect, much that is even erroneous. And the path of the just is often a haze and twilight at the first, yet is its light real, and one that shineth more and more unto the perfect day.

THE CONFESSION AND THE WARNING.

"And Jesus went forth, and His disciples, into the villages of Cæsarea Philippi : and in the way He asked His disciples, saying unto them, Who do men say that I am? And they told Him, saying, John the Baptist : and others, Elijah ; but others, One of the prophets. And He asked them, But Who say ye that I am ? Peter answereth and saith unto Him, Thou art the Christ. And He charged them that they should tell no man of Him. And He began to teach them, that the Son of man must suffer many things, and be rejected by the elders. and the chief priests, and the scribes, and be killed, and after three days rise again. And He spake the saying openly."—MARK viii. 27–32 (R.V.).

WE have now reached an important stage in the Gospel narrative, the comparative withdrawal from evangelistic effort, and the preparation of the disciples for an approaching tragedy. We find them in the wild country to the north of the Lake of Galilee, and even as far withdrawn as to the neighbourhood of the sources of the Jordan. Not without a deliberate intention has Jesus led them thither. He wishes them to realise their separation. He will fix upon their consciousness the failure of the world to comprehend Him, and give them the opportunity either to acknowledge Him, or sink back to the lower level of the crowd

This is what interests St. Mark ; and it is worthy of

notice that he, the friend of Peter, mentions not the
special honour bestowed upon him by Christ, nor the
first utterance of the memorable words " My Church."

"Who do men say that I am ? " Jesus asked.   The
answer would tell of acceptance or rejection, the
success or failure of His ministry, regarded in itself,
and apart from ultimate issues unknown to mortals.
From this point of view it had very plainly failed.   At
the beginning there was a clear hope that this was
He that should come, the Son of David, the Holy One
of God.   But now the pitch of men's expectation was
lowered.   Some said, John the Baptist, risen from the
dead, as Herod feared ; others spoke of Elijah, who
was to come before the great and notable day of the
Lord ; in the sadness of His later days some had
begun to see a resemblance to Jeremiah, lamenting the
ruin of his nation ; and others fancied a resemblance to
various of the prophets.   Beyond this the apostles confessed that men were not known to go.   Their enthusiasm had cooled, almost as rapidly as in the triumphal
procession, where they who blessed both Him, and
" the kingdom that cometh," no sooner felt the chill
of contact with the priestly faction, than their confession dwindled into " This is Jesus, the prophet of
Nazareth."   " But Who say ye that I am ? " He
added ; and it depended on the answer whether or not
there should prove to be any solid foundation, any
rock, on which to build His Church.   Much difference,
much error may be tolerated there, but on one subject
there must be no hesitation.   To make Him only a
prophet among others, to honour Him even as the first
among the teachers of mankind, is to empty His life
of its meaning, His death of its efficacy, and His
Church of its authority.   And yet the danger was real,

as we may see by the fervent blessing (unrecorded in our Gospel) which the right answer won. For it was no longer the bright morning of His career, when all bare Him witness and wondered; the noon was over now, and the evening shadows were heavy and lowering. To confess Him then was to have learned what flesh and blood could not reveal.

But Peter did not hesitate. In answer to the question, "Who say *ye*? Is your judgment like the the world's?" He does not reply, "We believe, we say," but with all the vigour of a mind at rest, "Thou art the Christ;" that is not even a subject of discussion: the fact is so.

Here one pauses to admire the spirit of the disciples, so unjustly treated in popular exposition because they were but human, because there were dangers which could appal them, and because the course of providence was designed to teach them how weak is the loftiest human virtue. Nevertheless, they could part company with all they had been taught to reverence and with the unanimous opinion of their native land, they could watch the slow fading out of public enthusiasm, and continue faithful, because they knew and revered the Divine life, and the glory which was hidden from the wise and prudent.

The confession of Peter is variously stated in the Gospels. St. Matthew wrote for Jews, familiar with the notion of a merely human Christ, and St. Luke for mixed Churches. Therefore the first Gospel gives the explicit avowal not only of Messiahship, but of divinity; and the third Gospel implies this. "Thou art the Christ, the Son of the living God"—"the Christ of God." But St. Mark wrote for Gentiles, whose first and only notion of the Messiah was derived

from Christian sources, and steeped in Christian attributes, so that, for their intelligence, all the great avowal
was implied in the title itself, Thou art the Christ.   Yet
it is instructive to see men insisting on the difference,
and even exaggerating it, who know that this Gospel
opens with an assertion of the Divine sonship of Jesus,
and whose theory is that its author worked with the
Gospel of St. Matthew before his eyes.   How then,
or why, do they suppose the confession to have been
weakened ?

This foundation of His Church being secured, His
Divine Messiahship being confessed in the face of an
unbelieving world, Jesus lost no time in leading His
apostles forward.   They were forbidden to tell any
man of Him : the vain hope was to be absolutely
suppressed of winning the people to confess their king.
The effort would only make it harder for themselves
to accept that stern truth which they were now to
learn, that His matchless royalty was to be won by
matchless suffering.   Never hitherto had Jesus proclaimed this truth, as He now did, in so many words.
It had been, indeed, the secret spring of many of His
sayings ; and we ought to mark what loving ingenuity
was lavished upon the task of gradually preparing
them for the dread shock of this announcement.   The
Bridegroom was to be taken away from them, and
then they should fast.   The temple of His body should
be destroyed, and in three days reared again.   The
blood of all the slaughtered prophets was to come
upon this generation.   It should suffice them when
persecuted unto death, that the disciple was as His
Master.   It was still a plainer intimation when He
said, that to follow Him was to take up a cross.   His
flesh was promised to them for meat and His blood

for drink. (Chap. ii. 20; John ii. 19; Luke xi. 50; Matt. x. 21, 25; 38; John vi. 54.) Such intimations Jesus had already given them, and doubtless many a cold shadow, many a dire misgiving had crept over their sunny hopes. But these it had been possible to explain away, and the effort, the attitude of mental antagonism thus forced upon them, would make the grief more bitter, the gloom more deadly, when Jesus spoke openly the saying, thenceforth so frequently repeated, that He must suffer keenly, be rejected formally by the chiefs of His creed and nation, and be killed. When He recurs to the subject (ix. 31), He adds the horror of being "delivered into the hands of men." In the tenth chapter we find Him setting His face toward the city outside which a prophet could not perish, with such fixed purpose and awful consecration in His bearing that His followers were amazed and afraid. And then He reveals the complicity of the Gentiles, who shall mock and spit upon and scourge and kill Him.

But in every case, without exception, He announced that on the third day He should arise again. For neither was He Himself sustained by a sullen and stoical submission to the worst, nor did He seek so to instruct His followers. It was for the joy that was set before Him that He endured the cross. And all the faithful who suffer with Him shall also reign together with Him, and are instructed to press toward the mark for the prize of their high calling. For we are saved by hope.

But now, contrast with the utmost courage of the martyrs, who braved the worst, when it emerged at the last suddenly from the veil which mercifully hides our future, and which hope can always gild with

starry pictures, this courage that looked steadily
forward, disguising nothing, hoping for no escape,
living through all the agony so long before it came,
seeing His wounds in the breaking of bread, and His
blood when wine was poured.   Consider how marvellous was the love, which met with no real sympathy,
nor even comprehension, as He spoke such dreadful
words, and forced Himself to repeat what must have
shaken the barb He carried in His heart, that by-
and-by His followers might be somewhat helped by
remembering that He had told them.

And yet again, consider how immediately the doctrine
of His suffering follows upon the confession of His
Christhood, and judge whether the crucifixion was
merely a painful incident, the sad close of a noble
life and a pure ministry, or in itself a necessary and
cardinal event, fraught with transcendent issues.

THE REBUKE OF PETER.

"And He spake the saying openly. And Peter took Him, and
began to rebuke Him." . . . "And He said unto them, Verily I say unto
you, There be some here of them that stand by, which shall in no
wise taste of death, till they see the kingdom of God come with
power."—MARK viii. 32–ix. 1 (R.V.).

THE doctrine of a suffering Messiah was strange in the
time of Jesus.   And to the warm-hearted apostle the
announcement that his beloved Master should endure a
shameful death was keenly painful.   Moreover, what
had just passed made it specially unwelcome then.
Jesus had accepted and applauded a confession which
implied all honour.   He had promised to build a new
Church upon a rock ; and claimed, as His to give away,
the keys of the kingdom of heaven.   Hopes were thus
excited which could not brook His stern repression ;

and the career which the apostle promised himself was very unlike that defence of a lost cause, and a persecuted and martyred leader, which now threatened him. The rebuke of Jesus clearly warns Peter, that he had miscalculated his own prospect as well as that of his Lord, and that he must prepare for the burden of a cross. Above all, it is plain that Peter was intoxicated by the great position just assigned to him, and allowed himself an utterly strange freedom of interference with his Master's plans. He "took Him and began to rebuke Him," evidently drawing Him aside for the purpose, since Jesus "turned about" in order to see the disciples whom He had just addressed. Thus our narrative implies that commission of the keys to him which it omits to mention, and we learn how absurd is the infidel contention that each evangelist was ignorant of all that he did not record. Did the appeal against those gloomy forebodings of Jesus, the protest that such evil must not be, the refusal to recognise a prophecy in His fears, awaken any answer in the sinless heart ? Sympathy was not there, nor approval, nor any shade of readiness to yield. But innocent human desire for escape, the love of life, horror of His fate, more intense as it vibrated in the apostle's shaken voice, these He assuredly felt. For He tells us in so many words that Peter was a stumbling-block to Him, although He, walking in the clear day, stumbled not. Jesus, let us repeat it again and again, endured not like a Stoic, deadening the natural impulses of humanity. Whatever outraged His tender and perfect nature was not less dreadful to Him than to us ; it was much more so, because His sensibilities were unblunted and ex- quisitely strung. At every thought of what lay before Him, his soul shuddered like a rudely touched instrument of most delicate structure. And it was necessary that He should throw back the temptation with indignation and even vehemence, with the rebuke of heaven set against the presumptuous rebuke of flesh, "Get thee behind Me. . . . for thou art mindful not of the things of God, but the things of men."

But what shall we say to the hard word, "Satan"? Assuredly Peter, who remained faithful to Him, did not take it for an outbreak of bitterness, an exaggerated epithet of unbridled and undisciplined resentment. The very time occupied in looking around, the "circumspection" which was shown, while it gave emphasis, removed passion from the saying.

Peter would therefore understand that Jesus heard, in his voice, the prompting of the great tempter, to whom He had once already spoken the same words. He would be warned that soft and indulgent sentiment, while seeming kind, may become the very snare of the destroyer.

And the strong word which sobered him will continue to be a warning to the end of time.

When love of ease or worldly prospects would lead us to discourage the self-devotion, and repress the zeal of any convert; when toil or liberality beyond the recognised level seems a thing to discountenance, not because it is perhaps misguided, but only because it is exceptional ; when, for a brother or a son, we are tempted to prefer an easy and prosperous life rather than a fruitful but stern and even perilous course, then we are in the same danger as Peter of becoming the mouthpiece of the Evil One.

Danger and hardness are not to be chosen for their own sake ; but to reject a noble vocation, because these are in the way, is to mind not the things of God but the things of men. And yet the temptation is one from which men are never free, and which intrudes into what seems most holy. It dared to assail Jesus ; and it is most perilous still, because it often speaks to us, as then to Him, through compassionate and loving lips.

But now the Lord calls to Himself all the multitude, and lays down the rule by which discipleship must to the end be regulated.

The inflexible law is, that every follower of Jesus must deny himself and take up his cross. It is not said, Let him devise some harsh and ingenious instrument of self-torture : wanton self-torture is cruelty, and is often due to the soul's readiness rather to endure any other suffering than that which God assigns. Nor is it said, Let him take up My cross, for the burden Christ bore devolves upon no other : the fight He fought is over.

But it speaks of some cross allotted, known, but not yet accepted, some lowly form of suffering, passive or active, against which nature pleads, as Jesus heard His own nature pleading when Peter spoke. In taking up this cross we must deny self, for it will refuse the dreadful burden. What it is, no man can tell his neighbour, for often what seems a fatal besetment is but a symptom and not the true disease ; and the angry man's irritability, and the drunkard's resort to stimulants, are due to remorse and self-reproach for a deeper-hidden evil gnawing the spiritual life away. But the man himself knows it. Our exhortations miss the mark when we bid him reform in this direction or in that, but conscience does not err ; and he well discerns the effort or the renouncement, hateful to him as the very cross itself, by which alone he can enter into life.

To him, that life seems death, the death of all for which he cares to live, being indeed the death of selfishness. But from the beginning, when God in Eden set a barrier against lawless appetite, it was announced that the seeming life of self-indulgence and of disobedience was really death. In the day when Adam ate of the forbidden fruit he surely died. And thus our Lord declared that whosoever is resolved to save his life—the life of wayward, isolated selfishness—he shall lose all its reality, the sap, the sweetness, and the glow of it. And whosoever is content to lose all this for the sake of the Great Cause, the cause of Jesus and His gospel, he shall save it.

It was thus that the great apostle was crucified with Christ, yet lived, and yet no longer he, for Christ Himself inspired in his breast a nobler and deeper life than that which he had lost, for Jesus and the gospel. The world knows, as the Church does, how much superior is self-devotion to self-indulgence, and that one crowded hour of glorious life is worth an age without a name. Its imagination is not inflamed by the picture of indolence and luxury, but by resolute and victorious effort. But it knows not how to master the rebellious senses, nor how to insure victory in the struggle, nor how to bestow upon the masses, plunged in their monotonous toils, the rapture of triumphant strife. That can only be done by revealing to them the spiritual responsibilities of life, and the beauty of His love Who calls the humblest to walk in His own sacred footsteps.

Very striking is the moderation of Jesus, Who does not refuse discipleship to self-seeking wishes but only to the self-seeking will, in which wishes have ripened into choice, nor does He demand that we should wel-

15

come the loss of the inferior life, but only that we should accept it. He can be touched with the feeling of our infirmities.

And striking also is this, that He condemns not the vicious life only : not alone the man whose desires are sensual and depraved ; but all who live for self. No matter how refined and artistic the personal ambitions be, to devote ourselves to them is to lose the reality of life, it is to become querulous or jealous or vain or forgetful of the claims of other men, or scornful of the crowd. Not self-culture but self-sacrifice is the vocation of the child of God.

Many people speak as if this text bade us sacrifice the present life in hope of gaining another life beyond the grave. That is apparently the common notion of saving our " souls." But Jesus used one word for the " life " renounced and gained. He spoke indeed of saving it unto life eternal, but His hearers were men who trusted that they had eternal life, not that it was a far-off aspiration (John vi. 47, 54).

And it is doubtless in the same sense, thinking of the freshness and joy which we sacrifice for worldliness, and how sadly and soon we are disillusionised, that He went on to ask, What shall it profit a man to gain the whole world and forfeit His life ? Or with what price shall he buy it back when he discovers his error ? But that discovery is too often postponed beyond the horizon of mortality. As one desire proves futile, another catches the eye, and somewhat excites again the often baffled hope. But the day shall come when the last self-deception shall be at an end. The cross of the Son of man, that type of all noble sacrifice, shall then be replaced by the glory of His Father with the holy angels ; and ignoble compromise, aware of Jesus and His words, yet ashamed of them in a vicious and self-indulgent age, shall in turn endure His averted face. What price shall they offer then, to buy back what they have forfeited ?

Men who were standing there should see the beginning of the end, the approach of the kingdom of God with power, in the fall of Jerusalem, and the removal of the Hebrew candlestick out of its place.

CHAPTER IX.

THE TRANSFIGURATION.

"**And** after six days Jesus taketh with Him Peter, and James, and John, and bringeth them up into a high mountain apart by themselves: and He was transfigured before them: and His garments became glistering, exceeding white: so as no fuller on earth can whiten them. And there appeared unto them Elijah with Moses: and they were talking with Jesus. And Peter answered and saith to Jesus, Rabbi, it is good for us to be here: and let us make three tabernacles; one for Thee, and one for Moses, and one for Elijah. For He wist not what to answer; for they became sore afraid. And there came a cloud overshadowing them: and there came a voice out of the cloud, This is My beloved Son: hear ye Him. And suddenly looking round about, they saw no one any more, save Jesus only with themselves."— MARK ix. 2–8 (R.V.).

THE Transfiguration is an event without a parallel in all the story of our Lord. This breaking forth of unearthly splendour in a life of self-negation, this miracle wrought without suffering to be relieved or want supplied, and in which He seems to be not the Giver of Help but the Receiver of Glory, arrests our attention less by the greatness of the marvel than by its loneliness.

But if myth or legend had to do with the making of our Gospels, we should have had wonders enough which bless no suppliant, but only crown the sacred head with laurels. They are as plentiful in the false Gospels as in the later stories of Mahomed or Gautama. Can we find a sufficient difference between these

romantic tales and this memorable event—causes
enough to lead up to it, and ends enough for it to
serve ?

An answer is hinted by the stress laid in all three
narratives upon the date of the Transfiguration. It
was "after six days" according to the first two.
St. Luke reckons the broken portions of the first day
and the last, and makes it "about eight days after
these sayings." A week has passed since the solemn
announcement that their Lord was journeying to a
cruel death, that self pity was discordant with the
things of God, that all His followers must in spirit
endure the cross, that life was to be won by losing it.
Of that week no action is recorded, and we may well
believe that it was spent in profound searchings of
heart. The thief Iscariot would more than ever be
estranged. The rest would aspire and struggle and
recoil, and explain away His words in such strange
ways, as when they presently failed to understand what
the rising again from the dead should mean (ver. 10).
But in the deep heart of Jesus there was peace, the
same which He bequeathed to all His followers, the
perfect calm of an absolutely surrendered will. He
had made the dread announcement and rejected the
insidious appeal; the sacrifice was already accomplished
in his inner self, and the word spoken, Lo, I come to do
Thy will, O God. We must steadily resist the notion
that the Transfiguration was required to confirm His
consecration; or, after six days had passed since He
bade Satan get behind Him, to complete and perfect
His decision. Yet doubtless it had its meaning for
Him also. Such times of more than heroic self-devotion make large demands upon the vital energies.
And He whom the angels more than once sustained,

now sought refreshment in the pure air and solemn
silence of the hills, and above all in communion with His
Father, since we read in St. Luke that He went up
to pray. Who shall say how far-reaching, how all-
embracing such a prayer would be ? What age, what
race may not hope to have shared its intercessions,
remembering how He once expressly prayed not for
His immediate followers alone. But we need not
doubt that now, as in the Garden, He prayed also for
Himself, and for support in the approaching death-
struggle. And the Twelve, so keenly tried, would be
especially remembered in this season. And even
among these there would be distinctions ; for we know
His manner, we remember that when Satan claimed
to have them all, Jesus prayed especially for Peter,
because his conversion would strengthen his brethren.
Now this principle of benefit to all through the selection
of the fittest, explains why three were chosen to be
the eye-witnesses of His glory. If the others had been
there, perhaps they would have been led away into
millennarian day-dreams. Perhaps the worldly aspirations of Judas, thus inflamed, would have spread far.
Perhaps they would have murmured against that return
to common life, which St. Peter was so anxious to
postpone. Perhaps even the chosen three were only
saved from intoxicating and delusive hopes by the
sobering knowledge that what they had seen was to
remain a secret until some intervening and mysterious
event. The unripeness of the others for special revelations was abundantly shown, on the morrow, by their
failure to cast out a devil. It was enough that their
leaders should have this grand confirmation of their
faith. There was among them, henceforth, a secret
fountain of encouragement and trust, amid the darkest

circumstances.   The panic in which all forsook Him
might have been final, but for this vision of His glory.
For it is noteworthy that these three are the foremost
afterwards in sincere though frail devotion : one offering
to die with Him, and the others desiring to drink of
His cup and to be baptized with His baptism.

While Jesus prays for them, He is Himself made
the source of their revival.   He had lately promised
that they who willed to lose their life should find it
unto life eternal.   And now, in Him who had perfectly
so willed, they beheld the eternal glory beaming forth,
until His very garments were steeped in light.   There
is no need of proof that the spirit has power over the
body ; the question is only of degree.   Vile passions
can permanently degrade human comeliness.   And there
is a beauty beyond that of line or colour, seen in vivid
hours of emotion, on the features of a mother beside
her sleeping babe, of an orator when his soul burns
within him, of a martyr when his face is as the face of
an angel, and often making fairer than youthful bloom
the old age that has suffered long and been kind.
These help us, however faintly, to believe that there is
a spiritual body, and that we may yet bear the image
of the heavenly.   And so once, if only once, it is given
to sinful men to see how a perfect spirit can illuminate
its fleshly tabernacle, as a flame illuminates a lamp,
and what the life is like in which self-crucifixion
issues.   In this hour of rapt devotion His body was
steeped in the splendour which was natural to holiness,
and which would never have grown dim but that the
great sacrifice had still to be carried out in action.
We shall best think of the glories of transfiguration
not as poured over Jesus, but as a revelation from
within.   Moreover, while they gaze, the conquering

chiefs of the Old Testament approach the Man of Sorrows. Because the spirit of the hour is that of self-devotion, they see not Abraham, the prosperous friend of God, nor Isaiah whose burning words befit the lips that were touched by fire from an unearthly altar, but the heroic law-giver and the lion-hearted prophet, the typical champions of the ancient dispensation. Elijah had not seen death; a majestic obscurity veiled the ashes of Moses from excess of honour; yet these were not offended by the cross which tried so cruelly the faith of the apostles. They spoke of His decease, and their word seems to have lingered in the narrative as strangely appropriate to one of the speakers; it is Christ's "exodus." *

But St. Mark does not linger over this detail, nor mention the drowsiness with which they struggled; he leans all the weight of his vivid narrative upon one great fact, the evidence now given of our Lord's absolute supremacy.

For, at this juncture Peter interposed. He " answered," a phrase which points to his consciousness that he was no unconcerned bystander, that the vision was in some degree addressed to him and his companions. But he answers at random, and like a man distraught. "Lord, it is good for us to be here," as if it were not always good to be where Jesus led, even though men should bear a cross to follow Him. Intoxicated by the joy of seeing the King in His beauty, and doubtless by the revulsion of new hope in the stead of his dolorous forebodings, he proposes to linger there. He will have

---

* Once besides in the New Testament this phrase was applied to death. That was by St. Peter speaking of his own, when the thought of the transfiguration was floating in his mind, and its voices lingered unconsciously in his memory (2 Pet. i. 15, cf. ver. 17). The phrase, though not unclassical, is not common.

more than is granted, just as, when Jesus washed his feet, he said "not my feet only, but also my hands and my head." And if this might be, it was fitting that these superhuman personages should have tabernacles made for them. No doubt the assertion that he wist not what to say, bears specially upon this strange offer to shelter glorified bodies from the night air, and to provide for each a place of separate repose. The words are incoherent, but they are quite natural from one who has so impulsively begun to speak that now he must talk on, because he knows not how to stop. They are the words of the very Peter whose actions we know so well. As he formerly walked upon the sea, before considering how boisterous were the waves, and would soon afterwards smite with the sword, and risk himself in the High Priest's palace, without seeing his way through either adventure, exactly so in this bewildering presence he ventures into a sentence without knowing how to close it.

Now this perfect accuracy of character, so dramatic and yet so unaffected, is evidence of the truth of this great miracle. To a frank student who knows human nature, it is a very admirable evidence. To one who knows how clumsily such effects are produced by all but the greatest masters of creative literature, it is almost decisive.

In speaking thus, he has lowered his Master to the level of the others, unconscious that Moses and Elijah were only attendants upon Jesus, who have come from heaven because He is upon earth, and who speak not of their achievements but of His sufferings. If Peter knew it, the hour had struck when their work, the law of Moses and the utterances of the prophets whom Elijah represented, should cease to be the chief impulse in religion, and without being destroyed, should be "fulfilled," and absorbed in a new system. He was there to whom Moses in the law, and the prophets bore witness, and in His presence they had no glory by reason of the glory that excelleth. Yet Peter would fain build equal tabernacles for all alike.

Now St. Luke tells us that he interposed just when they were departing, and apparently in the hope of staying them. But all the narratives convey a strong impression that his words hastened their disappearance, and decided the manner of it. For while he yet spake, as if all the vision were eclipsed on being thus misunderstood, a cloud swept over the three—bright, yet overshadowing them—and the voice of God proclaimed their Lord to be His beloved Son (not faithful only, like Moses, as a steward over the house), and bade them, instead of desiring to arrest the flight of rival teachers, hear Him.

Too often Christian souls err after the same fashion. We cling to authoritative teachers, familiar ordinances, and traditional views, good it may be, and even divinely given, as if they were not intended wholly to lead us up to Christ. And in many a spiritual eclipse, from many a cloud which the heart fears to enter, the great lesson resounds through the conscience of the believer, Hear Him !

Did the words remind Peter how he had lately begun to rebuke his Lord ? Did the visible glory, the ministration of blessed spirits and the voice of God, teach him henceforth to hear and to submit ? Alas, he could again contradict Jesus, and say Thou shalt never wash my feet. I never will deny Thee. And we, who wonder and blame him, as easily forget what we are taught.

Let it be observed that the miraculous and Divine
Voice reveals nothing new to them. For the words,
This is My beloved Son, and also their drift in raising
Him above all rivalry, were involved in the recent
confession of this very Peter that He was neither
Elijah nor one of the prophets, but the Son of the
Living God. So true is it that we may receive a truth
into our creed, and even apprehend it with such vital
faith as makes us "blessed," long before it grasps and
subdues our nature, and saturates the obscure regions
where impulse and excitement are controlled. What
we all need most is not clearer and sounder views, but
the bringing of our thoughts into subjection to the
mind of Jesus.

THE DESCENT FROM THE MOUNT.

"And as they were coming down from the mountain, He charged
them that they should tell no man what things they had seen, save
when the Son of man should have risen again from the dead. And they
kept the saying, questioning among themselves what the rising again
from the dead should mean. And they asked Him, saying, The scribes
say that Elijah must first come. And He said unto them, Elijah indeed
cometh first, and restoreth all things : and how is it written of the Son
of man, that He should suffer many things and be set at nought? But I
say unto you, that Elijah is come, and they have also done unto him
whatsoever they listed, even as it is written of Him."—MARK ix. 9-13
(R.V.).

IN what state of mind did the apostles return from beholding the glory of the Lord, and His ministers from
another world ? They seem to have been excited, de-
monstrative, ready to blaze abroad the wonderful event
which ought to put an end to all men's doubts.

They would have been bitterly disappointed, if they
had prematurely exposed their experience to ridicule,
cross-examination, conjectural theories, and all the controversy which reduces facts to logical form, but strips

them of their freshness and vitality. In the first age as in the nineteenth, it was possible to be witnesses for the Lord without exposing to coarse and irreverent handling all the delicate and secret experiences of the soul with Christ.

Therefore Jesus charged them that they should tell no man. Silence would force back the impression upon the depths of their own spirits, and spread its roots under the surface there.

Nor was it right to make such a startling demand upon the faith of others before public evidence had been given, enough to make scepticism blameworthy. His resurrection from the dead would suffice to unseal their lips. And the experience of all the Church has justified that decision. The resurrection is, in fact, the centre of all the miraculous narratives, the sun which keeps them in their orbit. Some of them, as isolated events, might have failed to challenge credence. But authority and sanction are given to all the rest by this great and publicly attested marvel, which has modified history, and the denial of which makes history at once untrustworthy and incoherent. When Jesus rose from the dead, the whole significance of His life and its events was deepened.

This mention of the resurrection called them away from pleasant day-dreams, by reminding them that their Master was to die. For Him there was no illusion. Coming back from the light and voices of heaven, the cross before Him was as visible as ever to His undazzled eyes, and He was still the sober and vigilant friend to warn them against false hopes. They however found means of explaining the unwelcome truth away. Various theories were discussed among them, what the rising from the dead should mean, what should be in fact the limit to their silence.   This very perplexity, and the chill upon their hopes, aided them to keep the matter close.

One hope was too strong not to be at least hinted to Jesus.   They had just seen Elias.   Surely they were right in expecting his interference, as the scribes had taught.   Instead of a lonely road pursued by the Messiah to a painful death, should not that great prophet come as a forerunner and restore all things ?   How then was murderous opposition possible ?

And Jesus answered that one day this should come to pass.   The herald should indeed reconcile all hearts, before the great and notable day of the Lord come. But for the present time there was another question. That promise to which they clung, was it their only light upon futurity ?   Was not the assertion quite as plain that the Son of Man should suffer many things and be set at nought ?   So far was Jesus from that state of mind in which men buoy themselves up with false hope.   No apparent prophecy, no splendid vision, deceived His unerring insight.   And yet no despair arrested His energies for one hour.

But, He added, Elias had already been offered to this generation in vain ; they had done to him as they listed.   They had re-enacted what history recorded of his life on earth.

Then a veil dropped from the disciples' eyes.   They recognised the dweller in lonely places, the man of hairy garment and ascetic life, persecuted by a feeble tyrant who cowered before his rebuke, and by the deadlier hatred of an adulterous queen.   They saw how the very name of Elias raised a probability that the second prophet should be treated "as it is written of" the first.

If then they had so strangely misjudged the preparation of His way, what might they not apprehend of the issue ? So should also the Son of man suffer of them.

Do we wonder that they had not hitherto recognised the prophet ? Perhaps, when all is made clear at last, we shall wonder more at our own refusals of reverence, our blindness to the meaning of noble lives, our moderate and qualified respect for men of whom the world is not worthy.

How much solid greatness would some of us overlook, if it went with an unpolished and unattractive exterior ? Now the Baptist was a rude and abrupt person, of little culture, unwelcome in kings' houses. Yet no greater had been born of woman.

THE DEMONIAC BOY.

"And when they came to the disciples, they saw a great multitude about them, and scribes questioning with them. And straightway all the multitude, when they saw Him, were greatly amazed, and running to Him saluted Him. And He asked them, What question ye with them ? And one of the multitude answered Him, Master, I brought unto Thee my son, which hath a dumb spirit ; and wheresoever it taketh him, it dasheth him down : and he foameth, and grindeth his teeth, and pineth away : and I spake to Thy disciples that they should cast it out ; and they were not able. And He answered them and saith, O faithless generation, how long shall I be with you? how long shall I bear with you? bring him unto Me. And they brought him unto Him : and when He saw him, straightway the spirit tare him grievously; and he fell on the ground, and wallowed foaming. And He asked his father, How long time is it since this hath come unto him ? And he said, From a child. And oft-times it hath cast him both into the fire and into the waters, to destroy him : but if Thou canst do anything, have compassion on us, and help us. And Jesus said unto him, If thou canst ! All things are possible to him that believeth. Straightway the father of the child cried out, and said, I believe ; help Thou mine unbelief. And when Jesus saw that a multitude came running together, He rebuked the unclean spirit, saying unto him, Thou dumb and deaf spirit, I command thee, come out of him, and enter no more into him.

And having cried out, and torn him much, he came out : and *the child* became as one dead ; insomuch that the more part said, He is dead. But Jesus took Him by the hand, and raised him up ; and he arose. And when He was come into the house, His disciples asked Him privately, *saying*, We could not cast it out.   And He said unto them, This kind can come out by nothing, save by prayer."—Mark ix. 14-29 (R.V.).

Peter soon had striking evidence that it would not have been "good" for them to linger too long upon the mountain.   And our Lord was recalled with painful abruptness from the glories of transfiguration to the scepticism of scribes, the failure and shame of disciples, and the triumph of the powers of evil.

To the Twelve He had explicitly given authority over devils, and even the Seventy, venturing by faith to cast them out, had told Him of their success with joy.   But now, in the sorrow and fear of these latter days, deprived of their Master and of their own foremost three, oppressed with gloomy forebodings, and infected with the worldliness which fails to pray, the nine had striven in vain.   It is the only distinct repulse recorded, and the scribes attacked them keenly.   Where was their Master at this crisis ?   Did not they profess equally to have the necessary power ?   Here was a test, and some failed, and the others did not present themselves. We can imagine the miserable scene, contrasting piteously with what passed on the summit of the hill. And in the centre was an agonized father and a tortured lad.

At this moment the crowds, profoundly moved, rushed to meet the Lord, and on seeing Him, became aware that failure was at an end.   Perhaps the exceeding brightness lingered still upon His face; perhaps it was but the unearthly and victorious calm of His consecration, visible in His mien ; what is certain is that they were greatly amazed, and ran to Him and did homage.

Jesus at once challenged a renewal of the attack which had been too much for His apostles. "What question ye with them?" But awe has fallen upon the scribes also, and misery is left to tell its own tale. Their attack by preference upon the disciples is very natural, and it by no means stands alone. They did not ask Him, but His followers, why He ate and drank with sinners, nor whether He paid the half-shekel (Mark ii. 16; Matt. xvii. 24). When they did complain to the Master Himself, it was commonly of some fault in His disciples: Why do Thy disciples fast not? Why they do on the Sabbath day that which is not lawful? Why do they eat with defiled hands? (Mark ii. 18, 24; vii. 5). Their censures of Himself were usually muttered or silent murmurings, which He discerned, as when He forgave the sins of the palsied man; when the Pharisee marvelled that He had not washed His hands; when He accepted the homage of the sinful woman, and again when He spoke her pardon (Mark ii. 8; Luke xi. 38; vii. 39-49). When He healed the woman whom a spirit of infirmity had bent down for eighteen years, the ruler of the synagogue spoke to the people, without venturing to address Jesus. (Luke xiii. 14).

It is important to observe such indications, unobtrusive, and related by various evangelists, of the majesty and impressiveness which surrounded our Lord, and awed even His bitter foes.

The silence is broken by an unhappy father, who had been the centre of the group, but whom the abrupt movement to meet Jesus has merged in the crowd again. The case of his son is among those which prove that demoniacal possession did not imply the exceptional guilt of its victims, for though still young, he has suffered long.   The demon which afflicts him is dumb ; it works in the guise of epilepsy, and as a disease it is affected by the changes of the moon ; a malicious design is visible in frequent falls into fire and water, to destroy him.   The father had sought Jesus with him, and since He was absent had appealed to His followers, but in vain.   Some consequent injury to his own faith, clearly implied in what follows, may possibly be detected already, in the absence of any further petition, and in the cold epithet, " Teacher," which he employs.

Even as an evidence the answer of Jesus is remarkable, being such as human ingenuity would not have invented, nor the legendary spirit have conceived.   It would have seemed natural that He should hasten to vindicate His claims and expose the folly of the scribes, or else have reproached His followers for the failure which had compromised Him.

But the scribes were entirely set aside from the moment when the Good Physician was invoked by a bleeding heart.   Yet the physical trouble is dealt with deliberately, not in haste, as by one whose mastery is assured.   The passing shadow which has fallen on His cause only concerns Him as a part of the heavy spiritual burden which oppresses Him, which this terrible scene so vividly exhibits.

For the true importance of His words is this, that they reveal sufferings which are too often forgotten, and which few are pure enough even to comprehend.   The prevalent evil weighed upon Him.   And here the visible power of Satan, the hostility of the scribes, the failure of His own, the suspense and agitation of the crowd, all breathed the spirit of that evil age, alien and harsh

16

to Him as an infected atmosphere. He blames none
more than others ; it is the " generation," so faithless
and perverse, which forces Him to exclaim: " How long
shall I be with you ? how long shall I bear with you ? "
It is the cry of the pain of Jesus. It bids us to consider Him Who endured such contradiction of sinners,
who were even sinners against Himself. So that the
distress of Jesus was not that of a mere eye-witness
of evil or sufferer by it. His priesthood established a
closer and more agonizing connection between our Lord
and the sins which tortured Him.

Do the words startle us, with the suggestion of a
limit to the forbearance of Jesus, well-nigh reached?
There *was* such a limit. The work of His messenger
had been required, lest His coming should be to smite
the world. His mind was the mind of God, and it
is written, Kiss the Son, lest He be angry.

Now if Jesus looked forward to shame and anguish
with natural shrinking, we here perceive another aspect
in which His coming Baptism of Blood was viewed,
and we discover why He was straitened until it was
accomplished. There is an intimate connection between
this verse and His saying in St. John, " If ye loved Me,
ye would rejoice, because I go unto My Father."

But swiftly the mind of Jesus recurs to the misery
which awaits help ; and He bids them bring the child
to Him. Now the sweet influence of His presence
would have soothed and mitigated any mere disease. It
is to such influence that sceptical writers are wont to
turn for an explanation, such as it is, of the works He
wrought. But it was the reverse in cases of possession.
There a wild sense of antagonism and revolt was wont
to show itself. And we might learn that this was something more than epilepsy, even were it left doubtful

otherwise, by the outburst of Satanic rage. When he saw Him, straightway the spirit convulsed him grievously, and he fell wallowing and foaming.

Yet Jesus is neither hurried nor agitated. In not one of His miracles does precipitation, or mere impulse, mingle with His grave and self-contained compassion. He will question the scribes while the man with a withered hand awaits His help. He will rebuke the disciples before quelling the storm. At Nain He will touch the bier and arrest the bearers. When He feeds the multitude, He will first command a search for loaves. He will stand still and call Bartimæus to Him. He will evoke, even by seeming harshness, the faith of the woman of Canaan. He will have the stone rolled away from the sepulchre of Lazarus. When He Himself rises, the grave-clothes are found folded up, and the napkin which bound His head laid in a place by itself, the last tribute of mortals to His mortality not being flung contemptuously aside. All His miracles are authenticated by the stamp of the same character— serene, not in haste nor tardy, since He saw the end from the beginning. In this case delay is necessary, to arouse the father, if only by interrogation, from his dull disappointment and hopelessness. He asks therefore "How long time is it since this came upon him?" and the answer shows that he was now at least a stripling, for he had suffered ever since he was a child. Then the unhappy man is swept away by his emotions: as he tells their sorrows, and thinks what a wretched life or miserable death lies before his son, he bursts into a passionate appeal. If Thou canst do anything, do this. Let pity for such misery, for the misery of father as well as child, evoke all Thy power to save. The form is more disrespectful than the substance of his cry; its very vehemence is evidence that some hope is working in his breast; and there is more real trust in its wild urgency than in many a reverential and carefully weighed prayer.

Yet how much rashness, self-assertion, and wilfulness (which is really unbelief) were mingled with his germinant faith and needed rebuke. Therefore Christ responded with his own word: " If *thou* canst: thou sayest it to Me, but I retort the condition upon thyself: with thee are indeed the issues of thine own application, for all things are possible to him that believeth."

This answer is in two respects important. There was a time when popular religion dealt too much with internal experience and attainment. But perhaps there are schools among us now which verge upon the opposite extreme. Faith and love are generally strongest when they forget themselves, and do not say "I am faithful and loving," but " Christ is trustworthy, Christ is adorable." This is true, and these virtues are becoming artificial, and so false, as soon as they grow self-complacent. Yet we should give at least enough attention to our own attainments to warn us of our deficiencies. And wherever we find a want of blessedness, we may seek for the reason within ourselves. Many a one is led to doubt whether Christ "can do anything" practical for him, since private prayer and public ordinances help him little, and his temptations continue to prevail, whose true need is to be roused up sharply to the consciousness that it is not Christ who has failed; it is he himself: his faith is dim, his grasp on his Lord is half hearted, he is straitened in his own affections. Our personal experiences should never teach us confidence, but they may often serve to humble and warn us.

This answer also impresses upon us the dignity of Him who speaks. Failure had already come through the spiritual defects of His disciples, but for Him, though " meek and lowly of heart," no such danger is even contemplated. No appeal to Him can be frustrated except through fault of the suppliant, since all things are possible to him that believeth.

Now faith is in itself nothing, and may even be pernicious ; all its effect depends upon the object. Trust reposed in a friend avails or misleads according to his love and his resources ; trust in a traitor is ruinous, and ruinous in proportion to its energy. And since trust in Jesus is omnipotent, Who and what is He ?

The word pierces like a two-edged sword, and reveals to the agitated father the conflict, the impurity of his heart. Unbelief is there, and of himself he cannot conquer it. Yet is he not entirely unbelieving, else what drew him thither ? What impulse led to that passionate recital of his griefs, that over-daring cry of anguish ? And what is now this burning sense within him of a great and inspiring Presence, which urges him to a bolder appeal for a miracle yet more spiritual and Divine, a cry well directed to the Author and Finisher of our faith ? Never was medicine better justified by its operation upon disease, than the treatment which converted a too-importunate clamour for bodily relief into a contrite prayer for grace. " I believe, help Thou mine unbelief." The same sense of mixed imperfect and yet real trust should exist in every one of us, or else our belief being perfect should be irresistible in the moral sphere, and in the physical world so resigned, so confident in the Love which governs, as never to be conscious of any gnawing importunate desire. And from the same sense of need, the same cry for help should spring.

Miraculous legends have gathered around the lives of many good and gracious men within Christendom and outside it. But they cannot claim to weigh against the history of Jesus, until at least one example can be produced of such direct spiritual action, so profound, penetrating and effectual, inextricably interwoven in the tissue of any fable.

All this time the agitation of the people had increased. A multitude was rushing forward, whose excitement would do more to distract the father's mind than further delay to help him. And Jesus, even in the midst of His treatment of souls, was not blind to such practical considerations, or to the influence of circumstances. Unlike modern dealers in sensation, He can never be shown to have aimed at religious excitement, while it was His custom to discourage it. Therefore He now rebuked the unclean spirit in the lad, addressing it directly speaking as a superior. "Thou deaf and dumb spirit, I command thee, come out of him," and adding, with explicitness which was due perhaps to the obstinate ferocity of "this kind," or perhaps was intended to help the father's lingering unbelief, "enter no more into him." The evil being obeys, yet proves his reluctance by screaming and convulsing his victim for the last time, so that he, though healed, lies utterly prostrate, and "the more part said, He is dead." It was a fearful exhibition of the disappointed malice of the pit. But it only calls forth another display of the power and love of Jesus, Who will not leave the sufferer to a gradual recovery, nor speak, as to the fiend, in words of mere authority, but reaches forth His benign hand, and raises him, restored. Here we discover the same heart which provided that the daughter of Jairus should have food, and delivered her

son to the widow of Nain, and was first to remind
others that Lazarus was encumbered by his grave-
clothes. The good works of Jesus were not melodram-
atic marvels for stage effect : they were the natural
acts of supernatural power and love.

JESUS AND THE DISCIPLES.

"And when He was come into the house, His disciples asked Him
privately, *saying*, We could not cast it out. And He said ur to them,
This kind can come out by nothing, save by prayer. And they went
forth from thence, and passed through Galilee ; and He would not that
any man should know it. For He taught His disciples, and said unto
them, The Son of man is delivered up into the hands of men, and they
shall kill Him ; and when He is killed, after three days He shall rise
again. But they understood not the saying, and were afraid to ask
Him. And they came to Capernaum : and when He was in the house
He asked them, What were ye reasoning in the way? But they held
their peace : for they had disputed one with another in the way, who
was the greatest. And He sat down, and called the twelve ; and He
saith unto them, If any man would be first, he shall be last of all, and
minister of all. And He took a little child, and set him in the midst
of them : and taking him in His arms, He said unto them, Whosoever
shall receive one of such little children in My name, receiveth Me ; and
whosoever receiveth Me, receiveth not Me but Him that sent Me."—
MARK ix. 28–37 (R.V.).

WHEN the apostles had failed to expel the demon from
the child, they gave a very natural expression to their
disappointment. Waiting until Jesus was in private
and in the house, they said, " We for our parts were
unable to cast it out." They take no blame to themselves. The tone is rather of perplexity and complaint
because the commission formerly received had not held
good. And it implies the question which is plainly
expressed by St. Matthew, Why could we not cast it
out ? Their very unconsciousness of personal blame
is ominous, and Jesus replies that the fault is entirely
their own. They ought to have stimulated, as He did

afterwards, what was flagging but not absent in the father, what their failure must have daunted further in him. Want of faith had overcome them, says the fuller account : the brief statement in St. Mark is, " This kind (of demon) can come out by nothing but by prayer"; to which fasting was added as a second condition by ancient copyists, but without authority. What is important is to observe the connection between faith and prayer; so that while the devil would only have gone out if they had prayed, or even perhaps only if they had been men of prayer, yet their failure was through unbelief. It plainly follows that prayer is the nurse of faith, and would have strengthened it so that it should prevail. Only in habitual communion with God can we learn to trust Him aright. There, as we feel His nearness, as we are reminded that He bends to hear our cry, as the sense of eternal and perfect power blends with that of immeasurable love, and His sympathy becomes a realized abiding fact, as our vain-glory is rebuked by confessions of sin, and of dependence, it is made possible for man to wield the forces of the spiritual world and yet not to be intoxicated with pride. The nearness of God is inconsistent with boastfulness of man. For want of this, it was better that the apostles should fail and be humbled, than succeed and be puffed up.

There are promises still unenjoyed, dormant and unexercised powers at the disposal of the Church to-day. If in many Christian families the children are not practically holy, if purity and consecration are not leavening our Christian land, where after so many centuries license is but little abashed and the faith of Jesus is still disputed, if the heathen are not yet given for our Lord's inheritance nor the uttermost parts of the earth for His possession—why are we unable to cast out the devils that afflict our race? It is because our efforts are so faithless. And this again is because they are not inspired and elevated by sufficient communion with our God in prayer.

Further evidences continued to be given of the dangerous state of the mind of His followers, weighed down by earthly hopes and fears, wanting in faith and prayer, and therefore open to the sinister influences of the thief who was soon to become the traitor. They were now moving for the last time through Galilee. It was a different procession from those glad circuits, not long before, when enthusiasm everywhere rose high, and sometimes the people would have crowned Him. Now He would not that any man should know it. The word which tells of His journey seems to imply that He avoided the main thoroughfares, and went by less frequented by-ways. Partly no doubt His motives were prudential, resulting from the treachery which He discerned. Partly it was because His own spirit was heavily weighed upon, and retirement was what He needed most. And certainly most of all because crowds and tumult would have utterly unfitted the apostles to learn the hard lesson, how vain their daydreams were, and what a trial lay before their Master.

We read that "He taught them" this, which implies more than a single utterance, as also perhaps does the remarkable phrase in St. Luke, "Let these sayings sink into your ears." When the warning is examined, we find it almost a repetition of what they had heard after Peter's great confession. Then they had apparently supposed the cross of their Lord to be such a figurative one as all His followers have to bear. Even after the

Transfiguration, the chosen three had searched for a meaning for the resurrection from the dead. But now, when the words were repeated with a naked, crude, resolute distinctness, marvellous from the lips of Him Who should endure the reality, and evidently chosen in order to beat down their lingering evasive hopes, when He says " They shall kill Him, and when He is killed, after three days He shall rise again," surely they ought to have understood.

In fact they comprehended enough to shrink from hearing more. They did not dare to lift the veil which covered a mystery so dreadful ; they feared to ask Him. It is a natural impulse, not to know the worst. Insolvent tradesmen leave their books unbalanced. The course of history would have run in another channel, if the great Napoleon had looked in the face the need to fortify his own capital while plundering others. No wonder that these Galileans recoiled from searching what was the calamity which weighed so heavily upon the mighty spirit of their Master. Do not men stifle the voice of conscience, and refuse to examine themselves whether they are in the faith, in the same abject dread of knowing the facts, and looking the inevitable in the face ? How few there are, who bear to think, calmly and well, of the certainties of death and judgment ?

But at the appointed time, the inevitable arrived for the disciples. The only effect of their moral cowardice was that it found them unready, surprised and therefore fearful, and still worse, prepared to forsake Jesus by having already in heart drawn away from Him, by having refused to comprehend and share His sorrows. It is easy to blame them, to assume that in their place we should not have been partakers in their evil deeds,

to make little of the chosen foundation stones upon
which Christ would build His New Jerusalem.   But
in so doing we forfeit the sobering lessons of their
weakness, who failed, not because they were less than
we, but because they were not more than mortal.   And
we who censure them are perhaps indolently refusing
day by day to reflect, to comprehend the meaning of
our own lives and of their tendencies, to realize a
thousand warnings, less terrible only because they continue to be conditional, but claiming more attention for
that very reason.

Contrast with their hesitation the noble fortitude
with which Christ faced His agony.   It was His, and
their concern in it was secondary.   Yet for their sakes
He bore to speak of what they could not bear to hear.
Therefore to Him there came no surprise, no sudden
shock ; His arrest found Him calm and reassured after
the conflict in the Garden, and after all the preparation
which had already gone forward through all these
latter days.

One only ingredient in His cup of bitterness is now
added to those which had been already mentioned :
" The Son of man is delivered up into the hands of
men."   And this is the same which He mentioned in the
Garden : " The Son of man is betrayed into the hands
of sinners."

It was that from which David recoiled when he said,
" Let me fall into the hands of God, but let me not fall
into the hands of men."   Suffering has not reached its
height until conscious malice designs the pang, and
says, " So would we have it."   Especially true was
this of the most tender of all hearts.   Yet this also
Jesus foreknew, while He steadfastly set His face to go
toward Jerusalem

Faithless inability to grapple with the powers of darkness, faithless unreadiness to share the cross of Jesus, what was to be expected next ?   Estrangement, jealousy and ambition, the passions of the world heaving in the bosom of the Church.   But while they fail to discern the spirit of Judas, the Lord discerned theirs, and asked them in the house, What were ye reasoning in the way ?   It was a sweet and gentle prudence, which had not corrected them publicly nor while their tempers were still ruffled, nor in the language of severe rebuke, for by the way they had not only reasoned but disputed one with another, who was the greatest.

Language of especial honour had been addressed to Peter.   Three had become possessed of a remarkable secret on the Holy Mount, concerning which hints on one side, and surmises on the other, may easily have excited jealousy.   The failure of the nine to cast out the devil would also, as they were not humbled, render them irritable and self-asserting.

But they held their peace.   No one asserted his right to answer on behalf of all.   Peter, who was so willingly their spokesman at other times, did not vindicate his boasted pre-eminence now.   The claim which seemed so reasonable while they forgot Jesus, was a thing to blush for in His presence.   And they, who feared to ask Him of His own sufferings, knew enough to feel the contrast between their temper, their thoughts and His. Would that we too by prayer and self-examination, more often brought our desires and ambitions into the searching light of the presence of the lowly King of kings.

The calmness of their Lord was in strange contrast with their confusion.   He pressed no further His inquiry, but left them to weigh His silence in this respect against their own. But importing by His action something deliberate and grave, He sat down and called the Twelve, and pronounced the great law of Christian rank, which is lowliness and the lowliest service. " If any man would be the first, he shall be the least of all, and the servant of all." When Kaisers and Popes ostentatiously wash the feet of paupers, they do not really serve, and therefore they exhibit no genuine lowliness. Christ does not speak of the luxurious nursing of a sentiment, but of that genuine humility which effaces itself that it may really become a servant of the rest. Nor does He prescribe this as a penance, but as the appointed way to eminence. Something similar He had already spoken, bidding men sit down in the lowest room, that the Master of the house might call them higher. But it is in the next chapter, when despite this lesson the sons of Zebedee persisted in claiming the highest places, and the indignation of the rest betrayed the very passion it resented, that Jesus fully explains how lowly service, that wholesome medicine for ambition, is the essence of the very greatness in pursuit of which men spurn it.

To the precept, which will then be more conveniently examined, Jesus now added a practical lesson of amazing beauty. In the midst of twelve rugged and unsympathetic men, the same who, despite this action, presently rebuked parents for seeking the blessing of Christ upon their babes, Jesus sets a little child. What but the grace and love which shone upon the sacred face could have prevented this little one from being utterly disconcerted? But children have a strange sensibility for love. Presently this happy child was caught up in His arms, and pressed to His bosom, and there He seems to have lain while John, possibly conscience-stricken, asked a question and received an unexpected answer. And the silent pathetic trust of this His lamb found its way to the heart of Jesus, who presently spoke of "these little ones who believe in Me" (v. 42).

Meanwhile the child illustrated in a double sense the rule of greatness which He had laid down. So great is lowliness that Christ Himself may be found in the person of a little child. And again, so great is service, that in receiving one, even one, of the multitude of children who claim our sympathies, we receive the very Master ; and in that lowly Man, who was among them as He that serveth, is manifested the very God : whoso receiveth Me receiveth not Me but Him that sent me.

OFFENCES.

"John said unto Him, Master, we saw one casting out devils in Thy Name : and we forbade him, because he followed not us. But Jesus said, Forbid him not : for there is no man which shall do a mighty work in My name, and be able quickly to speak evil of Me. For he that is not against us is for us. For whosoever shall give you a cup of water to drink, because ye are Christ's, verily I say unto you, he shall in no wise lose his reward. And whosoever shall cause one of these little ones that believe on Me to stumble, it were better for him if a great millstone were hanged about his neck, and he were cast into the sea. And if thy hand cause thee to stumble, cut it off : it is good for thee to enter into life maimed, rather than having thy two hands to go into hell, into the unquenchable fire. And if thy foot cause thee to stumble, cut it off : it is good for thee to enter into life halt, rather than having thy two feet to be cast into hell. And if thine eye cause thee to stumble, cast it out : it is good for thee to enter into the kingdom of God with one eye, rather than having two eyes to be cast into hell ; where their worm dieth not, and the fire is not quenched. For every one shall be salted with fire. Salt is good : but if the salt have lost its saltness, wherewith will ye season it ? Have salt in yourselves, and be at peace one with another."—MARK ix. 38-50 (R.V.).

When Jesus spoke of the blessedness of receiving in His name even a little child, the conscience of St. John became uneasy. They had seen one casting out devils in that name, and had forbidden him, "because he followeth not us." The spirit of partizanship which these words betray is somewhat softer in St. Luke, but it exists. He reports "because he followeth not (Jesus) with us."

The behaviour of the disciples all through this period is unsatisfactory. From the time when Peter contradicted and rebuked Jesus, down to their final desertion, there is weakness at every turn. And this is a curious example of it, that immediately after having failed themselves,* they should rebuke another for doing what their Master had once declared could not possibly be an evil work. If Satan cast out Satan his house was divided against itself: if the finger of God was there no doubt the kingdom of God was come unto them.

It is interesting and natural that St. John should have introduced the question. Others were usually more forward, but that was because he was more thoughtful. Peter went first into the sepulchre; but he first, seeing what was there, believed. And it was he who said "It is the Lord," although Peter thereupon plunged into the lake to reach Him. Discerning and grave : such is the character from which his Gospel would naturally come, and it belongs to him who first discerned the rebuke to their conduct implied in the words of Jesus. He was right. The Lord answered, " Forbid him not, for there is no man which shall do a mighty work in My name, and be able quickly to speak evil of Me:" his own action would seal his lips; he would have committed himself. Now this points out a very serious view of human life, too often overlooked.

---

* That the event was recent is implied in the present tense : " he followeth not " : " forbid him not " ; the matter is still fresh.

The deed of to-day rules to-morrow; one is half enslaved by the consequences of his own free will.   Let
no man, hesitating between two lines of action, ask,
What harm in this ? what use in that ? without adding,
And what future actions, good or evil, may they carry
in their train ?

The man whom they had rebuked was at least certain
to be for a time detached from the opponents of truth,
silent if not remonstrant when it was assailed, diluting
and enfeebling the enmity of its opponents.   And so
Christ laid down the principle, " He that is not against
us is for us."   In St. Luke the words are more plainly
pointed against this party spirit, " He that is not against
you is for you."

How shall we reconcile this principle with Christ's
declaration elsewhere, " He that is not with Me is
against Me, and he that gathereth not with Me
scattereth " ?

It is possible to argue that there is no contradiction
whatever, for both deny the existence of a neutral class,
and from this it equally follows that he who is not with
is against, and he who is not against is with us.   But
this answer only evades the difficulty, which is, that one
passage reckons seeming neutrality as friendship, while
the other denounces it as enmity.

A closer examination reveals a more profound reconciliation.   In St. Matthew, Christ announced His own
personal claim ; in St. Mark He declares that His people
must not share it.   Towards Christ Himself, indifference
is practical rejection.   The manifestation of God was
not made to be criticised or set aside : He loves them
who love Him ; He demands the hearts He died for ;
and to give Him less is to refuse Him the travail of His
soul.   Therefore He that is not with Christ is against

Him.   The man who boasts that he does no harm but
makes no pretence of religion, is proclaiming that one
may innocently refuse Christ.   And it is very noteworthy
that St. Matthew's aphorism was evoked, like this, by
a question about the casting out of devils.   There the
Pharisees had said that He cast out devils by Beelzebub.
And Jesus had warned all who heard, that in such a
controversy, to be indifferent was to deny him.   Here,
the man had himself appealed to the power of Jesus.
He had passed, long ago, the stage of cool semi-con-
temptuous indifference.   Whether he was a disciple of
the Baptist, not yet entirely won, or a later convert who
shrank from the loss of all things, what is plain is that
he had come far on the way towards Jesus.   It does not
follow that he enjoyed a saving faith, for Christ will at
last profess to many who cast out devils in His name,
that He never knew them.   But intellectual persuasion
and some active reliance were there.   Let them beware
of crushing the germs, because they were not yet developed.   Nor should the disciples suppose that loyalty
to their organization, although Christ was with them,
was the same as loyalty to Him.   " He that is not
against *you* is for you," according to St. Luke.   Nay
more, " He that is not against *us* is for us," according
to St. Mark.   But already He had spoken the stronger
word, " He that is not for *Me* is against Me."

No verse has been more employed than this in
sectarian controversy.   And sometimes it has been
pressed too far.   The man whom St. John would have
silenced was not spreading a rival organization ; and
we know how the same Apostle wrote, long afterwards,
of those who did so: " If they had been of us, they would
have continued with us ; but they went out that they
might be made manifest how all they are not of us "

17

(1 John ii. 19). This was simply a doer of good without ecclesiastical sanction, and the warning of the text
is against all who would use the name of discipline
or of order to bridle the zeal, to curb the energies, of
any Christian soul. But it is at least as often the new
movement as the old organization that would silence all
who follow not with it.

But the energies of Christ and His gospel can never
be monopolized by any organization whatsoever. Every
good gift and every perfect gift, wherever we behold it,
is from Him.

All help, then, is to be welcomed; not to hinder is to
speed the cause. And therefore Jesus, repeating a
former saying, adds that whosoever, moved by the
name of Christ, shall give His followers one cup of
water, shall be rewarded. He may be and continue
outside the Church; his after life may be sadly inconsistent with this one action: that is not the question;
the sole condition is the genuine motive—one impulse of
true respect, one flicker of loyalty, only decided enough
to speed the weary ambassador with the simplest possible
refreshment, should " in no wise lose its reward." Does
this imply that the giver should assuredly enter heaven?
Alas, no. But this it says, that every spark of fire in
the smoking flax is tended, every gracious movement
is answered by a gift of further grace, to employ or to
abuse. Not more surely is the thirsty disciple refreshed,
than the feverish worldliness of him who just attains to
render this service is fanned and cooled by breezes from
heaven, he becomes aware of a deeper and nobler life,
he is melted and drawn towards better things. Very
blessed, or very miserable is he who cannot remember
the holy shame, the yearning, the sigh because he is
not always thus, which followed naturally upon some

deed, small in itself perhaps, but good enough to be inconsistent with his baser self. The deepening of spiritual capacity is one exceeding great reward of every act of loyalty to Christ.

This was graciously said of a deed done to the apostles, despite their failures, rivalries, and rebukes of those who would fain speed the common cause. Not, however, because they were apostles, but " because ye are Christ's." And so was the least, so was the child who clung to Him. But if the slightest sympathy with these is thus laden with blessing, then to hinder, to cause to stumble one such little one, how terrible was that. Better to die a violent and shameful death, and never sleep in a peaceful grave.

There is a worse peril than from others. We ourselves may cause ourselves to stumble. We may pervert beyond recall things innocent, natural, all but necessary, things near and dear and useful to our daily life as are our very limbs. The loss of them may be so lasting a deprivation that we shall enter heaven maimed. But if the moral evil is irrevocably identified with the worldly good, we must renounce it.

The hand with its subtle and marvellous power may well stand for harmless accomplishments now fraught with evil suggestiveness; for innocent modes of livelihood which to relinquish means crippled helplessness, yet which have become hopelessly entangled with unjust or at least questionable ways; for the great possessions, honestly come by, which the ruler would not sell; for all endowments which we can no longer hope to consecrate, and which make one resemble the old Chaldeans, whose might was their god, who sacrificed to their net and burned incense to their drag.

And the foot, with its swiftness in boyhood, its plod-

ding walk along the pavement in maturer age, may
well represent the caprices of youth so hard to curb,
and also the half-mechanical habits which succeed to
these, and by which manhood is ruled, often to its
destruction. If the hand be capacity, resource, and
possession, the foot is swift perilous impulse, and also
fixed habitude, monotonous recurrence, the settled ways
of the world.

Cut off hand and foot, and what is left to the muti-
lated trunk, the ravaged and desolated life? Desire
is left; the desire of the eyes. The eyes may not
touch the external world; all may now be correct in
our actions and intercourse with men. But yet greed,
passion, inflamed imagination may desecrate the temple
of the soul. The eyes misled Eve when she saw that
the fruit was good, and David on his palace roof.
Before the eyes of Jesus, Satan spread his third and
worst temptation. And our Lord seems to imply that
this last sacrifice of the worst because the deepest evil
must be made with indignant vehemence; hand and
foot must be cut off, but the eye must be cast out,
though life be half darkened in the process.

These latter days have invented a softer gospel,
which proclaims that even the fallen err if they utterly
renounce any good creature of God, which ought to
be received with thanksgiving; that the duty of
moderation and self-control can never be replaced by
renunciation, and that distrust of any lawful enjoyment
revives the Manichean heresy. Is the eye a good
creature of God? May the foot be received with
thanksgiving? Is the hand a source of lawful enjoyment? Yet Jesus made these the types of what must,
if it has become an occasion of stumbling, be entirely
cast away.

He added that in such cases the choice is between mutilation and the loss of all. It is no longer a question of the full improvement of every faculty, the doubling of all the talents, but a choice between living a life impoverished and half spoiled, and going complete to Gehenna, to the charnel valley where the refuse of Jerusalem was burned in a continual fire, and the worm of corruption never died. The expression is too metaphorical to decide such questions as that of the eternal duration of punishment, or of the nature of the suffering of the lost. The metaphors of Jesus, however, are not employed to exaggerate His meaning, but only to express it. And what He said is this : The man who cherishes one dear and excusable occasion of offence, who spares himself the keenest spiritual surgery, shall be cast forth with everything that defileth, shall be ejected with the offal of the New Jerusalem, shall suffer corruption like the transgressors of whom Isaiah first used the tremendous phrase, " their worm shall not die, neither shall their fire be quenched," shall endure at once internal and external misery, as of decomposition and of burning.

Such is the most terrible menace that ever crossed the lips into which grace was poured. And it was not addressed to the outcast or the Pharisee, but to His own. They were called to the highest life ; on them the influences of the world was to be as constant and as disintegrating as that of the weather upon a mountain top. Therefore they needed solemn warning, and the counter-pressure of those awful issues known to be dependent on their stern self-discipline. They could not, He said in an obscure passage which has been greatly tampered with, they could not escape fiery suffering in some form. But the fire which tried would preserve and bless them if they endured it ; every one shall be salted with fire. But if they who ought to be the salt of the world received the grace of God in vain, if the salt have lost its saltness, the case is desperate indeed.

And since the need of this solemn warning sprang from their rivalry and partizanship, Jesus concludes with an emphatic charge to discipline and correct themselves and to beware of impeding others : to be searching in the closet, and charitable in the church : to have salt in yourselves, and be at peace with one another.

CHAPTER X.

DIVORCE.

' And He arose from thence, and cometh into the borders of Judæa and beyond Jordan : and multitudes come together unto Him again ; and, as He was wont, He taught them again. And there came unto Him Pharisees, and asked Him, Is it lawful for a man to put away his wife? tempting Him. And He answered and said unto them, What did Moses command you? And they said, Moses suffered to write a bill of divorcement, and to put her away. But Jesus said unto them, For your hardness of heart he wrote you this commandment. But from the beginning of the creation, Male and female made He them. For this cause shall a man leave his father and mother, and shall cleave to his wife ; and the twain shall become one flesh : so that they are no more twain, but one flesh. What therefore God hath joined together, let no man put asunder. And in the house the disciples asked Him again of this matter. And He saith unto them, Whosoever shall put away his wife, and marry another, committeth adultery against her : and if she herself shall put away her husband, and marry another, she committeth adultery."—MARK x. 1–12 (R.V).

IT is easy to read without emotion that Jesus arose from the scene of His last discourse, and came into the borders of Judæa beyond Jordan. But not without emotion did Jesus bid farewell to Galilee, to the home of His childhood and sequestered youth, the cradle of His Church, the centre of nearly all the love and faith He had awakened. When closer still to death, His heart reverted to Galilee, and He promised that when He was risen He would go thither before His disciples. Now He had to leave it. And we must not forget that every step He took towards Jerusalem was a deliberate approach to His assured and anticipated cross. He was not like other brave men, who endure death when it arrives, but are sustained until the crisis by a thousand flattering hopes and undefined possibilities. Jesus knew precisely where and how He should suffer. And now, as He arose from Galilee, every step said, Lo, I come to do Thy will, O God.

As soon as He entered Perea beyond Jordan, multitudes came to Him again. Nor did His burdened heart repress His zeal: rather He found relief in their importunity and in His Father's business, and so, "as He was wont, He taught them again." These simple words express the rule He lived by, the patient continuance in well-doing which neither hostilities nor anxieties could chill.

Not long was He left undisturbed. The Pharisees come to Him with a question dangerous in itself, because there is no conceivable answer which will not estrange many, and especially dangerous for Jesus, because already, on the Mount, He has spoken upon this subject words at seeming variance with His free views concerning sabbath observance, fasting, and ceremonial purity. Most perilous of all was the decision they expected when given by a teacher already under suspicion, and now within reach of that Herod who had, during the lifetime of his first wife, married the wife of a living man. "Is it lawful for a man to put away his wife for every cause?" It was a decision upon this very subject which had proved fatal to the forerunner.

But Jesus spoke out plainly. In a question and answer which are variously reported, what is clear is that He carefully distinguished between a command and a permission of Moses. Divorce had been allowed; yes, but some reason had been exacted, whatever dis-

putes might exist about its needful gravity, and deliberation had been enforced by demanding a legal
document, a writing of divorcement.   Thus conscience
was bidden to examine its motives, and time was gained
for natural relentings.   But after all, Jesus declared
that divorce was only a concession to their hardness of
heart.   Thus we learn that Old Testament institutions
were not all and of necessity an expression of the
Divine ideal.   They were sometimes a temporary concession, meant to lead to better things ; an expedient
rather than a revelation.

These words contain the germ of St. Paul's doctrine
that the law itself was a schoolmaster, and its function
temporary.

To whatever concessions Moses had been driven, the
original and unshaken design of God was that man and
woman should find the permanent completion of their
lives each in the other.   And this is shown by three
separate considerations.   The first is the plan of the
creation, making them male and female, and such that
body and soul alike are only perfect when to each its
complement is added, when the masculine element and
the feminine "each fulfils defect in each . . . the two-
celled heart beating with one full stroke life."   Thus
by anticipation Jesus condemned the tame-spirited
verdict of His disciples, that since a man cannot relieve
himself from a union when it proves galling, "it is not
good" to marry at all.   To this he distinctly answered
that such an inference could not prove even tolerable,
except when nature itself, or else some social wrong, or
else absorbing devotion to the cause of God, virtually
cancelled the original design.   But already he had here
shown that such prudential calculation degrades man,
leaves him incomplete, traverses the design of God

Who from the beginning of the creation made them male and female. In our own days, the relation between the sexes is undergoing a social and legislative revolution. Now Christ says not a word against the equal rights of the sexes, and in more than one passage St. Paul goes near to assert it. But equality is not identity, either of vocation or capacity. This text asserts the separate and reciprocal vocation of each, and it is worthy of consideration, how far the special vocation of womanhood is consistent with loud assertion of her "separate rights."

Christ's second proof that marriage cannot be dissolved without sin is that glow of heart, that noble abandonment, in which a man leaves even father and mother for the joy of his youth and the love of his espousals. In that sacred hour, how hideous and base a wanton divorce would be felt to be. Now man is not free to live by the mean, calculating, selfish afterthought, which breathes like a frost on the bloom of his noblest impulses and aspirations. He should guide himself by the light of his highest and most generous intuitions.

And the third reason is that no man, by any possibility, can undo what marriage does. They two are one flesh; each has become part of the very existence of the other; and it is simply incredible that a union so profound, so interwoven with the very tissue of their being, should lie at the mercy of the caprice or the calculations of one or other, or of both. Such a union arises from the profoundest depths of the nature God created, not from mean cravings of that nature in its degradation; and like waters springing up from the granite underneath the soil, it may suffer stain, but it is in itself free from the contamination of the fall. Despite of monkish and of Manichean slanders, impure dreams pretending to especial purity, God is He Who joins together man and woman in a bond which "no man," king or prelate, may without guilt dissolve.

Of what followed, St. Mark is content to tell us that in the house, the disciples pressed the question further. How far did the relaxation which Moses granted over-rule the original design? To what extent was every individual bound in actual life? And the answer, given by Jesus to guide His own people through all time, is clear and unmistakeable. The tie cannot be torn asunder without sin. The first marriage holds, until actual adultery poisons the pure life in it, and man or woman who breaks through its barriers commits adultery. The Baptist's judgment of Herod was confirmed.

So Jesus taught. Ponder well that honest unshrinking grasp of solid detail, which did not overlook the physical union whereof is one flesh, that sympathy with high and chivalrous devotion forsaking all else for its beloved one, that still more spiritual penetration which discerned a Divine purpose and a destiny in the correlation of masculine and feminine gifts, of strength and grace, of energy and gentleness, of courage and long-suffering—observe with how easy and yet firm a grasp He combines all these into one overmastering argument —remember that when He spoke, the marriage tie was being relaxed all over the ancient world, even as godless legislation is to-day relaxing it—reflect that with such relaxation came inevitably a blight upon the family, resulting in degeneracy and ruin for the nation, while every race which learned the lesson of Jesus grew strong and pure and happy—and then say whether this was only a Judæan peasant, or the Light of the World indeed.

CHRIST AND LITTLE CHILDREN.

" And they brought unto Him little children, that He should touch them : and the disciples rebuked them. But when Jesus saw it, He was moved with indignation, and said unto them, Suffer the little children to come unto Me ; forbid them not: for of such is the kingdom of God. Verily I say unto you, Whosoever shall not receive the kingdom of God as a little child, he shall in no wise enter therein. And He took them in His arms, and blessed them, laying His hands upon them."—MARK x. 13–16 (R.V.).

THIS beautiful story gains new loveliness from its context. The disciples had weighed the advantages and disadvantages of marriage, and decided in their calculating selfishness, that the prohibition of divorce made it " not good for a man to marry." But Jesus had regarded the matter from quite a different position ; and their saying could only be received by those to whom special reasons forbade the marriage tie. It was then that the fair blossom and opening flower of domestic life, the tenderness and winning grace of childhood, appealed to them for a softer judgment. Little children (St. Luke says " babes ") were brought to Him to bless, to touch them. It was a remarkable sight. He was just departing from Perea on His last journey to Jerusalem. The nation was about to abjure its King and perish, after having invoked His blood to be not on them only, but on their children. But here were some at least of the next generation led by parents who revered Jesus, to receive His blessing. And who shall dare to limit the influence exerted by that benediction on their future lives ? Is it forgotten that this very Perea was the haven of refuge for Jewish believers when the wrath fell upon their nation ? Meanwhile the fresh smile of their unconscious, un-

stained, unforeboding infancy met the grave smile of
the all-conscious, death-boding Man of Sorrows, as
much purer as it was more profound.

But the disciples were not melted. They were
occupied with grave questions. Babes could understand nothing, and therefore could receive no conscious
intelligent enlightenment. What then could Jesus do
for them ? Many wise persons are still of quite the
same opinion. No spiritual influences, they tell us, can
reach the soul until the brain is capable of drawing
logical distinctions. A gentle mother may breathe
softness and love into a child's nature, or a harsh
nurse may jar and disturb its temper, until the effects
are as visible on the plastic face as is the sunshine or
storm upon the bosom of a lake ; but for the grace of
God there is no opening yet. As if soft and loving
influences are not themselves a grace of God. As if
the world were given certain odds in the race, and the
powers of heaven were handicapped. As if the young
heart of every child were a place where sin abounds
(since he is a fallen creature, with an original tendency
towards evil), but where grace doth not at all abound.
Such is the unlovely theory. And as long as it prevails in the Church we need not wonder at the compensating error of rationalism, denying evil where so
many of us deny grace. It is the more amiable error
of the two. Since then the disciples could not believe
that edification was for babes, they naturally rebuked
those that brought them. Alas, how often still does
the beauty and innocence of childhood appeal to men
in vain. And this is so, because we see not the Divine
grace, " the kingdom of heaven," in these. Their
weakness chafes our impatience, their simplicity irri-
tates our worldliness, and their touching helplessness

and trustfulness do not find in us heart enough for any glad response.

In ancient times they had to pass through the fire to Moloch, and since then through other fires : to fashion when mothers leave them to the hired kindness of a nurse, to selfishness when their want appeals to our charities in vain, and to cold dogmatism, which would banish them from the baptismal font, as the disciples repelled them from the embrace of Jesus. But He was moved with indignation, and reiterated, as men do when they feel deeply, "Suffer the little children to come unto Me ; forbid them not." And He added this conclusive reason, "for of such," of children and childlike men, "is the kingdom of God."

What is the meaning of this remarkable assertion ? To answer aright, let us return in fancy to the morning of our days ; let our flesh, and all our primitive being, come back to us as those of a little child.

We were not faultless then. The theological dogma of original sin, however unwelcome to many, is in harmony with all experience. Impatience is there, and many a childish fault ; and graver evils develop as surely as life unfolds, just as weeds show themselves in summer, the germs of which were already mingled with the better seed in spring. It is plain to all observers that the weeds of human nature are latent in the early soil, that this is not pure at the beginning of each individual life. Does not our new-fangled science explain this fact by telling us that we have still in our blood the transmitted influences of our ancestors the brutes ?

But Christ never meant to say that the kingdom of heaven was only for the immaculate and stainless. If converted men receive it, in spite of many a haunting

appetite and recurring lust, then the frailties of our
babes shall not forbid us to believe the blessed assurance that the kingdom is also theirs.

How many hindrances to the Divine life fall away
from us, as our fancy recalls our childhood. What
weary and shameful memories, base hopes, tawdry
splendours, envenomed pleasures, entangling associations vanish, what sins need to be confessed no longer,
how much evil knowledge fades out that we never now
shall quite unlearn, which haunts the memory even
though the conscience be absolved from it. The days
of our youth are not those evil days, when anything
within us saith, My soul hath no pleasure in the
ways of God.

When we ask to what especial qualities of childhood
did Jesus attach so great value, two kindred attributes
are distinctly indicated in Scripture.

One is humility. The previous chapter showed us
a little child set in the midst of the emulous disciples,
whom Christ instructed that the way to be greatest was
to become like this little child, the least.

A child is not humble through affectation, it never
professes nor thinks about humility. But it understands, however imperfectly, that it is beset by mysterious and perilous forces, which it neither comprehends nor can grapple with. And so are we. Therefore
all its instincts and experiences teach it to submit, to
seek guidance, not to put its own judgment in competition with those of its appointed guides. To them,
therefore, it clings and is obedient.

Why is it not so with us ? Sadly we also know the
peril of self-will, the misleading power of appetite and
passion, the humiliating failures which track the steps
of self-assertion, the distortion of our judgments, the

feebleness of our wills, the mysteries of life and death amid which we grope in vain. Milton anticipated Sir Isaac Newton in describing the wisest

> "As children gathering pebbles on the shore."
>
> *Par. Reg.*, iv. 330.

And if this be so true in the natural world that its sages become as little children, how much more in those spiritual realms for which our faculties are still so infantile, and of which our experience is so rudimentary. We should all be nearer to the kingdom, or greater in it, if we felt our dependence, and like the child were content to obey our Guide and cling to Him.

The second childlike quality to which Christ attached value was readiness to receive simply. Dependence naturally results from humility. Man is proud of his independence only because he relies on his own powers ; when these are paralysed, as in the sickroom or before the judge, he is willing again to become a child in the hands of a nurse or of an advocate. In the realm of the spirit these natural powers are paralysed. Learning cannot resist temptation, nor wealth expiate a sin. And therefore, in the spiritual world, we are meant to be dependent and receptive.

Christ taught, in the Sermon on the Mount, that to those who asked Him, God would give His Spirit as earthly parents give good things to their children. Here also we are taught to accept, to receive the kingdom as little children, not flattering ourselves that our own exertions can dispense with the free gift, not unwilling to become pensioners of heaven, not distrustful of the heart which grants, not finding the bounties irksome which are prompted by a Fathers' love. What can be more charming in its gracefulness than the reception of a favour by an affectionate child. His glad and confident enjoyment are a picture of what ours might be.

Since children receive the kingdom, and are a pattern for us in doing so, it is clear that they do not possess the kingdom as a natural right, but as a gift. But since they do receive it, they must surely be capable of receiving also that sacrament which is the sign and seal of it. It is a startling position indeed which denies admission into the visible Church to those of whom is the kingdom of God. It is a position taken up only because many, who would shrink from any such avowal, half-unconsciously believe that God becomes gracious to us only when His grace is attracted by skilful movements upon our part, by conscious and well-instructed efforts, by penitence, faith and orthodoxy. But whatever soul is capable of any taint of sin must be capable of compensating influences of the Spirit, by Whom Jeremiah was sanctified, and the Baptist was filled, even before their birth into this world (Jer. i. 5 ; Luke i. 15). Christ Himself, in Whom dwelt bodily all the fulness of the Godhead, was not therefore incapable of the simplicity and dependence of infancy.

Having taught His disciples this great lesson, Jesus let His affections loose. He folded the children in His tender and pure embrace, and blessed them much, laying His hands on them, instead of merely touching them. He blessed them not because they were baptized. But we baptize our children, because all such have received the blessing, and are clasped in the arms of the Founder of the Church.

THE RICH INQUIRER.

"**And as** He was going forth into the way, there **ran one to Him,**
and kneeled to Him, and asked Him, Good Master, what shall I do
that I may inherit eternal life? And Jesus said unto him, Why callest
thou Me good? none is good save one, even God.   Thou knowest
the commandments, Do not kill, **Do not** commit adultery, Do not steal,
Do not bear false witness, Do not defraud, Honour thy father and
mother.   And He said unto him, Master, all these things have I observed from my youth.   And Jesus looking upon him loved him, and
said unto him, One thing thou lackest : go, sell whatsoever thou hast,
and give to the poor, and thou shalt have treasure in heaven : and
come, follow Me.   But his countenance fell at the saying, and he
went away sorrowful : for he was one that had great possessions."—
MARK x. 17–22 (R.V.).

THE excitement stirred by our Lord's teaching must
often have shown itself in a scene of eagerness like
this which St. Mark describes so well.   The Saviour
is just " ͼ ing forth " when one rushes to overtake Him,
and kneels down to Him, full of the hope of a great
discovery.   He is so frank, so innocent and earnest, as
to win the love of Jesus.   And yet he presently goes
away, not as he came, but with a gloomy forehead and
a heavy heart, and doubtless with slow reluctance.

The authorities were now in such avowed opposition that to be Christ's disciple was disgraceful if not
dangerous to a man of mark.   Yet no fear withheld
this young ruler who had so much to lose ; he would
not come by night, like Nicodemus before the storm
had gathered which was now so dark ; he openly
avowed his belief in the goodness of the Master, and
his own ignorance of some great secret which Jesus
could reveal.

There is indeed a charming frankness in his bearing,
so that we admire even his childlike assertion of his
own virtues, while the heights of a nobility yet un-

attained are clearly possible for one so dissatisfied, so anxious for a higher life, so urgent in his questioning, What shall I do ?   What lack I yet ?   That is what makes the difference between the Pharisee who thanks God that he is not as other men, and this youth who has kept all the commandments, yet would fain be other than he is, and readily confesses that all is not enough, that some unknown act still awaits achievement.   The goodness which thinks itself upon the summit will never toil much farther.   The conscience that is really awake cannot be satisfied, but is perplexed rather and baffled by the virtues of a dutiful and well-ordered life.   For a chasm ever yawns between the actual and the ideal, what we have done and what we fain would do.   And a spiritual glory, undefined and perhaps undefinable, floats ever before the eyes of all men whom the god of this world has not blinded. This inquirer honestly thinks himself not far from the great attainment ; he expects to reach it by some transcendant act, some great deed done, and for this he has no doubt of his own prowess, if only he were well directed.   What shall I do that I may have eternal life, not of grace, but as a debt—that I may inherit it ? Thus he awaits direction upon the road where heathenism and semi-heathen Christianity are still toiling, and all who would purchase the gift of God with money or toil or merit or bitterness of remorseful tears.

One easily foresees that the reply of Jesus will disappoint and humble him, but it startles us to see him pointed back to works and to the law of Moses.

Again, we observe that what this inquirer seeks he very earnestly believes Jesus to have attained.   And it is no mean tribute to the spiritual elevation of our Lord, no doubtful indication that amid perils and con-

tradictions and on His road to the cross the peace of
God sat visibly upon His brow, that one so pure and
yet so keenly aware that his own virtue sufficed not,
and that the kingdom of God was yet unattained, should
kneel in the dust before the Nazarene, and beseech
this good Master to reveal to him all his questioning.
It was a strange request, and it was granted in an un-
looked for way.   The demand of the Chaldean tyrant
that his forgotten dream should be interpreted was not
so extravagant as this, that the defect in an unknown
career should be discovered.   It was upon a lofty
pedestal indeed that this ruler placed our Lord.

And yet his question supplies the clue to that answer
of Christ which has perplexed so many.   The youth is
seeking for himself a purely human merit, indigenous
and underived.   And the same, of course, is what he
ascribes to Jesus, to Him who is so far from claiming
independent human attainment, or professing to be
what this youth would fain become, that He said, "The
Son can do nothing of Himself. . . I can of Mine own
self do nothing."   The secret of His human perfection
is the absolute dependence of His humanity upon God,
with Whom He is one.   No wonder then that He
repudiates any such goodness as the ruler had in view.

The Socinian finds quite another meaning in His
reply, and urges that by these words Jesus denied His
Deity.   There is none good but one, That is God, was
a reason why He should not be called so.   Jesus however does not remonstrate absolutely against being called
good, but against being thus addressed from this ruler's
point of view, by one who regards Him as a mere
teacher and expects to earn the same title for himself.
And indeed the Socinian who appeals to this text
grasps a sword by the blade.   For if it denied Christ's

divinity it must exactly to the same extent deny also
Christ's goodness, which he admits.   Now it is beyond
question that Jesus differed from all the saints in the
serene confidence with which He regarded the moral
law, from the time when He received the baptism of
repentance only that He might fulfil all righteousness,
to the hour when He cried, "Why hast Thou forsaken
Me?" and although deserted, claimed God as still His
God.   The saints of to-day were the penitents of
yesterday.   But He has finished the work that was
given Him to do.   He knows that God hears Him
always, and in Him the Prince of this world hath
nothing.   And yet there is none good but God.   Who
then is He?   If this saying does not confess what is
intolerable to a reverential Socinian, what Strauss and
Renan shrank from insinuating, what is alien to the
whole spirit of the Gospels, and assuredly far from
the mind of the evangelists, then it claims all that His
Church rejoices to ascribe to Christ.

Moreover Jesus does not deny even to ordinary men
the possibility of being "good."

A good man out of the good treasure of his heart
bringeth forth good things.   Some shall hear at last
the words, Well done, good and faithful servant.   The
children of the kingdom are good seed among the tares.
Clearly His repugnance is not to the epithet, but to the
spirit in which it is bestowed, to the notion that goodness can spring spontaneously from the soil of our
humanity.   But there is nothing here to discourage
the highest aspirations of the trustful and dependent
soul, who looks for more grace.

The doctrinal importance of this remarkable utterance is what most affects us, who look back through
the dust of a hundred controversies   But it was very

secondary at the time, and what the ruler doubtless felt most was a chill sense of repression and perhaps despair. It was indeed the death-knell of his false hopes. For if only God is good, how can any mortal inherit eternal life by a good deed? And Jesus goes on to deepen this conviction by words which find a wonderful commentary in St. Paul's doctrine of the function of the law. It was to prepare men for the gospel by a challenge, by revealing the standard of true righteousness, by saying to all who seek to earn heaven, "The man that doeth these things shall live by them." The attempt was sure to end in failure, for, "by the law is the knowledge of sin." It was exactly upon this principle that Jesus said "Keep the commandments," spiritualizing them, as St. Matthew tells us, by adding to the injunctions of the second table, "Thou shalt love thy neighbour as thyself," which saying, we know, briefly comprehends them all.

But the ruler knew not how much he loved himself: his easy life had met no searching and stern demand until now, and his answer has a tone of relief, after the ominous words he had first heard. "Master," and he now drops the questionable adjective, "all these have I kept from my youth;" these never were so burdensome that he should despair; not these, he thinks, inspired that unsatisfied longing for some good thing yet undone. We pity and perhaps blame the shallow answer, and the dull perception which it betrayed. But Jesus looked on him and loved him. And well it is for us that no eyes fully discern our weakness but those which were so often filled with sympathetic tears. He sees error more keenly than the sharpest critic, but he sees earnestness too. And the love which desired all souls was attracted especially by one who had felt from his youth up the obligation of the moral law, and had not consciously transgressed it.

This is not the teaching of those vile proverbs which declare that wild oats must be sown if one would reap good corn, and that the greater the sinner the greater will be the saint.

Nay, even religionists of the sensational school delight in the past iniquities of those they honour, not only to glorify God for their recovery, nor with the joy which is in the presence of the angels over one sinner that repenteth, but as if these possess through their former wickedness some passport to special service now. Yet neither in Scripture nor in the history of the Church will it appear that men of licentious revolt against known laws have attained to usefulness of the highest order. The Baptist was filled with the Holy Ghost from his mother's womb. The Apostle of the Gentiles was blameless as touching the righteousness of the law. And each Testament has a special promise for those who seek the Lord early, who seek His kingdom and righteousness first. The undefiled are nearest to the throne.

Now mark how endearing, how unlike the stern zeal of a propagandist, was Christ's tender and loving gaze; and hear the encouraging promise of heavenly treasure, and offer of His own companionship, which presently softened the severity of His demand; and again, when all failed, when His followers doubtless scorned the deserter, ponder the truthful and compassionate words, How hard it is!

Yet will Christ teach him how far the spirit of the law pierces, since the letter has not wrought the knowledge of sin. If he loves his neighbour as himself, let his needier neighbour receive what he most values. If he

loves God supremely, let him be content with treasure
in the hands of God, and with a discipleship which
shall ever reveal to him, more and more profoundly, the
will of God, the true nobility of man, and the way to
that eternal life he seeks.

The socialist would justify by this verse a universal
confiscation. But he forgets that the spirit which
seizes all is widely different from that which gives all
freely : that Zacchæus retained half his goods ; that
Joseph of Arimathea was rich ; that the property of
Ananias was his own, and when he sold it the price
was in his own power ; that St. James warned the rich
in this world only against trusting in riches instead of
trusting God, who gave them all richly, for enjoyment,
although not to be confided in. Soon after this Jesus
accepted a feast from his friends in Bethany, and
ebuked Judas who complained that a costly luxury
had not been sold for the benefit of the poor. Why
then is his demand now so absolute ? It is simply an
application of his bold universal rule, that every cause
of stumbling must be sacrificed, be it innocent as hand
or foot or eye. And affluent indeed would be all the
charities and missions of the Church in these latter
days, if the demand were obeyed in cases where it
really applies, if every luxury which enervates and all
pomp which intoxicates were sacrificed, if all who know
that wealth is a snare to them corrected their weakness
by rigorous discipline, their unfruitfulness by a sharp
pruning of superfluous frondage.

The rich man neither remonstrated nor defended
himself. His self-confidence gave way. He felt
that what he could not persuade himself to do was a
" good thing." And he who came running went away
sorrowful, and with a face " lowering " like the sky

which forebodes "foul weather." That is too often the issue of such vaunting offers. Yet feeling his weakness, and neither resisting nor upbraiding the faithfulness which exposes him, doubtless he was long disquieted by new desires, a strange sense of failure and unworthiness, a clearer vision of that higher life which had already haunted his reveries. Henceforward he had no choice but to sink to a baser contentment, or else rise to a higher self-devotion. Who shall say, because he failed to decide then, that he persisted for ever in the great refusal? Yet was it a perilous and hardening experience, and it was easier henceforward to live below his ideal, when once he had turned away from Christ. Nor is there any reason to doubt that the inner circle of our Lord's immediate followers was then for ever closed against him.

WHO THEN CAN BE SAVED?

"And Jesus looked round about, and saith unto His disciples, How hardly shall they that have riches enter into the kingdom of God! And the disciples were amazed at His words. But Jesus answereth again, and saith unto them, Children, how hard is it for them that trust in riches to enter into the kingdom of God! It is easier for a camel to go through a needle's eye, than for a rich man to enter into the kingdom of God. And they were astonished exceedingly, saying unto Him, Then who can be saved? Jesus looking upon them saith, With men it is impossible, but not with God: for all things are possible with God. Peter began to say unto Him, Lo, we have left all, and have followed thee. Jesus said, Verily I say unto you, There is no man that hath left house, or brethren, or sisters, or mother, or father, or children, or lands, for my sake, and for the gospel's sake, but he shall receive a hundredfold now in this time, houses, and brethren, and sisters, and mothers, and children, and lands, with persecutions; and in the world to come eternal life. But many that are first shall be last; and the last first."—MARK x. 23-31 (R.V.).

As the rich man turned away with the arrow in his breast, Jesus looked round about on His disciples.

The Gospels, and especially St. Mark, often mention the gaze of Jesus, and all who know the power of an intense and pure nature silently searching others, the piercing intuition, the calm judgment which sometimes looks out of holy eyes, can well understand the reason. Disappointed love was in His look, and that compassionate protest against harsh judgments which presently went on to admit that the necessary demand was hard. Some, perhaps, who had begun to scorn the ruler in his defeat, were reminded of frailties of their own, and had to ask, Shall I next be judged? And one was among them, pilfering from the bag what was intended for the poor, to whom that look of Christ must have been very terrible. Unless we remember Judas, we shall not comprehend all the fitness of the repeated and earnest warnings of Jesus against covetousness. Never was secret sin dealt with so faithfully as his.

And now Jesus, as He looks around, says, "How hardly shall they that have riches enter into the kingdom of God." But the disciples were amazed. To the ancient Jew, from Abraham to Solomon, riches appeared to be a sign of the Divine favour, and if the pathetic figure of Job reminded him how much sorrow might befall the just, yet the story showed even him at the end more prosperous than at the beginning. In the time of Jesus, the chiefs of their religion were greedily using their position as a means of amassing enormous fortunes. To be told that wealth was a positive hindrance on the way to God was wonderful indeed.

When Jesus modified His utterance, it was not to correct Himself, like one who had heedlessly gone beyond His meaning. His third speech reiterated the first, declaring that a manifest and proverbial physical impossibility was not so hard as for a rich

man to enter the kingdom of God, here or hereafter.
But He interposed a saying which both explained the
first one and enlarged its scope. "Children" He
begins, like one who pitied their inexperience and
dealt gently with their perplexities, "Children, how
hard is it for them that trust in riches to enter into the
kingdom of God." And therefore is it hard for all the
rich, since they must wrestle against this temptation to
trust in their possessions. It is exactly in this spirit
that St. James, who quoted Jesus more than any of the
later writers of Scripture, charges the rich that they
be not high-minded, nor trust in uncertain riches, but
in the living God. Immediately before, Jesus had
told them how alone the kingdom might be entered,
even by becoming as little children; lowly, dependent,
willing to receive all at the hands of a superior.
Would riches help them to do this? Is it easier to
pray for daily bread when one has much goods
laid up for many years? Is it easier to feel that
God alone can make us drink of true pleasures as
of a river, when a hundred luxuries and indulgences
lull us in sloth or allure us into excess? Hereupon
the disciples perceived what was more alarming still,
that not alone do rich men trust in riches, but all who
confound possessions with satisfaction, all who dream
that to have much is to be blessed, as if property were
character. They were right. We may follow the
guidance of Mammon beckoning from afar, with a trust
as idolatrous as if we held his hand. But who could
abide a principle so exacting? It was the revelation
of a new danger, and they were astonished exceedingly,
saying, Then who can be saved? Again Jesus looked
upon them, with solemn but reassuring gaze. They
had learned the secret of the new life, the natural

impossibility throwing us back in helpless appeal to
the powers of the world to come. "With men it is
impossible, but not with God, for all things are possible
with God."

Peter, not easily nor long to be discouraged, now saw
ground for hope. If the same danger existed for rich
and poor, then either might be encouraged by having
surmounted it, and the apostles had done what the rich
man failed to do—they had left all and followed Jesus.
The claim has provoked undue censure, as if too much
were made out of a very trifling sacrifice, a couple
of boats and a paltry trade. But the objectors have
missed the point ; the apostles really broke away from
the service of the world when they left their nets and
followed Jesus. Their world was perhaps a narrow
one, but He Who reckoned two mites a greater offering
than the total of the gifts of many rich casting in much,
was unlikely to despise a fisherman or a publican who
laid all his living upon the altar. The fault, if fault
there were, lay rather in the satisfaction with which
Peter contemplates their decision as now irrevocable and
secure, so that nothing remained except to claim the
reward, which St. Matthew tells us he very distinctly
did. The young man should have had treasure in
heaven : what then should they have ?

But in truth, their hardest battles with worldliness
lay still before them, and he who thought he stood might
well take heed lest he fell. They would presently unite
in censuring a woman's costly gift to Him, for Whom
they professed to have surrendered all. Peter himself
would shrink from his Master's side. And what a satire
upon this confident claim would it have been, could the
heart of Judas then and there have been revealed to
them.

The answer of our Lord is sufficiently remarkable. St. Matthew tells how frankly and fully He acknowledged their collective services, and what a large reward He promised, when they should sit with Him on thrones, judging their nation. So far was that generous heart from weighing their losses in a worldly scale, or criticizing the form of a demand which was not all unreasonable.

But St. Mark lays exclusive stress upon other and sobering considerations, which also St. Matthew has recorded.

There is a certain tone of egoism in the words, " Lo, we . . . what shall we have ? " And Jesus corrects this in the gentlest way, by laying down such a general rule as implies that many others will do the same, " there is no man " whose self sacrifice shall go without its reward.

Secondary and lower motives begin to mingle with the generous ardour of self-sacrifice as soon as it is careful to record its losses, and inquire about its wages. Such motives are not absolutely forbidden, but they must never push into the foremost place. The crown of glory animated and sustained St. Paul, but it was for Christ, and not for this that he suffered the loss of all things.

Jesus accordingly demands purity of motive. The sacrifice must not be for ambition, even with aspirations prolonged across the frontiers of eternity : it must be altogether " for My sake and for the gospel's sake." And here we observe once more the portentous demand of Christ's person upon His followers. They are servants of no ethical or theological system, however lofty. Christ does not regard Himself and them, as alike devoted to some cause above and external to them all. To Him they are to be consecrated, and to the gospel, which, as we have seen, is the story of His Life, Death and Resurrection. For Him they are to break the dearest and strongest of earthly ties. He had just proclaimed how indissoluble was the marriage bond. No man should sever those whom God had joined. But St. Luke informs us that to forsake even a wife for Christ's sake, was a deed worthy of being rewarded an hundredfold. Nor does He mention any higher being in whose name the sacrifice is demanded. Now this is at least implicitly the view of His own personality, which some profess to find only in St John.

Again, there was perhaps an undertone of complaint in Peter's question, as if no compensation for all their sacrifices were hitherto bestowed. What should their compensation be? But Christ declares that losses endured for Him are abundantly repaid on earth, in this present time, and even amid the fires of persecution. Houses and lands are replaced by the consciousness of inviolable shelter and inexhaustible provision. "Whither wilt thou betake thyself to find covert?" asks the menacing cardinal; but Luther answers, "Under the heaven of God." And if dearest friends be estranged, or of necessity abandoned, then, in such times of high attainment and strong spiritual insight, membership in the Divine family is felt to be no unreal tie, and earthly relationships are well recovered in the vast fraternity of souls. Brethren, and sisters, and mothers, are thus restored an hundredfold; but although a father is also lost, we do not hear that a hundred fathers shall be given back, for in the spiritual family that place is reserved for One.

Lastly, Jesus reminded them that the race was not yet over; that many first shall be last and the last first. We know how Judas by transgression fell, and how the persecuting Saul became not a whit behind the very chiefest apostle.   But this word remains for the warning and incitement of all Christians, even unto the end of the world.   There are " many" such.

Next after this warning, comes yet another prediction of His own suffering, with added circumstances of horror.   Would they who were now first remain faithful ? or should another take their bishopric ?

With a darkening heart Judas heard, and made his choice.

[MARK x. 32-34.   See MARK viii. 31, p. 219.]

CHRIST'S CUP AND BAPTISM.

" And there came near unto him James and John, the sons of Zebedee, saying unto him, Master, we would that Thou shouldst do for us whatsoever we shall ask of Thee.   And He said unto them, What would ye I should do for you ?   And they said unto Him, Grant unto us that we may sit, one on Thy right hand, and one on *Thy* left hand, in Thy glory.   But Jesus said unto them, Ye know not what ye ask.   Are ye able to drink the cup that I drink ? or to be baptized with the baptism that I am baptized with ?   And they said unto Him, We are able.   And Jesus said unto them, The cup that I drink ye shall drink ; and with the baptism that I am baptized withal shall ye be baptized : but to sit on My right hand or on My left hand is not Mine to give : but *it is for them* for whom it hath been prepared."—MARK x. 35-40 (R.V.).

WE learn from St. Matthew that Salome was associated with her sons, and was indeed the chief speaker in the earlier part of this incident.

And her request has commonly been regarded as the mean and shortsighted intrigue of an ambitious woman, recklessly snatching at an advantage for her family, and unconscious of the stern and steep road to honour in the kingdom of Jesus.

Nor can we deny that her prayer was somewhat presumptuous, or that it was especially unbecoming to aim at entangling her Lord in a blindfold promise, desiring Him to do something undefined, " whatsoever we shall ask of Thee. " Jesus was too discreet to answer otherwise than, "What would ye that I should do for you?" And when they asked for the chief seats in the glory that was yet to be their Master's, no wonder that the Ten hearing of it, had indignation. But Christ's answer, and the gentle manner in which He explains His refusal, when a sharp rebuke is what we would expect to read, alike suggest that there may have been some softening, half-justifying circumstance. And this we find in the period at which the daring request was made.

It was on the road, during the last journey, when a panic had seized the company ; and our Lord, apparently out of the strong craving for sympathy which possesses the noblest souls, had once more told the Twelve what insults and cruel sufferings lay before Him. It was a time for deep searching of hearts, for the craven to go back and walk no more with Him, and for the traitor to think of making His own peace, at any price, with His Master's foes.

But this dauntless woman could see the clear sky beyond the storm. Her sons shall be loyal, and win the prize, whatever be the hazard, and however long the struggle.

Ignorant and rash she may have been, but it was no base ambition which chose such a moment to declare its unshaken ardour, and claim distinction in the kingdom for which so much must be endured.

And when the stern price was plainly stated, she and her children were not startled, they conceived themselves able for the baptism and the cup ; and little as they dreamed of the coldness of the waters, and the bitterness of the draught, yet Jesus did not declare them to be deceived.   He said, Ye shall indeed share these.

Nor can we doubt that their faith and loyalty refreshed His soul amid so much that was sad and selfish.   He knew indeed on what a dreadful seat He was soon to claim His kingdom, and who should sit upon His right hand and His left.   These could not follow Him now, but they should follow Him hereafter— one by the brief pang of the earliest apostolic martyrdom, and the other by the longest and sorest experience of that faithless and perverse generation.

1. Very significant is the test of worth which Jesus propounds to them : not successful service but endurance ; not the active but the passive graces.   It is not *our* test, except in a few brilliant and conspicuous martyrdoms.   The Church, like the world, has crowns for learning, eloquence, energy ; it applauds the force by which great things are done.   The reformer who abolishes an abuse, the scholar who defends a doctrine, the orator who sways a multitude, and the missionary who adds a new tribe to Christendom,—all these are sure of honour.   Our loudest plaudits are not for simple men and women, but for high station, genius, and success.   But the Lord looketh upon the heart, not the brain or the hand ; He values the worker, not the work ; the love, not the achievement.   And, therefore, one of the tests He constantly applied was this, the capability for noble endurance.   We ourselves, in our saner moments, can judge whether it demands more grace to refute a heretic, or to sustain the long inglorious agonies of some disease which slowly gnaws away the heart of life.   And doubtless among the heroes for whom Christ is twining immortal garlands, there is many a pale and shattered creature, nerveless and unstrung,

19

tossing on a mean bed, breathing in imperfect English loftier praises than many an anthem which resounds through cathedral arches, and laying on the altar of burnt sacrifice all he has, even his poor frame itself, to be racked and tortured without a murmur. Culture has never heightened his forehead nor refined his face : we look at him, but little dream what the angels see, or how perhaps because of such an one the great places which Salome sought were not Christ's to give away except only to them for whom it was prepared. For these, at last, the reward shall be His to give, as He said, "To him that overcometh will I give to sit down with Me upon My throne."

2. Significant also are the phrases by which Christ expressed the sufferings of His people. Some, which it is possible to escape, are voluntarily accepted for Christ's sake, as when the Virgin mother bowed her head to slander and scorn, and said, " Behold the servant of the Lord, be it unto me according to Thy word." Such sufferings are a cup deliberately raised by one's own hand to the reluctant lips. Into other sufferings we are plunged : they are inevitable. Malice, ill-health, or bereavement plies the scourge ; they come on us like the rush of billows in a storm ; they are a deep and dreadful baptism. Or we may say that some woes are external, visible, we are seen to be submerged in them ; but others are like the secret ingredients of a bitter draught, which the lips know, but the eye of the bystander cannot analyze. But there is One Who knows and rewards ; even the Man of Sorrows Who said, The cup which My heavenly Father giveth, shall I not drink it ?

Now it is this standard of excellence, announced by Jesus, which shall give high place to many of the poor and ignorant and weak, when rank shall perish, when tongues shall cease, and when our knowledge, in the blaze of new revelations, shall utterly vanish away, not quenched, but absorbed like the starlight at noon.

3. We observe again that men are not said to drink of another cup as bitter, or to be baptized in other waters as chill, as tried their Master; but to share His very baptism and His cup. Not that we can add anything to His all-sufficient sacrifice. Our goodness extendeth not to God. But Christ's work availed not only to reconcile us to the Father, but also to elevate and consecrate sufferings which would otherwise have been penal and degrading. Accepting our sorrows in the grace of Christ, and receiving Him into our hearts, then our sufferings fill up that which is lacking of the afflictions of Christ (Col. i. 24), and at the last He will say, when the glories of heaven are as a robe around Him, " I was hungry, naked, sick, and in prison in the person of the least of these."

Hence it is that a special nearness to God has ever been felt in holy sorrow, and in the pain of hearts which, amid all clamours and tumults of the world, are hushed and calmed by the example of Him Who was led as a lamb to the slaughter.

And thus they are not wrong who speak of the Sacrament of Sorrow, for Jesus, in this passage, applies to it the language of both sacraments.

It is a harmless superstition even at the worst which brings to the baptism of many noble houses water from the stream where Jesus was baptized by John. But here we read of another and a dread baptism, consecrated by the fellowship of Christ, in depths which plummet never sounded, and into which the neophyte goes down sustained by no mortal hand.

Here is also the communion of an awful cup. No human minister sets it in our trembling hand; no human voice asks, "Are ye able to drink the cup that I drink?" Our lips grow pale, and our blood is chill; but faith responds, "We are able." And the tender and pitying voice of our Master, too loving to spare one necessary pang, responds with the word of doom: "The cup that I drink ye shall drink; and with the baptism that I am baptized withal shall ye be baptized." Even so: it is enough for the servant that he be as his Master.

THE LAW OF GREATNESS

"And when the ten heard it, they began to be moved with indignation concerning James and John. And Jesus called them to Him, and saith unto them, Ye know that they which are accounted to rule over the Gentiles lord it over them; and their great ones exercise authority over them. But it is not so among you: but whosoever would become great among you, shall be your minister: and whosoever would be first among you, shall be servant of all. For verily the Son of man came not to be ministered unto, but to minister, and to give His life a ransom for many."—MARK x. 41-45 (R.V.).

WHEN the Ten heard that James and John had asked for the chief places in the kingdom, they proved, by their indignation, that they also nourished the same ambitious desires which they condemned. But Jesus called them to Him, for it was not there that angry passions had broken out. And happy are they who hear and obey His summons to approach, when, removed from His purifying gaze by carelessness or wilfulness, ambition and anger begin to excite their hearts.

Now Jesus addressed them as being aware of their hidden emulation. And His treatment of it is remarkable.   He neither condemns, nor praises it, but simply teaches them what Christian greatness means, and the conditions on which it may be won.

The greatness of the world is measured by authority and lordliness.   Even there it is an uncertain test ; for the most real power is often wielded by some anonymous thinker, or by some crafty intriguer, content with the substance of authority while his puppet enjoys the trappings.   Something of this may perhaps be detected in the words, " They which are accounted to rule over the Gentiles lord it over them."   And it is certain that " their great ones exercise authority over them."   But the Divine greatness is a meek and gentle influence. To minister to the Church is better than to command it, and whoever desires to be the chief must become the servant of all.   Thus shall whatever is vainglorious and egoistic in our ambition defeat itself ; the more one struggles to be great the more he is disqualified : even benefits rendered to others with this object will not really be service done for them but for self ; nor will any calculated assumption of humility help one to become indeed the least, being but a subtle assertion that he is great, and like the last place in an ecclesiastical procession, when occupied in a self-conscious spirit. And thus it comes to pass that the Church knows very indistinctly who are its greatest sons.   As the gift of two mites by the widow was greater than that of large sums by the rich, so a small service done in the spirit of perfect self-effacement,—a service which thought neither of its merit nor of its reward, but only of a brother's need, shall be more in the day of reckoning than sacrifices which are celebrated by the historians and sung by the poets of the Church.   For it may avail nothing to give all my goods to feed the poor, and my body to be burned; while a cup of cold water, rendered by a loyal hand, shall in no wise lose its reward.

Thus Jesus throws open to all men a competition which has no charms for flesh and blood. And as He spoke of the entry upon His service, bearing a cross, as being the following of Himself, so He teaches us, that the greatness of lowliness, to which we are called, is His own greatness. "For verily the Son of Man came not to be ministered unto but to minister." Not here, not in this tarnished and faded world, would He Who was from everlasting with the Father have sought His own ease or honour. But the physician came to them that were sick, and the good Shepherd followed His lost sheep until He found it. Now this comparison proves that we also are to carry forward the same restoring work, or else we might infer that, because He came to minister to us, we may accept ministration with a good heart. It is not so. We are the light and the salt of the earth, and must suffer with Him that we may also be glorified together.

But He added another memorable phrase. He came "to give His life a ransom in exchange for many." It is not a question, therefore, of the inspiring example of His life. Something has been forfeited which must be redeemed, and Christ has paid the price. Nor is this done only on behalf of many, but in exchange for them.

So then the crucifixion is not a sad incident in a great career; it is the mark towards which Jesus moved, the power by which He redeemed the world.

Surely, we recognise here the echo of the prophet's words, "Thou shalt make His soul an offering for sin . . . by His knowledge shall My righteous servant justify many, and He shall bear their iniquities" (Isa. liii. 10, 11).

The elaborated doctrine of the atonement may not perhaps be here, much less the subtleties of theologians who have, to their own satisfaction, known the mind of the Almighty to perfection. But it is beyond reasonable controversy that in this verse Jesus declared that His sufferings were vicarious, and endured in the sinners' stead.

BARTIMÆUS.

"And they come to Jericho : and as He went out from Jericho, with His disciples and a great multitude, the son of Timæus, Bartimæus, a blind beggar, was sitting by the way side. And when he heard that it was Jesus of Nazareth, he began to cry out, and say, Jesus, Thou son of David, have mercy on me. And many rebuked him, that he should hold his peace : but he cried out the more a great deal, Thou son of David, have mercy on me. And Jesus stood still, and said, Call ye him. And they called the blind man, saying unto him, Be of good cheer ; rise, He calleth thee. And he, casting away his garment, sprang up, and came to Jesus. And Jesus answered him, and said, What wilt thou that I should do unto thee ? And the blind man said unto Him, Rabboni, that I may receive my sight. And Jesus said unto him, Go thy way ; thy faith hath made thee whole. And straightway he received his sight, and followed Him in the way."—MARK x. 46-52 (R.V.).

THERE is no miracle in the Gospels of which the accounts are so hard to reconcile as those of the healing of the blind at Jericho.

It is a small thing that St. Matthew mentions two blind men, while St. Mark and St. Luke are only aware of one. The same is true of the demoniacs at Gadara, and it is easily understood that only an eyewitness should remember the obscure comrade of a remarkable and energetic man, who would have spread far and wide the particulars of his own cure. The fierce and dangerous demoniac of Gadara was just such a man, and there is ample evidence of energy and vehemence in the brief account of Bartimæus. What is really perplexing is that St. Luke places the miracle at the entrance to Jericho, but St. Matthew and St. Mark, as Jesus came out of it. It is too forced and violent a theory which speaks of an old and a new town, so close together that one was entered and the other left at the same time.

It is possible that there were two events, and the success of one sufferer at the entrance to the town led others to use the same importunities at the exit. And this would not be much more remarkable than the two miracles of the loaves, or the two miraculous draughts of fish. It is also possible, though unlikely, that the same supplicant who began his appeals without success when Jesus entered, resumed His entreaties, with a comrade, at the gate by which He left.

Such difficulties exist in all the best authenticated histories : discrepancies of the kind arise continually between the evidence of the most trustworthy witnesses in courts of justice. And the student who is humble as well as devout will not shut his eyes against facts, merely because they are perplexing, but will remember that they do nothing to shake the solid narrative itself.

As we read St. Mark's account, we are struck by the vividness of the whole picture, and especially by the robust personality of the blind man. The scene is neither Jerusalem, the city of the Pharisees, nor Galilee, where they have persistently sapped the popularity of Jesus. Eastward of the Jordan, He has spent the last peaceful and successful weeks of His brief and stormy career, and Jericho lies upon the borders of that friendly district. Accordingly something is here of the old enthusiasm : a great multitude moves along with His disciples to the gates, and the rushing

concourse excites the curiosity of the blind son of
Timæus. So does many a religious movement lead to
inquiry and explanation far and wide. But when he,
sitting by the way, and unable to follow, knows that
the great Healer is at hand, but only in passing, and
for a moment, his interest suddenly becomes personal
and ardent, and "he began to cry out" (the expression
implies that his supplication, beginning as the crowd
drew near, was not one utterance but a prolonged
appeal), "and to say, Jesus, Thou Son of David,
have mercy on me." To the crowd his outcry seemed
to be only an intrusion upon One Who was too rapt,
too heavenly, to be disturbed by the sorrows of a blind
beggar. But that was not the view of Bartimæus,
whose personal affliction gave him the keenest interest
in those verses of the Old Testament which spoke of
opening the blind eyes. If he did not understand
their exact force as prophecies, at least they satisfied
him that his petition could not be an insult to the
great Prophet of Whom just such actions were told, for
Whose visit he had often sighed, and Who was now
fast going by, perhaps for ever. The picture is one of
great eagerness, bearing up against great discouragement. We catch the spirit of the man as he inquires
what the multitude means, as the epithet of his in-
formants, Jesus of Nazareth, changes on his lips into
Jesus, Thou Son of David, as he persists, without
any vision of Christ to encourage him, and amid the
rebukes of many, in crying out the more a great
deal, although pain is deepening every moment in his
accents, and he will presently need cheering. The
ear of Jesus is quick for such a call, and He stops.
He does not raise His own voice to summon him,
but teaches a lesson of humanity to those who would

fain have silenced the appeal of anguish, and says, Call
ye him.   And they obey with a courtier-like change of
tone, saying, Be of good cheer, rise, He calleth thee.
And Bartimæus cannot endure even the slight hindrance
of his loose garment, but flings it aside, and rises and
comes to Jesus, a pattern of the importunity which
prays and never faints, which perseveres amid all
discouragement, which adverse public opinion cannot
hinder.   And the Lord asks of him almost exactly the
same question as recently of James and John, What
wilt thou that I should do for thee?   But in his reply
there is no aspiring pride : misery knows how precious
are the common gifts, the every-day blessings which we
hardly pause to think about; and he replies, Rabboni,
that I may receive my sight.   It is a glad and eager
answer.   Many a petition he had urged in vain ; and
many a small favour had been discourteously bestowed ;
but Jesus, Whose tenderness loves to commend while
He blesses, shares with him, so to speak, the glory of
his healing, as He answers, Go thy way, thy faith hath
made thee whole.   By thus fixing his attention upon
his own part in the miracle, so utterly worthless as a
contribution, but so indispensable as a condition, Jesus
taught him to exercise hereafter the same gift of faith.

"Go thy way," He said.   And Bartimæus " followed
Him on the road."   Happy is that man whose eyes
are open to discern, and his heart prompt to follow, the
print of those holy feet.

CHAPTER XI.

THE TRIUMPHANT ENTRY.

"And when they draw nigh unto Jerusalem, unto Bethphage and Bethany, at the Mount of Olives, He sendeth two of His disciples, and saith unto them, Go your way into the village that is over against you: and straightway as ye enter into it, ye shall find a colt tied, whereon no man ever yet sat; loose him, and bring him. And if any one say unto you, Why do ye this? say ye, The Lord hath need of him; and straightway He will send him back hither. And they went away, and found a colt tied at the door without in the open street; and they loose him. And certain of them that stood there said unto them, What do ye, loosing the colt? And they said unto them even as Jesus had said: and they let them go. And they bring the colt unto Jesus, and cast on him their garments; and He sat upon him. And many spread their garments upon the way; and others branches, which they had cut from the fields. And they that went before, and they that followed, cried, Hosanna: Blessed *is* He that cometh in the name of the Lord: Blessed *is* the kingdom that cometh, *the kingdom* of our father David: Hosanna in the highest. And He entered into Jerusalem, into the temple; and when He had looked round about upon all things, it being now eventide, He went out unto Bethany with the twelve."—MARK xi. 1-11 (R.V.).

JESUS had now come near to Jerusalem, into what was possibly the sacred district of Bethphage, of which, in that case, Bethany was the border village. Not without pausing here (as we learn from the fourth Gospel), yet as the next step forward, He sent two of His disciples to untie and bring back an ass, which was fastened with her colt at a spot which He minutely described. Unless they were challenged they should

simply bring the animals away; but if any one remonstrated, they should answer, "The Lord hath need of them,"
and thereupon the owner would not only acquiesce,
but send them.   In fact they are to make a requisition,
such as the State often institutes for horses and cattle
during a campaign, when private rights must give way
to a national exigency.   And this masterful demand,
this abrupt and decisive rejoinder to a natural objection,
not arguing nor requesting, but demanding, this title
which they are bidden to give to Jesus, by which,
standing thus alone, He is rarely described in Scripture
(chiefly in the later Epistles, when the remembrance of
His earthly style gave place to the influence of habitual
adoration), all this preliminary arrangement makes us
conscious of a change of tone, of royalty issuing its
mandates, and claiming its rights.   But what a claim,
what a requisition, when He takes the title of Jehovah,
and yet announces His need of the colt of an ass.   It is
indeed the lowliest of all memorable processions which
He plans, and yet, in its very humility, it appeals to
ancient prophecy, and says unto Zion that her King
cometh unto her.   The monarchs of the East and the
captains of the West might ride upon horses as for war,
but the King of Sion should come unto her meek, and
sitting upon an ass, upon a colt, the foal of an ass.
Yet there is fitness and dignity in the use of "a colt
whereon never man sat," and it reminds us of other
facts, such as that He was the firstborn of a virgin
mother, and rested in a tomb which corruption had
never soiled.

Thus He comes forth, the gentlest of the mighty,
with no swords gleaming around to guard Him, or to
smite the foreigner who tramples Israel, or the worse
foes of her own household.   Men who will follow such

a King must lay aside their vain and earthly ambitions, and awake to the truth that spiritual powers are grander than any which violence ever grasped. But men who will not follow Him shall some day learn the same lesson, perhaps in the crash of their reeling commonwealth, perhaps not until the armies of heaven follow Him, as He goes forth, riding now upon a white horse, crowned with many diadems, smiting the nations with a sharp sword, and ruling them with an iron rod.

Lowly though His procession was, yet it was palpably a royal one. When Jehu was proclaimed king at Ramoth-Gilead, the captains hastened to make him sit upon the garments of every one of them, expressing by this national symbol their subjection. Somewhat the same feeling is in the famous anecdote of Sir Walter Raleigh and Queen Elizabeth. And thus the disciples who brought the ass cast on him their garments, and Jesus sat thereon, and many spread their garments in the way. Others strewed the road with branches; and as they went they cried aloud certain verses of that great song of triumph, which told how the nations, swarming like bees, were quenched like the light fire of thorns, how the right hand of the Lord did valiantly, how the gates of righteousness should be thrown open for the righteous, and, more significant still, how the stone which the builders rejected should become the head-stone of the corner. Often had Jesus quoted this saying when reproached by the unbelief of the rulers, and now the people rejoiced and were glad in it, as they sang of His salvation, saying, " Hosanna, blessed is He that cometh in the name of the Lord, Blessed is the kingdom that cometh, the Kingdom of our father David, Hosanna in the highest."

Such is the narrative as it impressed St. Mark. For

his purpose it mattered nothing that Jerusalem took
no part in the rejoicings, but was perplexed, and said,
Who is this ? or that, when confronted by this somewhat scornful and affected ignorance of the capital, the
voice of Galilee grew weak, and proclaimed no longer
the advent of the kingdom of David, but only Jesus, the
prophet of Nazareth ; or that the Pharisees in the
temple avowed their disapproval, while contemptuously
ignoring the Galilean multitude, by inviting Him to
reprove some children.　　What concerned St. Mark
was that now, at last, Jesus openly and practically
assumed rank as a monarch, allowed men to proclaim
the advent of His kingdom, and proceeded to exercise
its rights by calling for the surrender of property, and
by cleansing the temple with a scourge.　The same
avowal of kingship is almost all that he has cared to
record of the remarkable scene before His Roman
'udge.

After this heroic fashion did Jesus present Himself
to die.　Without a misleading hope, conscious of the
hollowness of His seeming popularity, weeping for the
impending ruin of the glorious city whose walls were
ringing with His praise, and predicting the murderous
triumph of the crafty faction which appears so helpless, He not only refuses to recede or compromise,
but does not hesitate to advance His claims in a
manner entirely new, and to defy the utmost animosity
of those who still rejected Him.

After such a scene there could be no middle course
between crushing Him, and bowing to Him.　He was
no longer a Teacher of doctrines, however revolutionary,
but an Aspirant to practical authority, Who must be
dealt with practically.

There was evidence also of His intention to proceed

upon this new line, when He entered into the temple, investigated its glaring abuses, and only left it for the moment because it was now eventide. To-morrow would show more of His designs.

Jesus is still, and in this world, King. And it will hereafter avail us nothir g to have received His doctrine, unless we have taken His yoke.

THE BARREN FIG-TREE.

" And on the morrow, when they were come out from Bethany, He hungered. And seeing a fig-tree afar off having leaves, He came, if haply He might find anything thereon : and when He came to it, He found nothing but leaves ; for it was not the season of figs. And He answered and said unto it, No man eat fruit from thee henceforward for ever. And His disciples heard it."

" And as they passed by in the morning, they saw the fig-tree withered away from the roots. And Peter calling to remembrance saith unto Him, Rabbi, behold, the fig-tree which Thou cursedst is withered away. And Jesus answering saith unto them, Have faith in God. Verily I say unto you, Whosoever shall sav unto this mountain, Be thou taken up and cast into the sea ; and shall not doubt in his heart, but shall believe that what he saith cometh to pass ; he shall have it. Therefore I say unto you, All things whatsoever ye pray and ask for, believe that ye have received them, and ye shall have them.   And whensoever ye stand praying, forgive, if ye have aught against any one ; that your Father also which is in heaven may forgive you your tres- passes."—MARK xi. 12–14, 20–25 (R.V.).

No sooner has Jesus claimed His kingdom, than He performs His first and only miracle of judgment. And it is certain that no mortal, informed that such a miracle was impending, could have guessed where the blow would fall. In this miracle an element is pre- dominant which exists in all, since it is wrought as an acted dramatized parable, not for any physical advan- tage, but wholly for the instruction which it conveys. Jesus hungered at the very outset of a day of toil, as

He came out from Bethany. And this was not due to poverty, since the disciples there had recently made Him a great feast, but to His own absorbing ardour. The zeal of God's house, which He had seen polluted and was about to cleanse, had either left Him indifferent to food until the keen air of morning aroused the sense of need, or else it had detained Him, all night long, in prayer and meditation out of doors. As He walks, He sees afar off a lonely fig-tree covered with leaves, and comes if haply He might find anything thereon. It is true that figs would not be in season for two months, but yet they ought to present themselves before the leaves did ; and since the tree was precocious in the show and profusion of luxuriance, it ought to bear early figs. If it failed, it would at least point a powerful moral ; and, therefore, when only leaves appeared upon it, Jesus cursed it with perpetual barrenness, and passed on. Not in the dusk of that evening as they returned, but when they passed by again in the morning the blight was manifest, the tree was withered from its very roots.

It is complained that by this act Jesus deprived some one of his property. But the same retributive justice of which this was an expression was preparing to blight, presently, all the possessions of all the nation. Was this unjust ? And of the numberless trees that are blasted year by year, why should the loss of this one only be resented ? Every physical injury must be intended to further some spiritual end ; but it is not often that the purpose is so clear, and the lesson so distinctly learned.

Others blame our Lord's word of sentence, because a tree, not being a moral agent, ought not to be punished. It is an obvious rejoinder that neither could it suffer pain ; that the whole action is symbolic ; and that we ourselves justify the Saviour's method of expression as often as we call one tree "good" and another "bad," and say that a third "ought" to bear fruit, while not much could be "expected of" a fourth. It should rather be observed that in this word of sentence Jesus revealed His tenderness. It would have been a false and cruel kindness never to work any miracle except of compassion, and thus to suggest the inference that He could never strike, whereas indeed, before that generation passed away, He would break His enemies in pieces like a potter's vessel.

Yet He came not to destroy men's lives but to save them. And, therefore, while showing Himself neither indifferent nor powerless against barren and false pretensions, He did this only once, and then only by a sign wrought upon an unsentient tree.

Retribution fell upon it not for its lack of fruit, since at that season it shared this with all its tribe, but for ostentatious, much-professing fruitlessness. And thus it pointed with dread significance to the condition of God's own people, differing from Greece and Rome and Syria, not in the want of fruit, but in the show of luxuriant frondage, in the expectation it excited and mocked. When the season of the world's fruitfulness was yet remote, only Israel put forth leaves, and made professions which were not fulfilled. And the permanent warning of the miracle is not for heathen men and races, but for Christians who have a name to live, and who are called to bear fruit unto God.

While the disciples marvelled at the sudden fulfilment of its sentence, they could not have forgotten the parable of a fig-tree in the vineyard, on which care and labour were lavished, but which must be destroyed after one year of respite if it continued to be a cumberer of the ground.

And Jesus drove the lesson home. He pointed to "this mountain" full in front, with the gold and marble of the temple sparkling like a diadem upon its brow, and declared that faith is not only able to smite barrenness with death, but to remove into the midst of the sea, to plant among the wild and stormswept races of the immeasurable pagan world, the glory and privilege of the realized presence of the Lord. To do this was the purpose of God, hinted by many a prophet, and clearly announced by Christ Himself. But its accomplishment was left to His followers, who should succeed in exact proportion to the union of their will and that of God, so that the condition of that moral miracle, transcending all others in marvel and in efficacy, was simple faith.

And the same rule covers all the exigencies of life. One who truly relies on God, whose mind and will are attuned to those of the Eternal, cannot be selfish, or vindictive, or presumptuous. As far as we rise to the grandeur of this condition we enter into the Omnipotence of God, and no limit need be imposed upon the prevalence of really and utterly believing prayer. The wishes that ought to be refused will vanish as we attain that eminence, like the hoar frost of morning as the sun grows strong.

To this promise Jesus added a precept, the admirable suitability of which is not at first apparent. Most sins are made evident to the conscience in the act of prayer. Drawing nigh to God, we feel our unfitness to be there, we are made conscious of what He frowns upon, and if we have such faith as Jesus spoke of, we at once resign what would grieve the Spirit of adoption. No saint is ignorant of the convicting power of prayer. But it is not of necessity so with resentment for real grievances. We may think we do well to be angry. We may confound our selfish fire with the pure flame of holy zeal, and begin, with confidence enough, yet not with the mind of Christ, to remove mountains, not because they impede a holy cause, but because they throw a shadow upon our own field. And, therefore, Jesus reminds us that not only wonder-working faith, but even the forgiveness of our sins requires from us the forgiveness of our brother. This saying is the clearest proof of how much is implied in a truly undoubting heart. And this promise is the sternest rebuke of the Church, endorsed with such ample powers, and yet after nineteen centuries confronted by an unconverted world.

THE SECOND CLEANSING OF THE TEMPLE.

"And they come to Jerusalem : and He entered into the temple, and began to cast out them that sold and them that bought in the temple, and overthrew the tables of the moneychangers, and the seats of them that sold the doves ; and He would not suffer that any man should carry a vessel through the temple. And He taught, and said unto them, Is it not written, My house shall be called a house of prayer for all the nations ? but ye have made it a den of robbers. And the chief priests and the scribes heard it, and sought how they might destroy Him : for they feared Him, for all the multitude was astonished at His teaching. And every evening He went forth out of the city."— MARK xi. 15-19. (R.V.).

WITH the authority of yesterday's triumph still about Him, Jesus returned to the temple, which He had then inspected. There at least the priesthood were not thwarted by popular indifference or ignorance : they had power to carry out fully their own views ; they were solely responsible for whatever abuses could be discovered. In fact, the iniquities which moved the indignation of Jesus were of their own contrivance, and they enriched themselves by a vile trade which robbed the worshippers and profaned the holy house.

Pilgrims from a distance needed the sacred money, the half-shekel of the sanctuary, still coined for this one purpose, to offer for a ransom of their souls (Exod. xxx. 13). And the priests had sanctioned a trade in the exchange of money under the temple roof, so fraudulent that the dealers' evidence was refused in the courts of justice.

Doves were necessary for the purification of the poor, who could not afford more costly sacrifices, and sheep and oxen were also in great demand. And since the unblemished quality of the sacrifices should be attested by the priests, they had been able to put a fictitious value upon these animals, by which the family of Annas in particular had accumulated enormous wealth.

To facilitate this trade, they had dared to bring the defilement of the cattle market within the precincts of the House of God. Not indeed into the place where the Pharisee stood in his pride and "prayed with himself," for that was holy ; but the court of the Gentiles was profane ; the din which distracted and the foulness which revolted Gentile worship was of no account to the average Jew. But Jesus regarded the scene with different eyes. How could the sanctity of that holy place not extend to the court of the stranger and the proselyte, when it was written, Thy house shall be called a house of prayer for all the nations ? Therefore Jesus had already, at the outset of His ministry, cleansed His Father's house. Now, in the fulness of His newly asserted royalty, He calls it My House : He denounces the iniquity of their traffic by branding it as a den of robbers ; He casts out the traders themselves, as well as the implements of their traffic ; and in so doing He fanned to a mortal heat the hatred of the chief priests and the scribes, who saw at once their revenues threatened and their reputation tarnished, and yet dared not strike, because all the multitude was astonished at His teaching.

But the wisdom of Jesus did not leave Him within their reach at night ; every evening He went forth out of the city.

From this narrative we learn the blinding force of self-interest, for doubtless they were no more sensible of their iniquity than many a modern slavedealer. And we must never rest content because our own conscience acquits us, unless we have by thought and prayer supplied it with light and guiding.

We learn reverence for sacred places, since the one exercise of His royal authority which Jesus publicly displayed was to cleanse the temple, even though upon the morrow He would relinquish it for ever, to be " your house "—and desolate.

We learn also how much apparent sanctity, what dignity of worship, splendour of offerings, and pomp of architecture may go along with corruption and un-reality.

And yet again, by their overawed and abject helpless-ness we learn the might of holy indignation, and the awakening power of a bold appeal to conscience. "The people hung upon Him, listening," and if all seemed vain and wasted effort on the following Friday, what fruit of the teaching of Jesus did not His followers gather in, as soon as He poured down on them the gifts of Pentecost.

Did they now recall their own reflections after the earlier cleansing of the temple ? and their Master's ominous words? They had then remembered how it was written, The zeal of thine house shall eat Me up. And He had said, Destroy this temple, and in three days I shall raise it up, speaking of the temple of His Body, which was now about to be thrown down.

THE BAPTISM OF JOHN, WHENCE WAS IT?

"And they come again to Jerusalem: and as He was walking in the temple, there come to Him the chief priests, and the scribes, and the elders; and they said unto Him, By what authority doest Thou these things? or who gave Thee this authority to do these things? And Jesus said unto them, I will ask of you one question, and answer Me, and I will tell you by what authority I do these things. The baptism of John, was it from heaven, or from men? answer Me. And they reasoned with themselves, saying, If we shall say, From heaven: He will say, Why then did ye not believe him? But should we say, From men—they feared the people: for all verily held John to be a prophet. And they answered Jesus and say, We know not. And Jesus saith unto them, Neither tell I you by what authority I do these things."— MARK xi. 27–33 (R.V.).

THE question put to Jesus by the hierarchy of Jerusalem is recorded in all the synoptic Gospels. But in some respects the story is most pointed in the narrative of St. Mark. And it is natural that he, the historian especially of the energies of Christ, should lay stress upon a challenge addressed to Him, by reason of His masterful words and deeds. At the outset, he had recorded the astonishment of the people because Jesus taught with authority, because "Verily I say" replaced the childish and servile methods by which the scribe and the Pharisee sustained their most wilful innovations.

When first he relates a miracle, he tells how their wonder increased, because with authority Jesus commanded the unclean spirits and they obeyed, respecting

His self-reliant word " I command thee to come out," more than the most elaborate incantations and exorcisms. St. Mark's first record of collision with the priests was when Jesus carried His claim still farther, and said " The Son of man hath authority" (it is the same word) "on earth to forgive sins." Thus we find the Gospel quite conscious of what so forcibly strikes a careful modern reader, the assured and independent tone of Jesus; His bearing, so unlike that of a disciple or a commentator; His consciousness that the Scriptures themselves are they which testify of Him, and that only He can give the life which men think they possess in these. In the very teaching of lowliness Jesus exempts Himself, and forbids others to be Master and Lord, because these titles belong to Him.

Impressive as such claims appear when we awake to them, it is even more suggestive to reflect that we can easily read the Gospels and not be struck by them. We do not start when He bids all the weary to come to Him, and offers them rest, and yet declares Himself to be meek and lowly. He is meek and lowly while He makes such claims. His bearing is that of the highest rank, joined with the most perfect graciousness; His great claims never irritate us, because they are palpably His due, and we readily concede the astonishing elevation whence He so graciously bends down so low. And this is one evidence of the truth and power of the character which the Apostles drew.

How natural is this also, that immediately after Palm Sunday, when the people have hailed their Messiah, royal and a Saviour, and when He has accepted their homage, we find new indications of authority in His bearing and His actions. He promptly took them at their word. It was now that He wrought His only miracle of judgment, and although it was but the withering of a tree (since He came not to destroy men's lives but to save them), yet was there a dread symbolical sentence involved upon all barren and unfruitful men and Churches.   In the very act of triumphal entry, He solemnly pronounced judgment upon the guilty city which would not accept her King.

Arrived at the temple, He surveyed its abuses and defilements, and returned on the morrow (and so not spurred by sudden impulse, but of deliberate purpose), to drive out them that sold and bought.   Two years ago He had needed to scourge the intruders forth, but now they are overawed by His majesty, and obey His word.   Then, too, they were rebuked for making His Father's house a house of merchandise, but now it is His own—"My House," but degraded yet farther into a den of thieves.

But while traffic and pollution shrank away, misery and privation were attracted to Him; the blind and the lame came and were healed in the very temple; and the centre and rallying-place of the priests and scribes beheld His power to save.   This drove them to extremities.   He was carrying the war into the heart of their territories, establishing Himself in their stronghold, and making it very plain that since the people had hailed Him King, and He had responded to their acclaims, He would not shrink from whatever His view of that great office might involve.

While they watched, full of bitterness and envy, they were again impressed, as at the beginning, by the strange, autocratic, spontaneous manner in which He worked, making Himself the source of His blessings, as no prophet had ever done since Moses expiated so dearly the offence of saying, Must we fetch you water

out of the rock ?   Jesus acted after the fashion of Him
Who openeth His hands and satisfieth the desire of
every living thing.   Why did He not give the glory to
One above ?   Why did He not supplicate, nor invoke,
but simply bestow ?   Where were the accustomed words
of supplication, " Hear me, O Lord God, hear me," or,
" Where is the Lord God of Israel ? "

Here they discerned a flaw, a heresy; and they would
force Him either to make a fatal claim, or else to moderate His pretensions at their bidding, which would
promptly restore their lost influence and leadership.

Nor need we shrink from confessing that our Lord
was justly open to such reproach, unless He was indeed
Divine, unless He was deliberately preparing His followers for that astonishing revelation, soon to come,
which threw the Church upon her knees in adoration
of her God manifest in flesh.   It is hard to understand
how the Socinian can defend his Master against the
charge of encroaching on the rights and honours of
Deity, and (to borrow a phrase from a different connection) sitting down at the right hand of the Majesty of
God, whereas every priest standeth ministering.   If He
were a creature, He culpably failed to tell us the conditions upon which He received a delegated authority,
and the omission has made His Church ever since
idolatrous.   It is one great and remarkable lesson
suggested by this verse : if Jesus were not Divine,
what was He ?

Thus it came to pass, in direct consequence upon
the events which opened the great week of the triumph
and the cross of Jesus, that the whole rank and
authority of the temple system confronted Him with a
stern question.   They sat in Moses' seat.   They were
entitled to examine the pretensions of a new and

aspiring teacher. They had a perfect right to demand " Tell us by what authority thou doest these things." The works are not denied, but the source whence they flow is questioned.

After so many centuries, the question is fresh to-day. For still the spirit of Christ is working in His world, openly, palpably, spreading blessings far and wide. It is exalting multitudes of ignoble lives by hopes that are profound, far-reaching, and sublime. When savage realms are explored, it is Christ Who hastens thither with His gospel, before the trader in rum and gunpowder can exhibit the charms of a civilization without a creed. In the gloomiest haunts of disease and misery, madness, idiotcy, orphanage, and vice, there is Christ at work, the good Samaritan, pouring oil and wine into the gaping wounds of human nature, acting quite upon His own authority, careless who looks askance, not asking political economy whether genuine charity is pauperisation, nor questioning the doctrine of development, whether the progress of the race demands the pitiless rejection of the unfit, and selection only of the strongest specimens for survival. That iron creed may be natural; but if so, ours is supernatural, it is a law of spirit and life, setting us free from that base and selfish law of sin and death. The existence and energy of Christian forces in our modern world is indisputable : never was Jesus a more popular and formidable claimant of its crown ; never did more Hosannas follow Him into the temple. But now as formerly His credentials are demanded : what is His authority and how has He come by it ?

Now we say of modern as of ancient inquiries, that they are right ; investigation is inevitable and a duty. But see how Jesus dealt with those men of old.

Let us not misunderstand Him. He did not merely set one difficulty against another, as if we should start some scientific problem, and absolve ourselves from the duty of answering any inquiry until science had disposed of this. Doubtless it is logical enough to point out that all creeds, scientific and religious alike, have their unsolved problems. But the reply of Jesus was not a dexterous evasion, it went to the root of things, and, therefore, it stands good for time and for eternity. He refused to surrender the advantage of a witness to whom He was entitled : He demanded that all the facts and not some alone should be investigated. In truth their position bound His interrogators to examine His credentials ; to do so was not only their privilege but their duty. But then they must begin at the beginning. Had they performed this duty for the Baptist ? Who or what was that mysterious, lonely, stern preacher of righteousness who had stirred the national heart sc profoundly, and whom all men still revered ? They themselves had sent to question him, and his answer was notorious : he had said that he was sent before the Christ ; he was only a voice, but a voice which demanded the preparation of a way before the Lord Himself, Who was approaching, and a highway for our God. What was the verdict of these investigators upon that great movement ? What would they make of the decisive testimony of the Baptist ?

As the perilous significance of this consummate rejoinder bursts on their crafty intelligence, as they recoil confounded from the exposure they have brought upon themselves, St. Mark tells how the question was pressed home, " Answer Me ! " But they dared not call John an impostor, and yet to confess him was to authenticate the seal upon our Lord's credentials. And Jesus is palpably within His rights in refusing to be questioned of such authorities as these. Yet immediately afterwards, with equal skill and boldness, He declared Himself, and yet defied their malice, in the story of the lord of a vineyard, who had vainly sent many servants to claim its fruit, and at the last sent his beloved son.

Now apply the same process to the modern opponents of the faith, and it will be found that multitudes of their assaults on Christianity imply the negation of what they will not and dare not deny. Some will not believe in miracles because the laws of nature work uniformly. But their uniformity is undisturbed by human operations; the will of man wields, without cancelling, these mighty forces which surround us. And why may not the will of God do the same, if there be a God? Ask them whether they deny His existence, and they will probably declare themselves Agnostics, which is exactly the ancient answer, "We cannot tell." Now as long as men avow their ignorance of the existence or non-existence of a Deity, they cannot assert the impossibility of miracles, for miracles are simply actions which reveal God, as men's actions reveal their presence.

Again, a demand is made for such evidence, to establish the faith, as cannot be had for any fact beyond the range of the exact sciences. We are asked, Why should we stake eternity upon anything short of demonstration? Yet it will be found that the objector is absolutely persuaded, and acts on his persuasion of many "truths which never can be proved"—of the fidelity of his wife and children, and above all, of the difference between right and wrong. That is a fundamental principle: deny it, and society becomes impossible. And yet sceptical theories are widely diffused

which really, though unconsciously, sap the very
foundations of morality, or assert that it is not from
heaven but of men, a mere expediency, a prudential
arrangement of society.

Such arguments may well "fear the people," for the
instincts of mankind know well that all such explanations of conscience do really explain it away.

And it is quite necessary in our days, when religion
is impugned, to see whether the assumptions of its
assailants would not compromise time as well as eternity,
and to ask, What think ye of all those fundamental
principles which sustain the family, society, and the
state, while they bear testimony to the Church of
Christ.

CHAPTER XII.

THE HUSBANDMEN.

"**And He** began to speak unto them in parables. A man planted a vineyard, and set a hedge about it, and digged a pit for the wine-press, and built a tower, and let it out to husbandmen, and went into another country. And at the season he sent to the husbandmen a servant, that he might receive from the husbandmen of the fruits of the vineyard. And they took him, and beat him, and sent him away empty. And again he sent unto them another servant : and him they wounded in the head, and handled shamefully. And he sent another; and him they killed : and many others ; beating some, and killing some. He had yet one, a beloved son : he sent him last unto them, saying, They will reverence my son. But those husbandmen said among themselves, This is the heir ; come, let us kill him, and the inheritance shall be ours. And they took him, and killed him, and cast him forth out of the vineyard. What, therefore, will the Lord of the vineyard do ? He will come and destroy the husbandmen, and will give the vineyard unto others. Have ye not read even this Scripture :

> The stone which the builders rejected,
> The same was made the head of the corner :
> This was from the Lord,
> And it is marvellous in our eyes ?

And they sought to lay hold on Him ; and they feared the multitude ; for they perceived that He spake the parable against them : and they left Him, and went away.—MARK xii. 1-12 (R.V.).

THE rulers of His people have failed to make Jesus responsible to their inquisition. He has exposed the hollowness of their claim to investigate His commission, and formally refused to tell them by what authority He did these things. But what He would not say for an unjust cross-examination, He proclaimed to all docile hearts ; and the skill which disarmed His enemies is not more wonderful than that which in their hearing answered their question, yet left them no room for accusation. This was achieved by speaking to them in parables. The indifferent might hear and not perceive : the keenness of malice would surely understand but could not easily impeach a simple story ; but to His own followers it would be given to know the mysteries of the kingdom of God.

His first words would be enough to arouse attention. The psalmist had told how God brought a vine out of Egypt, and cast out the heathen and planted it. Isaiah had carried the image farther, and sung of a vineyard in a very fruitful hill. The Well-beloved, Whose it was, cleared the ground for it, and planted it with the choicest vine, and built a tower, and hewed out a wine-press, and looked that it should bring forth grapes, but it had brought forth wild grapes. Therefore He would lay it waste. This well-known and recognized type the Lord now adopted, but modified it to suit His purpose. As in a former parable the sower slept and rose, and left the earth to bring forth fruit of itself, so in this, the Lord of the vineyard let it out to husbandmen and went into a far country. This is our Lord's own explanation of that silent time in which no special interpositions asserted that God was nigh, no prophecies were heard, no miracles startled the careless. It was the time when grace already granted should have been peacefully ripening. Now we live in such a period. Unbelievers desire a sign. Impatient believers argue that if our Master is as near us as ever, the same portents must attest His presence ; and, therefore, they recognise the gift of tongues in hysterical clamour, and stake the honour of religion upon faith-healing, and those various obscure phenomena which the annals of every fanaticism can rival. But the sober Christian understands that, even as the Lord of the vineyard went into another country, so Christ His Son (Who in spiritual communion is ever with His people) in another sense has gone into a far country to receive a kingdom and to return. In the interval, marvels would be simply an anachronism. The best present evidence of the faith lies in the superior fruitfulness of the vineyard He has planted, in the steady advance to rich maturity of the vine He has imported from another clime.

At this point Jesus begins to add a new significance to the ancient metaphor. The husbandmen are mentioned. Men there were in the ancient Church, who were specially responsible for the culture of the vineyard. As He spoke, the symbol explained itself. The imposing array of chief priests and scribes and elders stood by, who had just claimed as their prerogative that He should make good His commission to their scrutiny; and none would be less likely to mistake His meaning than these self-conscious lovers of chief seats in the synagogues. The structure of the parable, therefore, admits their official rank, as frankly as when Jesus bade His disciples submit to their ordinances because they sit in Moses' seat. But He passes on, easily and as if unconsciously, to record that special messengers from heaven had, at times, interrupted the self-indulgent quietude of the husbandmen. Because the fruit of the vineyard had not been freely rendered, a bondservant was sent to demand it. The epithet implies that the messenger was lower in rank, although his direct mission gave him authority even over the keepers of the vineyard. It expresses exactly the position of the prophets, few of them of priestly rank, some of them very

humble in extraction, and very rustic in expression,
but all sent in evil days to faithless husbandmen, to
remind them that the vineyard was not their own, and
to receive the fruits of righteousness.   Again and again
the demand is heard, for He sent "many others;" and
always it is rejected with violence, which sometimes
rises to murder.   As they listened, they must have felt
that all this was true, that while prophet after prophet
had come to a violent end, not one had seen the official
hierarchy making common cause with him.   And they
must also have felt how ruinous was this rejoinder to
their own demand that the people should forsake a
teacher when they rejected him.   Have any of the
rulers or of the Pharisees believed on Him ? was their
scornful question.   But the answer was plain, As long
as they built the sepulchres of the prophets, and gar-
nished the tombs of the righteous, and said, If we had
been in the days of our fathers, we would not have
been partakers with them in the blood of the prophets,
they confessed that men could not blindly follow a
hierarchy merely as such, since they were not the official successors of the prophets but of those who slew
them.   The worst charge brought against them was
only that they acted according to analogy, and filled up
the deeds of their fathers.   It had always been the
same.

The last argument of Stephen, which filled his judges
with madness, was but the echo of this great impeachment.   Which of the prophets did not your fathers
persecute ? and they killed them which showed
before of the coming of the Righteous One, of Whom
ye have now become the betrayers and murderers.

That last defiance of heaven, which Stephen thus
denounced, his Master distinctly foretold.   And He

21

added the appalling circumstance, that however they
might deceive themselves and sophisticate their conscience, they really knew Him Who He was. They
felt, at the very least, that into His hands should pass
all the authority and power they had so long monopolized : " This is the Heir; come let us kill Him and the
inheritance shall be ours." If there were no more, the
utterance of these words put forth an extraordinary claim.

All that should have been rendered up to heaven and
was withheld, all that previous messengers had demanded
on behalf of God without avail, all " the inheritance "
which these wicked husbandmen were intercepting, all
this Jesus announces to be His own, while reprehending
the dishonesty of any other claim upon it. And as a
matter of fact, if Jesus be not Divine, He has intercepted
more of the worship due to the Eternal, has attracted
to Himself more of the homage of the loftiest and profoundest minds, than any false teacher within the pale
of monotheism has ever done. It is the bounden duty
of all who revere Jesus even as a teacher, of all who have
eyes to see that His coming was the greatest upward
step in the progress of humanity, to consider well what
was implied, when, in the act of blaming the usurpers
of the heritage of God, Jesus declared that inheritance
to be His own. But this is not all, though it is what
He declares that the husbandmen were conscious of.
The parable states, not only that He is heir, but heir
by virtue of His special relationship to the Supreme.
Others are bondservants or husbandmen, but He is the
Son. He does not inherit as the worthiest and most
obedient, but by right of birth ; and His Father, in the
act of sending Him, expects even these bloodstained
outlaws to reverence His Son. In such a phrase, applied to such criminals, we are made to feel the lofty

rank alike of the Father and His Son, which ought to have overawed even them. And when we read that "He had yet one, a beloved Son," it seems as if the veil of eternity were uplifted, to reveal a secret and awful intimacy, of which, nevertheless, some glimmering consciousness should have controlled the most desperate heart.

But they only reckoned that if they killed the Heir, the inheritance would become their own. It seems the wildest madness, that men should know and feel Who He was, and yet expect to profit by desecrating His rights. And yet so it was from the beginning. If Herod were not fearful that the predicted King of the Jews was indeed born, the massacre of the Innocents was idle. If the rulers were not fearful that this counsel and work was of God, they would not, at Gamaliel's bidding, have refrained from the Apostles. And it comes still closer to the point to observe that, if they had attached no importance, even in their moment of triumph, to the prediction of His rising from the dead, they would not have required a guard, nor betrayed the secret recognition which Jesus here exposes. The same blind miscalculation is in every attempt to obtain profit or pleasure by means which are known to transgress the laws of the all-beholding Judge of all. It is committed every day, under the pressure of strong temptation, by men who know clearly that nothing but misery can result. So true is it that action is decided, not by a course of logic in the brain, but by the temperament and bias of our nature as a whole. We need not suppose that the rulers roundly spoke such words as these, even to themselves. The infamous motive lurked in ambush, too far in the back ground of the mind perhaps even for consciousness. But it was there, and it affected their decision, as lurking passions and self-interests always will, as surely as iron deflects the compass. "They caught Him and killed Him," said the unfaltering lips of their victim. And He added a circumstance of pain which we often overlook, but to which the great minister of the circumcision was keenly sensitive, and often reverted, the giving Him up to the Gentiles, to a death accursed among the Jews; "they cast Him forth out of the vineyard."

All evil acts are based upon an overestimate of the tolerance of God. He had seemed to remain passive while messenger after messenger was beaten, stoned, or slain. But now that they had filled up the iniquity of their fathers, the Lord of the vineyard would come in person to destroy them, and give the vineyard to others. This last phrase is strangely at variance with the notion that the days of a commissioned ministry are over, as, on the other hand, the whole parable is at variance with the notion that a priesthood can be trusted to sit in exclusive judgment upon doctrine for the Church.

At this point St. Mark omits an incident so striking, although small, that its absence is significant. The by-standers said, "God forbid!" and when the horrified exclamation betrayed their consciousness of the position, Jesus was content, without a word, to mark their self-conviction by His searching gaze. "He looked upon them." The omission would be unaccountable if St. Mark were simply a powerful narrator of graphic incidents; but it is explained when we think that for him the manifestation of a mighty Personage was all in all, and the most characteristic and damaging admissions of the hierarchy were as nothing compared with a word of his Lord. Thereupon he goes straight

on to record that, besides refuting their claim by the
history of the past, and asserting His own supremacy
in a phrase at once guarded in form and decisive in
import, Jesus also appealed to Scripture.   It was
written that by special and marvellous interposition of
the Lord a stone which the recognized builders had
rejected should crown the building.   And the quotation
was not only decisive as showing that their rejection
could not close the controversy; it also compensated,
with a promise of final v'·tory, the ominous words in
which their malice had seemed to do its worst.   Jesus
often predicted His death, but He never despaired of
His kingdom.

No wonder that the rulers sought to arrest Him,
and perceived that He penetrated and despised their
schemes.   And their next device is a natural outcome
from the fact that they feared the people, but did not
discontinue their intrigues; for this was a crafty and
dangerous attempt to estrange from Him the admiring
multitude.

THE TRIBUTE MONEY.

"And they send unto Him certain of the Pharisees and of the Herodians, that they might catch Him in talk.   And when they were come,
they say unto Him, Master, we know that Thou art true, and carest
not for any one : for Thou regardest not the person of men, but of a
truth teachest the way of God : Is it lawful to give tribute unto Cæsar,
or not?   Shall we give, or shall we not give?   But He, knowing their
hypocrisy, said unto them, Why tempt ye Me? bring Me a penny,
that I may see it.   And they brought it.   And He saith unto them,
Whose is this image and superscription?   And they said unto Him,
Cæsar's.   And Jesus said unto them, Render unto Cæsar the things
that are Cæsar's, and unto God the things that are God's.   And they
marvelled greatly at Him."—MARK xii. 13–17 (R.V.).

THE contrast is very striking between this incident and
the last.   Inst·ad of a challenge, Jesus is respectfully

consulted ; and instead of a formal concourse of the authorities of His religion, He is Himself the authority to Whom a few perplexed people profess to submit their difficulty. Nevertheless, it is a new and subtle effort of the enmity of His defeated foes. They have sent to Him certain Pharisees who will excite the popular indignation if He yields anything to the foreigner, and Herodians who will, if He refuses, bring upon Him the colder and deadlier vengeance of Rome. They flatter, in order to stimulate, that fearless utterance which must often have seemed to them so rash : " We know that Thou art true, and carest not for any one, for Thou regardest not the person of men, but of a truth teachest the way of God." And they appeal to a higher motive by representing the case to be one of practical and personal urgency. "Shall we give, or shall we not give ? "

Never was it more necessary to join the wisdom of the serpent to the innocence of the dove, for it would seem that He must needs answer directly, and that no direct answer can fail to have the gravest consequences. But in their eagerness to secure this menacing position, they have left one weak point in the attack. They have made the question altogether a practical one. The abstract doctrine of the right to drive out a foreign power, of the limits of authority and freedom, they have not raised. It is simply a question of the hour, Shall we give or shall we not give ?

And Jesus baffled them by treating it as such. There was no longer a national coinage, except only of the half shekel for the temple tax. When He asked them for a smaller coin, they produced a Roman penny stamped with the effigy of Cæsar. Thus they confessed the use of the Roman currency. Now since they

accepted the advantages of subjugation, they ought
also to endure its burdens: since they traded as
Roman subjects, they ought to pay the Roman tribute.
Not He had preached submission, but they had avowed
it; and any consequent unpopularity would fall not
upon Him but them. They had answered their own
question. And Jesus laid down the broad and simple
rule, "Render (pay back) unto Cæsar the things that
are Cæsar's, and unto God the things that are God's.
And they marvelled greatly at Him."   No wonder they
marvelled, for it would be hard to find in all the records
of philosophy so ready and practical a device to baffle
such cunning intriguers, such keenness in One Whose
life was so far removed from the schools of worldly
wisdom, joined with so firm a grasp on principle, in an
utterance so brief, yet going down so far to the roots
of action.

Now the words of Jesus are words for all time;
even when He deals with a question of the hour, He
treats it from the point of view of eternal fitness and
duty; and this command to render unto Cæsar the
things which are Cæsar's has become the charter of
the state against all usurpations of tyrannous eccle-
siastics. A sphere is recognized in which obedience
to the law is a duty to God. But it is absurd to pretend that Christ taught blind and servile obedience to
all tyrants in all circumstances, for this would often
make it impossible to obey the second injunction, and
to render unto God the things which are God's,—a
clause which asserts in turn the right of conscience
and the Church against all secular encroachments.
The point to observe is, that the decision of Jesus is
simply an inference, a deduction. St. Matthew has
inserted the word "therefore," and it is certainly

implied : render unto Cæsar the things which you confess to be his own, which bear his image upon their
face.

Can we suppose that no such inference gives point
to the second clause ? It would then become, like too
many of our pious sayings, a mere supplement, inappro-
priate, however excellent, a make weight, and a plati-
tude. No example of such irrelevance can be found
in the story of our Lord. When, finding the likeness
of Cæsar on the coin, He said, Render, therefore, unto
Cæsar the things that are Cæsar's, and unto God the
things that are God's, He at least suggested that the
reason for both precepts ran parallel, and the image of
the higher and heavenlier Monarch could be found on
what He claims of us. And it is so. He claims all
we have and all we are. "The earth is the Lord's,
and the fulness thereof:" and "I have made thee,
thou art Mine." And for us and ours alike the argument holds good. All the visible universe bears deeply
stamped into its substance His image and superscription. The grandeur of mountains and stars, the
fairness of violet and harebell, are alike revelations of
the Creator. The heavens declare His glory: the
firmament showeth His handiwork : the earth is full of
His riches: all the discoveries which expand our
mastery over nature and disease, over time and space,
are proofs of His wisdom and goodness, Who laid the
amazing plan which we grow wise by tracing out.
Find a corner on which contrivance and benevolence
have not stamped the royal image, and we may doubt
whether that bleak spot owes Him tribute. But no
desert is so blighted, no solitude so forlorn.

And we should render unto God the things which
are God's, seeing His likeness in His world. " For the

invisible things of Him since the creation of the world are clearly seen, being perceived through the things which are made, even His everlasting power and divinity."

And if most of all He demands the love, the heart of man, here also He can ask, "Whose image and super-scription is this?" For in the image of God made He man. It is sometimes urged that this image was quite effaced when Adam fell. But it was not to protect the unfallen that the edict was spoken "Whoso sheddeth man's blood, by man shall his blood be shed, for in the image of God made He man." He was not an unfallen man of whom St. Paul said that he "ought not to have his head veiled, forasmuch as he is the image and glory of God;" neither were they unfallen, of whom St. James said, "We curse men which are made after the likeness of God" (Gen. ix. 6; 1 Cor. xi. 7; James iii. 9). Common men, for whom the assassin lurks, who need instruction how to behave in church, and whom others scorn and curse, these bear upon them an awful likeness; and even when they refuse tribute to their king, He can ask them, Whose is this image?

We see it in the intellect, ever demanding new worlds to conquer, overwhelming us with its victories over time and space. "In apprehension how like a God." Alas for us! if we forget that the Spirit of knowledge and wisdom is no other than the Spirit of the Lord God.

We see this likeness far more in our moral nature. It is true that sin has spoiled and wasted this, yet there survives in man's heart, as nowhere else in our world, a strange sympathy with the holiness and love of God. No other of His attributes has the same power to thrill

us. Tell me that He lit the stars and can quench them
with a word, and I reverence, perhaps I fear Him ; yet
such power is outside and beyond my sphere ; it fails to
touch me, it is high, I cannot attain unto it. Even the
rarer human gifts, the power of a Czar, the wisdom of
Bacon, are thus beyond me, I am unkindléd, they do
not find me out. But speak of holiness, even the
stainless holiness of God, undefiled through all eternity,
and you shake the foundations of my being. And
why does the reflection that God is pure humble me
more than the knowledge that God is omnipotent ?
Because it is my spiritual nature which is most conscious of the Divine image, blurred and defaced
indeed, but not obliterated yet. Because while I
listen I am dimly conscious of my birthright, my
destiny, that I was born to resemble this, and all
is lost if I come short of it. Because every child and
every sinner feels that it is more possible for him to
be like his God than like Newton, or Shakespere, or
Napoleon. Because the work of grace is to call in
the worn and degraded coinage of humanity, and, as the
mint restamps and reissues the pieces which have
grown thin and worn, so to renew us after the image
of Him that created us.

CHRIST AND THE SADDUCEES.

"And there come unto Him Sadducees, which say that there is no
resurrection : and they asked Him, saying, Master, Moses wrote unto
us, If a man's brother die, and leave a wife behind him, and leave no
child, that his brother should take his wife, and raise up seed unto his
brother. There were seven brethren : and the first took a wife, and
dying left no seed ; and the second took her, and died, leaving no seed
behind him ; and the third likewise : and the seven left no seed. Last
of all the woman also died. In the resurrection whose wife shall she
be of them ? for the seven had her to wife. Jesus said unto them, Is it

not for this cause that ye err, that ye know not the Scriptures, nor the power of God? For when they shall rise from the dead, they neither marry, nor are given in marriage ; but are as angels in heaven. But as touching the dead, that they are raised; have ye not read in the book of Moses, in *the place concerning* the Bush, how God spake unto him, saying, I *am* the God of Abraham, and the God of Isaac, and the God of Jacob? He is not the God of the dead, but of the living : ye do greatly err."—MARK xii. 18–27 (R.V.).

CHRIST came that the thoughts of many hearts might be revealed. And so it was, that when He had silenced the examination of the hierarchy, and baffled their craft, the Sadducees were tempted to assail Him. Like the rationalists of every age, they stood coldly aloof from popular movements, and we seldom find them interfering with Christ or His followers, until their energies were roused by the preaching of His Resurrection, so directly opposed to their fundamental doctrines.

Their appearance now is extremely natural. The repulse of every other party left them the only champions of orthodoxy against the new movement, with every-thing to win by success, and little to lose by failure. There is a tone of quiet and confident irony in their interrogation, well befitting an upper-class group, a secluded party of refined critics, rather than practical teachers with a mission to their fellow-men. They break utterly new ground by raising an abstract and subtle question, a purely intellectual problem, but one which reduced the doctrine of a resurrection to an absurdity, if only their premises can be made good. And this peculiarity is often overlooked in criticism upon our Lord's answer. Its intellectual subtlety was only the adoption by Christ of the weapons of his adver-saries. But at the same time, He lays great and special stress upon the authority of Scripture, in this encounter with the party which least acknowledged it.

Their objection, stated in its simplest form, is the complication which would result if the successive ties for which death makes room must all revive together when death is abolished. If a woman has married a second time, whose wife shall she be? But their statement of the case is ingenious, not only because they push the difficulty to an absurd and ludicrous extent, but much more so because they base it upon a Divine ordinance. If there be a Resurrection, Moses must answer for all the confusion that will ensue, for Moses gave the commandment, by virtue of which a woman married seven times. No offspring of any union gave it a special claim upon her future life. "In the Resurrection, whose wife shall she be of them?" they ask, conceding with a quiet sarcasm that this absurd event must needs occur.

For these controversialists the question was solely of the physical tie, which had made of twain one flesh. They had no conception that the body can be raised otherwise than as it perished, and they rightly enough felt certain that on such a resurrection woeful complications must ensue.

Now Jesus does not rebuke their question with such stern words as He had just employed to others, "Why tempt ye me, ye hypocrites?" They were doubtless sincere in their conviction, and at least they had not come in the disguise of perplexed inquirers and almost disciples. He blames them, but more gently: "Is it not for this cause that ye err, because ye know not the Scriptures, nor the power of God?" They could not know one and not the other, but the boastful wisdom of this world, so ready to point a jibe by quoting Moses, had never truly grasped the meaning of the writer it appealed to.

Jesus, it is plain, does not quote Scripture only as having authority with His opponents : He accepts it heartily : He declares that human error is due to ignorance of its depth and range of teaching ; and He recognizes the full roll of the sacred books "the Scriptures."

It has rightly been said, that none of the explicit statements, commonly relied upon, do more to vindicate for Holy Writ the authority of our Lord, than this simple incidental question.

Jesus proceeded to restate the doctrine of the Resurrection and then to prove it ; and the more His brief words are pondered, the more they will expand and deepen.

St. Paul has taught us that the dead in Christ shall rise first (1 Thess. iv. 16). Of such attainment it is written, Blessed and holy is he that hath part in the first Resurrection (Rev. xx. 6).

Now since among the lost there could be no question of family ties, and consequent embarrassments, Jesus confines His statement to these happy ones, of whom the Sadducee could think no better than that their new life should be a reproduction of their existence here,— a theory which they did wisely in rejecting. He uses the very language taken up afterwards by His apostle, and says, "When they shall rise from the dead." And He asserts that marriage is at an end, and they are as the angels in heaven. Here is no question of the duration of pure and tender human affection, nor do these words compromise in any degree the hopes of faithful hearts, which cling to one another. Surely we may believe that in a life which is the outcome and resultant of this life, as truly as the grain is of the seed, in a life also where nothing shall be forgotten, but on the contrary we shall know what we know not now, there, tracing back the flood of their immortal energies to obscure fountains upon earth, and seeing all that each has owed half unconsciously to the fidelity and wisdom of the other, the true partners and genuine helpmeets of this world shall for ever drink some peculiar gladness, each from the other's joy. There is no reason why the close of formal unions which include the highest and most perfect friendships, should forbid such friendships to survive and flourish in the more kindly atmosphere of heaven.

What Christ asserts is simply the dissolution of the tie, as an inevitable consequence of such a change in the very nature of the blessed ones as makes the tie incongruous and impossible. In point of fact, marriage as the Sadducee thought of it, is but the counterpoise of death, renewing the face which otherwise would disappear, and when death is swallowed up, it vanishes as an anachronism. In heaven "they are as the angels," the body itself being made "a spiritual body," set free from the appetites of the flesh, and in harmony with the glowing aspirations of the Spirit, which now it weighs upon and retards. If any would object that to be as the angels is to be without a body, rather than to possess a spiritual body, it is answer enough that the context implies the existence of a body, since no person ever spoke of a resurrection of the soul. Moreover it is an utterly unwarrantable assumption that angels are wholly without substance. Many verses appear to imply the opposite, and the cubits of measurement of the New Jerusalem were "according to the measure of a man, that is of an angel" (Rev. xxi. 17), which seems to assert a very curious similarity indeed.

The objection of the Sadducees was entirely obviated, therefore by the broader, bolder, and more spiritual view of a resurrection which Jesus taught. And by far the greater part of the cavils against this same doctrine which delight the infidel lecturer and popular essayist of to-day would also die a natural death, if the free and spiritual teaching of Jesus, and its expansion by St. Paul, were understood. But we breathe a wholly different air when we read the speculations even of so great a thinker as St. Augustine, who supposed that we should rise with bodies somewhat greater than our present ones, because all the hair and nails we ever trimmed away must be diffused throughout the mass, lest they should produce deformity by their excessive proportions (*De Civitate Dei*, xxii. 19). To all such speculation, he who said, To every seed his own body, says, Thou fool, thou sowest not that body that shall be. But though Jesus had met these questions, it did not follow that His doctrine was true, merely because a certain difficulty did not apply. And, therefore, He proceeded to prove it by the same Moses to whom they had appealed, and whom Jesus distinctly asserts to be the author of the book of Exodus. God said, " I am the God of Abraham, and the God of Isaac, and the God of Jacob. He is not the God of the dead, but of the living : ye do greatly err."

The argument is not based upon the present tense of the verb *to be* in this assertion, for in the Greek the verb is not expressed. In fact the argument is not a verbal one at all ; or else it would be satisfied by the doctrine of the immortality of the spirit, and would not establish any resurrection of the body. It is based upon the immutability of God, and, therefore, the imperishability of all that ever entered into vital and real relationship with Him. To cancel such a relationship would introduce a change into the Eternal. And Moses,

to whom they appealed, had heard God expressly
proclaim Himself the God of those who had long since
passed out of time.   It was, therefore, clear that His
relationship with them lived on, and this guaranteed
that no portion, even the humblest, of their true
personality should perish.   Now the body is as real a
part of humanity, as the soul and spirit are, although a
much lowlier part.   And, therefore, it must not really die.

It is solemn to observe how Jesus, in this second
part of His argument, passes from the consideration of
the future of the blessed to that of all mankind; " as
touching the dead that they are raised."   With others
than the blessed, therefore, God has a real though a
dread relationship.   And it will prove hard to reconcile
this argument of Christ with the existence of any time
when any soul shall be extinguished.

" The body is for the Lord," said St. Paul, arguing
against the vices of the flesh, "and the Lord for the
body."   From these words of Christ he may well have
learned that profound and far-reaching doctrine, which
will never have done its work in the Church and in the
world, until whatever defiles, degrades, or weakens that
which the Lord has consecrated is felt to blaspheme
by implication the God of our manhood, unto Whom
all our life ought to be lived ; until men are no longer
dwarfed in mines, nor poisoned in foul air, nor massacred
in battle, men whose intimate relationship with God
the Eternal is of such a kind as to guarantee the
resurrection of the poor frames which we destroy.

How much more does this great proclamation frown
upon the sins by which men dishonour their own flesh.
" Know ye not," asked the apostle, carrying the same
doctrine to its utmost limit, " that your bodies are the
temples of the Holy Ghost ? "   So truly is God our God

THE DISCERNING SCRIBE.

"And one of the scribes came, and heard them questioning to-gether, and knowing that He had answered them well, asked Him, What commandment is the first of all? Jesus answered, The first is, Hear, O Israel; The Lord our God, the Lord is one : and thou shalt love the Lord thy God with all thy heart, and with all thy soul, and with all thy mind, and with all thy strength. The second is this, Thou shalt love thy neighbour as thyself. There is none other commandment greater than these. And the scribe said unto Him, Of a truth, Master, Thou hast well said that He is one ; and there is none other but He : and to love Him with all the heart, and with all the understanding, and with all the strength, and to love his neighbour as himself, is much more than all whole burnt offerings and sacrifices. And when Jesus saw that he answered discreetly, He said unto him, Thou art not far from the kingdom of God. And no man after that durst ask Him any question."—MARK xii. 28–34 (R.V.).

THE praise which Jesus bestowed upon this lawyer is best understood when we take into account the circumstances, the pressure of assailants with ensnaring questions, the sullen disappointment or palpable exasperation of the party to which the scribe belonged. He had probably sympathized in their hostility; and had come expecting and desiring the discomfiture of Jesus. But if so, he was a candid enemy; and as each new attempt revealed more clearly the spiritual insight, the self-possession and balanced wisdom of Him Who had been represented as a dangerous fanatic, his unfriendly opinion began to waver. For he too was at issue with popular views: he had learned in the Scriptures that God desireth not sacrifice, that incense might be an abomination to Him, and new moons and sabbaths things to do away with. And so, perceiving that He had answered them well, the scribe asked, upon his own account, a very different question, not rarely debated in their schools, and often

22

answered with grotesque frivolity, but which he felt
to go down to the very root of things.   Instead of
challenging Christ's authority, he tries His wisdom.
Instead of striving to entangle Him in dangerous
politics, or to assail with shallow ridicule the problems
of the life to come, he asks, What commandment is the
first of all ?   And if we may accept as complete this
abrupt statement of his interrogation, it would seem to
have been drawn from him by a sudden impulse, or
wrenched by an over-mastering desire, despite of reluctance and false shame.

The Lord answered him with great solemnity and
emphasis.   He might have quoted the commandment
only.   But He at once supported the precept itself and
also His own view of its importance by including the
majestic prologue, "Hear, O Israel; the Lord our God,
the Lord is one; and thou shalt love the Lord thy God
with all thy heart, and with all thy soul, and with all
thy mind, and with all thy strength."

The unity of God, what a massive and reassuring
thought !   Amid the debasements of idolatry, with its
deification of every impulse and every force, amid the
distractions of chance and change, seemingly so capri-
cious and even discordant, amid the complexities of the
universe and its phenomena, there is wonderful strength
and wisdom in the reflection that God is one.   All
changes obey His hand which holds the rein ; by Him
the worlds were made.   The exiled patriarch was
overwhelmed by the majesty of the revelation that his
fathers' God was God in Bethel even as in Beer-sheba :
it charmed away the bitter sense of isolation, it unsealed in him the fountains of worship and trust, and
sent him forward with a new hope of protection and
prosperity.   The unity of God, really apprehended, is

a basis for the human will to repose upon, and to become self-consistent and at peace. It was the parent of the fruitful doctrine of the unity of nature which underlies all the scientific victories of the modern world. In religion, St. Paul felt that it implies the equal treatment of all the human race, when he asked, "Is He the God of Jews only? Is He not the God of Gentiles also? Yea, of Gentiles also, if so be that God is one" (Rom iii. 29 R.V.). To be one, he seems to say, implies being universal also. And if it thus excludes the reprobation of races, it disproves equally that of individual souls, and all thought of such unequal and partial treatment as should inspire one with hope of indulgence in guilt, or with fear that his way is hid from the Lord.

But if this be true, if there be one fountain of all life and loveliness and joy, of all human tenderness and all moral glory, how are we bound to love Him. Every other affection should only deepen our adoring loyalty to Him Who gives it. No cold or formal service can meet His claim, Who gives us the power to serve. No, we must love Him. And as all our nature comes from Him, so must all be consecrated : that love must embrace all the affections of "heart and soul" panting after Him, as the hart after the waterbrooks; and all the deep and steady convictions of the "mind," musing on the work of His hand, able to give a reason for its faith; and all the practical homage of the "strength," living and dying to the Lord. How easy, then, would be the fulfilment of His commandments in detail, and how surely it would follow. All the precepts of the first table are clearly implied in this.

In such another commandment were summed up also the precepts which concerned our neighbour

When we love him as ourselves (neither exaggerating his claims beyond our own, nor allowing our own to trample upon his), then we shall work no ill to our neighbour, and so love shall fulfil the law. There is none other commandment greater than these.

The questioner saw all the nobility of this reply; and the disdain, the anger, and perhaps the persecution of his associates could not prevent him from an admiring and reverent repetition of the Saviour's words, and an avowal that all the ceremonial observances of Judaism were as nothing compared with this.

While he was thus judging, he was being judged. As he knew that Jesus had answered well, so Jesus saw that he answered discreetly; and in view of his unprejudiced judgment, his spiritual insight, and his frank approval of One Who was then despised and rejected, He said, Thou art not far from the kingdom of God. But he was not yet within it, and no man knows his fate.

Sad yet instructive it is to think that he may have won the approval of Christ, and heard His words, so full of discernment and of desire for his adherence, and yet never crossed the invisible and mysterious boundary which he then approached so nearly. But we also may know, and admire, and confess the greatness and goodness of Jesus, without forsaking all to follow Him.

His enemies had been defeated and put to shame, their murderous hate had been denounced, and the nets of their cunning had been rent like cobwebs; they had seen the heart of one of their own order kindled into open admiration, and they henceforth renounced as hopeless the attempt to conquer Jesus in debate. No man after that durst ask Him any questions.

He will now carry the war into their own country. It will be for them to answer Jesus.

DAVID'S LORD.

" And Jesus answered and said, as He taught in the temple, **How say the scribes that the Christ is the Son of David ?** David himself said in the Holy Spirit,—

> The Lord said unto my Lord,
> Sit Thou on my right hand,
> Till I make Thine enemies the footstool of Thy feet.

David himself calleth Him Lord ; and whence is He His son? And the common people heard Him gladly. And in His teaching He said, Beware of the scribes, which desire to walk in long robes, and *to have* salutations in the marketplaces, and chief seats in the synagogues, and chief places at feasts : they which devour widows' houses, and for a pretence make long prayers ; these shall receive greater condemnation. MARK xii. 35-40 (R.V.).

JESUS, having silenced in turn His official interrogators and the Sadducees, and won the heart of His honest questioner, proceeded to submit a searching problem to His assailants. Whose son was the Messiah ? And when they gave Him an obvious and shallow answer, He covered them with confusion publicly. The event is full of that dramatic interest which St. Mark is so well able to discern and reproduce. How is it then that he passes over all this aspect of it, leaves us ignorant of the defeat and even of the presence of the scribes, and free to suppose that Jesus stated the whole problem in one long question, possibly without an opponent at hand to feel its force ?

This is a remarkable proof that his concern was not really for the pictorial element in the story, but for the manifestation of the power of his Master, the " authority " which resounds through his opening chapters, the royalty which he exhibits at the close. To him the vital point is that Jesus, upon openly claiming to be the Christ, and repelling the vehement attacks which were made upon Him as such, proceeded to unfold the astonishing greatness which this implied; and that after asserting the unity of God and His claim upon all hearts, He demonstrated that the Christ was sharer of His throne.

The Christ, they said, was the Son of David, and this was not false: Jesus had wrought many miracles for suppliants who addressed Him by that title. But was it all the truth? How then did David call Him Lord? A greater than David might spring from among his descendants, and hold rule by an original and not merely an ancestral claim: He might not reign as a son of David. Yet this would not explain the fact that David, who died ages before His coming, was inspired to call Him *My* Lord. Still less would it satisfy the assertion that God had bidden Him sit beside Him on His throne. For the scribes there was a serious warning in the promise that His enemies should be made His footstool, and for all the people a startling revelation in the words which follow, and which the Epistle to the Hebrews has unfolded, making this Son of David a priest for ever, after another order than that of Aaron.

No wonder that the multitude heard with gladness teaching at once so original, so profound, and so clearly justified by Scripture.

But it must be observed how remarkably this question of Jesus follows up His conversation with the scribe. Then He had based the supreme duty of love to God upon the supreme doctrine of the Divine Unity. He now proceeds to show that the throne of Deity is not a lonely throne, and to demand, Whose Son is He Who shares it, and Whom David in Spirit accosts by the same title as his God?

St. Mark is now content to give the merest indication of the final denunciation with which the Lord turned His back upon the scribes of Jerusalem, as He previously broke with those of Galilee. But it is enough to show how utterly beyond compromise was the rupture. The people were to beware of them : their selfish objects were betrayed in their very dress, and their desire for respectful salutations and seats of honour. Their prayers were a pretence, and they devoured widows' houses, acquiring under the cloke of religion what should have maintained the friendless. But their affected piety would only bring upon them a darker doom.

It is a tremendous impeachment. None is entitled to speak as Jesus did, who is unable to read hearts as He did. And yet we may learn from it that mere softness is not the meekness He demands, and that, when sinister motives are beyond doubt, the spirit of Jesus is the spirit of burning.

There is an indulgence for the wrongdoer which is mere feebleness and half compliance, and which shares in the guilt of Eli. And there is a dreadful anger which sins not, the wrath of the Lamb.

THE WIDOW'S MITE.

"And He sat down over against the treasury, and beheld how the multitude cast money into the treasury : and many that were rich cast in much. And there came a poor widow, and she cast in two mites, which make a farthing. And He called unto Him His disciples, and said unto them, Verily I say unto you, This poor widow cast in more than all they which are casting into the treasury ; for they all did cast in of their superfluity ; but she of her want did cast in all that she had, *even* all her living."—MARK xii. 41-44 (R.V.).

WITH words of stern denunciation Jesus for ever left the temple. Yet He lingered, as if reluctant, in the outer court; and while the storm of His wrath was still resounding in all hearts, observed and pointed out an action of the lowliest beauty, a modest flower of Hebrew piety in the vast desert of formality. It was not too modest, however, to catch, even in that agitating hour, the eye of Jesus; and while the scribes were devouring widows' houses, a poor widow could still, with two mites which make a farthing, win honourable mention from the Son of God. Thus He ever observes realities among pretences, the pure flame of love amid the sour smoke which wreathes around it. What He saw was the last pittance, cast to a service which in reality was no longer God's, yet given with a noble earnestness, a sacrifice pure from the heart.

1. His praise suggests to us the unknown observation, the unsuspected influences which surround us. She little guessed herself to be the one figure, amid a glittering group and where many were rich, who really interested the all-seeing Eye. She went away again, quite unconscious that the Lord had converted her two mites into a perennial wealth of contentment for lowly hearts, and instruction for the Church, quite ignorant that she was approved of Messiah, and that her little gift was the greatest event of all her story. So are we watched and judged in our least conscious and our most secluded hours.

2. We learn St. Paul's lesson, that, " if the readiness is there, it is acceptable according as a man hath, and not according as he hath not."

In war, in commerce, in the senate, how often does an accident at the outset blight a career for ever. One is taken in the net of circumstances, and his clipped wings can never soar again. But there is no such disabling accident in religion. God seeth the heart.

The world was redeemed by the blighted and thwarted career of One Who would fain have gathered His own city under His wing, but was refused and frustrated. And whether we cast in much, or only possess two mites, an offering for the rich to mock, He marks, understands, and estimates aright.

And while the world only sees the quantity, He weighs the motive of our actions. This is the true reason why we can judge nothing before the time, why the great benefactor is not really pointed out by the splendid benefaction, and why many that are last shall yet be first, and the first last.

3. The poor widow gave not a greater proportion of her goods, she gave all ; and it has been often remarked that she had still, in her poverty, the opportunity of keeping back one half. But her heart went with her two mites. And, therefore, she was blessed. We may picture her return to her sordid drudgery, unaware of the meaning of the new light and peace which followed her, and why her heart sang for joy. We may think of the Spirit of Christ which was in her, leading her afterwards into the Church of Christ, an obscure and perhaps illiterate convert, undistinguished by any special gift, and only loved as the first Christians all loved each other. And we may think of her now, where the secrets of all hearts are made known, followed by myriads of the obscure and undistinguished whom her story has sustained and cheered, and by some who knew her upon earth, and were astonished to learn that this was she. Then let us ask ourselves, Is there any such secret of unobtrusive lowly service, born of love, which the future will associate with me ?

CHAPTER XIII.

THINGS PERISHING AND THINGS STABLE.

"And as He went forth out of the temple, one of His disciples saith unto Him, Master, behold, what manner of stones and what manner of buildings! And Jesus said unto him, Seest thou these great buildings? there shall not be left here one stone upon another, which shall not be thrown down. And as He sat on the Mount of Olives over against the temple, Peter and James and John and Andrew asked Him privately, Tell us, when shall these things be? and what *shall be* the sign when these things are all about to be accomplished? And Jesus began to say unto them, Take heed that no man lead you astray. Many shall come in My name, saying, I am *He;* and shall lead many astray. And when ye shall hear of wars and rumours of wars, be not troubled : *these things* must needs come to pass : but the end is not yet."—MARK xiii. 1–7 (R.V.).

NOTHING is more impressive than to stand before one of the great buildings of the world, and mark how the toil of man has rivalled the stability of nature, and his thought its grandeur. It stands up like a crag, and the wind whistles through its pinnacles as in a grove, and the rooks float and soar about its towers as they do among the granite peaks. Face to face with one of these mighty structures, man feels his own pettiness, shivering in the wind, or seeking a shadow from the sun, and thinking how even this breeze may blight or this heat fever him, and how at the longest he shall have crumbled into dust for ages, and his name, and possibly his race, have perished, while this same pile shall stretch the same long shadow across the plain.

No wonder that the great masters of nations have all delighted in building, for thus they saw their power, and the immortality for which they hoped, made solid, embodied and substantial, and it almost seemed as if they had blended their memory with the enduring fabric of the world.

Such a building, solid, and vast, and splendid, white with marble, and blazing with gold, was the temple which Jesus now forsook.   A little afterwards, we read that its Roman conqueror, whose race were the great builders of the world, in spite of the rules of war, and the certainty that the Jews would never remain quietly in subjection while it stood, " was reluctant to burn down so vast a work as this, since this would be a mischief to the Romans themselves, as it would be an ornament to their government while it lasted."

No wonder, then, that one of the disciples, who had seen Jesus weep for its approaching ruin, and who now followed His steps as He left it desolate, lingered, and spoke as if in longing and appeal, " Master, see what manner of stones, and what manner of buildings."

But to the eyes of Jesus all was evanescent as a bubble, doomed and about to perish : " Seest thou these great buildings, there shall not be left here one stone upon another that shall not be thrown down."

The words were appropriate to His solemn mood, for He had just denounced its guilt and flung its splendour from Him, calling it no longer " My house," nor " My Father's house," but saying, " Your house is left unto you desolate."   Little could all the solid strength of the very foundations of the world itself avail against the thunderbolt of God.   Moreover, it was a time when He felt most keenly the consecration, the approaching surrender of His own life. In such an hour no splendours distract the penetrating vision; all the world is brief and frail and hollow to the man who has consciously given himself to God. It was the fitting moment at which to utter such a prophecy.

But, as He sat on the opposite slope, and gazed back upon the towers that were to fall, His three favoured disciples and Andrew came to ask Him privately when should these things be, and what would be the sign of their approach.

It is the common assertion of all unbelievers that the prophecy which followed has been composed since what passes for its fulfilment. When Jesus was murdered, and a terrible fate befel the guilty city, what more natural than to connect the two events? And how easily would a legend spring up that the sufferer foretold the penalty? But there is an obvious and complete reply. The prediction is too mysterious, its outlines are too obscure; and the ruin of Jerusalem is too inexplicably complicated with the final visitation of the whole earth, to be the issue of any vindictive imagination working with the history in view.

We are sometimes tempted to complain of this obscurity. But in truth it is wholesome and designed. We need not ask whether the original discourse was thus ambiguous, or they are right who suppose that a veil has since been drawn between us and a portion of the answer given by Jesus to His disciples. We know as much as it is meant that we should know. And this at least is plain, that any process of conscious or unconscious invention, working backwards after Jerusalem fell, would have given us far more explicit predictions than we possess. And, moreover, that

what we lose in gratification of our curiosity, we gain
in personal warning to walk warily and vigilantly.

Jesus did not answer the question, When shall these
things be? But He declared, to men who wondered
at the overthrow of their splendid temple, that all
earthly splendours must perish. And He revealed to
them where true permanence may be discovered.
These are two of the central thoughts of the discourse,
and they are worthy of much more attention from its
students than they commonly receive, being overlooked
in the universal eagerness "to know the times and
the seasons." They come to the surface in the distinct
words, "Heaven and earth shall pass away, but My
words shall not pass away."

Now, if we are to think of this great prophecy as a
lurid reflection thrown back by later superstition on
the storm-clouds of the nation's fall, how shall we
account for its solemn and pensive mood, utterly free
from vindictiveness, entirely suited to Jesus as we
think of Him, when leaving for ever the dishonoured
shrine, and moving forward, as His meditations would
surely do, beyond the occasion which evoked them?
Not such is the manner of resentful controversialists,
eagerly tracing imaginary judgments. They are narrow,
and sharp, and sour.

1. The fall of Jerusalem blended itself, in the thought
of Jesus, with the catastrophe which awaits all that appears to be great and stable. Nation shall rise against
nation, and kingdom against kingdom, so that, although
armies set their bodies in the gap for these, and heroes
shed their blood like water, yet they are divided among
themselves and cannot stand. This prediction, we must
remember, was made when the iron yoke of Rome imposed quiet upon as much of the world as a Galilean

was likely to take into account, and, therefore, was by no means so easy as it may now appear to us.

Nature itself should be convulsed. Earthquakes should rend the earth, blight and famine should disturb the regular course of seed-time and harvest. And these perturbations should be the working out of a stern law, and the sure token of sorer woes to come, the beginning of pangs which should usher in another dispensation, the birth-agony of a new time. A little later, and the sun should be darkened, and the moon should withdraw her light, and the stars should " be falling " from heaven, and the powers that are in the heavens should be darkened. Lastly, the course of history should close, and the affairs of earth should come to an end, when the elect should be gathered together to the glorified Son of Man.

2. It was in sight of the ruin of all these things that He dared to add, My word shall not pass away.

Heresy should assail it, for many should come in the name of Christ, saying, I am He, and should lead many astray. Fierce persecutions should try His followers, and they should be led to judgment and delivered up. The worse afflictions of the heart would wring them, for brother should deliver up brother to death, and the father his child, and children should rise up against parents and cause them to be put to death. But all should be too little to quench the immortality bestowed upon His elect. In their sore need, the Holy Ghost should speak in them : when they were caused to be put to death, he that endureth to the end, the same shall be saved.

Now these words were treasured up as the utterances of One Who had just foretold His own approaching murder, and Who died accordingly amid circumstances full of horror and shame. Yet His followers rejoiced to think that when the sun grew dark, and the stars were falling, He should be seen in the clouds coming with great glory.

It is the reversal of human judgment : the announcement that all is stable which appears unsubstantial, and all which appears solid is about to melt like snow.

And yet the world itself has since grown old enough to know that convictions are stronger than empires, and truths than armed hosts. And this is the King of Truth. He was born and came into the world to bear witness to the truth, and every one that is of the truth heareth His voice. He is the Truth become vital, the Word which was with God in the beginning.

THE IMPENDING JUDGMENT.

" For nation shall rise against nation, and kingdom against kingdom ; there shall be earthquakes in divers places ; there shall be famines : these things are the beginning of travail. But take ye heed to yourselves : for they shall deliver you up to councils ; and in synagogues shall ye be beaten ; and before governors and kings shall ye stand for My sake, for a testimony unto them. And the gospel must first be preached unto all the nations. And when they lead you *to judgment,* and deliver you up, be not anxious beforehand what ye shall speak : but whatsoever shall be given you in that hour, that speak ye : for it is not ye that speak, but the Holy Ghost. And brother shall deliver up brother to death, and the father his child ; and children shall rise up against parents, and cause them to be put to death. And ye shall be hated of all men for My name's sake ; but he that endureth to the end, the same shall be saved. But when ye see the abomination of desolation standing where he ought not (let him that readeth understand), then let them that are in Judæa flee unto the mountains : and let him that is on the housetop not go down, nor enter in, to take anything out of his house : and let him that is in the field not return back to take his cloke."—MARK xiii. 8–16 (R.V.).

WHEN we perceive that one central thought in our Lord's discourse about the last things is the contrast between material things which are fleeting, and spiritual realities which abide, a question naturally arises, which ought not to be overlooked. Was the prediction itself anything more than a result of profound spiritual insight? Are we certain that prophecy in general was more than keenness of vision? There are flourishing empires now which perhaps a keen politician, and certainly a firm believer in retributive justice governing the world, must consider to be doomed. And one who felt the transitory nature of earthly resources might expect a time when the docks of London will resemble the lagoons of Venice, and the State which now predominates in Europe shall become partaker of the decrepitude Spain. But no such presage is a prophecy in the Christian sense. Even when suggested by religion, it does not claim any greater certainty than that of sagacious inference.

The general question is best met by pointing to such specific and detailed prophecies, especially concerning the Messiah, as the twenty-second Psalm, the fifty-third of Isaiah, and the ninth of Daniel.

But the prediction of the fall of Jerusalem, while we have seen that it has none of the minuteness and sharpness of an after-thought, is also too definite for a presentiment. The abomination which defiled the Holy Place, and yet left one last brief opportunity for hasty flight, the persecutions by which that catastrophe would be heralded, and the precipitating of the crisis for the elect's sake, were details not to be conjectured. So was the coming of the great retribution, the beginning of His kingdom within that generation, a limit which was foretold at least twice besides (Mark ix. 1 and xiv. 62), with which the "henceforth" in Matthew xxvi. 64 must be compared. And so was another circumstance which is not enough considered: the fact that between the fall of Jerusalem and the Second Coming, however long or short the interval, no second event of a similar character, so universal in its effect upon Christianity, so epoch-making, should intervene. The coming of the Son of man should be "in those days after that tribulation."

The intervening centuries lay out like a plain country between two mountain tops, and did not break the vista, as the eye passed from the judgment of the ancient Church, straight on to the judgment of the world. Shall we say then that Jesus foretold that His coming would follow speedily? and that He erred? Men have been very willing to bring this charge, even in the face of His explicit assertions. "After a long time the Lord of that servant cometh. . . While the bridegroom tarried they all slumbered and slept. . . . If that wicked servant shall say in his heart, My Lord delayeth His coming."

It is true that these expressions are not found in St. Mark. But instead of them stands a sentence so startling, so unique, that it has caused to ill-instructed orthodoxy great searchings of heart. At least, however, the flippant pretence that Jesus fixed an early date for His return, ought to be silenced when we read, "Of that day or that hour knoweth no one, not even the angels of heaven, nor the Son, but the Father."

These words are not more surprising than that He increased in wisdom; and marvelled at the faith of some, and the unbelief of others (Luke ii. 52; Matt. viii. 10; Mark vi. 6). They are involved in the great assertion, that He not only took the form of a servant, but emptied Himself (Phil. ii. 7). But they decide the question of the genuineness of the discourse; for when could

23

they have been invented ?   And they are to be taken
in connection with others, which speak of Him not
in His low estate, but as by nature and inherently,
the Word and the Wisdom of God ; aware of all that
the Father doeth ; and Him in Whom dwelleth all the
fulness of the Godhead bodily (John i. 1 ; Luke xi. 49 ;
John v. 20; Col. ii. 9).

But these were "the days of His flesh ;" and that
expression is not meant to convey that He has since
laid aside His body, for He says, "A spirit hath
not flesh . . . as ye see Me have" (Heb. v. 7 ;
Luke xxiv. 39).   It must therefore express the limitations, now removed, by which He once condescended to
be trammelled.   What forbids us, then, to believe that
His knowledge, like His power, was limited by a lowliness not enforced, but for our sakes chosen ; and that
as He could have asked for twelve legions of angels,
yet chose to be bound and buffeted, so He could have
known that day and hour, yet submitted to ignorance,
that He might be made like in all points to His
brethren ?   Souls there are for whom this wonderful
saying, "the Son knoweth not," is even more affecting
than the words, "The Son of man hath not where to
lay His head."

But now the climax must be observed which made
His ignorance more astonishing than that of the angels
in heaven.   The recent discourse must be remembered,
which had asked His enemies to explain the fact that
David called Him Lord, and spoke of God as occupying
no lonely throne.   And we must observe His emphatic
expression, that His return shall be that of the Lord
of the House (ver. 35), so unlike the temper which He
impressed on every servant, and clearly teaching the
Epistle to the Hebrews to speak of His fidelity as

that of a Son over His house, and to contrast it sharply with that of the most honourable servant (iii. 6).

It is plain, however, that Jesus did not fix, and renounced the power to fix, a speedy date for His second coming.   He checked the impatience of the early Church by insisting that none knew the time.

But He drew the closest analogy between that event and the destruction of Jerusalem, and required a like spirit in those who looked for each.

Persecution should go before them.   Signs would indicate their approach as surely as the budding of the fig tree told of summer.   And in each case the disciples of Jesus must be ready.   When the siege came, they should not turn back from the field into the city, nor escape from the housetop by the inner staircase. When the Son of man comes, their loins should be girt, and their lights already burning.   But if the end has been so long delayed, and if there were signs by which its approach might be known, how could it be the practical duty of all men, in all the ages, to expect it ?   What is the meaning of bidding us to learn from the fig tree her parable, which is the approach of summer when her branch becomes tender, and yet asserting that we know not when the time is, that it shall come upon us as a snare, that the Master will surely surprise us, but need not find us unprepared, because all the Church ought to be always ready ?

What does it mean, especially when we observe, beneath the surface, that our Lord was conscious of addressing more than that generation, since He declared to the first hearers, "What I say unto you I say unto all, Watch ?"   It is a strange paradox.   But yet the history of the Church supplies abundant proof that in no age has the expectation of the Second Advent disappeared, and the faithful have always been mocked by the illusion, or else keen to discern the fact, that He is near, even at the doors. It is not enough to reflect that, for each soul, dissolution has been the preliminary advent of Him who has promised to come again and receive us unto Himself, and the Angel of Death is indeed the Angel of the Covenant. It must be asserted that for the universal Church, the feet of the Lord have been always upon the threshold, and the time has been prolonged only because the Judge *standeth* at the door. The "birth pangs" of which Jesus spoke have never been entirely stilled. And the march of time has not been towards a far-off eternity, but along the margin of that mysterious ocean, by which it must be engulfed at last, and into which, fragment by fragment, the beach it treads is crumbling.

Now this necessity, almost avowed, for giving signs which should only make the Church aware of her Lord's continual nearness, without ever enabling her to assign the date of His actual arrival, is the probable explanation of what has been already remarked, the manner in which the judgment of Jerusalem is made to symbolize the final judgment. But this symbolism makes the warning spoken to that age for ever fruitful. As they were not to linger in the guilty city, so we are to let no earthly interests arrest our flight,—not to turn back, but promptly and resolutely to flee unto the everlasting hills. As they should pray that their flight through the mountains should not be in the winter, so should we beware of needing to seek salvation in the winter of the soul, when the storms of passion and appetite are wildest, when evil habits have made the road slippery under foot, and sophistry and selfwill have hidden the gulfs in a treacherous wreath of snow.

Heedfulness, a sense of surrounding peril and of the danger of the times, is meant to inspire us while we read. The discourse opens with a caution against heresy : " Take heed that no man deceive you." It goes on to caution them against the weakness of their own flesh " Take heed to yourselves, for they shall deliver you up." It bids them watch, because they know not when the time is. And the way to watchfulness is prayerfulness ; so that presently, in the Garden, when they could not watch with Him one hour, they were bidden to watch and pray, that they enter not into temptation.

So is the expectant Church to watch and pray. Nor must her mood be one of passive idle expectation, dreamful desire of the promised change, neglect of duties in the interval. The progress of all art and science, and even the culture of the ground, is said to have been arrested by the universal persuasion that the year One Thousand should see the return of Christ. The luxury of millennarian expectation seems even now to relieve some consciences from the active duties of religion. But Jesus taught His followers that on leaving His house, to sojourn in a far country, He regarded them as His servants still, and gave them every one his work. And it is the companion of that disciple to whom Jesus gave the keys, and to whom especially He said, " What, couldest thou not watch with Me one hour ? " St. Mark it is who specifies the command to the porter that he should watch. To watch is not to gaze from the roof across the distant roads. It is to have girded loins and a kindled lamp ; it is not measured by excited expectation, but by readiness. Does it seem to us that the world is no longer hostile, because persecution and torture are at an end ? That the need is over for a clear distinction between her and us? This very belief may prove that we are falling asleep. Never was there an age to which Jesus did not say Watch. Never one in which His return would be other than a snare to all whose life is on the level of the world.

Now looking back over the whole discourse, we come to ask ourselves, What is the spirit which it sought to breathe into His Church? Clearly it is that of loyal expectation of the Absent One. There is in it no hint, that because we cannot fail to be deceived without Him, therefore His infallibility and His Vicar shall for ever be left on earth. His place is empty until He returns. Whoever says, Lo, here is Christ, is a deceiver, and it proves nothing that he shall deceive many. When Christ is manifested again, it shall be as the blaze of lightning across the sky. There is perhaps no text in this discourse which directly assails the Papacy; but the atmosphere which pervades it is deadly alike to her claims, and to the instincts and desires on which those claims rely.

CHAPTER XIV.

THE CRUSE OF OINTMENT.

"Now after two days was *the feast of* the passover and the un-leavened bread : and the chief priests and the scribes sought how they might take Him with subtilty, and kill Him : for they said, Not during the feast, lest haply there shall be a tumult of the people. And while He was in Bethany in the house of Simon the leper, as He sat at meat, there came a woman having an alabaster cruse of ointment of spikenard very costly ; *and* she brake the cruse, and poured it over His head. But there were some that had indignation among themselves, *saying*, To what purpose hath this waste of the ointment been made ? For this ointment might have been sold for above three hundred pence, and given to the poor. And they murmured against her. But Jesus said, Let her alone ; why trouble ye her ? she hath wrought a good work on Me. For ye have the poor always with you, and whensoever ye will ye can do them good : but Me ye have not always. She hath done what she could : she hath anointed My body aforehand for the burying. And verily I say unto you, Wheresoever the gospel shall be preached throughout the whole world, that also which this woman hath done shall be spoken of for a memorial of her."—MARK xiv. 1-9 (R.V.).

PERFECTION implies not only the absence of blemishes, but the presence, in equal proportions, of every virtue and every grace. And so the perfect life is full of the most striking, and yet the easiest transitions. We have just read predictions of trial more startling and intense than any in the ancient Scripture. If we knew of Jesus only by the various reports of that discourse, we should think of a recluse like Elijah or the Baptist, and imagine that His disciples, with girded loins, should be more ascetic than St. Anthony. We are next shown Jesus at a supper gracefully accepting the graceful homage of a woman.

From St. John we learn that this feast was given six days before the passover. The other accounts postponed the mention of it, plainly because of an incident which occurred then, but is vitally connected with a decision arrived at somewhat later by the priests. Two days before the passover, the council finally determined that Jesus must be destroyed. They recognised all the dangers of that course. It must be done with subtlety; the people must not be aroused; and therefore they said, Not on the feast-day. It is remarkable, however, that at the very time when they so determined, Jesus clearly and calmly made to His disciples exactly the opposite announcement. "After two days the passover cometh, and the Son of man is delivered up to be crucified" (Matt. xxvi. 2). Thus we find at every turn of the narrative that their plans are over-ruled, and they are unconscious agents of a mysterious design, which their Victim comprehends and accepts. On one side, perplexity snatches at all base expedients; the traitor is welcomed, false witnesses are sought after, and the guards of the sepulchre bribed. On the other side is clear foresight, the deliberate unmasking of Judas, and at the trial a circumspect composure, a lofty silence, and speech more majestic still.

Meanwhile there is a heart no longer light (for He foresees His burial), yet not so burdened that He should decline the entertainment offered Him at Bethany.

This was in the house of Simon the leper, but St. John tells us that Martha served, Lazarus sat at meat, and the woman who anointed Jesus was Mary. We naturally infer some relationship between Simon and this favoured family ; but the nature of the tie we know not, and no purpose can be served by guessing.   Better far to let the mind rest upon the sweet picture of Jesus, at home among those who loved Him ; upon the eager service of Martha ; upon the man who had known death, somewhat silent, one fancies, a remarkable sight for Jesus, as He sat at meat, and perhaps suggestive of the thought which found utterance a few days afterwards, that a banquet was yet to come, when He also, risen from the grave, should drink new wine among His friends in the kingdom of God.   And there the adoring face of her who had chosen the better part was turned to her Lord with a love which comprehended His sorrow and His danger, while even the Twelve were blind—an insight which knew the awful presence of One upon his way to the sepulchre, as well as one who had returned thence.   Therefore she produced a cruse of very precious ointment, which had been "kept" for Him, perhaps since her brother was embalmed.   And as such alabaster flasks were commonly sealed in making, and only to be opened by breaking off the neck, she crushed the cruse between her hands and poured it on His head.   On His feet also, according to St. John, who is chiefly thinking of the embalming of the body, as the others of the anointing of the head.   The discovery of contradiction here is worthy of the abject "criticism" which detects in this account a variation upon the story of her who was a sinner.   As if two women who loved much might not both express their loyalty, which could not speak, by so fair and feminine a device; or as if it were inconceivable that the blameless Mary should consciously imitate the gentle penitent.

But even as this unworthy controversy breaks in

upon the tender story, so did indignation and murmuring spoil that peaceful scene. "Why was not this ointment sold for much, and given to the poor?" It was not common that others should be more thoughtful of the poor than Jesus.

He fed the multitudes they would have sent away; He gave sight to Bartimæus whom they rebuked. But it is still true, that whenever generous impulses express themselves with lavish hands, some heartless calculator reckons up the value of what is spent, and especially its value to "the poor;" the poor, who would be worse off if the instincts of love were arrested and the human heart frozen. Almshouses are not usually built by those who declaim against church architecture; nor is utilitarianism famous for its charities. And so we are not surprised when St. John tells us how the quarrel was fomented. Iscariot, the dishonest pursebearer, was exasperated at the loss of a chance of theft, perhaps of absconding without being so great a loser at the end of his three unrequited years. True that the chance was gone, and speech would only betray his estrangement from Jesus, upon Whom so much good property was wasted. But evil tempers must express themselves at times, and Judas had craft enough to involve the rest in his misconduct. It is the only indication in the Gospels of intrigue among the Twelve which even indirectly struck at their Master's honour.

Thus, while the fragrance of the ointment filled the house, their parsimony grudged the homage which soothed His heart, and condemned the spontaneous impulse of Mary's love.

It was for her that Jesus interfered, and His words went home.

The poor were always with them: opportunities

would never fail those who were so zealous; and whensoever they would they could do them good,—whensoever Judas, for example, would. As for her, she had wrought a good work (a high-minded and lofty work is implied rather than a useful one) upon Him, Whom they should not always have. Soon His body would be in the hands of sinners, desecrated, outraged. And she only had comprehended, however dimly, the silent sorrow of her Master; she only had laid to heart His warnings; and, unable to save Him, or even to watch with Him one hour, she (and through all that week none other) had done what she could. She had anointed His body beforehand for the burial, and indeed with clear intention " to prepare Him for burial" (Matt. xxvi. 12).

It was for this that His followers had chidden her. Alas, how often do our shrewd calculations and harsh judgments miss the very essence of some problem which only the heart can solve, the silent intention of some deed which is too fine, too sensitive, to explain itself except only to that sympathy which understands us all. Men thought of Jesus as lacking nothing, and would fain divert His honour to the poor; but this woman comprehended the lonely heart, and saw the last inexorable need before Him. Love read the secret in the eyes of love, and this which Mary did shall be told while the world stands, as being among the few human actions which refreshed the lonely One, the purest, the most graceful, and perhaps the last.

THE TRAITOR.

" And Judas Iscariot, he that was one of the twelve, went away unto the chief priests, that he might deliver Him unto them. And they, when they heard it, were glad, and promised to give him money. And he sought how he might conveniently deliver Him *unto them.* And on the first day of unleavened bread, when they sacrificed the passover, His disciples say unto Him, Where wilt Thou that we go and make ready that Thou mayest eat the passover? And He sendeth two of His disciples, and saith unto them, Go into the city, and there shall meet you a man bearing a pitcher of water : follow him ; and wheresoever he shall enter in, say to the goodman of the house, the Master saith, Where is My guest-chamber, where I shall eat the passover with My disciples ? And he will himself shew you a large upper room furnished and ready : and there make ready for us. And the disciples went forth, and came into the city, and found as He had said unto them : and they made ready the passover."—MARK xiv. 10-16 (R.V.).

IT was when Jesus rebuked the Twelve for censuring Mary, that the patience of Judas, chafing in a service which had grown hateful, finally gave way. He offered a treacherous and odious help to the chiefs of his religion, and these pious men, too scrupulous to cast blood-money into the treasury or to defile themselves by entering a pagan judgment hall, shuddered not at the contact of such infamy, warned him not that perfidy will pollute the holiest cause, cared as little then for his ruin as when they asked what to them was his remorseful agony ; but were glad, and promised to give him money. By so doing, they became accomplices in the only crime by which it is quite certain that a soul was lost. The supreme "offence" was planned and perpetrated by no desperate criminal. It was the work of an apostle, and his accomplices were the heads of a divinely given religion. What an awful example of the deadening power, palsying the conscience, petrifying the heart, of religious observances devoid of real trust and love.

The narrative, as we saw, somewhat displaced the story of Simon's feast, to connect this incident more closely with the betrayal. And it now proceeds at once to the passover, and the final crisis. In so doing, it pauses at a curious example of circumspection, intimately linked also with the treason of Judas. The disciples, unconscious of treachery, asked where they should prepare the paschal supper. And Jesus gave them a sign by which to recognise one who had a large upper room prepared for that purpose, to which he would make them welcome. It is not quite impossible that the pitcher of water was a signal preconcerted with some disciple in Jerusalem, although secret understandings are not found elsewhere in the life of Jesus. What concerns us to observe is that the owner of the house which the bearer entered was a believer. To him Jesus is "the Master," and can say "Where is My guest-chamber?"

So obscure a disciple was he, that Peter and John required a sign to guide them to his house. Yet his upper room would now receive such a consecration as the Temple never knew. With strange feelings would he henceforth enter the scene of the last supper of his Lord. But now, what if he had only admitted Jesus with hesitation and after long delay? We should wonder; yet there are lowlier doors at which the same Jesus stands and knocks, and would fain come in and sup. And cold is His welcome to many a chamber which is neither furnished nor made ready.

The mysterious and reticent indication of the place is easily understood. Jesus would not enable His enemies to lay hands upon Him before the time. His

nights had hitherto been spent at Bethany; now first
it was possible to arrest Him in the darkness, and
hurry on the trial before the Galileans at the feast,
strangers and comparatively isolated, could learn the
danger of their "prophet of Galilee." It was only too
certain that when the blow was struck, the light and
fickle adhesion of the populace would transfer itself to
the successful party. Meanwhile, the prudence of
Jesus gave Him time for the Last Supper, and the
wonderful discourse recorded by St. John, and the
conflict and victory in the Garden. When the priests
learned, at a late hour, that Jesus might yet be arrested
before morning, but that Judas could never watch Him
any more, the necessity for prompt action came with
such surprise upon them, that the arrest was accomplished while they still had to seek false witnesses, and
to consult how a sentence might best be extorted from
the Governor. It is right to observe at every point,
the mastery of Jesus, the perplexity and confusion of
His foes.

And it is also right that we should learn to include,
among the woes endured for us by the Man of Sorrows,
this haunting consciousness that a base vigilance was
to be watched against, that He breathed the air of
treachery and vileness.

Here then, in view of the precautions thus forced
upon our Lord, we pause to reflect upon the awful fall
of Judas, the degradation of an apostle into a hireling,
a traitor, and a spy. Men have failed to believe that
one whom Jesus called to His side should sink so low.

They have not observed how inevitably great goodness rejected brings out special turpitude, and dark
shadows go with powerful lights; how, in this supreme
tragedy, all the motives, passions, moral and immoral

impulses are on the tragic scale; what gigantic forms of baseness, hypocrisy, cruelty, and injustice stalk across the awful platform, and how the forces of hell strip themselves, and string their muscles for a last desperate wrestle against the powers of heaven, so that here is the very place to expect the extreme apostasy. And so they have conjectured that Iscariot was only half a traitor. Some project misled him of forcing his Master to turn to bay. Then the powers which wasted themselves in scattering unthanked and unprofitable blessings would exert themselves to crush the foe. Then he could claim for himself the credit deserved by much astuteness, the consideration due to the only man of political resource among the Twelve. But this well-intending Judas is equally unknown to the narratives and the prophecies, and this theory does not harmonise with any of the facts. Profound reprobation and even contempt are audible in all the narratives; they are quite as audible in the reiterated phrase, "which was one of the Twelve," and in almost every mention of his name, as in the round assertion of St. John, that he was a thief and stole from the common purse. Only the lowest motive is discernible in the fact that his project ripened just when the waste of the ointment spoiled his last hope from apostleship,—the hope of unjust gain, and in his bargaining for the miserable price which he still carried with him when the veil dropped from his inner eyes, when he awoke to the sorrow of the world which worketh death, to the remorse which was not penitence.

One who desired that Jesus should be driven to counter-measures and yet free to take them, would probably have favoured His escape when once the attempt to arrest Him inflicted the necessary spur

and certainly he would have anxiously avoided any
appearance of insult.   But it will be seen that Judas
carefully closed every door against his Lord's escape,
and seized Him with something very like a jibe on
his recreant lips.

No, his infamy cannot be palliated, but it can be
understood.   For it is a solemn and awful truth, that in
every defeat of grace the reaction is equal to the action ;
they who have been exalted unto heaven are brought
down far below the level of the world ; and the principle
is universal that Israel cannot, by willing it, be as the
nations that are round about, to serve other gods.   God
Himself gives him statutes that are not good.   He makes
fat the heart and blinds the eyes of the apostate.   Therefore it comes that religion without devotion is the
mockery of honest worldlings ; that hypocrisy goes so
constantly with the meanest and most sordid lust of
gain, and selfish cruelty ; that publicans and harlots
enter heaven before scribes and pharisees ; that salt
which has lost its savour is fit neither for the land nor
for the dung-hill.   Oh, then, to what place of shame
shall a recreant apostle be thrust down ?

Moreover it must be observed that the guilt of Judas,
however awful, is but a shade more dark than that of
his sanctimonious employers, who sought false witnesses
against Christ, extorted by menace and intrigue a
sentence which Pilate openly pronounced to be unjust,
mocked His despairing agony, and on the resurrection
morning bribed a pagan soldiery to lie for the Hebrew
faith   It is plain enough that Jesus could not and did
not choose the apostles through foreknowledge of what
they would hereafter prove, but by His perception of
what they then were, and what they were capable of
becoming, if faithful to the light they should receive.

Not one, when chosen first, was ready to welcome the purely spiritual kingdom, the despised Messiah, the life of poverty and scorn. They had to learn, and it was open to them to refuse the discipline. Once at least they were asked, Will ye also go away? How severe was the trial may be seen by the rebuke of Peter, and the petition of "Zebedee's children" and their mother. They conquered the same reluctance of the flesh which overcame the better part in Judas. But he clung desperately to secular hope, until the last vestige of such hope was over. Listening to the warnings of Christ against the cares of this world, the lust of other things, love of high places and contempt of lowly service, and watching bright offers rejected and influential classes estranged, it was inevitable that a sense of personal wrong, and a vindictive resentment, should spring up in his gloomy heart. The thorns choked the good seed. Then came a deeper fall. As he rejected the pure light of self-sacrifice, and the false light of his romantic daydreams faded, no curb was left on the baser instincts which are latent in the human heart. Self-respect being already lost, and conscience beaten down, he was allured by low compensations, and the apostle became a thief. What better than gain, however sordid, was left to a life so plainly frustrated and spoiled? That is the temptation of disillusion, as fatal to middle life as the passions are to early manhood. And this fall reacted again upon his attitude towards Jesus. Like all who will not walk in the light, he hated the light; like all hirelings of two masters, he hated the one he left. Men ask how Judas could have consented to accept for Jesus the bloodmoney of a slave. The truth is that his treason itself yielded him a dreadful satisfaction, and the insulting kiss, and the

24

sneering " Rabbi," expressed the malice of his heart.
Well for him if he had never been born. For when his
conscience awoke with a start and told him what thing
he had become, only self-loathing remained to him.
Peter denying Jesus was nevertheless at heart His own ;
a look sufficed to melt him. For Judas, Christ was
become infinitely remote and strange, an abstraction,
"the innocent blood," no more than that. And so,
when Jesus was passing into the holiest through the
rent veil which was His flesh, this first Antichrist
had already torn with his own hands the tissue of
the curtain which hides eternity.

Now let us observe that all this ruin was the result
of forces continually at work upon human hearts.
Aspiration, vocation, failure, degradation—it is the
summary of a thousand lives. Only it is here exhibited
on a vast and dreadful scale (magnified by the light
which was behind, as images thrown by a lantern upon
a screen) for the instruction and warning of the
world.

THE SOP.

"And when it was evening He cometh with the twelve. And as they
sat and were eating, Jesus said, Verily I say unto you, One of you shall
betray Me, *even* he that eateth with Me. They began to be sorrowful,
and to say unto Him one by one, Is it I ? And He said unto them, *It
is* one of the twelve, he that dippeth with Me in the dish. For the Son
of man goeth, even as it is written of Him : but woe unto that man
through whom the Son of man is betrayed ! good were it for that man
if he had not been born."—MARK xiv. 17-21 (R.V.).

IN the deadly wine which our Lord was made to drink,
every ingredient of mortal bitterness was mingled.
And it shows how far is even His Church from com-
prehending Him, that we think so much more of the

physical than the mental and spiritual horrors which gather around the closing scene.

But the tone of all the narratives, and perhaps especially of St. Mark's, is that of the exquisite Collect which reminds us that our Lord Jesus Christ was contented to be betrayed, and given up into the hands of wicked men, as well as to suffer death on the cross. Treason and outrage, the traitor's kiss and the weakness of those who loved Him, the hypocrisy of the priest and the ingratitude of the mob, perjury and a mock trial, the injustice of His judges, the brutal outrages of the soldiers, the worse and more malignant mockery of scribe and Pharisee, and last and direst, the averting of the face of God, these were more dreadful to Jesus than the scourging and the nails.

And so there is great stress laid upon His anticipation of the misconduct of His own.

As the dreadful evening closes in, having come to the guest chamber " with the Twelve "—eleven whose hearts should fail them and one whose heart was dead, it was " as they sat and were eating " that the oppression of the traitor's hypocrisy became intolerable, and the outraged One spoke out. " Verily I say unto you, One of you shall betray Me, even he that eateth with Me." The words are interpreted as well as predicted in the plaintive Psalm which says, " Mine own familiar friend in whom I trusted, which did also eat of My bread, hath lifted up his heel against Me." And perhaps they are less a disclosure than a cry.

Every attempt to mitigate the treason of Judas, every suggestion that he may only have striven too wilfully to serve our Lord by forcing Him to take decided measures, must fail to account for the sense of utter wrong which breathes in the simple and piercing complaint "one of you . . . even he that eateth with Me." There is a tone in all the narratives which is at variance with any palliation of the crime.

No theology is worth much if it fails to confess, at the centre of all the words and deeds of Jesus, a great and tender human heart. He might have spoken of teaching and warnings lavished on the traitor, and miracles which he had beheld in vain. What weighs heaviest on His burdened spirit is none of these; it is that one should betray Him who had eaten His bread.

When Brutus was dying he is made to say—

> "My heart doth joy, that yet, in all my life,
> I found no man, but he was true to me."

But no form of innocent sorrow was to pass Jesus by.

The vagueness in the words "one of you shall betray Me," was doubtless intended to suggest in all a great searching of heart. Coming just before the institution of the Eucharistic feast, this incident anticipates the command which it perhaps suggested: "Let a man examine himself, and so let him eat." It is good to be distrustful of one's self. And if, as was natural, the Eleven looked one upon another doubting of whom He spake, they also began to say to Him, one by one (first the most timid, and then others as the circle narrowed), Is it I? For the prince of this world had something in each of them,—some frailty there was, some reluctance to bear the yoke, some longing for the forbidden ways of worldliness, which alarmed each at this solemn warning, and made him ask, Is it, can it be possible, that it is I? Religious self-sufficiency was not then the apostolic mood. Their questioning is also remarkable as a proof how little they suspected Judas, how firmly he bore himself even

as those all-revealing words were spoken, how strong
and wary was the temperament which Christ would
fain have sanctified.   For between the Master and him
there could have been no more concealment.

The apostles were right to distrust themselves, and
not to distrust another.   They were right, because they
were so feeble, so unlike their Lord.   But for Him
there is no misgiving : His composure is serene in
the hour of the power of darkness.   And His perfect
spiritual sensibility discerned the treachery, unknown
to others, as instinctively as the eye resents the presence of a mote imperceptible to the hand.

The traitor's iron nerve is somewhat strained as he
feels himself discovered, and when Jesus is about to
hand a sop to him, he stretches over, and their hands
meet in the dish.   That is the appointed sign : " It is
one of the Twelve, he that dippeth with Me in the
dish," and as he rushes out into the darkness, to seek
his accomplices and his revenge, Jesus feels the awful
contrast between the betrayer and the Betrayed.   For
Himself, He goeth as it is written of Him.   This
phrase admirably expresses the co-operation of Divine
purpose and free human will, and by the woe that
follows He refutes all who would make of God's
fore-knowledge an excuse for human sin.   He then is
not walking in the dark and stumbling, though men
shall think Him falling.   But the life of the false one
is worse than utterly cast away : of him is spoken the
dark and ominous word, never indisputably certain of
any other soul, " Good were it for him if that man had
not been born."

" That man ! " The order and emphasis are very
strange.   The Lord, who felt and said that one of His
chosen was a devil, seems here to lay stress upon the

warning thought, that he who fell so low was human,
and his frightful ruin was evolved from none but human
capabilities for good and evil. In "the Son of man"
and "that man," the same humanity was to be found.

For Himself, He is the same to-day as yesterday.
All that we eat is His. And in the most especial and
far-reaching sense, it is His bread which is broken for
us at His table. Has He never seen traitor except one
who violated so close a bond? Alas, the night when
the Supper of the Lord was given was the same night
when He was betrayed.

BREAD AND WINE.

"And as they were eating, He took bread, and when He had blessed,
He brake it, and gave to them, and said, Take ye : this is My body.
And He took a cup, and when He had given thanks, He gave to them :
and they all drank of it. And He said unto them, This is My blood
of the covenant, which is shed for many. Verily I say unto you, I
will no more drink of the fruit of the vine, until that day when I drink
it new in the kingdom of God."—MARK xiv. 22-25 (R.V.).

How much does the Gospel of St. Mark tell us about
the Supper of the Lord? He is writing to Gentiles.
He is writing probably before the sixth chapter of
St. John was penned, certainly before it reached his
readers. Now we must not undervalue the reflected
light thrown by one Scripture upon another. Still less
may we suppose that each account conveys all the
doctrine of the Eucharist. But it is obvious that
St. Mark intended his narrative to be complete in
itself, even if not exhaustive. No serious expositor
will ignore the fulness of any word or action in which
later experience can discern meanings, truly involved,
although not apparent at the first. That would be
to deny the inspiring guidance of Him who sees the

end from the beginning.   But it is reasonable to omit
from the interpretation of St. Mark whatever is not
either explicitly there, or else there in germ, waiting
underneath the surface for other influences to develope
it.   For   instance,   the   "remembrance"   of   Christ
in St. Paul's narrative may (or it may not) mean a
sacrificial memorial to God of His Body and His Blood.
If it be, this notion was to be conveyed to the readers
of this Gospel hereafter, as a quite new fact, resting
upon other authority.   It has no place whatever here,
and need only be mentioned to point out that St. Mark
did not feel bound to convey the slightest hint of it.
A communion, therefore, could be profitably celebrated
by persons who had no glimmering of any such conception.   Nor does he rely, for an understanding of
his narrative, upon such familiarity with Jewish ritual
as would enable his readers to draw subtle analogies
as they went along.   They were so ignorant of these
observances that he had just explained to them on
what day the passover was sacrificed (ver. 12).

But this narrative conveys enough to make the
Lord's Supper, for every believing heart, the supreme
help to faith, both intellectual and spiritual, and the
mightiest of promises, and the richest gift of grace.

It is hard to imagine that any reader would conceive
that the bread in Christ's hands had become His body,
which still lived and breathed ; or that His blood, still
flowing in His veins, was also in the cup He gave to
His disciples.   No resort could be made to the glorification of the risen Body as an escape from the perplexities
of such a notion, for in whatever sense the words are
true, they were spoken of the body of His humiliation,
before which still lay the agony and the tomb.

Instinct would revolt yet more against such a gross

explanation, because the friends of Jesus are bidden to eat and drink. And all the analogy of Christ's language would prove that His vivid style refuses to be tied down to so lifeless and mechanical a treatment. Even in this Gospel they could discover that seed was teaching, and fowls were Satan, and that they were themselves His mother and His brethren. Further knowledge of Scripture would not impair this natural freedom of interpretation. For they would discover that if animated language were to be frozen to such literalism, the partakers of the Supper were themselves, though many, one body and one loaf, that Onesimus was St. Paul's very heart, that leaven is hypocrisy, that Hagar is Mount Sinai, and that the veil of the temple is the flesh of Christ (1 Cor. x. 17 ; Philem. ver. 12 ; Luke xii. 1 ; Gal. iv. 25 ; Heb. x. 20). And they would also find, in the analogous institution of the paschal feast, a similar use of language (Exod. xii. 11).

But when they had failed to discern the doctrine of a transubstantiation, how much was left to them. The great words remained, in all their spirit and life, " Take ye, this is My Body . . . this is My Blood of the Covenant, which is shed for many."

(1) So then, Christ did not look forward to His death as to ruin or overthrow. The Supper is an institution which could never have been devised at any later period. It comes to us by an unbroken line from the Founder's hand, and attested by the earliest witnesses. None could have interpolated a new ordinance into the simple worship of the early Church, and the last to suggest such a possibility should be those sceptics who are deeply interested in exaggerating the estrangements which existed from the first, and which made

the Jewish Church a keen critic of Gentile innovation, and the Gentiles of a Jewish novelty.

Nor could any genius have devised its vivid and pictorial earnestness, its copious meaning, and its pathetic power over the heart, except His, Who spoke of the Good Shepherd and of the Prodigal Son. And so it tells us plainly what Christ thought about His own death. Death is to most of us simply the close of life. To Him it was itself an achievement, and a supreme one. Now it is possible to remember with exultation a victory which cost the conqueror's life. But on the Friday which we call Good, nothing happened except the crucifixion. The effect on the Church, which is amazing and beyond dispute, is produced by the death of her Founder, and by nothing else. The Supper has no reference to Christ's resurrection. It is as if the nation exulted in Trafalgar, not in spite of the death of our great Admiral, but solely because he died; as if the shot which slew Nelson had itself been the overthrow of hostile navies. Now the history of religions offers no parallel to this. The admirers of the Buddha love to celebrate the long spiritual struggle, the final illumination, and the career of gentle helpfulness. They do not derive life and energy from the somewhat vulgar manner of his death. But the followers of Jesus find an inspiration (very displeasing to some recent apostles of good taste) in singing of their Redeemer's blood. Remove from the Creed (which does not even mention His three years of teaching) the proclamation of His death, and there may be left, dimly visible to man, the outline of a sage among the sages, but there will be no longer a Messiah, nor a Church. It is because He was lifted up that He draws all men unto Him. The perpetual nourishment of the Church, her bread and wine, are beyond question the slain body of her Master and His blood poured out for man.

What are we to make of this admitted fact, that from the first she thought less of His miracles, His teaching, and even of His revelation of the Divine character in a perfect life, than of the doctrine that He who thus lived, died for the men who slew Him? And what of this, that Jesus Himself, in the presence of imminent death, when men review their lives and set a value on their achievements, embodied in a solemn ordinance the conviction that all He had taught and done was less to man than what He was about to suffer? The Atonement is here proclaimed as a cardinal fact in our religion, not worked out into doctrinal subtleties, but placed with marvellous simplicity and force, in the forefront of the consciousness of the simplest. What the Incarnation does for our bewildering thoughts of God, the absolute and unconditioned, that does the Eucharist for our subtle reasonings upon the Atonement.

(2) The death of Christ is thus precious, because He Who is sacrificed for us can give Himself away. "Take ye" is a distinct offer. And so the communion feast is not a mere commemoration, such as nations hold for great deliverances. It is this, but it is much more, else the language of Christ would apply worse to that first supper whence all our Eucharistic language is derived, than to any later celebration. When He was absent, the bread would very aptly remind them of His wounded body, and the wine of His blood poured out. It might naturally be said, Henceforward, to your loving remembrance this shall be my Body, as indeed, the words, As oft as ye drink it, are actually linked with the injunction to do this in remembrance. But scarcely could it have been said by Jesus, looking His disciples

in the face, that the elements were then His body and blood, if nothing more than commemoration were in His mind. And so long as popular Protestantism fails to look beyond this, so long will it be hard pressed and harassed by the evident weight of the words of institution. These are given in Scripture solely as having been spoken then, and no interpretation is valid which attends chiefly to subsequent celebrations, and only in the second place to the Supper of Jesus and the Eleven.

Now the most strenuous opponent of the doctrine that any change has passed over the material substance of the bread and wine, need not resist the palpable evidence that Christ appointed these to represent Himself. And how ? Not only as sacrificed for His people, but as verily bestowed upon them. Unless Christ mocks us, "Take ye" is a word of absolute assurance. Christ's Body is not only slain, and His Blood shed on our behalf; He gives Himself *to* us as well as *for* us; He is ours. And therefore whoever is convinced that he may take part in "the sacrament of so great a mystery" should realize that he there receives, conveyed to him by the Author of that wondrous feast, all that is expressed by the bread and wine.

(3) And yet this very word "Take ye," demands our co-operation in the sacrament. It requires that we should receive Christ, as it declares that He is ready to impart Himself, utterly, like food which is taken into the system, absorbed, assimilated, wrought into bone, into tissue and into blood. And if any doubt lingered in our minds of the significance of this word, it is removed when we remember how belief is identified with feeding, in St. John's Gospel. "I am the bread of life: he that cometh to Me shall not hunger, and he that believeth on Me shall never thirst. . . . He that

believeth hath eternal life. I am the bread of life."
(John vi. 35, 47, 48.) If it follows that to feed upon
Christ is to believe, it also follows quite as plainly that
belief is not genuine unless it really feeds upon Christ.

It is indeed impossible to imagine a more direct and
vigorous appeal to man to have faith in Christ than
this, that He formally conveys, by the agency of His
Church, to the hands and lips of His disciples, the
appointed emblem of Himself, and of Himself in the act
of blessing them. For the emblem is food in its most
nourishing and in its most stimulating form, in a form
the best fitted to speak of utter self-sacrifice, by the
bruised corn of broken bread, and by the solemn resemblance to His sacred blood. We are taught to
see, in the absolute absorption of our food into our
bodily system, a type of the completeness wherewith
Christ gives Himself to us.

That gift is not to the Church in the gross, it is
"divided among" us; it individualizes each believer;
and yet the common food expresses the unity of the
whole Church in Christ. Being many we are one bread.

Moreover, the institution of a meal reminds us that
faith and emotion do not always exist together. Times
there are when the hunger and thirst of the soul are
like the craving of a sharp appetite for food. But the
wise man will not postpone his meal until such a keen
desire returns, and the Christian will seek for the
Bread of life, however his emotions may flag, and his
soul cleave unto the dust. Silently and often unaware,
as the substance of the body is renovated and restored
by food, shall the inner man be strengthened and
built up by that living Bread.

(4) We have yet to ask the great question, what
is the specific blessing expressed by the elements, and

therefore surely given to the faithful by the sacramen:.
Too many are content to think vaguely of Divine
help, given us for the merit of the death of Christ.
But bread and wine do not express an indefinite
Divine help, they express the body and blood of Christ,
they have to do with His Humanity.   We must
beware, indeed, of limiting the notion overmuch.   At
the Supper He said not " My flesh," but " My body,"
which is plainly a more comprehensive term.   And
in the discourse when He said My Flesh is meat
indeed," He also said " I am the bread of life. . . .
He that eateth Me, the same shall live by Me."   And
we may not so carnalize the Body as to exclude the
Person, who bestows Himself.   Yet is all the language
so constructed as to force the conviction upon us that
His body and blood, His Humanity, is the special
gift of the Lord's Supper.   As man He redeemed us,
and as man He imparts Himself to man.

Thus we are led up to the sublime conception of a new
human force working in humanity.   As truly as the
life of our parents is in our veins, and the corruption
which they inherited from Adam is passed on to us, so
truly there is abroad in the world another influence,
stronger to elevate than the infection of the fall is to
degrade ; and the heart of the Church is propelling to
its utmost extremities the pure life of the Second Adam,
the Second Man, the new Father of the race.   As in
Adam all die, even so in Christ shall all be made alive ;
and we who bear now the image of our earthy pro-
genitor shall hereafter bear the image of the heavenly.
Meanwhile, even as the waste and dead tissues of our
bodily frame are replaced by new material from every
meal, so does He, the living Bread, impart not only
aid from heaven, but nourishment, strength to our poor

human nature, so weary and exhausted, and renovation to what is sinful and decayed. How well does such a doctrine of the sacrament harmonize with the declarations of St. Paul : " I live, and yet no longer I, but Christ liveth in me." " The Head, from whom all the body being supplied and knit together through the joints and bands, increaseth with the increase of God " (Gal. ii 20 ; Col. ii 19).

(5) In the brief narrative of St. Mark, there are a few minor points of interest.

Fasting communions may possibly be an expression of reverence only. The moment they are pressed further, or urged as a duty, they are strangely confronted by the words, " While they were eating, Jesus took bread."

The assertion that " they all drank," follows from the express commandment recorded elsewhere. And while we remember that the first communicants were not laymen, yet the emphatic insistence upon this detail, and with reference only to the cup, is entirely at variance with the Roman notion of the completeness of a communion in one kind.

It is most instructive also to observe how the far-reaching expectation of our Lord looks beyond the Eleven, and beyond His infant Church, forward to the great multitude which no man can number, and speaks of the shedding of His blood " for many." He, who is to see of the travail of His soul and to be satisfied, has already spoken of a great supper when the house of God shall be filled. And now He will no more drink of the fruit of the vine until that great day when the marriage of the Lamb having come, and His Bride having made herself ready, He shall drink it new in the consummated kingdom of God.

With the announcement of that kingdom He began His gospel: how could the mention of it be omitted from the great gospel of the Eucharist? or how could the Giver of the earthly feast be silent concerning the banquet yet to come?

THE WARNING

"And when they had sung a hymn, they went out into the mount of Olives. And Jesus saith unto them, All ye shall be offended : for it is written, I will smite the shepherd, and the sheep shall be scattered abroad. Howbeit, after I am raised up, I will go before you into Galilee. But Peter said unto Him, Although all shall be offended, yet will not I. And Jesus saith unto him, Verily I say unto thee, that thou to-day, *even* this night, before the cock crow twice, shalt deny me thrice. But he spake exceeding vehemently, If I must die with Thee, I will not deny Thee. And in like manner also said they all."—MARK xiv. 26-31 (R.V.).

SOME uncertainty attaches to the position of Christ's warning to the Eleven in the narrative of the last evening. Was it given at the supper, or on Mount Olivet; or were there perhaps premonitory admonitions on His part, met by vows of faithfulness on theirs, which at last led Him to speak out so plainly, and elicited such vainglorious protestations, when they sat together in the night air?

What concerns us more is the revelation of a calm and beautiful nature, at every point in the narrative. Jesus knows and has declared that His life is now closing, and His blood already "being shed for many." But that does not prevent Him from joining with them in singing a hymn. It is the only time when we are told that our Saviour sang, evidently because no other occasion needed mention; a warning to those who draw confident inferences from such facts as that " none ever said He smiled," or that there is no record of His having been sick. It would surprise such theorists to observe the number of biographies much longer than any of the Gospels, which also mention nothing of the kind. The Psalms usually sung at the close of the feast are cxv. and the three following. The first tells how the dead praise not the Lord, but we will praise Him from this time forth for ever. The second proclaims that the Lord hath delivered my soul from death, mine eyes from tears, and my feet from falling. The third bids all the nations praise the Lord, for his merciful kindness is great and His truth endureth for ever. And the fourth rejoices because, although all nations compassed me about, yet I shall not die, but live and declare the works of the Lord; and because the stone which the builders rejected is become the head stone of the corner. Memories of infinite sadness were awakened by the words which had so lately rung around His path : " Blessed is He that cometh in the name of the Lord ; " but His voice was strong to sing, " Bind the sacrifice with cords, even to the horns of the altar ; " and it rose to the exultant close, " Thou art my God, and I will praise Thee : Thou art my God, I will exalt Thee. O give thanks unto the Lord for He is good, for His mercy endureth for ever."

This hymn, from the lips of the Perfect One, could be no " dying swan-song." It uplifted that more than heroic heart to the wonderful tranquillity which presently said, " When I am risen, I will go before you into Galilee." It is full of victory. And now they go unto the Mount of Olives.

Is it enough considered how much of the life of Jesus was passed in the open air ? He preached on the hill side ; He desired that a boat should be at His command upon the lake ; He prayed upon the mountain ; He was transfigured beside the snows of Hermon ; He oft-times resorted to a garden which had not yet grown awful ; He met His disciples on a Galilean mountain ; and He finally ascended from the Mount of Olives. His unartificial normal life, a pattern to us, not as students but as men—was spent by preference neither in the study nor the street.

In this crisis, most solemn and yet most calm, He leaves the crowded city into which all the tribes had gathered, and chooses for His last intercourse with His disciples, the slopes of the opposite hill side, while overhead is glowing, in all the still splendour of an Eastern sky, the full moon of Passover. Here then is the place for one more emphatic warning. Think how He loved them. As His mind reverts to the impending blow, and apprehends it in its most awful form, the very buffet of God Who Himself will smite the Shepherd, He remembers to warn His disciples of their weakness. We feel it to be gracious that He should think of them at such a time. But if we drew a little nearer, we should almost hear the beating of the most loving heart that ever broke. They were all He had. In them He had confided utterly. Even as the Father had loved Him, He also had loved them, the firstfruits of the travail of His soul. He had ceased to call them servants and had called them friends. To them He had spoken those affecting words, "Ye are they which have continued with me in My temptations." How intensely He clung to their sympathy, imperfect though it was, is best seen by His repeated appeals to it in the Agony. And He knew that they loved Him, that the spirit was willing, that they would weep and lament for Him, sorrowing

25

with a sorrow which He hastened to add that He would turn into joy.

It is the preciousness of their fellowship which reminds Him how this, like all else, must fail Him. If there is blame in the words, " Ye shall be offended," this passes at once into exquisite sadness when He adds that He, Who so lately said, " Them that Thou gavest Me, I have guarded," should Himself be the cause of their offence, " All ye shall be caused to stumble because of Me." And there is an unfathomable tenderness, a marvellous allowance for their frailty in what follows. They were His sheep, and therefore as helpless, as little to be relied upon, as sheep when the shepherd is stricken. How natural it was for sheep to be scattered.

The world has no parallel for such a warning to comrades who are about to leave their leader, so faithful and yet so tender, so far from estrangement or reproach.

If it stood alone it would prove the Founder of the Church to be not only a great teacher, but a genuine Son of man.

For Himself, He does not share their weakness, nor apply to Himself the lesson of distrustfulness which He teaches them; He is of another nature from these trembling sheep, the Shepherd of Zechariah, " Who is My fellow, saith the Lord of Hosts." He does not shrink from applying to Himself this text, which awakens against Him the sword of God (Zechariah xiii. 7).

Looking now beyond the grave to the resurrection, and unestranged by their desertion, He resumes at once the old relation; for as the shepherd goeth before his sheep, and they follow him, so He will go before them into Galilee, to the familiar places, far from the city where men hate Him.

This last touch of quiet human feeling completes an utterance too beautiful, too characteristic to be spurious, yet a prophecy, and one which attests the ancient predictions, and which involves an amazing claim.

At first sight it is surprising that the Eleven who were lately so conscious of weakness that each asked was he the traitor, should since have become too self-confident to profit by a solemn admonition. But a little examination shows the two statements to be quite consistent. They had wronged themselves by that suspicion, and never is self-reliance more boastful than when it is reassured after being shaken. The institution of the Sacrament had invested them with new privileges, and drawn them nearer than ever to their Master. Add to this the infinite tenderness of the last discourse in St. John, and the prayer which was for them and not for the world. How did their hearts burn within them as He said, "Holy Father, keep them in Thy name whom Thou hast given Me." How incredible must it then have seemed to them, thrilling with real sympathy and loyal gratitude, that they should forsake such a Master.

Nor must we read in their words merely a loud and indignant self-assertion, all unworthy of the time and scene. They were meant to be a solemn vow. The love they professed was genuine and warm. Only they forgot their weakness; they did not observe the words which declared them to be helpless sheep, entirely dependent on the Shepherd, whose support would speedily seem to fail.

Instead of harsh and unbecoming criticism, which

repeats almost exactly their fault by implying that we should not yield to the same pressure, let us learn the lesson, that religious exaltation, a sense of special privilege, and the glow of generous emotions, have their own danger. Unless we continue to be as little children, receiving the Bread of Life, without any pretence to have deserved it, and conscious still that our only protection is the staff of our Shepherd, then the very notion that we are something, when we are nothing, will betray us to defeat and shame.

Peter is the loudest in his protestations; and there is a painful egoism in his boast, that even if the others fail, he will never deny Him. So in the storm, it is he who should be called across the waters. And so an early reading makes him propose that he alone should build the tabernacles for the wondrous Three.

Naturally enough, this egoism stimulates the rest. For them, Peter is among those who may fail, while each is confident that he himself cannot. Thus the pride of one excites the pride of many.

But Christ has a special humiliation to reveal for his special self-assertion. That day, and even before that brief night was over, before the second cock-crowing ("the cock-crow" of the rest, being that which announced the dawn) he shall deny his Master twice. Peter does not observe that his eager contradictions are already denying the Master's profoundest claims. The others join in his renewed protestations, and their Lord answers them no more. Since they refuse to learn from Him, they must be left to the stern schooling of experience. Even before the betrayal, they had an opportunity to judge how little their good intentions might avail. For Jesus now enters Gethsemane.

IN THE GARDEN.

" And they come unto a place which was named Gethsemane : and He saith unto His disciples, Sit ye here, while I pray. And He taketh with Him Peter and James and John, and began to be greatly amazed, and sore troubled. And He saith unto them, My soul is exceeding sorrow‑ful even unto death : abide ye here, and watch. And He went forward a little, and fell on the ground, and prayed that, if it were possible, the hour might pass away from Him. And He said, Abba, Father, all things are possible unto Thee : remove this cup from Me : howbeit not what I will, but what Thou wilt. And He cometh, and findeth them sleeping, and saith unto Peter, Simon, sleepest thou ? couldest thou not watch one hour ? Watch and pray, that ye enter not into temptation : the spirit indeed is willing, but the flesh is weak. And again He went away, and prayed, saying the same words. And again He came, and found them sleeping, for their eyes were very heavy ; and they wist not what to answer Him. And He cometh the third time, and saith unto them, Sleep on now, and take your rest : it is enough ; the hour is come ; behold, the Son of man is betrayed into the hands of sinners. Arise, let us be going : behold, he that betrayeth Me is at hand."— MARK xiv. 32–42 (R.V.).

ALL Scripture, given by inspiration of God, is profitable ; yet must we approach with reverence and solemn shrinking, the story of our Saviour's anguish. It is a subject for caution and for reticence, putting away all over-curious surmise, all too-subtle theorizing, and choosing to say too little rather than too much.

It is possible so to argue about the metaphysics of the Agony as to forget that a suffering human heart was there, and that each of us owes his soul to the victory which was decided if not completed in that fearful place. The Evangelists simply tell us how He suffered.

Let us begin with the accessories of the scene, and gradually approach the centre.

In the warning of Jesus to His disciples there was an undertone of deep sorrow. God will smite Him, and

they will all be scattered like sheep. However dauntless be the purport of such words, it is impossible to
lose sight of their melancholy. And when the Eleven
rejected His prophetic warning, and persisted in trusting
the hearts He knew to be so fearful, their professions
of loyalty could only deepen His distress, and intensify
His isolation.

In silence He turns to the deep gloom of the olive
grove, aware now of the approach of the darkest and
deadliest assault.

There was a striking contrast between the scene of
His first temptation and His last ; and His experience
was exactly the reverse of that of the first Adam, who
began in a garden, and was driven thence into the
desert, because he failed to refuse himself one pleasure
more beside ten thousand. Jesus began where the
transgression of men had driven them, in the desert
among the wild beasts, and resisted not a luxury, but
the passion of hunger craving for bread. Now He is
in a garden, but how different from theirs. Close by
is a city filled with foemen, whose messengers are
already on His track. Instead of the attraction of
a fruit good for food, and pleasant, and to be desired
to make one wise, there is the grim repulsion of death,
and its anguish, and its shame and mockery. He is
now to be assailed by the utmost terrors of the flesh
and of the spirit. And like the temptation in the
wilderness, the assault is three times renewed.

As the dark " hour " approached, Jesus confessed
the two conflicting instincts of our human nature in its
extremity—the desire of sympathy, and the desire of
solitude. Leaving eight of the disciples at some distance,
He led still nearer to the appointed place His elect
of His election, on whom He had so often bestowed

special privilege, and whose faith would be less shaken by the sight of His human weakness, because they had beheld His Divine glory on the holy mount. To these He opened His heart. "My soul is exceeding sorrowful, even unto death; abide ye here and watch." And He went from them a little. Their neighbourhood was a support in His dreadful conflict, and He could at times return to them for sympathy; but they might not enter with Him into the cloud, darker and deadlier than that which they feared on Hermon. He would fain not be desolate, and yet He must be alone.

But when He returned, they were asleep. As Jesus spoke of watching for one hour, some time had doubt-less elapsed. And sorrow is exhausting. If the spirit do not seek for support from God, it will be dragged down by the flesh into heavy sleep, and the brief and dangerous respite of oblivion.

It was the failure of Peter which most keenly affected Jesus, not only because his professions had been so loud, but because much depended on his force of cha-racter. Thus, when Satan had desired to have them, that he might sift them all like wheat, the prayers of Jesus were especially for Simon, and it was he when he was converted who should strengthen the rest. Surely then he at least might have watched one hour. And what of John, His nearest human friend, whose head had reposed upon His bosom? However keen the pang, the lips of the Perfect Friend were silent; only He warned them all alike to watch and pray, because they were themselves in danger of temptation.

That is a lesson for all time. No affection and no zeal are a substitute for the presence of God realised, and the protection of God invoked. Loyalty and love are not enough without watchfulness and prayer, for even when the spirit is willing, the flesh is weak, and needs to be upheld.

Thus, in His severest trial and heaviest oppression, there is neither querulousness nor invective, but a most ample recognition of their good will, a most generous allowance for their weakness, a most sedulous desire, not that He should be comforted, but that they should escape temptation.

With His yearning heart unsoothed, with another anxiety added to His heavy burden, Jesus returned to His vigil. Three times He felt the wound of unrequited affection, for their eyes were very heavy, and they wist not what to answer Him when He spoke.

Nor should we omit to contrast their bewildered stupefaction, with the keen vigilance and self-possession of their more heavily burdened Lord.

If we reflect that Jesus must needs experience all the sorrows that human weakness and human wickedness could inflict, we may conceive of these varied wrongs as circles with a common centre, on which the cross was planted. And our Lord has now entered the first of these; He has looked for pity but there was no man; His own, although it was grief which pressed them down, slept in the hour of His anguish, and when He bade them watch.

It is right to observe that our Saviour had not bidden them to pray with Him. They should watch and pray. They should even watch with Him. But to pray for Him, or even to pray with Him, they were not bidden. And this is always so. Never do we read that Jesus and any mortal joined together in any prayer to God. On the contrary, when two or three of them asked anything in His name, He took for Himself the position of the Giver of their petition. And we know certainly that He did not invite them to join His prayers, for it was as He was praying in a certain place that when He ceased, one of His disciples desired that they also might be taught to pray (Luke xi. 1). Clearly then they were not wont to approach the mercy seat hand in hand with Jesus. And the reason is plain. He came directly to His Father; no man else came unto the Father but by Him; there was an essential difference between His attitude towards God and ours.

Has the Socinian ever asked himself why, in this hour of His utmost weakness, Jesus sought no help from the intercession of even the chiefs of the apostles?

It is in strict harmony with this position, that St. Matthew tells us, He now said not Our Father, but My Father. No disciple is taught, in any circumstances to claim for himself a monopolized or special sonship. He may be in his closet and the door shut, yet must he remember his brethren and say, Our Father. That is a phrase which Jesus never addressed to God. None is partaker of His Sonship; none joined with Him in supplication to His Father.

THE AGONY.

"And He saith unto them, My soul is exceeding sorrowful, even unto death: abide ye here, and watch. And He went forward a little, and fell on the ground, and prayed that, if it were possible, the hour might pass away from Him. And He said, Abba, Father, all things are possible unto Thee; remove this cup from Me: howbeit not what I will, but what Thou wilt. And He cometh, and findeth them sleeping, and saith unto Peter, Simon, sleepest thou? couldest thou not watch one hour? Watch and pray, that ye enter not into temptation: the spirit indeed is willing, but the flesh is weak. And again He went away, and prayed, saying the same words. And again He came, and found them sleeping, for their eyes were very heavy; and they wist not what to answer Him. And He cometh the third time, and saith unto them, Sleep on now, and take your rest: it is enough; the hour is come ; behold, the Son of man is betrayed into the hands of sinners. Arise, let us be going : behold, he that betrayeth Me is at hand."— MARK xiv. 34–42 (R.V.).

SCEPTICS and believers have both remarked that St. John, the only Evangelist who was said to have been present, gives no account of the Agony.

It is urged by the former, that the serene composure of the discourse in his Gospel leaves no room for subsequent mental conflict and recoil from suffering, which are inconsistent besides with his conception of a Divine man, too exalted to be the subject of such emotions.

But do not the others know of composure which bore to speak of His Body as broken bread, and seeing in the cup the likeness of His Blood shed, gave it to be the food of His Church for ever ?

Was the resignation less serene which spoke of the smiting of the Shepherd, and yet of His leading back the flock to Galilee ? If the narrative was rejected as inconsistent with the calmness of Jesus in the fourth Gospel, it should equally have repelled the authors of the other three.

We may grant that emotion, agitation, is inconsistent with unbelieving conceptions of the Christ of the fourth Gospel. But this only proves how false those conceptions are. For the emotion, the agitation, is already there. At the grave of Lazarus the word which tells that when He groaned in spirit He was troubled, describes one's distress in the presence of some palpable opposing force (John xi. 34). There was, however, a much closer approach to His emotion in the garden, when the Greek world first approached Him. Then He contrasted its pursuit of self-culture with His own doctrine of self-sacrifice, declaring that even a grain of wheat must either die or abide by itself alone. To Jesus that doctrine was no smooth, easily announced theory, and so He adds, " Now is My soul troubled, and what shall I say ?   Father save Me from this hour.   But for this cause came I unto this hour " (John xii. 27).

Such is the Jesus of the fourth Gospel, by no means that of its modern analysts.   Nor is enough said, when we remind them that the Speaker of these words was capable of suffering ; we must add that profound agitation at the last was inevitable, for One so resolute in coming to this hour, yet so keenly sensitive of its dread.

The truth is that the silence of St. John is quite in his manner.   It is so that he passes by the Sacraments, as being familiar to his readers, already instructed in the gospel story.   But he gives previous discourses in which the same doctrine is expressed which was embodied in each Sacrament,—the declaration that Nicodemus must be born of water, and that the Jews must eat His flesh and drink His blood.   It is thus that instead of the agony, he records that earlier agitation.   And this threefold recurrence of the same expedient is almost incredible except by design.   St. John was therefore not forgetful of Gethsemane.

A coarser infidelity has much to say about the shrinking of our Lord from death.   Such weakness is pronounced unworthy, and the bearing of multitudes of brave men and even of Christian martyrs, unmoved in the flames, is contrasted with the strong crying and tears of Jesus.

It would suffice to answer that Jesus also failed not when the trial came, but before Pontius Pilate witnessed a good confession, and won upon the cross the adoration of a fellow-sufferer and the confession of a Roman soldier.   It is more than enough to answer that His story, so far from relaxing the nerve of human

fortitude, has made those who love Him stronger to
endure tortures than were emperors and inquisitors
to invent them.   What men call His weakness has
inspired ages with fortitude.   Moreover, the censure
which such critics, much at ease, pronounce on Jesus
expecting crucifixion, arises entirely from the magnifi-
cent and unique standard by which they try Him ; for
who is so hard-hearted as to think less of the valour
of the martyrs because it was bought by many a lonely
and intense conflict with the flesh ?

For us, we accept the standard ; we deny that Jesus
in the garden came short of absolute perfection ; but
we call attention to the fact that much is conceded to us,
when a criticism is ruthlessly applied to our Lord which
would excite indignation and contempt if brought to
bear on the silent sufferings of any hero or martyr but
Himself.

Perfection is exactly what complicates the problem
here.

Conscious of our own weakness, we not only justify
but enjoin upon ourselves every means of attaining as
much nobility as we may.   We " steel ourselves to
bear," and therefore we are led to expect the same of
Jesus.   We aim at some measure of what, in its lowest
stage, is callous insensibility.   Now that word is negative ; it asserts the absence or paralysis of a faculty, not
its fulness and activity.   Thus we attain victory by a
double process ; in part by resolutely turning our mind
away, and only in part by its ascendancy over appre-
ciated distress.   We administer anodynes to the soul.
But Jesus, when he had tasted thereof, would not drink.
The horrors which were closing around Him were
perfectly apprehended, that they might perfectly be
overcome.

Thus suffering, He became an example for gentle womanhood, and tender childhood, as well as man boastful of his stoicism.   Moreover, He introduced into the world a new type of virtue, much softer and more emotional than that of the sages.   The stoic, to whom pain is no evil, and the Indian laughing and singing at the stake, are partly actors and partly perversions of humanity.   But the good Shepherd is also, for His gentleness, a lamb.   And it is His influence which has opened our eyes to see a charm unknown before, in the sensibility of our sister and wife and child.   Therefore, since the perfection of manhood means neither the ignoring of pain nor the denying of it, but the union of absolute recognition with absolute mastery of its fearfulness, Jesus, on the approach of agony and shame, and who shall say what besides, yields Himself beforehand to the full contemplation of His lot.   He does so, while neither excited by the trial, nor driven to bay by the scoffs of His murderers, but in solitude, in the dark, with stealthy footsteps approaching through the gloom.

And ever since, all who went farthest down into the dread Valley, and on whom the shadow of death lay heaviest, found there the footsteps of its conqueror. It must be added that we cannot measure the keenness of the sensibility thus exposed to torture.   A physical organization and a spiritual nature fresh from the creative hand, undegraded by the transmitted heritage of ages of artificial, diseased and sinful habit, unblunted by one deviation from natural ways, undrugged by one excess, was surely capable of a range of feeling as vast in anguish as in delight.

The sceptic supposes that a torrent of emotion swept our Saviour off His feet.   The only narratives he can go upon give quite the opposite impression. He is seen to fathom all that depth of misery, He allows the voice of nature to utter all the bitter earnestness of its reluctance, yet He never loses self-control, nor wavers in loyalty to His Father, nor renounces His submission to the Father's will. Nothing in the scene is more astonishing than its combination of emotion with self-government. Time after time He pauses, gently and lovingly admonishes others, and calmly returns to His intense and anxious vigil.

Thus He has won the only perfect victory. With a nature so responsive to emotion, He has not refused to feel, nor abstracted His soul from suffering, nor silenced the flesh by such an effort as when we shut our ears against a discord. Jesus sees all, confesses that He would fain escape, but resigns Himself to God.

In the face of all asceticisms, as of all stoicisms, Gethsemane is the eternal protest that every part of human nature is entitled to be heard, provided that the spirit retains the arbitration over all.

Hitherto nothing has been assumed which a reasonable sceptic can deny. Nor should such a reader fail to observe the astonishing revelation of character in the narrative, its gentle pathos, its intensity beyond what commonly belongs to gentleness, its affection, its mastery over the disciples, its filial submission. Even the rich imaginative way of thinking, which invented the parables and sacraments, is in the word " this cup."

But if the story of Gethsemane can be vindicated from such a point of view, what shall be said when it is viewed as the Church regards it? Both Testaments declare that the sufferings of the Messiah were supernatural. In the Old Testament it was pleasing to the Father to bruise Him. The terrible cry of Jesus to a

God who had forsaken Him is conclusive evidence from the New Testament. And if we ask what such a cry may mean, we find that He is a curse for us, and made to be sin for us, Who knew no sin.

If the older theology drew incredible conclusions from such words, that is no reason why we should ignore them. It is incredible that God was angry with His Son, or that in any sense the Omniscient One confused the Saviour with the sinful world. It is incredible that Jesus ever endured estrangement as of lost souls from the One Whom in Gethsemane He called Abba Father, and in the hour of utter darkness, My God, and into whose Fatherly hands He committed His Spirit. Yet it is clear that He is being treated otherwise than a sinless Being, as such, ought to expect. His natural standing-place is exchanged for ours. And as our exceeding misery, and the bitter curse of all our sin fell on Him, Who bore it away by bearing it, our pollution surely affected His purity as keenly as our stripes tried His sensibility. He shuddered as well as agonized. The deep waters in which He sank were defiled as well as cold. Only this can explain the agony and bloody sweat. And as we, for whom He endured it, think of this, we can only be silent and adore.

Once more, Jesus returns to His disciples, but no longer to look for sympathy, or to bid them watch and pray. The time for such warnings is now past: the crisis, "the hour" is come, and His speech is sad and solemn. "Sleep on now and take your rest, it is enough." Had the sentence stopped there, none would ever have proposed to treat it as a question, "Do ye now sleep on and take your rest?" It would plainly have mean, "Since ye refuse My counsel and will none of my reproof, I strive no further to arouse the torpid will, the inert conscience, the inadequate affection. Your resistance prevails against My warning."

But critics fail to reconcile this with what follows, " Arise, let us be going." They fail through supposing that words of intense emotion must be interpreted like a syllogism or a lawyer's parchment.

" For My part, sleep on ; but your sleep is now to be rudely broken : take your rest so far as respect for your Master should have kept you watchful ; but the traitor is at hand to break such repose, let him not find you ignobly slumbering. 'Arise, he is at hand that doth betray Me.' "

This is not sarcasm, which taunts and wounds. But there is a lofty and profound irony in the contrast between their attitude and their circumstances, their sleep and the eagerness of the traitor.

And so they lost the most noble opportunity ever given to mortals, not through blank indifference nor unbelief, but by allowing the flesh to overcome the spirit. And thus do multitudes lose heaven, sleeping until the golden hours are gone, and He who said, " Sleep on now," says, " He that is unrighteous, let him be unrighteous still."

Remembering that defilement was far more urgent than pain in our Saviour's agony, how sad is the meaning of the words, " the Son of man is betrayed into the hands of sinners," and even of " the sinners," the representatives of all the evil from which He had kept Himself unspotted.

The one perfect flower of humanity is thrown by treachery into the polluted and polluting grasp of wickedness in its many forms ; the traitor delivers Him to hirelings ; the hirelings to hypocrites ; the hypo-

crites to an unjust and sceptical pagan judge ; the judge
to his brutal soldiery ; who expose Him to all that
malice can wreak upon the most sensitive organization,
or ingratitude upon the most tender heart.

At every stage an outrage. Every outrage an appeal
to the indignation of Him who held them in the hollow
of His hand. Surely it may well be said, Consider
Him who endured such contradiction ; and endured it
from sinners against Himself.

THE ARREST.

"And straightway, while He yet spake, cometh Judas, one of the
twelve, and with him a multitude with swords and staves, from the
chief priests and the scribes and the elders. Now he that betrayed
Him had given them a token, saying, Whomsoever I shall kiss, that is
He ; take Him, and lead Him away safely. And when he was come,
straightway he came to Him, and saith, Rabbi ; and kissed Him. And
they laid hands on Him, and took Him. But a certain one of them
that stood by drew his sword, and smote the servant of the high priest,
and struck off his ear. And Jesus answered and said unto them, Are
ye come out, as against a robber, with swords and staves to seize Me?
I was daily with you in the temple teaching, and ye took Me not : but
this is done that the scriptures might be fulfilled. And they all left Him
and fled. And a certain young man followed with Him, having a linen
cloth cast about him, over *his* naked *body* : and they lay hold on him ;
but he left the linen cloth, and fled naked."—MARK xiv. 43-52 (R.V.).

ST. MARK has told this tragical story in the most
pointed and the fewest words. The healing of the ear
of Malchus concerns him not, that is bu. one miracle
among many ; and Judas passes from sight unfollowed :
the thought insisted on is of foul treason, pitiable
weakness, brute force predominant, majestic remonstrance and panic flight. From the central events no
accessories can distract him.

There cometh, he tells us, " Judas, one of the Twelve."
Who Judas was, we knew already, but we are to con-

sider how Jesus felt it now. Before His eyes is the catastrophe which His death is confronted to avert— the death of a soul, a chosen and richly dowered soul for ever lost—in spite of so many warnings—in spite of that incessant denunciation of covetousness which rings through so much of His teaching, which only the presence of Judas quite explains, and which His terrible and searching gaze must have made like fire, to sear since it could not melt—in spite of the outspoken utterances of these last days, and doubtless in spite of many prayers, he is lost: one of the Twelve.

And the dark thought would fall cold upon Christ's heart, of the multitudes more who should receive the grace of God, His own dying love, in vain. And with that, the recollection of many an hour of loving-kindness wasted on this familiar friend in whom He trusted, and who now gave Him over, as he had been expressly warned, to so cruel a fate. Even toward Judas, no unworthy bitterness could pollute that sacred heart, the fountain of unfathomable compassions, but what speechless grief must have been there, what inconceivable horror. For the outrage was dark in form as in essence. Judas apparently conceived that the Eleven might, as they had promised, rally around their Lord ; and he could have no perception how impossible it was that Messiah should stoop to escape under cover of their devotion, how frankly the good Shepherd would give His life for the sheep. In the night, he thought, evasion might yet be attempted, and the town be raised. But he knew how to make the matter sure. No other would as surely as himself recognise Jesus in the uncertain light. If he were to lay hold on Him rudely, the Eleven would close in, and in the struggle, the prize might yet be lost. But approaching a little in advance, and peaceably, he would ostentatiously kiss his Master, and so clearly point Him out that the arrest would be accomplished before the disciples realized what was being done.

But at every step the intrigue is overmastered by the clear insight of Jesus. As He foretold the time of His arrest, while yet the rulers said, Not on the feast day, so He announced the approach of the traitor, who was then contriving the last momentary deception of his polluting kiss.

We have already seen how impossible it is to think of Judas otherwise than as the Church has always regarded him, an apostate and a traitor in the darkest sense. The milder theory is at this stage shattered by one small yet significant detail. At the supper, when conscious of being suspected, and forced to speak, he said not, like the others, "Lord," but "Rabbi, is it I?" Now they meet again, and the same word is on his lips, whether by design and in Satanic insolence, or in hysterical agitation and uncertainty, who can say?

But no loyalty, however misled, inspired that halting and inadequate epithet, no wild hope of a sudden blazing out of glories too long concealed is breathed in the traitor's Rabbi!

With that word, and his envenomed kiss, the "much kissing," which took care that Jesus should not shake him off, he passes from this great Gospel. Not a word is here of his remorse, or of the dreadful path down which he stumbled to his own place. Even the lofty remonstrance of the Lord is not recorded: it suffices to have told how he betrayed the Son of man with a kiss, and so infused a peculiar and subtle poison into Christ's draught of deadly wine. That, and not the punishment of that, is what St. Mark recorded for the

Church, the awful fall of an apostle, chosen of Christ; the solemn warning to all privileged persons, richly endowed and highly placed; the door to hell, as Bunyan has it, from the very gate of Heaven.

A great multitude with swords and staves had come from the rulers. Possibly some attempt at rescue was apprehended from the Galileans who had so lately triumphed around Jesus. More probably the demonstration was planned to suggest to Pilate that a dangerous political agitation had to be confronted.

At all events, the multitude did not terrify the disciples : cries arose from their little band, " Lord shall we smite with the sword ? " and if Jesus had consented, it seems that with two swords the Eleven whom declaimers make to be so craven, would have assailed the multitude in arms.

Now this is what points the moral of their failure. Few of us would confess personal cowardice by accepting a warning from the fears of the fearful. But the fears of the brave must needs alarm us. It is one thing to defy death, sword in hand, in some wild hour of chivalrous effort—although the honours we shower upon the valiant prove that even such fortitude is less common than we would fain believe. But there is a deep which opens beyond this. It is a harder thing to endure the silent passive anguish to which the Lamb, dumb before the shearers, calls His followers. The victories of the spirit are beyond animal strength of nerve. In their highest forms they are beyond the noble reach of intellectual resolution. How far beyond it we may learn by contrasting the excitement and then the panic of the Eleven with the sublime composure of their Lord.

One of them, whom we know to have been the

impulsive Simon, showed his loss of self-control by what would have been a breach of discipline, even had resistance been intended.   While others asked should they smite with the sword, he took the decision upon himself, and struck a feeble and abortive blow, enough to exasperate but not to disable.   In so doing he added, to the sorrows of Jesus, disobedience, and the inflaming of angry passion among His captors.

Strange it is, and instructive, that the first act of violence in the annals of Christianity came not from her assailants but from her son.   And strange to think with what emotions Jesus must have beheld that blow.

St. Mark records neither the healing of Malchus nor the rebuke of Peter.   Throughout the events which now crowd fast upon us, we shall not find him careful about fulness of detail.   This is never his manner, though he loves any detail which is graphic, characteristic, or intensifying.   But his concern is with the spirit of the Lord and of His enemies : he is blind to no form of injustice or insult which heightened the sufferings of Jesus, to no manifestation of dignity and self-control overmastering the rage of hell.   If He is unjustly tried by Caiaphas, it matters nothing that Annas also wronged Him.   If the soldiers of Pilate insulted Him, it matters nothing that the soldiers of Herod also set Him at nought.   Yet the flight of a nameless youth is recorded, since it adds a touch to the picture of His abandonment.

And therefore he records the indignant remonstrance of Jesus upon the manner of His arrest.   He was no man of violence and blood, to be arrested with a display of overwhelming force.   He needed not to be sought in concealment and at midnight.

He had spoken daily in the temple, but then their

malice was defeated, their snares rent asunder, and the people witnessed their exposure. But all this was part of His predicted suffering, for Whom not only pain but injustice was foretold, Who should be taken from prison and from judgment.

It was a lofty remonstrance. It showed how little could danger and betrayal disturb His consciousness, and how clearly He discerned the calculation of His foes.

At this moment of unmistakable surrender, His disciples forsook Him and fled. One young man did indeed follow Him, springing hastily from slumber in some adjacent cottage, and wrapped only in a linen cloth. But he too, when seized, fled away, leaving his only covering in the hands of the soldiers.

This youth may perhaps have been the Evangelist himself, of whom we know that, a few years later, he joined Paul and Barnabas at the outset, but forsook them when their journey became perilous.

It is at least as probable that the incident is recorded as a picturesque climax to that utter panic which left Jesus to tread the winepress alone, deserted by all, though He never forsook any.

BEFORE CAIAPHAS.

"And they led Jesus away to the high priest : and there come together with him all the chief priests and the elders and the scribes. And Peter had followed Him afar off, even within, into the court of the high priest ; and he was sitting with the officers, and warming himself in the light *of the fire.* Now the chief priests and the whole council sought witness against Jesus to put Him to death ; and found it not. For many bare false witness against Him, and their witness agreed not together. And there stood up certain, and bare false witness against Him, saying, We heard Him say, I will destroy this temple that is made with hands, and in three days I will build another made without hands. And not even so did their witness agree together. And the high priest stood up in the midst, and asked Jesus, saying, Answerest Thou nothing? what is it which these witness against Thee? But He held His peace and answered nothing. Again the high priest asked Him, and saith unto Him, Art Thou the Christ, the Son of the Blessed? And Jesus said, I am : and ye shall see the Son of man sitting at the right hand of power, and coming with the clouds of heaven. And the high priest rent his clothes, and saith, What further need have we of witnesses? Ye have heard the blasphemy : what think ye? And they all condemned Him to be worthy of death. And some began to spit on Him, and to cover His face, and to buffet Him, and to say unto Him, Prophesy : and the officers received Him with blows of their hands "—MARK xiv. 53-65 (R.V.).

WE have now to see the Judge of quick and dead taken from prison and judgment, the Preacher of liberty to the captives bound, and the Prince of Life killed. It is the most solemn page in earthly story ; and as we read St. Mark's account, it will concern us less to reconcile his statements with those of the other three, than to see what is taught us by his especial manner of regarding it. Reconciliation, indeed, is quite unnecessary, if we bear in mind that to omit a fact is not to contradict it. For St. Mark is not writing a history but a Gospel, and his readers are Gentiles, for whom the details of Hebrew intrigue matter nothing, and the trial before a Galilean Tetrarch would be only half intelligible.

St. John, who had been an eye-witness, knew that the private inquiry before Annas was vital, for there the decision was taken which subsequent and more formal assemblies did but ratify. He therefore, writing last, threw this ray of explanatory light over all that the others had related. St. Luke recorded in the Acts (iv. 27) that the apostles recognised, in the consent of Romans and Jews, and of Herod and Pilate, what the Psalmist had long foretold, the rage of the heathen

and the vain imagination of the peoples, and the conjunction of kings and rulers. His Gospel therefore
lays stress upon the part played by all of these. And
St. Matthew's readers could appreciate every fulfilment of prophecy, and every touch of local colour.
St. Mark offers to us the essential points : rejection
and cruelty by His countrymen, rejection and cruelty
over again by Rome, and the dignity, the elevation, the
lofty silence and the dauntless testimony of his Lord.
As we read, we are conscious of the weakness of His
crafty foes, who are helpless and baffled, and have no
resort except to abandon their charges and appeal to
His own truthfulness to destroy Him.

He shows us first the informal assembly before
Caiaphas, whither Annas sent Him with that sufficient
sign of his own judgment, the binding of His hands,
and the first buffet, inflicted by an officer, upon His
holy face. It was not yet daylight, and a formal
assembly of the Sanhedrim was impossible. But what
passed now was so complete a rehearsal of the tragedy,
that the regular meeting could be disposed of in a
single verse.

There was confusion and distress among the conspirators. It was not their intention to have arrested
Jesus on the feast day, at the risk of an uproar
among the people. But He had driven them to do so
by the expulsion of their spy, who, if they delayed
longer, would be unable to guide their officers. And
so they found themselves without evidence, and had
to play the part of prosecutors when they ought to
be impartial judges. There is something frightful in
the spectacle of these chiefs of the religion of Jehovah
suborning perjury as the way to murder ; and it
reminds us of the solemn truth, that no wickedness is

so perfect and heartless as that upon which sacred
influences have long been vainly operating, no corruption so hateful as that of a dead religion.   Presently
they would cause the name of God to be blasphemed
among the heathen, by bribing the Roman guards to
lie about the corpse.   And the heart of Jesus was
tried by the disgraceful spectacle of many false
witnesses, found in turn and paraded against Him,
but unable to agree upon any consistent charge, while
yet the shameless proceedings were not discontinued.
At the last stood up witnesses to pervert what He had
spoken at the first cleansing of the temple, which the
second cleansing had so lately recalled to mind.   They
represented Him as saying, " I am able to destroy this
temple made with hands,"— or perhaps, "I will
destroy " it, for their testimony varied on this grave
point—" and in three days I will build another made
without hands."   It was for blaspheming the Holy
Place that Stephen died, and the charge was a grave
one ; but His words were impudently manipulated to
justify it.   There had been no proposal to substitute
a different temple, and no mention of the temple made
with hands.   Nor had Jesus ever proposed to destroy
anything.   He had spoken of their destroying the
Temple of His Body, and in the use they made of
the prediction they fulfilled it.

As we read of these repeated failures before a tribunal
so unjust, we are led to suppose that opposition must
have sprung up to disconcert them ; we remember the
councillor of honourable estate, who had not consented
to their counsel and deed, and we think, What if, even
in that hour of evil, one voice was uplifted for righteousness ?   What if Joseph confessed Him in the
conclave, like the penitent thief upon the cross ?

And now the high priest, enraged and alarmed by imminent failure, rises in the midst, and in the face of all law cross-questions the prisoner, Answerest Thou nothing? What is it which these witness against Thee? But Jesus will not become their accomplice; He maintains the silence which contrasts so nobly with their excitement, which at once sees through their schemes and leaves them to fall asunder. And the urgency of the occasion, since hesitation now will give the city time to rise, drives them to a desperate expedient. Without discussion of His claims, without considering that some day there *must* be some Messiah, (else what is their faith and who are they?) they will treat it as blasphemous and a capital offence simply to claim that title. Caiaphas adjures Him by their common God to answer, Art thou the Christ, the Son of the Blessed? So then they were not utterly ignorant of the higher nature of the Son of David: they remembered the words, Thou art My Son, this day have I begotten Thee. But the only use they ever made of their knowledge was to heighten to the uttermost the Messianic dignity which they would make it death to claim. And the prisoner knew well the consequences of replying. But He had come into the world to bear witness to the truth, and this was the central truth of all. "And Jesus said, I am." Now Renan tells us that He was the greatest religious genius who ever lived, or probably ever shall live. Mill tells us that religion cannot be said to have made a bad choice in pitching on this Man as the ideal representative and guide of humanity. And Strauss thinks that we know enough of Him to assert that His consciousness was unclouded by the memory of any sin. Well then, if anything in the life of Jesus is beyond controversy, it is this, that the sinless Man, our ideal representative and guide, the greatest religious genius of the race, died for asserting upon oath that He was the Son of God. A good deal has been said lately, both wise and foolish, about Comparative Religion : is there anything to compare with this ? Lunatics, with this example before their eyes, have conceived wild and dreadful infatuations. But these are the words of Him whose character has dominated nineteen centuries, and changed the history of the world. And they stand alone in the records of mankind.

As Jesus spoke the fatal words, as malice and hatred lighted the faces of His wicked judges with a base and ignoble joy, what was His own thought ? We know it by the warning that He added. They supposed themselves judges and irresponsible, but there should yet be another tribunal, with justice of a far different kind, and there they should occupy another place. For all that was passing before His eyes, so false, hypocritical and murderous, there was no lasting victory, no impunity, no escape : " Ye shall see the Son of man sitting at the right hand of power and coming with the clouds of heaven." Therefore His apostle Peter tells us that in this hour, when He was reviled and reviled not again, " He committed Himself to Him that judgeth righteously " (1 Peter ii. 23).

He had now quoted that great vision in which the prophet Daniel saw Him brought near unto the Ancient of Days, and invested with an everlasting dominion (Dan. vii. 13, 14.) But St. Matthew adds one memorable word. He did not warn them, and He was not Himself sustained, only by the mention of a far-off judgment : He said they should behold Him thus " henceforth." And that very day they saw the veil of their temple rent, felt the world convulsed, and re-membered in their terror that He had foretold His own death and His resurrection, against which they had still to guard. And in the open sepulchre, and the supernatural vision told them by its keepers, in great and notable miracles wrought by the name of Jesus, in the desertion of a great multitude even of priests, and their own fear to be found fighting against God, in all this the rise of that new power was thenceforth plainly visible, which was presently to bury them and their children under the ruins of their temple and their palaces. But for the moment the high-priest was only relieved; and he proceeded, rending his clothes, to announce his judgment, before consulting the court, who had no further need of witnesses, and were quite content to become formally the accusers before themselves. The sentence of this irregular and informal court was now pronounced, to fit them for bearing part, at sunrise, in what should be an unbiassed trial; and while they awaited the dawn Jesus was abandoned to the brutality of their servants, one of whom He had healed that very night. They spat on the Lord of Glory. They covered His face, an act which was the symbol of a death sen-tence (Esther vii. 8), and then they buffeted Him, and invited Him to prophesy who smote Him. And the officers "received Him" with blows.

What was the meaning of this outburst of savage cruelty of men whom Jesus had never wronged, and some of whose friends must have shared His super-human gifts of love? Partly it was the instinct of low natures to trample on the fallen, and partly the result of partizanship. For these servants of the priests must have seen many evidences of the hate and dread with which their masters regarded Jesus. But there was doubtless another motive. Not without fear, we may be certain, had they gone forth to arrest at midnight the Personage of whom so many miraculous tales were universally believed. They must have remembered the captains of fifty whom Elijah consumed with fire. And in fact there was a moment when they all fell prostrate before His majestic presence. But now their terror was at an end: He was helpless in their hands; and they revenged their fears upon the Author of them.

Thus Jesus suffered shame to make us partakers of His glory; and the veil of death covered His head, that He might destroy the face of the covering cast over all peoples, and the veil that was spread over all nations. And even in this moment of bitterest outrage He remembered and rescued a soul in the extreme of jeopardy, for it was now that the Lord turned and looked upon Peter.

THE FALL OF PETER.

" And as Peter was beneath in the court, there cometh one of the maids of the high priest ; and seeing Peter warming himself, she looked upon him, and saith, Thou also wast with the Nazarene, *even* Jesus. But he denied, saying, I neither know, nor understand what thou sayest : and he went out into the porch ; and the cock crew. And the maid saw him, and began again to say to them that stood by, This is *one* of them. But he again denied it. And after a little while again they that stood by said to Peter, Of a truth thou art *one* of them ; for thou art a Galilæan. But he began to curse, and to swear, I know not this man of whom ye speak. And straightway the second time the cock crew. And Peter called to mind the word, how that Jesus said unto him, Before the cock crow twice, thou shalt deny Me thrice. And when he thought thereon, he wept "—MARK xiv. 66–72 (R.V.).

THE fall of Peter has called forth the easy scorn of multitudes who never ran any risk for Christ. But if he had been a coward, and his denial a dastardly weakness, it would not be a warning for the whole Church, but only for feeble natures. Whereas the lesson which it proclaims is this deep and solemn one, that no natural endowments can bear the strain of the spiritual life. Peter had dared to smite when only two swords were forthcoming against the band of Roman soldiers and the multitude from the chief priests. After the panic in which all forsook Jesus, and so fulfilled the prediction "ye shall leave Me alone," none ventured so far as Peter. John indeed accompanied him ; but John ran little risk, he had influence and was therefore left unassailed, whereas Peter was friendless and a mark for all men, and had made himself conspicuous in the garden. Of those who declaim about his want of courage few indeed would have dared so much. And whoever misunderstands him, Jesus did not. He said to him, "Satan hath desired to have you (all) that he may sift you like wheat, but I have prayed for thee (especially) that thy strength fail not." Around him the fiercest of the struggle was to rage, as around some point of vantage on a battlefield ; and it was he, when once he had turned again, who should stablish his brethren (Luke xxii. 31, 32).

God forbid that we should speak one light or scornful word of this great apostle ! God grant us, if our footsteps slip, the heart to weep such tears as his.

Peter was a loving, brave and loyal man. But the circumstances were not such as human bravery could deal with. Resistance, which would have kindled his spirit, had been forbidden to him, and was now impossible. The public was shut out, and he was practically alone among his enemies. He had come "to see the end," and it was a miserable sight that he beheld. Jesus was passive, silent, insulted : His foes fierce, unscrupulous and confident.   And Peter was more and more conscious of being alone, in peril, and utterly without resource.   Moreover sleeplessness and misery lead to physical languor and cold,* and as the officers had kindled a fire, he was drawn thither, like a moth, by the double wish to avoid isolation and to warm himself.   In thus seeking to pass for one of the crowd, he showed himself ashamed of Jesus, and incurred the menaced penalty, " of him shall the Son of man be ashamed, when He cometh."   And the method of self-concealment which he adopted only showed his face, strongly illuminated, as St. Mark tells us, by the flame.

If now we ask for the secret of his failing resolution, we can trace the disease far back.   It was self-confidence.   He reckoned himself the one to walk upon the waters.   He could not be silent on the holy mount, when Jesus held high communion with the inhabitants of heaven.   He rebuked the Lord for dark forebodings. When Jesus would wash his feet, although expressly told that he should understand the act hereafter, he rejoined, Thou shalt never wash my feet, and was only sobered by the peremptory announcement that further rebellion would involve rejection.   He was sure that if all the rest were to deny Jesus, he never should deny Him.   In the garden he slept, because he failed to pray and watch.   And then he did not wait to be directed, but strove to fight the battle of Jesus with the weapons of the flesh.   Therefore he forsook Him and fled.   And the consequences of that hasty blow were heavy upon him now.   It marked him for the attention of the servants : it drove him to merge himself in the crowd.   But his bearing was too suspicious to

---

* " By the fire the children sit
Cold in that atmosphere of death."—*In Memoriam,* **xx.**

enable him to escape unquestioned. The first assault came very naturally, from the maid who kept the door, and had therefore seen him with John. He denied indeed, but with hesitation, not so much affirming that the charge was false as that he could not understand it. And thereupon he changed his place, either to escape notice or through mental disquietude ; but as he went into the porch the cock crew. The girl however was not to be shaken off : she pointed him out to others, and since he had forsaken the only solid ground, he now denied the charge angrily and roundly. An hour passed, such an hour of shame, perplexity and guilt, as he had never known, and then there came a still more dangerous attack. They had detected his Galilean accent, while he strove to pass for one of them. And a kinsman of Malchus used words as threatening as were possible without enabling a miracle to be proved, since the wound had vanished : " Did I myself not see thee in the garden with Him ? " Whereupon, to prove that his speech had nothing to do with Jesus, he began to curse and swear, saying, I know not the man. And the cock crew a second time, and Peter remembered the warning of his Lord, which then sounded so harsh, but now proved to be the means of his salvation. And the eyes of his Master, full of sorrow and resolution, fell on him. And he knew that he had added a bitter pang to the sufferings of the Blessed One. And the crowd and his own danger were forgotten, and he went out and wept.

It was for Judas to strive desperately to put himself right with man : the sorrow of Peter was for himself and God to know.

What lessons are we taught by this most natural and humbling story ? That he who thinketh he standeth must take heed lest he fall. That we are in most danger when self-confident, and only strong when we are weak. That the beginning of sin is like the letting out of water. That Jesus does not give us up when we cast ourselves away, but as long as a pulse of love survives, or a spark of loyalty, He will appeal to that by many a subtle suggestion of memory and of providence, to recall His wanderer to Himself.

And surely we learn by the fall of this great and good apostle to restore the fallen in the spirit of meekness, considering ourselves lest we also be tempted, remembering also that to Peter, Jesus sent the first tidings of His resurrection, and that the message found him in company with John, and therefore in the house with Mary. What might have been the issue of his anguish if these holy ones had cast Him off?

CHAPTER XV.

PILATE.

" **And** straightway in the morning the chief priests with the elders **and** scribes, and the whole council, held a consultation, and bound Jesus, and carried Him away, and delivered Him up to Pilate."

" . . . And they lead Him out to crucify Him."—MARK xv. 1-20 (R.V.).

WITH morning came the formal assembly, which St. Mark dismisses in a single verse. It was indeed a disgraceful mockery. Before the trial began its members had prejudged the case, passed sentence by anticipation, and abandoned Jesus, as one condemned, to the brutality of their servants. And now the spectacle of a prisoner outraged and maltreated moves no indignation in their hearts.

Let us, for whom His sufferings were endured, reflect upon the strain and anguish of all these repeated examinations, these foregone conclusions gravely adopted in the name of justice, these exhibitions of greed for blood. Among the "unknown sufferings" by which the Eastern Church invokes her Lord, surely not the least was His outraged moral sense.

As the issue of it all, they led Him away to Pilate, meaning, by the weight of such an accusing array, to overpower any possible scruples of the governor, but in fact fulfilling His words, "they shall deliver Him unto the Gentiles." And the first question recorded by St. Mark expresses the intense surprise of Pilate. "Thou," so meek, so unlike the numberless conspirators that I have tried,—or perhaps, " Thou," Whom no sympathising multitude sustains, and for Whose death the disloyal priesthood thirsts, " Art *Thou* the King of the Jews ? " We know how carefully Jesus disentangled His claim from the political associations which the high priests intended that **it** should suggest, how the King of Truth would not exaggerate any more than understate the case, and explained that His kingdom was not of this world, that His servants did not fight, that His royal function was to uphold the truth, not to expel conquerors.   The eyes of a practised Roman governor saw through the accusation very clearly.   Before him, Jesus was accused of sedition, but that was a transparent pretext ; Jews did **not** hate Him for enmity to Rome : He was a rival teacher and a successful one, and for envy they had delivered Him.   So far all was well.   Pilate investigated the charge, arrived at the correct judgment, and it only remained that he should release the innocent man.   In reaching this conclusion Jesus had given him the most prudent and skilful help, but as soon as the facts became clear, He resumed His impressive and mysterious silence.   Thus, before each of his judges in turn, Jesus avowed Himself the Messiah and then held His peace.   It was an awful silence, which would not give that which was holy to the dogs, nor profane the truth by unavailing protests or controversies.   It was, however, a silence only possible to an exalted nature full of self-control, since the words actually spoken redeem it from any suspicion or stain of sullenness. It is the conscience of Pilate which must henceforth speak.   The Romans were the lawgivers of the ancient world, and a few years earlier their greatest poet had boasted that their mission was to spare the helpless and to crush the proud. In no man was an act of deliberate injustice, of complaisance to the powerful at the cost of the good, more unpardonable than in a leader of that splendid race, whose laws are still the favourite study of those who frame and administer our own. And the conscience of Pilate struggled hard, aided by superstitious fear. The very silence of Jesus amid many charges, by none of which His accusers would stand or fall, excited the wonder of His judge. His wife's dream aided the effect. And he was still more afraid when he heard that this strange and elevated Personage, so unlike any other prisoner whom he had ever tried, laid claim to be Divine. Thus even in his desire to save Jesus, his motive was not pure, it was rather an instinct of self-preservation than a sense of justice. But there was danger on the other side as well; since he had already incurred the imperial censure, he could not without grave apprehensions contemplate a fresh complaint, and would certainly be ruined if he were accused of releasing a conspirator against Cæsar. And accordingly he stooped to mean and crooked ways, he lost hold of the only clue in the per-plexing labyrinth of expediencies, which is principle, and his name in the creed of Christendom is spoken with a shudder—" crucified under Pontius Pilate ! "

It was the time for him to release a prisoner to them, according to an obscure custom, which some suppose to have sprung from the release of one of the two sacrificial goats, and others from the fact that they now celebrated their own deliverance from Egypt. At this moment the people began to demand their usual indulgence, and an evil hope arose in the heart of Pilate. They would surely welcome One who was in danger as a patriot: he would himself make the offer;

and he would put it in this tempting form, " Will ye
that I release unto you the King of the Jews?" Thus
would the enmity of the priests be gratified, since
Jesus would henceforth be a condemned culprit, and
owe His life to their intercession with the foreigner.
But the proposal was a surrender. The life of Jesus
had not been forfeited; and when it was placed at
their discretion, it was already lawlessly taken away.
Moreover, when the offer was rejected, Jesus was in
the place of a culprit who should not be released. To
the priests, nevertheless, it was a dangerous proposal,
and they needed to stir up the people, or perhaps
Barabbas would not have been preferred.

Instigated by their natural guides, their religious
teachers, the Jews made the tremendous choice, which
has ever since been heavy on their heads and on their
children's. Yet if ever an error could be excused by
the plea of authority, and the duty of submission to
constituted leaders, it was this error. They followed
men who sat in Moses' seat, and who were thus entitled,
according to Jesus Himself, to be obeyed. Yet that
authority has not relieved the Hebrew nation from the
wrath which came upon them to the uttermost. The
salvation they desired was not moral elevation or
spiritual life, and so Jesus had nothing to bestow upon
them; they refused the Holy One and the Just. What
they wanted was the world, the place which Rome held,
and which they fondly hoped was yet to be their own.
Even to have failed in the pursuit of this was better
than to have the words of everlasting life, and so the
name of Barabbas was enough to secure the rejection
of Christ. It would almost seem that Pilate was ready
to release both, if that would satisfy them, for he asks,
in hesitation and perplexity, " What shall I do then

with Him Whom ye call the King of the Jews ? " Surely
in their excitement for an insurgent, that title, given
by themselves, will awake their pity. But again and
again, like the howl of wolves, resounds their ferocious
cry, Crucify Him, crucify Him.

The irony of Providence is known to every student
of history, but it never was so manifest as here. Under
the pressure of circumstances upon men whom principle
has not made firm, we find a Roman governor striving to
kindle every disloyal passion of his subjects, on behalf
of the King of the Jews,—appealing to men whom he
hated and despised, and whose charges have proved
empty as chaff, to say, What evil has He done ? and
even to tell him, on his judgment throne, what he shall
do with their King; we find the men who accused Jesus
of stirring up the people to sedition, now shamelessly
agitating for the release of a red-handed insurgent ;
forced moreover to accept the responsibility which they
would fain have devolved on Pilate, and themselves to
pronounce the hateful sentence of crucifixion, unknown
to their law, but for which they had secretly intrigued ;
and we find the multitude fiercely clamouring for a
defeated champion of brute force, whose weapon has
snapped in his hands, who has led his followers to
the cross, and from whom there is no more to hope.
What satire upon their hope of a temporal Messiah
could be more bitter than their own cry, " We have no
king but Cæsar " ? And what satire upon this profession
more destructive than their choice of Barabbas and
refusal of Christ ? And all the while, Jesus looks on
in silence, carrying out His mournful but effectual plan,
the true Master of the movements which design to
crush Him, and which He has foretold. As He ever
receives gifts for the rebellious, and is the Saviour of

all men, though especially of them that believe, so now
His passion, which retrieved the erring soul of Peter,
and won the penitent thief, rescues Barabbas from the
cross.   His suffering was made visibly vicarious.

One is tempted to pity the feeble judge, the only
person who is known to have attempted to rescue Jesus,
beset by his old faults, which will make an impeachment
fatal, wishing better than he dares to act, hesitating,
sinking inch by inch, and like a bird with broken wing.
No accomplice in this frightful crime is so suggestive
of warning to hearts not entirely hardened.

But pity is lost in sterner emotion as we remember
that this wicked governor, having borne witness to the
perfect innocence of Jesus, was content, in order to
save himself from danger, to watch the Blessed One
enduring all the horrors of a Roman scourging, and
then to yield Him up to die.

It is now the unmitigated cruelty of ancient paganism which has closed its hand upon our Lord.   When
the soldiers led Him away within the court, He was
lost to His nation, which had renounced Him.   It is
upon this utter alienation, even more than the locality
where the cross was fixed, that the Epistle to the
Hebrews turns our attention, when it reminds us that
"the bodies of those beasts whose blood is brought
into the holy place by the high priest as an offering for
sin, are burned without the camp.   Wherefore Jesus
also, that He might sanctify the people through His
own blood, suffered without the gate."   The physical
exclusion, the material parallel points to something
deeper, for the inference is that of estrangement.
Those who serve the tabernacle cannot eat of our altar.
Let us go forth unto Him, bearing His reproach.
(Heb. xii. 10–13).

Renounced by Israel, and about to become a curse under the law, He has now to suffer the cruelty of wantonness, as He has already endured the cruelty of hatred and fear. Now, more than ever perhaps, He looks for pity and there is no man. None responded to the deep appeal of the eyes which had never seen misery without relieving it. The contempt of the strong for the weak and suffering, of coarse natures for sensitive ones, of Romans for Jews, all these were blended with bitter scorn of the Jewish expectation that some day Rome shall bow before a Hebrew conqueror, in the mockery which Jesus now underwent, when they clad Him in such cast-off purple as the Palace yielded, thrust a reed into His pinioned hand, crowned Him with thorns, beat these into His holy head with the sceptre they had offered Him, and then proceeded to render the homage of their nation to the Messiah of Jewish hopes. It may have been this mockery which suggested to Pilate the inscription for the cross. But where is the mockery now? In crowning Him King of sufferings, and Royal among those who weep, they secured to Him the adherence of all hearts. Christ was made perfect by the things which He suffered; and it was not only in spite of insult and anguish but by means of them that He drew all men unto Him.

CHRIST CRUCIFIED.

" And they compel one passing by, Simon of Cyrene, coming from the country, the father of Alexander and Rufus, to go *with them*, that he might bear His cross. And they bring Him unto the place Golgotha, which is, being interpreted, The place of a skull. And they offered Him wine mingled with myrrh : but He received it not. And they crucify Him, and part His garments among them, casting lots upon them, what each should take. And it was the third hour, and they crucified Him. And the superscription of His accusation was written over, THE KING OF THE JEWS. And with Him they crucify two robbers ; one on His right hand, and one on His left.   And they that passed by railed on Him, wagging their heads, and saying, Ha ! Thou that destroyest the temple, and buildest it in three days, save Thyself, and come down from the cross.   In like manner also the chief priests mocking *Him* among themselves with the scribes said, He saved others ; Himself He cannot save.   Let the Christ, the King of Israel, now come down from the cross, that we may see and believe.   And they that were crucified with Him reproached Him."—MARK xv. 21–32 (R.V.).

AT last the preparations were complete and the interval of mental agony was over.   They led Him away to crucify Him.   And upon the road an event of mournful interest took place.   It was the custom to lay the two arms of the cross upon the doomed man, fastening them together at such an angle as to pass behind His neck, while his hands were bound to the ends in front. And thus it was that Jesus went forth bearing His cross.   Did He think of this when He bade us take His yoke upon us ?   Did He wait for events to explain the words, by making it visibly one and the same to take His yoke and to take up our cross and follow Him ?

On the road, however, they forced a reluctant stranger to go with them that he might bear the cross.   The traditional reason is that our Redeemer's strength gave way, and it became physically impossible for Him to proceed ; but this is challenged upon the ground that to fail would have been unworthy of our Lord, and would mar the perfection of His example.   How so, when the failure was a real one ?   Is there no fitness in the belief that He who was tempted in all points like as we are, endured this hardness also, of struggling with the impossible demands of human cruelty, the spirit indeed willing but the flesh weak ?   It is not easy to believe that any other reason than manifest

inability, would have induced his persecutors to spare
Him one drop of bitterness, one throb of pain. The
noblest and most delicately balanced frame, like all
other exquisite machines, is not capable of the rudest
strain ; and we know that Jesus had once sat wearied
by the well, while the hardy fishers went into the town,
and returned with bread. And this night our gentle
Master had endured what no common victim knew.
Long before the scourging, or even the buffeting began,
His spiritual exhaustion had needed that an angel from
heaven should strengthen Him. And the utmost possibility of exertion was now reached : the spot where
they met Simon of Cyrene marks this melancholy limit;
and suffering henceforth must be purely passive.

We cannot assert with confidence that Simon and
his family were saved by this event. The coercion put
upon him, the fact that he was seized and "impressed"
into the service, already seems to indicate sympathy with
Jesus. And we are fain to believe that he who received
the honour, so strange and sad and sacred, the unique
privilege of lifting some little of the crushing burden
of the Saviour, was not utterly ignorant of what he did.
We know at least that the names of his children,
Alexander and Rufus, were familiar in the Church for
which St. Mark was writing, and that in Rome a
Rufus was chosen in the Lord, and his mother was
like a mother to St. Paul (Rom. xvi. 13). With what
feelings may they have recalled the story, " him they
compelled to bear His cross."

They led Him to a place where the rounded summit
of a knoll had its grim name from some resemblance to
a human skull, and prepared the crosses there.

It was the custom of the daughters of Jerusalem,
who lamented Him as He went, to provide a stupefying

draught for the sufferers of this atrocious cruelty. "And they offered Him wine mixed with myrrh, but He received it not," although that dreadful thirst, which was part of the suffering of crucifixion, had already begun, for He only refused when He had tasted it.

In so doing He rebuked all who seek to drown sorrows or benumb the soul in wine, all who degrade and dull their sensibilities by physical excess or indulgence, all who would rather blind their intelligence than pay the sharp cost of its exercise. He did not condemn the use of anodynes, but the abuse of them. It is one thing to suspend the senses during an operation, and quite another thing by one's own choice to pass into eternity without consciousness enough to commit the soul into its Father's hands.

"And they crucify Him." Let the words remain as the Evangelist left them, to tell their own story of human sin, and of Divine love which many waters could not quench, neither could the depths drown it.

Only let us think in silence of all that those words convey.

In the first sharpness of mortal anguish, Jesus saw His executioners sit down at ease, all unconscious of the dread meaning of what was passing by their side, to part His garments among them, and cast lots for the raiment which they had stripped from His sacred form. The Gospels are content thus to abandon those relics about which so many legends have been woven. But indeed all through these four wonderful narratives the self-restraint is perfect. When the Epistles touch upon the subject of the crucifixion they kindle into flame. When St. Peter soon afterwards referred to it, his indignation is beyond question, and Stephen called the rulers betrayers and murderers (Acts ii. 23, 24;

iii. 13, 14; vii. 51–53) but not one single syllable of complaint or comment mingles with the clear flow of narrative in the four Gospels. The truth is that the subject was too great, too fresh and vivid in their minds, to be adorned or enlarged upon. What comment of St. Mark, what mortal comment, could add to the weight of the words "they crucify Him"? Men use no figures of speech when telling how their own beloved one died. But it was differently that the next age wrote about the crucifixion; and perhaps the lofty self-restraint of the Evangelists has never been attained again.

St. Mark tells us that He was crucified at the third hour, whereas we read in St. John that it was "about the sixth hour" when Pilate ascended the seat of judgment (xix. 14). It seems likely that St. John used the Roman reckoning, and his computation does not pretend to be exact; while we must remember that mental agitation conspired with the darkening of the sky, to render such an estimate as he offers even more than usually vague.

It has been supposed that St. Mark's "third hour" goes back to the scourging, which, as being a regular part of Roman crucifixion, he includes, although inflicted in this case before the sentence. But it will prove quite as hard to reconcile this distribution of time with "the sixth hour" in St. John, while it is at variance with the context in which St. Mark asserts it.

The small and bitter heart of Pilate keenly resented his defeat and the victory of the priests. Perhaps it was when his soldiers offered the scornful homage of Rome to Israel and her monarch, that he saw the way to a petty revenge. And all Jerusalem was scandalized by reading the inscription over a crucified malefactor's head, The King of the Jews.

It needs some reflection to perceive how sharp the taunt was.   A few years ago they had a king, but the sceptre had departed from Judah; Rome had abolished him.   It was their hope that soon a native king would for ever sweep away the foreigner from their fields.   But here the Roman exhibited the fate of such a claim, and professed to inflict its horrors not upon one whom they disavowed, but upon their king indeed.   We know how angrily and vainly they protested ; and again we seem to recognise the solemn irony of Providence.   For this was their true King, and they, who resented the superscription, had fixed their Anointed there.

All the more they would disconnect themselves from Him, and wreak their passion upon the helpless One whom they hated.   The populace mocked Him openly : the chief priests, too cultivated to insult avowedly a dying man, mocked Him "among themselves," speaking bitter words for Him to hear.   The multitude repeated the false charge which had probably done much to inspire their sudden preference for Barabbas, " Thou that destroyest the temple and buildest it again in three days, save Thyself and come down from the cross."

They little suspected that they were recalling words of consolation to His memory, reminding Him that all this suffering was foreseen, and how it was all to end. The chief priests spoke also a truth full of consolation, "He saved others, Himself He cannot save," although it was no physical bar which forbade Him to accept their challenge.   And when they flung at Him His favourite demand for faith, saying " Let the Christ, the King of Israel, now come down from the cross, that we may see and believe " surely they reminded Him of the great multitude who should not see, and yet should

believe, when He came back through the gates of
death.

Thus the words they spoke could not afflict Him.
But what horror to the pure soul to behold these yawning
abysses of malignity, these gulfs of pitiless hate. The
affronts hurled at suffering and defeat by prosperous and
exultant malice are especially Satanic. Many diseases
inflict more physical pain than torturers ever invented,
but they do not excite the same horror, because gentle
ministries are there to charm away the despair which
human hate and execration conjure up.

To add to the insult of His disgraceful death, the
Romans had crucified two robbers, doubtless from the
band of Barabbas, one upon each side of Jesus. We
know how this outrage led to the salvation of one of
them, and refreshed the heavy laden soul of Jesus,
oppressed by so much guilt and vileness, with the visible
firstfruit of His passion, giving Him to see of the travail
of His soul, by which He shall yet be satisfied.

But in their first agony and despair, when all voices
were unanimous against the Blessed One, and they
too must needs find some outlet for their frenzy, they
both reproached Him. Thus the circle of human
wrong was rounded.

The traitor, the deserters, the forsworn apostle, the
perjured witnesses, the hypocritical pontiff professing
horror at blasphemy while himself abjuring his national
hope, the accomplices in a sham trial, the murderer
of the Baptist and his men of war, the abject ruler
who declared Him innocent yet gave Him up to die,
the servile throng who waited on the priests, the
soldiers of Herod and of Pilate, the pitiless crowd
which clamoured for His blood, and they who mocked
Him in His agony,—not one of them whom Jesus did

not compassionate, whose cruelty had not power to wring His heart. Disciple and foeman, Roman and Jew, priest and soldier and judge, all had lifted up their voice against Him. And when the comrades of His passion joined the cry, the last ingredient of human cruelty was infused into the cup which James and John had once proposed to drink with Him.

THE DEATH OF JESUS.

"And when the sixth hour was come, there was darkness over the whole land until the ninth hour. And at the ninth hour Jesus cried with a loud voice, Eloi, Eloi, lama sabachthani? which is, being interpreted, My God, My God, why hast Thou forsaken Me? And some of them that stood by, when they heard it, said, Behold, He calleth Elijah. And one ran, and filling a sponge full of vinegar, put it on a reed, and gave Him to drink, saying, Let be; let us see whether Elijah cometh to take Him down. And Jesus uttered a loud voice, and gave up the ghost. And the veil of the temple was rent in twain from the top to the bottom. And when the centurion, which stood by over against Him, saw that He so gave up the ghost, he said, Truly this man was the Son of God. And there were also women beholding from afar: among whom *were* both Mary Magdalene, and Mary the mother of James the less and of Joses, and Salome; who, when He was in Galilee, followed Him, and ministered unto Him; and many other women which came up with Him unto Jerusalem."—MARK xv. 33–41 (R.V.).

THREE hours of raging human passion, endured with Godlike patience, were succeeded by three hours of darkness, hushing mortal hatred into silence, and perhaps contributing to the penitence of the reviler at His side. It was a supernatural gloom, since an eclipse of the sun was impossible during the full moon of Passover. Shall we say that, as it shall be in the last days, nature sympathized with humanity, and the angel of the sun hid his face from his suffering Lord?

Or was it the shadow of a still more dreadful eclipse,

for now the eternal Father veiled His countenance from the Son in whom He was well pleased?

In some true sense God forsook Him. And we have to seek for a meaning of this awful statement—inadequate no doubt, for all our thoughts must come short of such a reality, but free from prevarication and evasion.

It is wholly unsatisfactory to regard the verse as merely the heading of a psalm, cheerful for the most part, which Jesus inaudibly recited. Why was only this verse uttered aloud? How false an impression must have been produced upon the multitude, upon St. John, upon the penitent thief, if Jesus were suffering less than the extreme of spiritual anguish. Nay, we feel that never before can the verse have attained its fullest meaning, a meaning which no experience of David could more than dimly shadow forth, since we ask in our sorrows, Why have we forsaken God? but Jesus said, Why hast Thou forsaken Me?

And this unconsciousness of any reason for desertion disproves the old notion that He felt Himself a sinner, and "suffered infinite remorse, as being the chief sinner in the universe, all the sins of mankind being His." One who felt thus could neither have addressed God as "My God," nor asked why He was forsaken.

Still less does it allow us to believe that the Father perfectly identified Jesus with sin, so as to be "wroth" with Him, and even "to hate Him to the uttermost." Such notions, the offspring of theories carried to a wild and irreverent extreme, when carefully examined impute to the Deity confusion of thought, a mistaking of the Holy One for a sinner or rather for the aggregate of sinners. But it is very different when we pass from the Divine consciousness to the bearing of God toward Christ our representative, to the outshining or eclipse

of His favour.   That this was overcast is manifest from
the fact that Jesus everywhere else addresses Him as
My Father, here only as My God.   Even in the garden
it was Abba Father, and the change indicates not indeed estrangement of heart, but certainly remoteness.
Thus we have the sense of desertion, combined with
the assurance which once breathed in the words, O God,
Thou art my God.

Thus also it came to pass that He who never forfeited
the most intimate communion and sunny smile of
heaven, should yet give us an example at the last
of that utmost struggle and sternest effort of the soul,
which trusts without experience, without emotion, in
the dark, because God is God, not because I am happy.

But they who would empty the death of Jesus of its
sacrificial import, and leave only the attraction and inspiration of a sublime life and death, must answer the
hard questions, How came God to forsake the Perfect
One ?   Or, how came He to charge God with such
desertion ?   His follower, twice using this very word,
could boast that he was cast down yet not forsaken, and
that at his first trial all men forsook him, yet the Lord
stood by him (2 Cor. iv. 9; 2 Tim. iv. 16, 17).   How
came the disciple to be above his Master ?

The only explanation is in His own word, that His
life is a ransom in exchange for many (Mark x. 45).
The chastisement of our peace, not the remorse of our
guiltiness, was upon Him.   No wonder that St. Mark,
who turns aside from his narrative for no comment,
no exposition, was yet careful to preserve this alone
among the dying words of Christ.

And the Father heard His Son.   At that cry the mysterious darkness passed away; and the soul of Jesus was
relieved from its burden, so that He became conscious

28

of physical suffering; and the mockery of the multitude was converted into awe. It seemed to them that His Eloi might indeed bring Elias, and the great and notable day, and they were willing to relieve the thirst which no stoical hardness forbade that gentlest of all sufferers to confess. Thereupon the anguish that redeemed the world was over; a loud voice told that exhaustion was not complete; and yet Jesus "gave up the ghost." *

Through the veil, that is to say His flesh, we have boldness to enter into the holy place; and now that He had opened the way, the veil of the temple was rent asunder by no mortal hand, but downward from the top. The way into the holiest was visibly thrown open, when sin was expiated, which had forfeited our right of access.

And the centurion, seeing that His death itself was abnormal and miraculous, and accompanied with miraculous signs, said, Truly this was a righteous man. But such a confession could not rest there: if He was this, He was all He claimed to be; and the mockery of His enemies had betrayed the secret of their hate; He was the Son of God.

"When the centurion saw" . . . "There were also many women beholding." Who can overlook the connection? Their gentle hearts were not to be utterly overwhelmed: as the centurion saw and drew his inference, so they beheld, and felt, however dimly, amid sorrows that benumb the mind, that still, even in such wreck and misery, God was not far from Jesus.

When the Lord said, It is finished, there was not only an end of conscious anguish, but also of contempt and

---

* The ingenious and plausible attempt to show that His death was caused by a physical rupture of the heart has one fatal weakness. Death came too late for this; the severest pressure was already relieved.

insult. His body was not to see corruption, nor was a
bone to be broken, nor should it remain in hostile hands.

Respect for Jewish prejudice prevented the Romans
from leaving it to moulder on the cross, and the
approaching Sabbath was not one to be polluted. And
knowing this, Joseph of Arimathæa boldly went in to
Pilate and asked for the body of Jesus. It was only
secretly and in fear that he had been a disciple, but the
deadly crisis had developed what was hidden, he had
opposed the crime of his nation in their council, and in
the hour of seeming overthrow he chose the good part.
Boldly the timid one " went in," braving the scowls of
the priesthood, defiling himself moreover, and forfeiting
his share in the sacred feast, in hope to win the further
defilement of contact with the dead.

Pilate was careful to verify so rapid a death ; but when
he was certain of the fact, " he granted the corpse to
Joseph," as a worthless thing. His frivolity is expressed
alike in the unusual verb* and substantive : he " freely-
bestowed," he " gave away " not " the body " as when
Joseph spoke of it, but " the corpse," the fallen thing,
like a prostrated and uprooted tree that shall revive no
more. Wonderful it is to reflect that God had entered
into eternal union with what was thus given away to
the only man of rank who cared to ask for it. Wonderful to think what opportunities of eternal gain men
are content to lose ; what priceless treasures are given
away, or thrown away as worthless. Wonderful to
imagine the feelings of Joseph in heaven to-day, as he
gazes with gratitude and love upon the glorious Body
which once, for a little, was consigned to his reverent care.

St. John tells us that Nicodemus brought a hundred
pound weight of myrrh and aloes, and they together

---

* *I.e.* in the New Testament, where it occurs but once besides.

wrapped Him in these, in the linen which had been provided; and Joseph laid Him in his own new tomb, undesecrated by mortality.

And there Jesus rested. His friends had no such hope as would prevent them from closing the door with a great stone. His enemies set a watch, and sealed the stone. The broad moon of Passover made the night as clear as the day, and the multitude of strangers, who thronged the city and its suburbs, rendered any attempt at robbery even more hopeless than at another season.

What indeed could the trembling disciples of an executed pretender do with such an object as a dead body? What could they hope from the possession of it? But if they did not steal it, if the moral glories of Christianity are not sprung from deliberate mendacity, why was the body not produced, to abash the wild dreams of their fanaticism? It was fearfully easy to identify. The scourging, the cross, and the spear, left no slight evidence behind, and the broken bones of the malefactors completed the absolute isolation of the sacred body of the Lord.

The providence of God left no precaution unsupplied to satisfy honest and candid inquiry. It remained to be seen, would He leave Christ's soul in Hades, or suffer His Holy One (such is the epithet applied to the body of Jesus) to see corruption?

Meantime, through what is called three days and nights—a space which touched, but only touched, the confines of a first and third day, as well as the Saturday which intervened, Jesus shared the humiliation of common men, the divorce of soul and body. He slept as sleep the dead, but His soul was where He promised that the penitent should come, refreshed in Paradise.

CHAPTER XVI.

CHRIST RISEN.

"And when the sabbath was past, Mary Magdalene, and Mary the *mother* of James, and Salome, bought spices, that they might come and anoint Him. And very early on the first day of the week, they come to the tomb when the sun was risen. And they were saying among themselves, Who shall roll us away the stone from the door of the tomb? and looking up, they see that the stone is rolled back : for it was exceeding great. And entering into the tomb, they saw a young man sitting on the right side, arrayed in a white robe, and they were amazed. And he saith unto them, Be not amazed ; ye seek Jesus, the Nazarene, Which hath been crucified : He is risen ; He is not here : behold, the place where they laid Him! But go, tell His disciples and Peter, He goeth before you into Galilee : there shall ye see Him, as He said unto you. And they went out, and fled from the tomb; for trembling and astonishment had come upon them ; and they said nothing to any one ; for they were afraid. Now when He was risen early on the first day of the week, He appeared first to Mary Magdalene, from whom He had cast out seven devils. She went and told them that had been with Him, as they mourned and wept. And they, when they heard that He was alive, and had been seen of her, disbelieved. And after these things He was manifested in another form unto two of them, as they walked, on their way into the country. And they went away and told it unto the rest : neither believed they them. And afterward He was manifested unto the eleven themselves as they sat at meat; and He upbraided them with their unbelief and hardness of heart, because they believed not them which had seen Him after He was risen. And He said unto them, Go ye into all the world, and preach the gospel to the whole creation. He that believeth and is baptized shall be saved; but he that disbelieveth shall be condemned. And these signs shall follow them that believe : in My name shall they cast out devils; they shall speak with new tongues ; they shall take up serpents, and if they drink any deadly thing, it shall in no wise hurt them ; they shall lay hands on the sick, and they shall recover."—MARK xvi. 1-18 (R.V.).

THE Gospels were not written for the curious but for the devout. They are most silent therefore where myth and legend would be most garrulous, and it is instructive to seek, in the story of Jesus, for anything similar to the account of the Buddha's enlightenment under the Bo tree. We read nothing of the interval in Hades; nothing of the entry of His crowned and immortal body into the presence chamber of God; nothing of the resurrection. Did He awake alone? Was He waited upon by the hierarchy of heaven, who robed Him in raiment unknown to men? We are only told what concerns mankind, the sufficient manifestation of Jesus to His disciples.

And to harmonise the accounts a certain effort is necessary, because they tell of interviews with men and women who had to pass through all the vicissitudes of despair, suspense, rapturous incredulity,* and faith. Each of them contributes a portion of the tale.

From St. John we learn that Mary Magdalene came early to the sepulchre, from St. Matthew that others were with her, from St. Mark that these women, dissatisfied with the unskilful ministrations of men (and men whose rank knew nothing of such functions), had brought sweet spices to anoint Him Who was about to claim their adoration; St. John tells how Mary, seeing the empty sepulchre, ran to tell Peter and John of its desecration; the others, that in her absence an angel told the glad tidings to the women; St. Mark, that Mary was the first to whom Jesus Himself appeared. And thenceforth the narrative more easily falls into its place.

---

* Can anything surpass that masterstroke of insight and descriptive power, "they still disbelieved for joy" (Luke xxiv. 41).

This confusion, however perplexing to thoughtless readers, is inevitable in the independent histories of such events, derived from the various parties who delighted to remember, each what had befallen himself.

But even a genuine contradiction would avail nothing to refute the substantial fact. When the generals of Henry the Fourth strove to tell him what passed after he was wounded at Aumale, no two of them agreed in the course of events which gave them victory. Two armies beheld the battle of Waterloo, but who can tell when it began? At ten o'clock, said the Duke of Wellington. At half past eleven, said General Alava, who rode beside him. At twelve according to Napoleon and Drouet; and at one according to Ney.

People who doubt the reality of the resurrection, because the harmony of the narratives is underneath the surface, do not deny these facts. They are part of history. Yet it is certain that the resurrection of Jesus colours the history of the world more powerfully to-day, than the events which are so much more recent.

If Christ were not risen, how came these despairing men and women by their new hope, their energy, their success among the very men who slew Him? If Christ be not risen, how has the morality of mankind been raised? Was it ever known that a falsehood exercised for ages a quickening and purifying power which no truth can rival?

From the ninth verse to the end of St. Mark's account it is curiously difficult to decide on the true reading. And it must be said that the note in the Revised Version, however accurate, does not succeed in giving any notion of the strength of the case in favour of the remainder of the Gospel. It tells us that the two oldest manuscripts omit them, but we do not read that in one of these a space is left for the insertion of something, known by the scribe to be wanting there. Nor does it mention the twelve manuscripts of almost equal antiquity in which they are contained, nor the early date at which they were quoted.

The evidence appears to lean towards the belief that they were added in a later edition, or else torn off in an early copy from which some transcribers worked. But unbelief cannot gain anything by converting them into a separate testimony, of the very earliest antiquity, to events related in each of the other Gospels.

And the uncertainty itself will be wholesome if it reminds us that saving faith is not to be reposed in niceties of criticism, but in a living Christ, the power and wisdom of God. Jesus blamed men for thinking that they had eternal life in their inspired Scriptures, and so refusing to come for life to Him, of Whom those Scriptures testified. Has sober criticism ever shaken for one hour that sacred function of Holy Writ ?

What then is especially shown us in the closing words of St. Mark ?

Readiness to requite even a spark of grace, and to bless with the first tidings of a risen Redeemer the love which sought only to embalm His corpse. Tender care for the fallen and disheartened, in the message sent especially to Peter. Immeasurable condescension, such as rested formerly, a Babe, in a peasant woman's arms, and announced its Advent to shepherds, now appearing first of all to a woman "out of whom He had cast seven devils."

A state of mind among the disciples, far indeed from that rapt and hysterical enthusiasm which men have fancied, ready to be whirled away in a vortex of religious propagandism (and to whirl the whole world after it), upon the impulse of dreams, hallucinations, voices mistaken on a misty shore, longings which begot convictions. Jesus Himself, and no second, no messenger from Jesus, inspired the zeal which kindled mankind. The disciples, mourning and weeping, found the glad tidings incredible, while Mary who had seen Him, believed. When two, as they walked, beheld Him in another shape, the rest remained incredulous, announcing indeed that He had actually risen and appeared unto Peter, yet so far from a true conviction that when He actually came to them, they supposed that they beheld a spirit (Luke xxiv. 34, 37). Yet He looked in the face those pale discouraged Galileans, and bade them go into all the world, bearing to the whole creation the issues of eternal life and death. And they went forth, and the power and intellect of the world are won. Whatever unbelievers think about individual souls, it is plain that the words of the Nazarene have proved true for communities and nations, He that believeth and is baptised has been saved, He that believeth not has been condemned. The nation and kingdom that has not served Christ has perished.

Nor does any one pretend that the agents in this marvellous movement were insincere. If all this was a dream, it was a strange one surely, and demands to be explained. If it was otherwise, no doubt the finger of God has come unto us.

THE ASCENSION.

"So then the Lord Jesus, after He had spoken unto them, was received up into heaven, and sat down at the right hand of God. And they went forth, and preached everywhere, the Lord working with them, and confirming the word by the signs that followed. Amen."— MARK xvi. 19-20 (R.V.)

WE have reached the close of the great Gospel of the energies of Jesus, His toils, His manner, His searching gaze, His noble indignation, His love of children, the consuming zeal by virtue of which He was not more truly the Lamb of God than the Lion of the tribe of Judah. St. Mark has just recorded how He bade His followers carry on His work, defying the serpents of the world, and renewing the plague-stricken race of Adam. In what strength did they fulfil this commission ? How did they fare without the Master ? And what is St. Mark's view of the Ascension ?

Here, as all through the Gospel, minor points are neglected. Details are only valued when they carry some aid for the special design of the Evangelist, who presses to the core of his subject at once and boldly. As he omitted the bribes with which Satan tempted Jesus, and cared not for the testimony of the Baptist when the voice of God was about to peal from heaven over the Jordan, as on the holy mount he told not the subject of which Moses and Elijah spoke, but how Jesus Himself predicted His death to His disciples, so now He is silent about the mountain slope, the final benediction, the cloud which withdrew Him from their sight and the angels who sent back the dazed apostles to their homes and their duties. It is not caprice nor haste that omits so much interesting information. His mind is fixed on a few central thoughts ; what concerns him is to link the mighty story of the life and death of Jesus with these great facts, that He was received up into Heaven, that He there sat down upon the right hand of God, and that His disciples were never forsaken of Him at all, but proved, by the miraculous spread of the early Church, that His power was among them still.   St. Mark does not record the promise, but he asserts the fact that Christ was with them all the days.   There is indeed a connection between his two closing verses, subtle and hard to render into English, and yet real, which suggests the notion of balance, of relation between the two movements, the ascent of Jesus, and the evangelisation of the world, such as exists, for example, between detachments of an army co-operating for a common end, so that our Lord, for His part, ascended, while the disciples, for their part, went forth and found Him with them still.

But the link is plainer which binds the Ascension to His previous story of suffering and conflict.   It was "then," and "after He had spoken unto them," that "the Lord Jesus was received up."   In truth His ascension was but the carrying forward to completion of His resurrection, which was not a return to the poor conditions of our mortal life, but an entrance into glory, only arrested in its progress until He should have quite convinced His followers that "it is I indeed," and made them understand that "thus it is written that the Christ should suffer, and rise again from the dead the third day," and filled them with holy shame for their unbelief, and with courage for their future course, so strange, so weary, so sublime.

There is something remarkable in the words, "He was received up into heaven."   We habitually speak of Him as ascending, but Scripture more frequently

declares that He was the subject of the action of
another, and was taken up. St. Luke tells us that,
"while they worshipped, He was carried up into
heaven," and again "He was received up. . . . He
was taken up" (Luke xxiv. 51 ; Acts i. 2, 9). Physical
interference is not implied : no angels bore Him aloft ;
and the narratives make it clear that His glorious Body,
obedient to its new mysterious nature, arose unaided.
But the decision to depart, and the choice of a time,
came not from Him : He did not go, but was taken.
Never hitherto had He glorified Himself. He had
taught His disciples to be contented in the lowest room
until the Master of the house should bid them come up
higher. And so, when His own supreme victory is
won, and heaven held its breath expectant and astonished, the conquering Lord was content to walk with
peasants by the Lake of Galilee and on the slopes of
Olivet until the appointed time. What a rebuke to us
who chafe and fret if the recognition of our petty merits
be postponed.

"He was received up into heaven !" What sublime
mysteries are covered by that simple phrase. It was
He who taught us to make, even of the mammon of
unrighteousness, friends who shall welcome us, when
mammon fails and all things mortal have deserted us,
into everlasting habitations. With what different greet-
ings, then, do men enter the City of God. Some converts of the death bed perhaps there are, who scarcely
make their way to heaven, alone, unhailed by one
whom they saved or comforted, and like a vessel which
struggles into port, with rent cordage and tattered sails,
only not a wreck. Others, who aided some few, spar-
ing a little of their means and energies, are greeted and
blessed by a scanty group. But even our chieftains and

leaders, the martyrs, sages and philanthropists whose
names brighten the annals of the Church, what is their
influence, and how few have they reached, compared
with that great multitude whom none can number, of
all nations and tribes and peoples and tongues, who
cry with a loud voice, Salvation unto our God who
sitteth upon the throne, and unto the Lamb. Through
Him it pleased the Father to reconcile all things unto
Himself, through Him, whether things upon the earth
or things in the heavens. And surely the supreme
hour in the history of the universe was when, in flesh,
the sore stricken but now the all-conquering Christ re-
entered His native heaven.

And He sat down at the right hand of God. The
expression is, beyond all controversy, borrowed from
that great Psalm which begins by saying, "The Lord
said unto my Lord, Sit thou at My right hand," and
which presently makes the announcement never
revealed until then, "Thou art a Priest for ever after
the order of Melchizedec" (Ps. cx. 1, 4). It is therefore an anticipation of the argument for the royal
Priesthood of Jesus which is developed in the Epistle
to the Hebrews. Now priesthood is a human function:
every high priest is chosen from among men. And
the Ascension proclaims to us, not the Divinity of the
Eternal Word but the glorification of "the Lord
Jesus;" not the omnipotence of God the Son, but that
all power is committed unto Him Who is not ashamed
to call us brethren, that His human hands wield the
sceptre as once they held the reed, and the brows then
insulted and torn with thorns are now crowned with
many crowns. In the overthrow of Satan He won
all, and infinitely more than all, of that vast bribe
which Satan once offered for His homage, and the

angels for ever worship Him who would not for a moment bend His knee to evil.

Now since He conquered not for Himself but as Captain of our Salvation, the Ascension also proclaims the issue of all the holy suffering, all the baffled efforts, all the cross-bearing of all who follow Christ.

His High Priesthood is with authority. "Every high priest standeth," but He has for ever sat down on the right hand of the throne of the majesty in the heavens, a Priest sitting upon His throne (Heb. viii. 1 ; Zech. vi. 13). And therefore it is His office, Who pleads for us and represents us, Himself to govern our destinies. No wonder that His early followers, with minds which He had opened to understand the Scriptures, were mighty to cast down strongholds. Against tribulation and anguish and persecution and famine and nakedness and peril and sword they were more than conquerors through Him. For He worked with them and confirmed His word with signs. And we have seen that He works with His people still, and still confirms His gospel, only withdrawing signs of one order as those of another kind are multiplied. Wherever they wage a faithful battle, He gives them victory. Whenever they cry to Him in anguish, the form of the Son of God is with them in the furnace, and the smell of fire does not pass upon them. Where they come, the desert blossoms as a rose ; and where they are received, the serpents of life no longer sting, its fevers grow cool, and the demons which rend it are cast out.

IMPORTANT RELIGIOUS WORKS.

The Dragon, Image and Demon;

OR, THE THREE RELIGIONS OF CHINA.

CONFUCIANISM, BUDDHISM, and TAOISM.

Giving an account of the *Mythology, Idolatry,* and *Demonolatry* of the Chinese. By Rev. HAMPDEN C. DU BOSE, 14 years a Missionary in China. With **188 Illustrations, Engraved in China.** Crown octavo. Beautifully bound. Cloth, full gilt side. $2.00.

"The writer has drawn his water from native wells, the facts being mostly gathered from Chinese sources. The pen is not held by one seated in a professor's study, but by a plain man, who daily walks to and fro among idolators, and testifies of what he has seen and heard, written in a plain style, so that the young as well as the old may understand it."

"As a writer, he has drawn largely on native sources. There is much here that will be of value, even to those familiar with the literature on the subject. One walks as with a familiar friend with every thing in the country, who simply talks to him about these religions as known by the literati and the common people. The style is remarkably lucid, and the interest is sustained from the first to the last."—*Northern Christian Advocate.*

"We commend it as a clear and popular presentation of the subject about which such vague views prevail."—*Lutheran Quarterly.*

"The work will make a valuable addition to our young people's libraries, and will afford much food for reflection."—*Zion's Herald.*

"Here is a vast store of information about the Chinese manners and customs in all the phases of life. The author has also studied the writings of Edkins, Eitet, Legge, and Beal, and the various Chinese sages."—*N. Y. Commercial.*

London Saturday Review—"It is a book likely to be widely read. Of the author's minute description of popular and household deities, and the mass of legend connected with them, the book and its curious illustrations can alone speak. Mr. Du Bose has much to say that is fresh and suggestive, and he says it with force and conviction."

MOMENTS ON THE MOUNT.

A Series of 108 Devotional Meditations.

By Rev. GEO. MATHESON, D.D. (From 2d English edition.) 12mo, cloth. $1.25.

"In 'Moments on the Mount' we are brought into contact with a writer whose whole soul is saturated with Divine ideas, and to whom Scriptural images are the exponents and symbols of spiritual conceptions. This volume is not one to be read through at a sitting and then laid aside; rather, each meditation is to be pondered over and enjoyed singly and separately, and to be dwelt upon until it becomes a permanent possession."—THE SCOTSMAN.

Rev. Dr. John Hall says each section is self-contained, practical, starting with a Bible word and bringing out in a meditative form its meaning. For the sick-room, the aged, or for the closet-table of any Christian, it is a thoroughly fit and good book.

Copies sent by mail on receipt of price.

A. C. ARMSTRONG & SON.

IMPORTANT RELIGIOUS WORKS.

MR. SPURGEON'S NEW BOOK:
The Cheque-Book of the Bank of Faith.

BEING PRECIOUS PROMISES ARRANGED FOR DAILY USE.
With Brief Experimental Comments. Nearly 400 pages, 12mo, $1.50.

"*When it is stated that this well-named book contains a Scripture Promise for each day in the year, commented on, in his best vein, by the prince of practical and experimental preachers, enough has been said to commend it as first in its class.*"—N. Y. Christian Intelligencer.

"It is done in the great preacher's inimitable style, and SPEAKS HOME ON EVERY PAGE to the heart and need of the believer."—*N. Y. Independ't.*

"*Mr. Spurgeon's words are so plain, his style so sparkling, and his spirit so devout, that the reading of his productions is almost sure to excite a mental glow and awaken holy aspirations. This book is brimful of quickening, soothing, soul-lifting power.*"—N. Y. Witness.

"As there are three hundred and sixty-five cheques in this book, the man who makes right use of them is rich indeed."—*N. Y. Observer.*

Palestine in the Time of Christ.

By EDMUND STAPFER, D. D., of the Protestant Faculty, Paris. With map, and plans. Uniform with *Stanley's "Sinai and Palestine."* Crown 8vo, cloth, $2.50.

"*There is so much here of accurate learning, and of matter extremely valuable in respect to the personal and every-day life of the people, that 'it fills a place not filled' by any other volume within our knowledge. It is an excellent book for reference for all who would like to interpret biblical passages for homiletic purposes with minute and accurate statement.*"—N. Y. Christian Advocate and Journal.

"Dr. STAPFER may be congratulated on the successful way in which he has accomplished his task. He has studied the diversified topics he treats of, and has generally drawn his material from the best authorities, arranging it in lucid order. Few guides will be found more useful in surveying the varied details into which a comprehensive subject leads him. There is no English book that can be put beside it as occupying the same ground."—*London Athenæum.*

"De Pressense's Brilliant Book."

THE ANCIENT WORLD AND CHRISTIANITY. By E. DE PRESSENSE, D. D., author of a "Study of Origins," etc. Cr. 8vo, 500 pages, $1.75.

"It is an admirable hand-book of comparative religion. It is a substantial, learned, and instructive treatment of a most important subject."—*British Weekly.*

"*A brilliant book. . . . No one who opens the book is likely to fail to admire the ingenuity of the treatment of the beliefs of the primitive man.*"—London Literary World.

"Brilliant in style, lucid in exposition, comprehensive in philosophic grasp, it presents a fair specimen of what modern scholarship and scientific thought can accomplish, together with a firm belief in the fundamental propositions of Christianity."—*Boston Advertiser.*

"This book is a great treasury of gathered learning, presented in a popular form."—*N. Y. Observer.*

Copies sent by mail, post-paid, on receipt of price.

A. C. ARMSTRONG & SON, 51 East 10th Street, New York.